GLENN ROBINSON

Divided Loyalties

Divided Loyalties

Nationalism and Mass Politics in Syria at the Close of Empire

JAMES L. GELVIN

University of California Press
BERKELEY LOS ANGELES LONDON

University of California Press
Berkeley and Los Angeles, California

University of California Press, Ltd.
London, England

Library of Congress Cataloging-in-Publication Data

Gelvin, James L., 1951–
Divided loyalties : nationalism and mass politics in Syria at the close of Empire / James L. Gelvin.
p. cm.
Includes bibliographical references and index.
ISBN 0–520-21069-7 (alk. paper). — ISBN 0-520-21070-0 (alk. paper)
1. Syria—History—20th century. 2. Nationalism—Syria. 3. Mandates—Syria. 4. Elites (Social sciences)—Syria. I. Title.
DS98.G45 1999
956.9104—dc21 98-3204
CIP

Printed in the United States of America
9 8 7 6 5 4 3 2 1

The paper used in this publication meets the minimum requirements of American National Standards for Information Sciences—Permanence of Paper for Printed Library Materials, ANSI Z39.48-1984.

Contents

Contents

Acknowledgments

This book could not have been written without the assistance and support of friends and colleagues. Since the book is based upon my doctoral dissertation, I would like to begin by thanking the two members of my committee, Zachary Lockman and Philip S. Khoury. The guidance both provided from the dissertation stage through the final revisions of the book manuscript was invaluable, and I am particularly grateful for their enthusiasm and for their continued support. In addition, I would like to thank David Commins, Leila Fawaz, R. Stephen Humphreys, Fred Lawson, David W. Lesch, Anne McCants, Michael Morony, Roger Owen, Chase Robinson, Eugene Rogan, Malcolm Russell, Nina Safran, Linda Schatkowski Schilcher, and Peter Sluglett, who took the time to read and comment on all or parts of the manuscript during its preparation. Ronald Mellor of the UCLA History Department and Lynne Withey of UC Press offered encouragement and backing throughout the process of preparing this manuscript that expedited its publication.

I undertook research for this book in Syria, Egypt, Jordan, Britain, France, and the United States, and I wish to thank those who facilitated my research in these places. In particular, I would like to extend my gratitude to those Syrians who consented to be interviewed (their names appear in the bibliography) and to Najate Kassab-Hassan, Fakhri Nuri al-Kaylani, Muhammad Kamal al-Qasimi, and 'Umar Khadim al-Saruji, who helped me arrange those interviews. I am also deeply indebted to Sylva Oghlanian Bolz of Maktabat al-Asad in Damascus and to the proprietors and personnel of the Salafiyya Library/Bookstore in Cairo for their graciousness and efficiency, as well as to Abdul-Karim Rafeq and Khairia Kasmieh who guided me through the Syrian bureaucracy.

Grants for research and write-up were provided by the Fulbright-Hays Dissertation Research Committee, the Social Science Research Council, and the Charlotte W. Newcombe Foundation. I also wish to express belated thanks to Robert Faulkner and Dennis Hale of the Political Science Department at Boston College, William Graham of the Center for Middle Eastern Studies at Harvard University, and the faculty and staff of the History Departments at Massachusetts Institute of Technology and the University of California, Los Angeles, who provided me with an environment in which I could learn from my colleagues and test my ideas.

Most of all, I would like to thank Najwa al-Qattan, who has put up with me despite my grousing about the progress of this project and has suffered through countless unsolicited disquisitions on nationalism in Syria. To list her immeasurable contributions to the writing of this book would only trivialize them.

• • •

Some of the material contained in this book has appeared before. I would like to thank the editors and publishers of three publications for granting me permission to draw from the following works:

"Demonstrating Communities in Post-Ottoman Syria," *Journal of Interdisciplinary History* 25(1) (summer 1994), 23–44. Copyright © by Massachusetts Institute of Technology Press and the editors of *The Journal of Interdisciplinary History.*

"The Social Origins of Popular Nationalism in Syria: Evidence for a New Framework," *International Journal of Middle East Studies* 26 (November 1994), 645–662. Copyright © by Cambridge University Press and the editors of *International Journal of Middle East Studies.*

"The Other Arab Nationalism: Syrian/Arab Populism in Its Historical and International Contexts," in *Rethinking Nationalisms in the Arab World,* edited by James Jankowski and Israel Gershoni. Copyright © 1997 by Columbia University Press. Reprinted by permission of the publisher.

Abbreviations

AD	Archives diplomatiques, Nantes, France
BL	British Library
DU SA	Durham University, Sudan Archives
FO	Foreign Office, London
GCC	Général commandant en chef, armée du Levant
GHQ	General Headquarters—Egypt
HC	Haut commissionaire
IO	India Office, London
MAE	Ministère des affaires étrangères, Paris
MD	Ministère de la défense, Vincennes, France
SL:LD	Salafiyya Library, Cairo: Lajnat al-Difāʿ file
SL:LW	Salafiyya Library, Cairo: Lajna Waṭaniyya file
USNA	U.S. National Archives, Washington, D.C.
WO	War Office, London

Map 1. Syria within Its Natural Boundaries

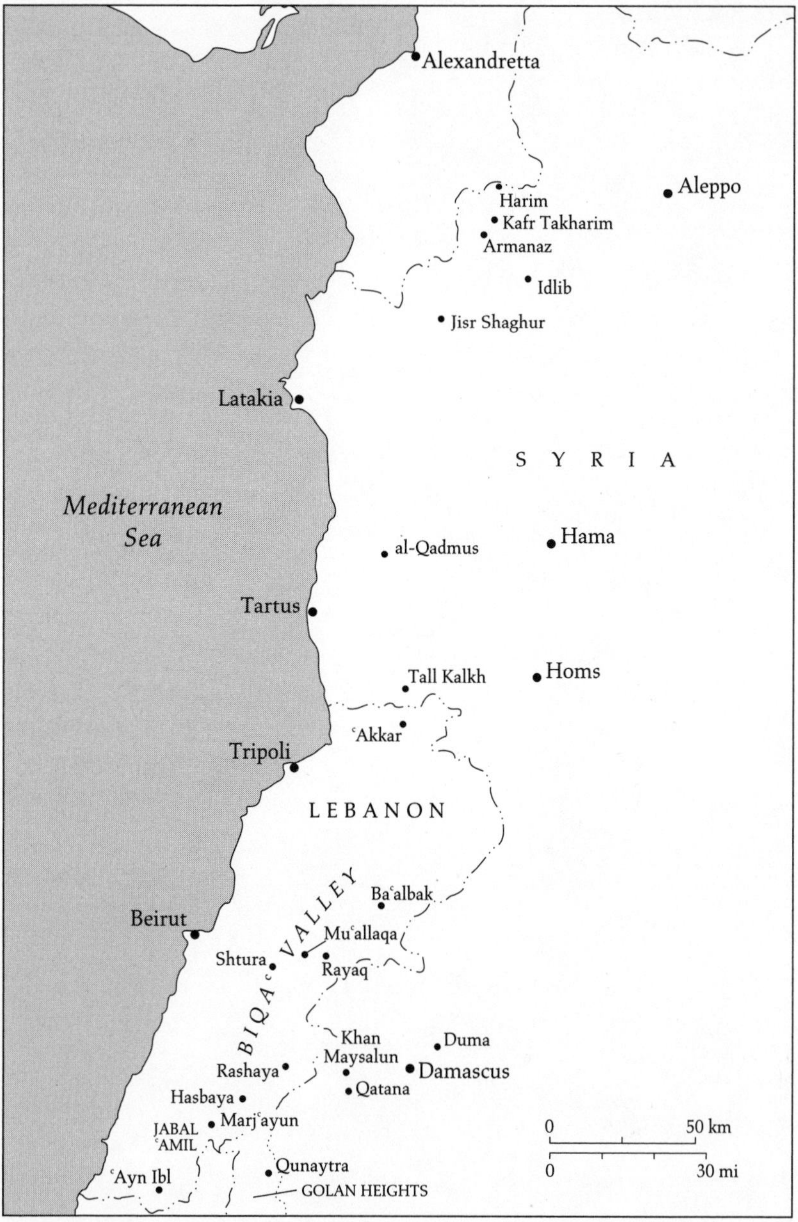

Map 2. Western Syria and Lebanon

Introduction

Although this book focuses on events that occurred in Syria[1] between October 1918 and July 1920—the period during which an Arab government ruled in Damascus—I have neither structured it as a narrative account nor intended it to be one. Such narratives have already been written, with greater or lesser success.[2] The purpose of this book is much different: it is an examination of contending constructions of nation and nationalism in early twentieth-century Syria and of the origins and early evolution of mass politics and popular nationalism in the same region. The need for such an investigation becomes evident by juxtaposing two incidents, separated by only a few months, that took place on opposite sides of the Atlantic.

On 20 July 1920, six days after the initial French ultimatum to the Arab government of Amir Faysal and four days before French troops entered Damascus to begin their quarter-century occupation, insurrection erupted in the Syrian capital. Throughout the city, petit-bourgeois mer-

1. I shall be using the term *Syria* to refer to several different geographic areas. Usually, it will refer to the territory under the administration of Occupied Enemy Territory Administration—East (OETA-E). At other times, particularly in discussions of contemporaneous notions of geographic divisions, *Syria* refers to "Syria within its natural boundaries"—the territory that comprises present-day Syria, Lebanon, Jordan, Israel, the "Palestinian Entity," the Israeli occupied territories, a small section of the Republic of Turkey south of the Taurus Mountains and the province of Alexandretta, and western Iraq. The reader should be able to determine which definition is appropriate from the context.

2. See, for example, Malcolm Russell, *The First Modern Arab State: Syria under Faysal 1918–1920;* Khairia Kasmieh (Khayriyya Qāsimiyya), *al-Ḥukūma al-ʿarabiyya fī Dimashq bayna 1918–1920;* ʿAlī Sulṭān, *Tārīkh Sūriyya 1918–1920: Ḥukm Fayṣal b. Ḥusayn;* Zeine N. Zeine, *The Struggle for Arab Independence: Western Diplomacy and the Rise and Fall of Faisal's Kingdom in Syria.*

chants, neighborhood toughs, unemployed youths, refugees from the Biqaʿ Valley, and recently demobilized soldiers from the regular Arab army took to the streets, while former members of the prorogued Syrian General Congress, ulama, and political agitators denounced the government that had acceded to French demands from minbars and street corners. Popular leaders raised sanjaks[3] and distributed leaflets that warned of conspiracies threatening the nation and described atrocities committed by French soldiers stationed to the west. Newspapers, printed as broadsheets, taunted the enemy with patriotic bluster: "Tell the Pope, the clericalists, the capitalists, and the politicians who aim at conquest," *al-Kināna* announced in a two-page, bold-faced spread, "that young Syria will never submit to old France."[4] In the quarters of Shaghur and the Maydan, where less than two weeks before residents had disarmed and beaten military policemen who had attempted to enforce the Arab government's despised conscription policy, the same residents now attacked a contingent of troops loyal to the traitorous (*khāʾin*) amir because they believed him to be collaborating with the enemies of the nation.[5]

When the Arab government tried to retake the streets, fighting broke out between regular army units (such as the bedouin and Yemeni troops that had fought alongside the amir during the Arab Revolt) and the population. One group of insurrectionists, shouting anti-Faysal slogans, attacked the royal palace (on the roof of which the amir, anticipating rebellion, had placed machine guns). Another group stormed the Damascus citadel where arms and ammunition were stored and where, the rebels assumed, the government had interned the popular leader Kamil al-Qassab, along with other political prisoners. According to British estimates, over

3. A sanjak consisted of a broad banner which was suspended from a wooden crossbeam. The crossbeam was carried by one man, while two others assisted by holding ropes attached to the bottom of the cloth to ensure that the news or slogan printed on the banner could be read. Sanjaks were usually displayed in areas of heavy traffic, near mosques, or in cemeteries. Ḥasan al-Amīn, *Dhikrayāt, al-Juzʾ al-awwal: Min al-ṭufūla ilā al-ṣibā*, 27.

4. MD 4H114/695, "Renseignements," n.d.; MD 4H114/4/691, Cousse to Gouraud, 13 July 1920; MD 4H114/5/282–283, Cousse to Gouraud, 15 July 1920; al-Amīn, *Dhikrayāt*, 27; Iḥsān Hindī, *Maʿrakat Maysalūn*, 59–60.

5. MD 4H114/4/662, Cousse to Gouraud, 8 July 1920; FO 371/5037/E8509/74, Mackereth (Beirut) to FO, 16 July 1920; MD 4H114/5, Cousse to Gouraud, 20 July 1920; FO 371/5037/E8880/80, Mackereth to FO, 23 July 1920; MD 4H60/1, "Bulletin quotidien 1270," 23 July 1920. According to Ghalib al-ʿIyashi, the crowd also called for the downfall of *murrāq* (turncoats) and *mutaʾāmirūn* (conspirators). al-ʿIyāshī, *al-Īḍāḥāt al-siyāsiyya wa asrār al-intidāb al-faransī ʿalā Sūriyya*, 105–106.

100 Damascenes died in the clashes; Faysal himself later estimated 120 killed and 200 injured.[6]

The next day, a similar insurrection, launched by the local committee of national defense and inspired by events in Damascus, broke out in Aleppo. Mobilized by the district governor, the chief of police, and popular leaders, an estimated four thousand men from the mostly lower-class district of Bab al-Nayrab—estimated to be about one-third of the population of the district—attacked the citadel of Aleppo and looted and distributed the weapons found within. A raid by another group of rebels on an arms depot the following morning triggered an explosion that reportedly claimed between five and six hundred casualties.[7]

On the afternoon of 21 July, popular leaders toured the quarters of Damascus, encouraging residents to assemble at Baramki Station to await transportation west to Khan Maysalun, where General Yusuf al-ʿAzma was organizing a stand against the invading French. At Baramki, Shaykh Kamal al-Khatib led evening prayers and, in anticipation of the coming battle, prayers for the dead. Of the seventeen hundred volunteers from one Damascus neighborhood, only seven hundred carried weapons. Many of the volunteers who had earlier resisted conscription into the army of the Arab government now departed for the front, anticipating heroic death in *"al-jihād al-waṭanī."*[8]

6. MD 4H114/5, Cousse to Gouraud, 20 July 1920; MD 4H60/1, "Bulletin quotidien 1266," 20 July 1920; MD 4H60/1, "Bulletin quotidien 1270," 23 July 1920; IO L/PS/10/802/P5841, GHQ to WO, 24 July 1920; Maḥmūd al-Charkas, *al-Dalīl al-muṣawwar lil-bilād al-ʿarabiyya,* vol. 1, 119–121; Asʿad Dāghir, *Mudhakkarātī ʿalā hāmish al-qaḍiyya al-ʿarabiyya,* 122, 139–142; Muḥammad ʿAlī al-ʿAjlūnī, *Dhikrayāt ʿan al-thawra al-ʿarabiyya al-kubrā,*98; Hindī, *Maʿrakat Maysalūn,* 59, 61–62.

7. Jules Kersante, "Syrie: L'occupation d'Alep," 172–173; Dāghir, *Mudhakkarātī,* 139; MD 4H114/9/70SP, Cousse to GCC, 21 July 1920; IO L/PS/10/802.P5841, GHQ to WO, 24 July 1920; FO 371/5039/E10316/38, J. B. Jackson (U.S. Consul, Aleppo), 30 July 1920; MAE L:SL/vol. 33/107–305, Gouraud, "Note au sujet des rapports entre le haut commissionaire de la République Française en Syrie-Cilicie et l'emir Fayçal," 22 September 1920; *al-ʿĀṣima,* 13 November 1919, 6; Sulaymān Mūsā, *al-Murāsalāt al-tārīkhiyya,* vol. 3: 1920–1923, 144. For higher estimates of casualties in Damascus, see FO 371/5040/E11756, Gertrude Bell, 6 August 1920; John de Vere Loder, *The Truth about Mesopotamia, Palestine and Syria,* 78. Insurrections also broke out in Homs and Hama. For details of the former, see P. G. Angelil, "L'occupation d'Homs: Angoisses et délivrance."

8. Interviews with Muhammad Rida al-Khatib, descendant of Kamal al-Khatib (6 January 1990); Kamil Daghmush (2 November 1989) and Abu Ribah al-Jaza'iri (15 November 1989), veterans of the Battle of Maysalun; Hindī, *Maʿrakat Maysalūn,* 113; Ilyās al-Fāḍil and Rāmiz Ḥīthāwī, *al-Kitāb al-dhahabī lil-mujāhidīn*

Just five months after these events, Stephen P. Duggan of the Institute of International Education delivered an address to the American Historical Association in which he outlined the evolution of nationalism in Syria from the late nineteenth century through the first months of French occupation.[9] Duggan's lecture had what Hayden White, drawing from the work of Northrop Frye, has described as the "pre-generic plot-structure" of tragedy.[10] He thus began by tracing the auspicious origins and early promise of "Arab nationalism" (the nineteenth-century Arab literary renaissance, the appeal of "the principles of liberty, equality and fraternity under a national and representative government"), pursued his narrative through false hopes (the Arab Congress of 1913, the Arab Revolt, the Anglo-French Declaration of November 1918, the King-Crane Commission) and trials (repression by the Committee of Union and Progress [C.U.P.], the defensive politicization of the movement through secret societies, the *seferberlik,*[11] the passion of the Syrian martyrs), and concluded by recounting betrayal and, ultimately, disaster (the wartime agreements, Zionism and the Balfour Declaration, British abandonment and French occupation).[12] Duggan failed to mention the July insurrections in his remarks: since every plot-structure circumscribes and defines the array of options available to the historian—from the questions to be investigated to the selection and organization of data—Duggan could only regard the July events, if he regarded them at all, as irrelevant or anomalous. Insurrectionists who had claimed the title "*thuwwār*" (revolutionaries) subsequently became "extremists," or "the mob" to the infrequent historian who did include them in his or her account.

---

al-sūriyyīn; Jān Alexān, "Zaynab fī Maysalūn," *al-Jundī,* 19 April 1960, 32–33. Neither historians nor contemporary observers agree on the number of volunteers who fought at the Battle of Maysalun. Amir Faysal, for example, put the number at two thousand. See "The Case of Emir Feisal."

9. Duggan's speech was later published under the title "Syria and its Tangled Problems."

10. See the discussion of the use of "pre-generic plot-structures" in the writing of history in Hayden White, "Interpretation in History," 51–80.

11. "*Seferberlik*" (literally "travel by land") refers to the suffering endured by Syrians during the period of World War I, including famine and deportation. See L. Schatkowski Schilcher, "The Famine of 1915–1918 in Greater Syria," 229–258.

12. To underscore Duggan's conceptual plan, the editors of *Current History* subtitled his article, "Story of the Allies' Promises, Mustapha Kemal's Ambitions, Emir Feisal's Disappointment, the Franco-British Rivalry and the Zionists in Palestine—French Difficulties in Syria."

Duggan's address is not noteworthy because of its novelty; to the contrary, Duggan's address is noteworthy because it represents one of the earliest examples of the predominant strategy that has been used to emplot the story of nationalism in the Arab Middle East from the *nahḍa* (the Arab literary renaissance of the late nineteenth century) through the mandate period. Not only did Duggan's colleagues—historians and advocates of "the Arab cause" such as T. E. Lawrence, John de Vere Loder, Hans Kohn, Richard Coke, and Elizabeth P. MacCallum—also situate their accounts within the selfsame narrative structure, but after more than seventy years, many contemporary historians of nationalism in the region continue to do so as well.[13] As a result, the various assumptions and inferences derived from the application of this structure—including the tendency to treat the history of nationalism in the Arab world as intellectual (idealist) history and to look to a select group of indigenous elites as the sole originators, carriers, and disseminators of nationalism—are shared by several generations of historians.

Both idealist and elitist assumptions have served to circumscribe historical inquiry. In the process of privileging an essentialized "Arab nationalism" above all other constructions of nationalism, idealist historians have taken the claims of its proponents at face value. This has, in effect, predisposed them to accept the existence of a nationalism that is rooted in an immutable and singular Arab identity—what sociologist Anthony D. Smith would call an Arab *ethnie*.[14] According to Zeine N. Zeine, for example,

> Nationalism has undergone several changes in meaning during the course of its evolution in various states. But if we take into consideration, basically, the racial, cultural, and spiritual elements of nationalism, we find that Arab nationalism is one of the oldest nationalisms in the world. The true birth of Arab nationalism took place with the rise of Islam. . . . What the educated and enlightened Arabs were waking up to [at the turn of the century] was not to Arab consciousness, which had never "slept" but to an independent political life.[15]

13. T. E. Lawrence, "Emir Feisal II: The Sykes-Picot Treaty, Impatient Arabs," *Times* (London), 11 August 1920, 9; T. E. Lawrence, *Evolution of a Revolt;* Loder, *Truth About Mesopotamia;* Hans Kohn, *A History of Nationalism in the East;* Richard Coke, *The Arab's Place in the Sun;* Elizabeth P. MacCallum, "The Arab National Movement." Edward Said makes a similar point but draws different inferences; see *Culture and Imperialism,* 252.

14. Anthony D. Smith, *National Identity,* 19–42.

15. Zeine N. Zeine, *The Emergence of Arab Nationalism with a Background Study of Arab-Turkish Relations in the Near East,* 129–130, 133.

Because the full recovery of the Arab *ethnie* merely awaited the proper speculative advancement and political conjuncture, historians of nationalism in the region have spent an inordinate amount of time attempting to uncover the contributions made by various intellectuals to the "rediscovery" and elucidation of that identity, the chain through which an Arab "protonationalism" and nationalism were transmitted from generation to generation, and the timing of the diffusion of a paradigmatic nationalism throughout the population of the Arab Middle East.

The preoccupation with this narrow range of issues has provided the narrative focus for countless expositions about the "rise of Arab nationalism," including *The Arab Awakening* of George Antonius, perhaps the most famous and influential treatment of the movement's origins and early history.[16] In his work, Antonius cites many of the same predicates and utilizes the same narrative structure as had Stephen P. Duggan almost two decades before. Although briefly alluding to the "false starts" that preceded the authentic evolutionary path followed by the "Arab national movement"—Antonius finds what might be called a "proto-protonationalism" in the Wahhabi movement of Arabia and in the propaganda disseminated by Muhammad ʿAli and his son Ibrahim during their conquest of Syria—his tale really begins with Christian Arab circles whose attraction to nationalism was a natural outgrowth of their affinity with the West and Western ideas; thus, "[t]he story of the Arab national movement opens in Syria in 1847, with the foundation in Bairut [sic] of a modest literary society under American patronage."[17] According to Antonius, in the decades following its initial crystallization and articulation, Arab protonationalism and nationalism traversed communal boundaries and began to percolate through the larger Muslim community.

Although historians writing in the wake of *The Arab Awakening* have generally accepted Antonius's methodological presuppositions, they have continually fussed with the details of his narrative. In contrast to Antonius, Hisham Sharabi and C. Ernest Dawn, for example, have posited very different roots and evolutionary course for "Arab nationalism," counterposing their contention that (in the words of Dawn), "[t]here is convincing evidence that the prevailing ideology of Arab nationalists in the twentieth

16. George Antonius, *The Arab Awakening: The Story of the Arab National Movement.* See also Albert Hourani, "*The Arab Awakening* Forty Years After." For an insightful description of Antonius's milieu and motives, see Edward Said, "Third World Intellectuals and Metropolitan Culture."

17. Antonius, *Arab Awakening,* 13.

century was formed in the 1920s, at the latest, from Islamic modernist roots."[18] Still others, such as Bassam Tibi and Sylvia Haim, have combined the trajectories outlined by Antonius and Sharabi/Dawn, thereby tracing a chain of transmission that synthesizes Christian secularism and Islamic modernism.[19] Whatever the source and the path chosen by historians, however, they have commonly ignored or glossed over fundamental differences that divided proponents of the Arab cause—and the ideologies that they advocated—from one another. As a result, nationalism in the Arab Middle East has achieved a retrospective homogeneity and coherence through their works that it had never achieved in actuality.[20]

The focus placed by historians on the activities of a small elite that played a conspicuous role in the synthesis and dissemination of nationalist ideology has, over the past two decades, been reinforced by the work of historians such as Dawn, Philip S. Khoury, and Rashid Khalidi, who have analyzed the social strata from which many of the earliest advocates of the Arab cause emerged.[21] According to Dawn and Khoury, the strongest proponents of "Arabism" (the precursor to "Arab nationalism") in Syria came from a thin fraction of the urban-based, landowning-bureaucratic notability that "had failed to achieve power and influence commensurate with their expectations."[22] These elites expressed their dissatisfaction by rein-

18. C. Ernest Dawn, "The Origins of Arab Nationalism;" Hisham Sharabi, *Arab Intellectuals and the West: The Formative Years 1875–1914,* 58–60, 64–65.

19. Bassam Tibi, *Arab Nationalism: A Critical Enquiry,* 58–68; Sylvia Haim, *Arab Nationalism: An Anthology,* ix–x, 25–27.

20. One recent effort to revise this ascription of homogeneity is Eliezer Tauber's three-volume history of nationalism in the Arab Middle East from the founding of the early nationalist societies through 1920. Rather than privileging "Arab" nationalism, Tauber identifies four competing nationalist strands: "Arabism," "Syrianism," "Lebanonism," and "Iraqism." While a step in the right direction and a rich source of detail, Tauber's books still maintain the elitist bias of their predecessors. Furthermore, his analysis does not recognize the conditional nature of identity. His substitution of four essential nationalist strands for one is thus reminiscent of attempts made by pre-Copernican astronomers to save the Ptolemaic map of the universe by proposing additional epicycles to explain "irregular" planetary behavior. See Tauber, *The Emergence of the Arab Movements; The Arab Movements in World War I; The Formation of Modern Syria and Iraq.*

21. See in particular Ç. Ernest Dawn, *From Ottomanism to Arabism: Essays on the Origins of Arab Nationalism;* Philip S. Khoury, *Urban Notables and Arab Nationalism: The Politics of Damascus 1860–1920.*

22. Khoury, *Urban Notables,* 67–68. Coined by Dawn, the term *Arabism* is a rather loose conception. Dawn first used the term in counterposition to the doctrine of "Ottomanism" to which, he maintained, it was a reaction. While both ideologies germinated from the common root of Islamic modernism, Dawn traces the distinct lineage of Arabism from Rifaʿa Rafiʿ al-Tahtawi through Muhammad ʿAbduh and

terpreting the doctrine of "Ottomanism" (according to which all localist, religious, and ethnic identities within the empire would be subsumed in a distinctive Ottoman identity), by rejecting the centralization policies of the Committee of Union and Progress, and by supporting policies that promised looser administrative controls that would increase local autonomy.

In contrast to Dawn and Khoury, Khalidi has persistently championed the part played by a circle of professionals, particularly journalists, in the development and promotion of Arabism.[23] This circle comprised the "new middle classes," the "middle strata," or perhaps less agreeably, the "marginal men" whom Western historians of nationalism have frequently credited with defining national goals, sparking nationalist agitation, and organizing nationalist movements throughout the late colonial world. As Khalidi and others demonstrate, those who might be included in this circle were not elite in the sense that they held positions of economic, social, or political preeminence. Indeed, because these professionals often hailed from less than prestigious social backgrounds, scholars of nationalism have frequently attributed their nationalist activities, like those of Khoury's landowning-bureaucrats, to resentments engendered by their exclusion from positions of influence.[24] Whatever their motivation, their relatively modest social background underscores the fact that it was privileged access to Western-style education, characteristic worldview, and self-ascription—determinants that did not necessarily coincide with birthright—that distinguished those who might be included in the category "nationalist elites."

Although some of the findings of idealist historians, when applied with circumspection, have contributed to the understanding of select intellectual currents extant in the Arab world during the late nineteenth and early twentieth centuries, the attempt to locate nationalism in the region solely within the domain of nationalist elites is essentially ill-conceived. While the role played by these elites in nationalist politics cannot be dismissed, it

Rashid Rida, defining Arabism as a doctrine that maintains that the Arabs "were a special people who possessed peculiar virtues and rights." See Dawn, *From Ottomanism to Arabism*, 122–123, 133, 136–140, 142–144, 147–148. Rashid Khalidi has added that Arabism was a "protonationalism rather than full-fledged nationalism" and that Ottomanism and Arabism were not mutually exclusive, but instead were "ideal types" separated by a fluid boundary. See "The Origins of Arab Nationalism: Introduction," ix; "Ottomanism and Arabism in Syria before 1914: A Reassessment," 51, 61–63.

23. See Rashid Khalidi, "ʿAbd al-Ghani al-ʿUraisi and *al-Mufid:* The Press and Arab Nationalism before 1914"; "Society and Ideology in Late Ottoman Syria" (particularly 123).

24. See Elie Kedourie, *Nationalism in Asia and Africa*, 80–92.

was, notwithstanding the formidable powers attributed to "charisma" and to the efficacy of vertical mobilization, far from comprehensive. Because the capacity of these nationalist elites to define and dominate the political field was ultimately circumscribed by the ability of their ideas to articulate with the aspirations of other elements of the population, histories that place nationalist politics solely within the domain of these elites fail because they present only one moment of the nationalist dialectic. They omit the other moment, the domain of popular politics, the manifold attributes of which cannot entirely be ascribed to elite designs. The reintegration into the nationalist dialectic of political movements that included this moment, such as those represented by the July insurrectionists, their predecessors, and their successors, as well as an exposition of the contributions made by these movements to a consequent nationalist synthesis, are the subject of this book.

The book is divided into three sections. In Part I, I discuss how the nature of political organizing changed in Syria before, during, and after World War I. In the wake of these changes, complex and comprehensive political organizations frequently replaced, marginalized, or recontextualized traditional and parochial modes of organization, facilitating the programmatic mobilization of large numbers of constituents. These organizations not only induced the expansion of political participation, they broke the monopoly on authority held by the previously dominant categories of elites and redefined and politicized the ties that bound non-elites to their leaders. As a result, mass politics not only became possible in Syria during the immediate post-World War I period, it became inevitable.

Because the new popular organizations were comprehensive and ideological, and because they incorporated their followers through a variety of customary and original bonds of loyalty, they acted to verify, intensify, actualize, and hone the possible meanings that could be derived from a coherent set of symbols that were frequently distinctive. Those associated with the popular groups thus were not an amorphous "mob," but were rather members of a discretely constituted discursive community that, although very different from the discursive community composed of members of the Arab government and its supporters, must also be considered part of the nationalist tendency. In Part II, I compare the two main nationalist discursive communities that arose in Syria during the Faysali period. Through the use of leaflets, graffiti, newspaper editorials, speeches, rumors, and other texts, I compare the most important symbols ("key symbols") and slogans and the fields in which these symbols and slogans were situated to trace the evolution of these rival discursive communities.

Part III, a discussion of activities such as demonstrations, public celebrations, and theater carried out in public/symbolic space integrates themes that were developed separately in the first two parts. Because ceremonies balance in various proportions celebratory and didactic elements, and because they not only contain symbols but act as symbols, I use the analysis of ceremony to add a new dimension to the understanding of the efficacy of competing integrated symbol systems promoted by political rivals to instruct their political base or to enlist political support. Furthermore, through an analysis of public ceremonies, I outline the unique attributes that allowed the new political formations to attract a mass following and the process by which competing political factions contributed—both intentionally and unintentionally—to the creation of the new political public.

Before these particular analyses can be undertaken, however, it is necessary to address two preliminary tasks. Since, as discussed above, previous histories of the origins and early evolution of nationalism in the Arab Middle East have been too encumbered by idealist, essentialist, and elitist assumptions to present anything but a narrow and distorted glimpse of what they have sought to examine, the first task is to formulate a replacement paradigm that avoids these pitfalls. The second task is somewhat more prosaic: the presentation of an outline of the most important political, diplomatic, social, and economic events that took place in Syria during and immediately following World War I, events that formed the context for the phenomena analyzed in the subsequent chapters.

• • •

The past two decades have witnessed a veritable renaissance in the field of nationalist studies. As a result of the introduction of new methodological strategies (ranging from world-systems and neo-Marxist approaches to postmodern and postcolonial critiques) and the proliferation of interdisciplinary and comparative studies, not only have suppositions previously accepted as certainties been called into question, but essential categories, including "nation," "nationalism," and "national identity," have been subjected to renewed scrutiny and/or subsumed in heretofore unconventional analytical frameworks. Four aspects of the current debate about nationalism and national identity are particularly relevant to the argument presented in this book.

First, for the past twenty years, scholars studying nationalism have approached the object of their research with heightened skepticism. Numerous recent contributors to the field of nationalist studies have directed their efforts toward deconstructing official national histories and deflating the teleological pretensions of state-supported nationalisms that represent themselves as the inevitable and singular historically inscribed expressions of national destiny. Others have made the hegemonizing process itself, as well as resistances to it, the object of their scrutiny. As a result, phrases such as "the invention of tradition," and "peasants into Frenchmen" have by now become a familiar part of the academic discourse on nationalism. Because of these efforts, the ferreting out of less successful and frequently neglected alternative constructions of nation and national identity, such as those held by groups subordinated on account of social status, gender, class, ethnic or religious affiliation, and/or geographic placement, has become a virtual cottage industry as social scientists and historians have increasingly approached nationalism not as it has been presented in official histories but rather, in the words of Prasenjit Duara, as "the site where different representations of the nation contest and negotiate with each other."[25] This book conforms to this deconstructive agenda.

Second, most observers now agree that nationalisms are "Janus-faced." Like the ancient Roman deity, nationalisms bear two faces, one looking backward to the past, the other looking ahead to the future. On the one hand, nationalist movements represent themselves as the heirs to an ancient and distinctive national history. In keeping with this principle, they reconstruct ("revive") ancient national glories, traditions, symbols, and myths. On the other hand, such movements simultaneously embrace Enlightenment and post-Enlightenment rationalism and its progressive and universalist pretensions, thereby situating themselves within the global modernist project.[26]

It is necessary to add, however, that while nationalist movements combine both the past and the future, uniqueness and universalism, the manner in which they unite these seemingly contradictory elements varies from movement to movement. For some nationalist movements, such as secular Zionism, the modernist component nearly overwhelms the traditionalist component, whose presence in nationalist discourse provides little more than an historical pretext for the modernizing effort. Even the resurrection of the ancient language of Hebrew was largely undertaken for the purpose of differentiating secular Zionists from their more "backward" Yiddish-speaking brethren in the Jewish diaspora. In contrast, other nationalist movements—among which some contemporary Islamicist move-

25. Prasenjit Duara, *Rescuing History from the Nation: Questioning Narratives of Modern China,* 8.

26. See Tom Nairn, "The Modern Janus."

ments must be counted—emphasize their traditionalism, in the process obscuring the fact that the very principles that enable their movements are themselves anything but traditional. As will be seen below, in the aftermath of World War I, rival nationalist factions in Syria effected the reconciliation of the "traditionalist" and "modern" faces of nationalism in disparate ways, in effect constructing distinct but coincident nationalist movements that competed for the loyalty of the Syrian population.

Third, most contemporary scholars also argue that identity is circumstantial. In other words, identity is not permanently fixed ("primordial"), nor does the assertion of a national identity necessarily preclude an individual from asserting other forms of identity. Nevertheless, periods of national crisis and/or mobilization may effect a temporary reification of the boundaries separating self-ascribed national subjects from an external "other" and induce those subjects to privilege the bonds of nation over other attachments.[27] As I shall argue in the following pages, one such period occurred in the Arab Middle East in the immediate aftermath of World War I.

Finally, the shift from primordialist to constructivist theories of national origins—from the belief that nations are natural and ancient entities to the belief that nations are created and a relatively new phenomenon in world history—has inspired a number of studies exploring the social and historical conditions necessary for the emergence and propagation of the nation form and nationalist ideologies. As Benedict Anderson, Ernest Gellner, Etienne Balibar, and others argue, nationalism appertains to a specific framework for the organization of social relations and social reproduction, and by implication, for the diffusion and allocation of power.[28] To understand the emergence of nationalisms in the Middle East or any other region, therefore, it is necessary to step outside the nationalist narrative and to focus on those factors that prompted the transition from a social system that was not conducive to nationalism to one that was apposite to the ideology. This is where I shall begin.

The appearance of nationalisms in the Middle East can be traced to the same preconditions that foreshadowed the appearance of nationalisms in

27. See, for example, Stuart Hall, "Ethnicity: Identity and Difference"; John L. Comaroff, "Of Totemism and Ethnicity"; Duara, *Rescuing History from the Nation*, 55, 65–66; Zdzislaw Mach, *Symbols, Conflict, and Identity: Essays in Political Anthropology*, 15–16.

28. See Benedict Anderson, *Imagined Communities: Reflections on the Origin and Spread of Nationalism*; Ernest Gellner, *Nations and Nationalism;* Etienne Balibar, "The Nation Form: History and Ideology."

other regions. During the nineteenth century, two interconnected processes induced far-reaching economic, political, and social changes within the Ottoman Empire. First, the accelerating rate of integration of the empire into the periphery of the capitalist world system hastened, albeit unevenly, the ongoing integration of local marketplace economies into a broader market economy.[29] The salience of commercial relations and associated institutions thus increased for many inhabitants of the empire who now produced crops destined for regional and international markets, competed with workers overseas, sold their labor, loaned or borrowed money at usurious rates, and participated as middlemen and factors in foreign trade. The expansion of commercial relations was facilitated by the second phenomenon, the attempts made by the Ottoman government throughout the century to strengthen and rationalize central control. While the regulations promulgated in Istanbul often had desultory and even antithetic effects when applied in the provinces (perhaps the most notorious example being the application of the Ottoman Land Code of 1858), over the course of the late nineteenth and early twentieth centuries they enabled government on all levels to expand substantially its role in society and its control over the citizenry. Furthermore, because government policies promoted the construction of institutions that were congruent with those of Europe, they abetted the further penetration of European capital and, consequently, the diffusion of commercial relations throughout the empire.[30]

The spread of the market economy and the expansion of state authority effected a variety of well-documented consequences. For example, the twin processes altered the size and nature of cities. Coastal cities and extramural urban areas expanded as a result of shifting economic patterns and migration. As a result of the growth of international trade, Beirut expanded from a "rather insignificant" town of 6,000 in the last quarter of the eighteenth century to a city of 120,000 at the beginning of the twentieth. Although

29. I have borrowed this phrase from Winifred Barr Rothenberg, *From Market-Places to a Market Economy: The Transformation of Rural Massachusetts, 1750–1850.*

30. See, inter alia, Roger Owen, *The Middle East in the World Economy, 1800–1914*, 153–179, 244–272; Moshe Maʿoz, "The Impact of Modernization on Syrian Politics and Society during the Early Tanzimat Period"; Shimon Shamir, "The Modernization of Syria: Problems and Solutions in the Early Period of Abdulhamid"; Gabriel Baer, "Village and Countryside in Egypt and Syria: 1500–1900"; Linda Schatkowski Schilcher, *Families in Politics: Damascene Factions and Estates of the 18th and 19th Century*, 60–86; James Anthony Reilly, "Origins of Peripheral Capitalism in the Damascus Region, 1830–1914."

definitive data are lacking, it appears that the population of Damascus increased 60–100 percent or more between the mid-nineteenth century and 1917.[31] Newcomers to cities frequently settled in neighborhoods (such as the Maydan in Damascus and al-Kallasa in Aleppo) in which ties of patronage were tenuous at best. In addition, the construction and reconstruction of cities (sometimes, as in the case of districts of Cairo and Istanbul, along European lines) and urban renewal efforts (such as those undertaken in Damascus before and during World War I[32]) transformed the nature of urban space, facilitated the breakdown of quarter-based loyalties, and created public areas in which, for example, ceremonies could take place, thereby expediting, to borrow a phrase from historian George L. Mosse, the "nationalization of the masses."[33]

In addition, urbanization and the expansion and intensification of commercial relations encouraged the proliferation of newpapers, literary salons, private clubs, and coffeehouses, through which news was disseminated and information exchanged. In conjunction with the efforts of the Ottoman state to reconstitute the foundations of its legitimacy through the promulgation of official secular and religiously-based Ottomanist ideologies,[34] the literary salons and political clubs that turned political neophytes into political activists; the newpaper headlines that shouted on street corners in Beirut, Damascus, and other cities; and the didactic theatrical productions written for and performed in coffeehouses all contributed to a

31. See Y. Eyup Ozveren, "Beirut"; Schilcher, *Families in Politics,* 5–6; Owen, *Middle East in the World Economy,* 244.

32. During the late nineteenth and early twentieth centuries, the map of the central rectangle of Damascus was deliberately redrawn, and tramway, telegraph, and telephone systems and municipal lighting were installed. Shariʿ Nasr, one of the major arteries of Damascus, which during the Faysali period would be used for public demonstrations, was built by the Ottoman administration during World War I; simultaneously, the Ministry of Awqaf ordered the destruction of all houses and other buildings surrounding the Umayyad Mosque, creating huge areas suitable for ceremonial space. See *al-Qibla,* 22 dhu al-ḥijja 1334, 4; Muḥammad Adīb Āl Taqī al-Dīn al-Ḥuṣnī, *Kitāb muntakhabāt al-tawārīkh li-Dimashq,* 1:286. For other physical changes, see Nazīh al-Kawākibī, "al-Maẓhar al-ʿumrānī li-Dimashq fī al-muntaṣaf al-thānī lil-qarn al-tāsiʿ ʿashr"; Qatība al-Shihābī, *Dimashq: Tārīkh wa ṣuwar.*

33. See George L. Mosse, *The Nationalization of the Masses: Political Symbolism and Mass Movements in Germany from the Napoleonic Wars through the Third Reich.*

34. Kemal H. Karpat, "The Transformation of the Ottoman State, 1789–1908"; Selim Deringel, "Legitimacy Structures in the Ottoman State: The Reign of Abdulhamid II (1876–1909)."

heightened political atmosphere and the emergence of an ever-widening modern "public sphere" in Syria. It was within this emergent public sphere that a small but steadily increasing number of Syrians at the turn of the century began to contest a multiplicity of ideas and ideologies, including a variety of nationalist ideologies.

The spread of commercial relations and the attempt to impose a uniform apparatus of power throughout the Ottoman Empire concurrently induced the redrawing of boundaries that had previously divided state from civil society. The state imposed new obligations, such as the much-detested policy of conscription, and with varying degrees of commitment and success took charge of functions that had previously been outside its domain, including education and certain types of public works. Government on all levels even supervised a variety of welfare policies, such as the provision of poor relief and agricultural assistance and the payment of pensions to widows and orphans.[35] The expansion of the breadth and magnitude of the jurisdiction of government, and its assumption of responsibilities associated with modern states, contributed to the rending of parochial loyalties and, again in the words of Mosse, helped make "political action into a drama supposedly shared by the people themselves."[36]

Finally, the transformation of Ottoman society, particularly in the second half of the nineteenth century, affected both the role and the composition of local economic and political elites. In coastal cities such as Beirut, for example, the size and economic power of the so-called Christian bourgeoisie swelled as European governments extorted favorable terms for trade and special privileges for their clients from the Ottoman government. In Damascus, Aleppo, and the smaller cities of Syria, the status and prerogatives of those families that both derived their wealth from landed investment and fostered good relations with the central Ottoman administration in Istanbul—the absentee landowning-bureaucratic elite mentioned above—also expanded, eclipsing in status and prerogatives those families that lacked one asset or the other. Concurrently, the "middle strata," composed of the skilled professionals, belletrists, civil servants (those whom Nietzsche aptly called the "state nomads without homes"[37]), and trained military officers whose skills both were made possible by and were neces-

35. These policies (and their breach) are discussed on the pages of such Syrian newspapers as *al-Bashīr* and *al-Muqtabas.*
36. Mosse, *Nationalization of the Masses,* 2.
37. Friedrich Nietzsche, *The Will to Power,* 40.

sary for the continued expansion of market relations and the administrative apparatus, emerged.[38]

According to most conventional narratives, what attracted one or more of the above categories of elites to Arabism, "Arab nationalism," and the antecedent literary/cultural revival (the previously mentioned *nahḍa*) was the inherent appeal of "the principles of liberty, equality and fraternity"; elective ties of affinity rooted in the common religious affiliation, education, or experience that bonded Middle Eastern elites to their European counterparts; or an instinctive aversion to alien (i.e., Turkish, European) control. However, while it is unarguable that over time many from these social categories did align themselves with various nationalist currents, explanations based solely on deliberate choice or instinctive anti-imperialism are inadequate. What at these narratives fail to take into account is that nationalism is not fare to be selected or rejected freely from an ideological menu, and that while elective ties frequently strengthened the bonds connecting Middle Eastern elites with their counterparts in the West and with derivative nationalist tenets, these ties were themselves adjunctive.

Because the so-called Christian bourgeoisie, the landowning-bureaucratic elite, and the middle strata all originated as the result of the expansion of peripheral capitalism and the attempt to introduce uniform institutions of governance throughout the Ottoman Empire, the specific categories and constellation of categories used by individuals within these groupings to organize their world and order their society naturally cohered with, and in some cases even duplicated, those enjoined by the dominant culture within the *métropole.* These categories sanctioned a multiplicity of fundamentally analogous ideologies—Ottomanism, Arabism, Phoenicianism, and so on—the survival and propagation of which depended on factors external to the ideologies themselves (the degree to which the ideology was institutionalized, the resources available to those who promoted the ideology, and the political environment in which competing ideologies were situated). As a result, the fundamental ideological divide within Middle Eastern society during the late nineteenth and early twentieth centuries did not separate Ottomanists from Arabists; rather, the fundamental ideological divide separated Ottomanists, Arabists, and their ilk from the remainder of society, whose transformation and integration had been less thoroughly accom-

38. See Leila Tarazi Fawaz, *Merchants and Migrants in Nineteenth Century Beirut;* Khoury, *Urban Notables;* Khalidi, "Society and Ideology"; Ruth Roded, "Ottoman Service as a Vehicle for the Rise of New Upstarts among the Urban Elite Families of Syria in the Last Decades of Ottoman Rule."

plished or whose experience of the transformation was less felicitous. For example, according to historian James Reilly,

> Engineers formed part of a new civil service elite who lived well and earned high salaries. . . . The contrast between these engineers, versed in modern technology, and agricultural laborers in the Ghuta who labored with traditional tools for 3½ piasters a day, underscores the uneven development which had begun to take root in Damascus and Syria by the First World War, eventually creating an historically unprecedented gap between town and country that would color the political and economic history of Syria in the twentieth century.[39]

As will be seen in Parts II and III of this book, many of the nationalist elites that were affiliated with the Arab government of Amir Faysal during the immediate post-Ottoman period themselves recognized the centrality of this cleavage. Not only did they, through discourse and ritual activity, divide the Syrian population between those fit to rule (a select group of notables and a self-identified grouping drawn from the middle strata, the so-called "men of culture" [*mutanawwirūn,* etc.]) and the vast majority of the population that was fit only to be ruled, but the descriptions of the Syrian future that they proffered reflected their Comteanism and technocratic pragmatism:

> [Looking into the future,] I saw . . . the people now turning their attention to the founding of schools and colleges until no village remained without an excellent primary school. I saw prosperity spreading throughout the country and railroads connecting populous villages and farms. I saw farmers using the most modern agricultural techniques, extensive trade, and flourishing industry. Damascus appeared to me to be the most advanced of cities in terms of its construction. Its streets and lanes were paved with asphalt and the Barada River was like the Seine, traversing the city from east to west. On its banks was a corniche on which towering buildings stood. I saw Aleppo: its water, brought by canals from the Euphrates, sustained its gardens and parks and anointed its waterless desert. . . . Factories were founded throughout the kingdom so that the country had no need for manufactured goods from the West, but instead exported its products to China, India, and Africa. Its people grew rich, its power increased, and it moved to the forefront of advanced nations.[40]

These aspirations for the Syrian future cohered with a host of other attitudes, including the advocacy of free market economics, the celebration of "self-made men" (*ʿiṣāmiyyūn*) and "republican motherhood," and denun-

39. Reilly, "Origins of Peripheral Capitalism," 174.
40. *al-ʿĀṣima,* 7 May 1919, 1–2.

ciations of worker indolence and amusements that were pronounced daily in speeches and disseminated through print by those nationalist elites allied with the Arab government of Amir Faysal.[41] For the nationalist elites active after World War I, according to Albert Hourani, "[t]o be independent was to be accepted by European states on a level of equality, to have the Capitulations, the legal privileges of foreign citizens, abolished, to be admitted to the League of Nations. To be modern was to have a political and social life similar to those of the countries of Western Europe."[42] Yet because these nationalist elites infused their discourse with appeals to such recondite concepts as "progress" and "secularism," and because of the narrow range of interests their discourse represented, their ideology not only appeared to be "imported" and "imitative," but lacked resonance for many Syrians more attuned to the discourse emanating from their adversaries within the nationalist tendency.

The aforementioned elites were not, of course, the only strata to be affected by the transformation of Ottoman society. Over the course of the nineteenth century, particularly after the onset of the Great Depression of 1873, non-elites within the empire who increasingly found themselves at the mercy of market and state vented their rage by undertaking acts of resistance that ranged from draft evasion and emigration to open rebellion. Strikes for higher wages were common among Damascene journeymen weavers, who were threatened not only by a decline in real wages but by the weakening of guilds and guild-sponsored welfare programs, proletarianization, and unemployment or employment in sweatshops. In the Hawran, the grain-producing region of Syria south of Damascus, the decade of the 1890s brought increased taxation and more efficient tax collection, a severely depressed international market for wheat, and the restructuring of land tenure and the renegotiation of cultivation rights. As a result, peasants abandoned their harvests, withheld taxes, and even fought pitched battles with Ottoman troops deployed into the region to quell the disturbances—in one case inflicting more than six hundred casualties.[43]

41. See, for example, *al-Kawkab*, 13 January 1919, 11; *al-ʿĀṣima*, 7 May 1919, 1–2; *al-ʿĀṣima*, 16 June 1919, 1–2; *al-ʿĀṣima*, 25 August 1919, 1–2; *al-ʿĀṣima*, 28 August 1919, 5–6; *al-ʿĀṣima*, 11 September 1919, 1; *al-Kawkab*, 30 September 1919, 7–8; *al-Kawkab*, 21 October 1919, 7–8; *al-Kawkab*, 28 October 1919, 7–8; *al-Kawkab*, 11 November 1919, 11; *al-ʿĀṣima*, 5 February 1920, 5; *al-ʿĀṣima*, no. 24 (n.d.).

42. Albert Hourani, *A History of the Arab Peoples*, 343–344.

43. Reilly, "Origins of Peripheral Capitalism," 120, 155–158; Sherry Vatter, "Militant Journeymen in Nineteenth-Century Damascus: Implications for the

Strikes, tax revolts, and the wholesale abandonment of villages are examples of what Charles Tilly calls "reactive collective actions." Undertaken to defend a customary social order or moral economy, these acts of resistance lack both the political program and organizational structure that would enable participants to maintain large-scale, long-term mobilization.[44] But the very factors that provoked reactive collective actions in Syria also presaged the appearance of conditions necessary for programmatic and complex mobilization. The expanding influence of the "merchants and statemakers" and the policies with which they were associated contributed to the breakdown of the parochialism and verticality that, according to most historians, had previously characterized the predominant pattern of political and social relations in the Middle East. Simultaneously, the weakening and/or dissolution of customary bonds of patronage and consanguinity brought about by, for example, increased physical mobility and the aforementioned status revolution, facilitated the emergence among Syrians of horizontal and associational ties whose boundaries were delimited only by the furthest extent of regional market relations and informal migratory circuits. Particularly during periods of crisis, such as during the second year after the establishment of an Arab government in Damascus, these recast ties came to rival, subsume, and even replace the narrower vertical ties that were incompatible with the transformed social and economic landscape.[45]

Urban areas in which vertical ties of patronage were particularly weak or absent as a result of immigration and/or rapid growth often served as epicenters for sustained political mobilization. For example, because the Maydan quarter of Damascus increasingly assumed the role of entrepôt for grain and immigrants from the Hawran during the late nineteenth and early twentieth centuries, the quarter contained a large population of newcomers and transients whose connections with the rural hinterland from which they had come frequently superseded those within their new urban

Middle Eastern Labor History Agenda"; Aḥmad Ḥilmī al-ʿAllāf, *Dimashq fī maṭlaʿ al-qarn al-ʿishrīn*, 137; Linda Schatkowski Schilcher, "Violence in Rural Syria in the 1880s and 1890s: State Centralization, Rural Integration, and the World Market."

44. Charles Tilly, Louise Tilly, and Richard Tilly, *The Rebellious Century, 1830–1930*, 50, 253–254; E. J. Hobsbawm, *Primitive Rebels: Studies in Archaic Forms of Social Movement in the Nineteenth and Twentieth Centuries*, 1–10, 108–125.

45. Schilcher, "Violence in Rural Syria," 76; James L. Gelvin, "The Social Origins of Popular Nationalism in Syria: Evidence for a New Framework."

environment. As a result, during the months preceding the French invasion of inland Syria, Maydanis provided reliable, and often enthusiastic, support for organizations that pioneered unmediated and horizontal forms of political mobilization, and Maydani volunteers, trained and equipped in Damascus, joined guerrilla bands, such as the Druze-led units operating in the areas surrounding Rashaya and Hasbaya and a squadron of cavalry led by Mahmud Faʿur in the Golan, raised to harass the French army occupying the Syrian littoral. The Maydan, designated a *"faubourg révolutionnaire"* by French diplomats, continued its anti-French resistance after most other quarters of Damascus had been "pacified," and residents of the quarter played a prominent role in the 1925 Syrian Great Revolt as well.[46]

Thus, by the first decades of the twentieth century, a social and economic framework that would permit sustained and proactive political mobilization was in place throughout much of Syria. Accordingly, in the wake of the economic and political crises that engulfed the Faysali state in the autumn of 1919, a broad coalition of Syrians—antigovernment intellectuals and professionals (many of whom who resented a government that they claimed was controlled by outsiders, i.e., Hijazis, Iraqis, and Palestinians), lower-middle-class religious dignitaries and shopkeepers, local toughs, conservative notables, and textile and grain merchants from a wide range of socioeconomic backgrounds—could unite to form popular committees such as the Higher National Committee (*al-lajna al-waṭaniyya al-ʿulyā*), local branches of the Higher National Committee (*al-lijān al-waṭaniyya al-farʿiyya*), and committees of national defense (*lijān al-difāʿ al-waṭanī*), which successfully solicited the active participation of non-elites in politics. Through their mobilization of dense familial, market, and geographically derived networks, these organizations not only provided their constituents with a model for political community appropriate to the radically altered circumstances in which Syrians found themselves, they also sanctioned the

46. MAE L:SL/12/32–38, Cousse to HC, 6 April 1919; AD 2344/C1/305–306, Cousse to Picot, 31 October 1919; AD 2344/C1/311, Cousse to Picot, 3 November 1919; AD 2430/dossier confidentiel—départ/325–326, Cousse (?) to HC, 10 November 1919; AD 2375/chemise: division de la Syrie 1919–1920/442/2, Arlabosse to gen. cmdt. div. Syrie, 25 January 1920; AD 2375/chemise: division de la Syrie 1919–1920/445/2, Haak to GCC, 26 January 1920; MD 4H58/2, Haut commissionaire et armée du Levant état-major (deuxième bureau), "Rapport hebdomadaire," 503, 29 July-4 August 1920; Schilcher, *Families in Politics*, 9, 11, 16; Philip S. Khoury, *Syria and the French Mandate: The Politics of Arab Nationalism, 1920–1945*, 180, 191, 291–292; Albert Hourani, "Ottoman Reform and the Politics of Notables," 53; Jean-Paul Pascual, "La Syrie à l'époque ottomane (le XIXe siècle)," 39.

reappropriation by civil society of a variety of tasks, from the guaranteeing of a "fair price" for grain to the mustering of volunteer militias to provide internal security and national defense—tasks that had previously been entrusted to or commandeered by the state or state-connected notables. The July insurrection might be seen as a natural consequence of the mobilization and propaganda efforts of these committees.

Perhaps most tellingly, the popular committees that appeared in Faysali Syria displayed the same attributes that, according to historian Eric Hobsbawm, characterized the "mass parties-cum-movements" that had accompanied the popularization of politics in Europe during the late nineteenth century.[47] As with their European counterparts, a schematic rendering of the structure of the Syrian popular organizations would show a pyramid, with neighborhood committees at the base, municipal and regional committees at midsection, and a national committee at the summit. This structure not only expedited the mobilization of large numbers of constituents, the coordination of their activities, and their democratic participation (albeit within controlled conditions), it redirected their focus away from local concerns to the national arena. Thus, like other popular movements, the Syrian popular mobilization "shattered the old localized or regional framework of politics, or pushed it to the margin, or integrated it" into a wider context.

Furthermore, through a combination of replacement and co-optation, the popular committees (with the earlier assistance of the Faysali government, which, as will be seen in Part III, had both wittingly and unwittingly initiated this process for very different reasons) broke the monopoly of political authority held by local elites and substituted in its stead an arrangement in which factions of the older elites and the educated "middle strata," on the one hand, and organizers for the popular committees, on the other hand, shared, often uneasily, urban political power. Thus, as noted by Hobsbawm, the ensuing nationalization of politics partially transformed the role of the traditional local notability, which now had to reach a modus vivendi with upstart "bosses" attached to a national political machine.

Finally, the popular organizations were ideological, offering their constituents a "total vision of the world." This enabled the organizations to incorporate members by taking advantage of multiple and complex bonds of loyalty, including the familial, market, and spatially derived networks that combined vertical and emergent horizontal linkages and that facilitated the

47. Eric Hobsbawm, *The Age of Empire, 1875–1914*, 92–94.

synthesis of a new model of political community. It also endowed the organizations with a capacity for symbol generation and symbol acquisition far greater than that of simple pressure or special-interest groups.

Thus, except perhaps for supplying a rich and seemingly bottomless mythopoetic wellspring from which both nationalist historians and subsequent regimes in the Arab Middle East might draw, the most enduring legacy of the Faysali years in Syria was the formation of these popular committees, committees that not only displayed in microcosm the social and political transformation that Syrians had experienced during the preceding three-quarters of a century, but acted to expedite the emergence of mass politics.

• • •

Syria had been part of the Ottoman Empire for nearly four hundred years when the government in Istanbul made the ill-fated decision to enter World War I on the side of the central powers. The effects of this decision, and of the ensuing war-related economic and political turmoil, had enduring consequences for all inhabitants of Syria.

From 1914 through 1918, economic crises buffeted the popular classes of Syria, simultaneously lowering their standard of living and widening the gap that separated rich and poor. Prices for all basic commodities rose during the war, while other goods, such as coffee, sugar, and rice, were virtually unobtainable.[48] At the same time, the scarcity of labor and transport, the impounding of farm animals by the Ottoman Fourth Army headquartered in Damascus, and a series of natural disasters—a ruinous drought during the harvest of 1914–1915, a locust plague in 1915, and a crop-destroying heat wave in 1916—reduced harvests in the interior. The entente naval blockade of the eastern Mediterranean, which had particularly devastating effects on coastal cities and which remained in place in one form or another through February 1919, further exacerbated food shortages, while currency depreciation, speculation, and forced government requisitioning drove commodity prices even higher.[49] In July 1917, at a time when

48. FO 371/2771, "Arab Bureau Intelligence Survey 10," 14 July 1916; FO 371/3058/137867, "Internal Conditions," 11 May 1917.

49. FO 861/63, Vice Consul, Aleppo to L. Mallet, 31 August 1914; *al-Muqtabas*, 23 June 1915, 2; FO 371/2770/104598/296, "Internal Conditions: Enemy Countries (Athens)," 28 May 1916; FO 371/2771, "Arab Bureau Intelligence Survey 10," 14 July 1916; FO 371/2781/193557, "Information from Two Arab Officers Recently Arrived in England from the Caucasus and Examined by Sir M. Sykes," 25 September 1916; *Arab Bulletin*, 4 December 1916, 504–507; FO

Ottoman paper currency was worth approximately 25 percent of its face value, Hawrani farmers resisted selling wheat for anything but gold. By 1918, when the value of Ottoman currency fell to approximately 14 percent of its face value, merchants commonly refused to accept Ottoman paper even when threatened with harsh penalties, thus restricting most transactions to barter.[50]

For many, life in the interior cities of Syria was nightmarish. The Ottoman government frequently denied widows, orphans, state functionaries, and pensioners all or part of their customary stipends. Even when disbursed, stipends were paid in depreciated Ottoman paper currency and were therefore hardly sufficient for subsistence.[51] Lower nutritional levels (aggravated both by the common practice of adulterating flour and, after 1916, by a system of rationing that reduced per capita consumption) and a breakdown of municipal services opened up the coastal and interior cities of Syria to epidemics of dysentery, typhus, smallpox, diphtheria, malaria, and cholera.[52] The press reported a rise in the rates of suicide, crime, and vagrancy in Damascus. By midwar, gangs of deserters from the Ottoman army threatened the security of villages surrounding the city and all but smothered local trade. Rural insecurity, in turn, loosed a flood of refugees on the city, raising the size of the urban population (according to one probably exaggerated account) to as many as half a million. Overcrowding, combined with speculation in real estate, also boosted the cost of housing both inside the walls of Damascus and in the immediate environs so high that by 1918, the average rate of profit on urban real estate had doubled from 4 percent to 8 percent.[53]

371/3058/137867, "Internal Conditions," 11 May 1917; FO 371/2783/221220, "Report of an Inhabitant of Athlit, Mt. Carmel, Syria," n.d.; MAE L:SL/vol. 78/1840, Amiral Gauchet to président de la république, 21 February 1919.

50. See Schilcher, "Famine of 1915–1918"; FO 371/2771, "Arab Bureau Intelligence Survey 10," 14 July 1916; FO 371/3050/142519, "Notes of an Interview with Mr. Edelman," 6 July 1917; FO 371/3050/158286, William Yale, "Palestine-Syria Situation," 10 July 1917; DU SA 493/15/85–98, G. B. Stewart (Treasurer, Syrian Protestant College) to Saʿid Shuqayr, 7 June 1919.

51. *al-Muqtabas,* 15 March 1915, 2; *al-Muqtabas,* 13 June 1915, 2.

52. *al-Muqtabas,* 10 January 1915, 2; *The Near East,* 28 April 1916, 701; *Arab Bulletin,* 30 June 1916, 2; *Arab Bulletin,* 14 July 1916, 3–4; FO 371/2779/165094, "Arabian Report N.S. No. V. (Week Ending August 16, 1916)"; FO 371/2779/170425, Dr. Franklin Hoskins, 29 August 1916; FO 371/3058/117734, "Memorandum of Conversation with Mr. Samuel Edelman, U.S. Consul at Damascus," 10 June 1917.

53. *al-Muqtabas,* 16 January 1915, 1; *al-Qibla,* 12 rajab 1335, 2; *al-Qibla,* 16 rajab 1335, 3; FO 371/2783/221220, "Report of an Inhabitant of Athlit, Mt. Carmel,

While generally devastating for the popular classes, the war had a mixed effect on the upper classes. On the one hand, the Ottoman government exiled the families of "economic criminals" (speculators), political criminals, and deserters, and confiscated their property.[54] In December 1916, for example, according to a report in the (pro-Sharifian) Meccan newspaper *al-Qibla,* Ottoman authorities arrested 150 Damascene notables and sent 100 families into exile in Anatolia. By November 1917, according to another report in the same newspaper, 450 families had been exiled and their property confiscated.[55] On the other hand, some merchants did grow rich from speculation, smuggling, and the sale of supplies to the Ottoman Fourth Army. According to journalist Muhammad Kurd ʿAli, "Many of the merchants, functionaries, and middlemen in the administration became wealthy. . . . [Gold came into Damascus through disbursements to both the Ottoman and Arab armies] until the country became, in the last two years of the war, a nation of ease and opulence."[56]

In addition to the direct social and economic effects that the war had on the lives of the inhabitants of Syria, two relevant political effects followed from the outbreak of hostilities. First, in anticipation of the defeat of the central powers and the dismemberment of the Ottoman Empire, Britain, France, and other entente powers entered into a series of secret agreements that outlined plans for the orderly partition of the Ottoman Empire. One such agreement, the Sykes-Picot Agreement of 1916, stipulated the division of the Arab provinces of the empire into areas of direct and indirect British and French control.[57] Although later modified to accommodate con-

---

Syria," n.d.; MAE L:SL/vol. 64/20, "Note sur les finances municipales, les travaux urbains, et la nécessité d'un crédit communal," 8 January 1920(?); Schilcher, "Famine of 1915–1918," 241. According to the newspaper *al-Kawkab,* after the establishment of the Arab government, the municipal government of Damascus attempted to formulate some sort of rent control program because "[i]t is true that rent increases in this city crowded with thousands of people has become the subject of widespread chatter and gossip." *al-Kawkab,* 28 October 1919, 10.

54. *al-Muqtabas,* 9 April 1915, 2; FO 371/2779/165094, "Arabian Report N.S. No. V. (Week Ending August 16, 1916)"; FO 371/3050/161668, "Mr. (William) Hall's Report on Syria," 1 August 1917; Schilcher, *Families in Politics,* 17.

55. *al-Qibla,* 15 ṣafar 1335, 2; *al-Qibla,* 16 muḥarram 1336, 3.

56. Muḥammad Kurd ʿAlī, *Khiṭaṭ al-Shām,* 4:255; FO 371/3050/161668, "Mr. (William) Hall's Report on Syria," 1 August 1917; FO 371/3413/179133, "Translation of a Document Captured by Desert Mounted Corps During Operation 19th to 21st September 1918."

57. For the text of the Sykes-Picot Agreement and subsequent modifications, see J. C. Hurewitz, *The Middle East and North Africa in World Politics: A Documentary Record,* 2:60–64, 118–128, 158–166.

tingencies unforeseen at the time of its negotiation, the Sykes-Picot Agreement provided the rationale for rival national claims and diplomatic maneuverings during the immediate postwar period.

The second relevant political consequence of the war was the installation of a representative of the Hashemite family of Mecca in Damascus. In 1916, as part of the larger campaign against the Ottoman Empire, the British encouraged the rebellion of Sharif Husayn and his sons against their Ottoman overlords—the highly-touted "Arab Revolt." In an exchange of letters, the British pledged their support for the military campaign and for the establishment of an independent Arab state or states after the termination of hostilities.[58] One of the sharif's sons, Amir Faysal, was placed in charge of the Northern Arab Army, which participated in the British-led campaign that drove north from the Hijaz through Palestine to present-day Syria. According to prevailing assessments (in this case, that of an American observer who wrote his summary sketch shortly after the amir entered Damascus), Faysal was "pleasing of manner and appearance, liberal minded and kindly disposed to all parties. But he is not a strong man and is surrounded by clever, shrewd, and unscrupulous politicians, who can easily influence him."[59] Although after the capture of Damascus the chain of command linking the British, Faysal, and the appointed military governor of Syria was confused, British recognition, in conjunction with familial (sharifian) and military prestige and, initially, the judicious use of force, endowed the young amir with sufficient leverage to establish himself as the "supreme authority over all Arab matters in Syria, both administrative and military."[60]

This arrangement was not uncontested. By the time British, Australian, and Arab troops entered Damascus, the Turks had already abandoned the city.[61] To maintain order during the brief interregnum, several groups at-

58. See ibid., 46–56.

59. USNA 165/112/2075–2088, U.S. Military Attaché (Cairo), "The Political Situation in Syria," 9 November 1918.

60. Russell, *First Modern Arab State*, 19.

61. The best description of the last days of Turkish government in Damascus and the events of late September 1918 is in Wajīh al-Ḥaffār, "al-Ḥukūmāt allatī taʿāqabat ʿalā al-ḥukm fī Sūriyya," *al-Shurṭa wal-amn al-ʿāmm* 1 (2 ramadan 1372): 12–13 and (3 shuwwāl 1372): 18–19, 47. See also Muḥammad Jamīl Bayhum, *Sūriyya wa Lubnān, 1918–1922*, 44–48; Elie Kedourie, "The Capture of Damascus, 1 October 1918"; Anwar al-Rifāʿī, *Jihād nuṣf qarn: Sumūw al-amīr Saʿīd al-Jazāʾirī*, 96–104; ʿAbd al-ʿAzīz al-ʿAẓma, *Mirʾāt al-Shām: Tārīkh Dimashq wa*

tempted to organize a governing authority in the city. With the fall of Damascus imminent, Jamal Pasha (al-Saghir), the last Ottoman governor of Syria, commissioned Saʿid al-Jazaʾiri to form a civil guard from among his clients to maintain order. Although the Jazaʾiris were relative newcomers to Damascus, the family had gained prominence in local affairs for its role in quelling the intercommunal riots that had racked the city in 1860.[62] Saʿid al-Jazaʾiri enlisted the assistance of Shaykh Rida al-ʿAttar, an officer in the Ottoman army and scion of a prominent family of Damascus qadis, and Amin al-Tarabulsi, the leader of the local constabulary. Their efforts were soon joined by those of other distinguished Damascus residents, including Faris al-Khuri, Tahir al-Jazaʾiri, ʿAta al-Ayyubi, Badiʿ al-Muʾayyad, Shakir al-Hanbali, Saʿada Kahala, Amin al-Tamimi, and Shaykh ʿAbd al-Qadir al-Khatib, the former *khaṭīb* (preacher) at the Umayyad Mosque whom the Jazaʾiris appointed president of the Damascus municipality. Several of these men had previously met in the home of Mahmud al-Barudi, one of the wealthiest landowners in Damascus, where they established a "national committee" (*lajna waṭaniyya*) to secure the peaceable surrender of the city to the advancing Anglo-Arab army. After the national committee had negotiated an agreement between Saʿid al-Jazaʾiri and a representative of the Arab army, Shukri al-Ayyubi,[63] al-Jazaʾiri appointed a government from among the above-mentioned individuals with himself as "President of the Syrian Arab government," his brother, ʿAbd al-Qadir al-Jazaʾiri, as commander of the Arab cavalry, and Shukri al-Ayyubi as military governor.

The true attitude of the Jazaʾiris and their government to Faysal and the Arab Revolt will probably never be known; likewise, it is difficult to assess whether or not the two sides might eventually have been able to reach some form of accommodation had they been shielded from British interference.[64] Whatever the possibilities, this did not occur: T. E. Lawrence,

---

ahlihā, 235; Sulṭān, *Tārīkh Sūriyya 1918–1920*, 18; FO 882/7/352ff., T. E. Lawrence, "The Destruction of the Fourth Army"; FO 371/3383/169562/559ff., Clayton to FO, 8 October 1918.

62. Saʿid al-Jazaʾiri's grandfather, ʿAbd al-Qadir al-Jazaʾiri, had led the Algerian resistance to French colonial ambitions in the 1830s. After his capture, he settled in Damascus in 1855. See John Ruedy, *Modern Algeria: The Origins and Development of a Nation*, 57–66.

63. According to al-Haffar, the leader of the departing Ottoman army had also designated al-Ayyubi to secure the city.

64. Al-Haffar claims that, while outwardly pledging their support for the Hashemites, the Jazaʾiris were, in fact, preparing for civil war. See al-Ḥaffār, "al-Ḥukūmāt allatī taʿāqabat" 1(3 shuwwāl 1372): 47.

whose role as British liaison with the Arab army belied the extent of his influence on the young amir, regarded the Jaza'iris and their Damascene and "Moorish" supporters as a threat to his protégé, and thus treated the brothers and their government with undisguised contempt. "They are both insane, and as well pro-Turkish, and religious fanatics of the most unpleasant sort," he wrote.

> In consequence I sent for them, and before the beladiyeh and the sheukh el harrat, announced that as Feisal's representative I declared Shukri el-Ayubi Arab Military Governer (Ali Riza, the intended governer, missing) and the provisional civil administration of the Algerians dissolved. They took it rather hard and had to be sent home.[65]

Although Faysal and his followers were soon able, with British assistance, to eliminate their rivals from positions of power (ʿAbd al-Qadir al-Jaza'iri was shot and killed under disputed circumstances soon after the arrival of the Anglo-Arab army in Damascus, while the British exiled Saʿid al-Jaza'iri to Haifa), many prominent Damascenes remained resentful of their new rulers who, they felt, had been imposed on them by force of arms.

After the Anglo-Arab army entered Damascus, units of the Arab army raced north to seize control of Homs, Hama, and Aleppo. Concurrently, the British army relinquished control of Amman in the south to a local representative of the amir. On 22 October 1918, General Sir Edmund H. Allenby, commander of the Egyptian Expeditionary Force that conducted the Syria campaign, divided the former Ottoman territories under his authority into two administrative districts. He placed the inland territory stretching from the Hijaz north through Damascus and Aleppo under the authority of the Occupied Enemy Territory Administration—East (OETA-East). To the west, Allenby created a coastal zone that included the prewar Ottoman province of Beirut and, initially, the inland towns of Hasbaya, Rashaya, Muʿallaqa, and Baʿalbak, to be supervised by the Occupied Enemy Territory Administration—West (OETA-West). While this second zone came under French administration, the British sanctioned the establishment of a temporary Arab government under Amir Faysal in the inland (eastern) zone.[66]

65. FO 882/7/352ff, T. E. Lawrence, "The Destruction of the Fourth Army," n.d.

66. A third authority, Occupied Enemy Territory Administration—North, was established in January 1919. Both the British and the Arab governments claimed jurisdiction over Palestine. See Russell, *First Modern Arab State*, 17–21, 26–27. Perhaps the most readable account of the diplomatic maneuvering that took place after World War I is David Fromkin's *A Peace to End All Peace: The Fall of the*

Even before the Arab administration was fully functioning, Faysal, his closest associates from the Arab army, and a select group of nonmilitary appointees attempted to win popular favor and establish direct links with the inhabitants of their zone. Faysal's government recommenced Ottoman welfare programs that had been suspended during the war and resumed the payment of pensions to war widows, orphans, and former Ottoman functionaries and their families.[67] The government also attempted to maintain the stability of prices and prevent food shortages in urban centers by buying grain directly from farmers in the Hawran, establishing committees in each quarter to oversee distribution of foodstuffs, and periodically dispensing grain from captured granaries to the urban poor and distributing seed to impoverished farmers.[68]

To ensure that the population understood who was responsible for the largesse disbursed by the Arab government, high-ranking officials, often joined by a retinue of bureaucrats, journalists, and even poets who had been commissioned to compose and recite paeans to Amir Faysal or the government, visited the quarters of Damascus and other cities and traveled the countryside where they distributed gifts in ceremonies designed to solemnize the occasion. For example, ʿAli Rida al-Rikabi, the first military governor of the eastern zone, toured Syria in January 1919. According to an account written by the journalist who accompanied him, upon entering a village, al-Rikabi convoked the local cultivators to discuss conditions and problems, urging them to petition him directly if they suffered any grievance. In Homs, al-Rikabi announced a general amnesty for criminals, awarded honors, and distributed money for the transport and settlement of those Syrian soldiers returning from Anatolia who had fought in the Ottoman army. In Hama and Aleppo, he distributed seed to local villagers, offered a moratorium on farmers' debt, contributed to local charities, and or-

---

Ottoman Empire and the Creation of the Modern Middle East. For the division of the occupied territory, see 338–339.

67. *al-ʿĀṣima,* 17 April 1919, 3; DU SA 493/16/13–15, Saʿid Shuqayr, "Points to Be Discussed with Col. Waters-Taylor at Haifa on the 11th August, 1919"; *al-ʿĀṣima,* 23 February 1920, 4; DU SA 493/15/5, n.d.

68. FO 371/3412/180073/148, Clayton to FO, 28 October 1918; FO 371/3412/189713/184, Clayton to FO, 14 November 1918; FO 371/4143/104019, Major General Sir Walter Lawrence to Commander in Chief (Egypt), 13 May 1919; DU SA 493/15/28–9, General Director of Agricultural Bank to Minister of Finance, 9 July 1919; *al-ʿĀṣima,* 1 December 1919, 7; *al-ʿĀṣima,* 29 December 1919, 2; *al-ʿĀṣima,* 10 June 1920, 2; Suhayla al-Rīmāwī, *al-Tajriba al-fayṣaliyya fī bilād al-Shām,* 41.

dered the installation of public works.[69] Al-Rikabi continued his travels as late as spring 1920. During his last recorded tour, once again made in the presence of journalists, al-Rikabi visited various quarters of Damascus, inspecting bakers' ovens. When he discovered the use of adulterated flour or short weights, he publicly ordered the arrest of those responsible. Other high government officials, including Amir Faysal himself, made similar tours.[70]

The Arab government did not direct its beneficence and propaganda only at the peasantry and urban masses, however. British officials frequently complained that too much of the subsidy that they were paying to the Arab government was being used to buy the loyalty of wealthy and powerful Syrians as well. The government paid off leaders of tribes, politicians, members of political and cultural associations, religious leaders, and journalists. The records of the financial adviser to the Arab government, Saʿid Shuqayr, are replete with notations of political payoffs: 16,000 Egyptian pounds (P.E.) distributed to notables at Junia; 100 P.E. to the grand rabbi of Damascus; 25,000 P.E. for propaganda work in Beirut; 1,500 P.E. to the Orthodox church in Damascus.[71] For the month of June 1919 alone, Shuqayr recorded as "Donations" or "Irregular or Extraordinary Expenditures" payments to Nasib al-Atrash, ʿAdil Arslan, and other Druze leaders; shaykhs of the al-Diab, Dahamisha and Majalib tribes; ʿAwda Abi Tayah and Ibn ʿAwda Abi Tayah of the Huwaytat tribe; Nuri al-Shaʿlan of the Ruwalla tribe; the Greek Catholic Club, Moslem-Christian Committee, Alliance Committee (*Alliance israélite*?), and Literary Society; ʿAbd al-Qadir al-Khatib; Yusuf al-ʿAzma, whom Faysal later appointed head of the Arab government's war council; Arab Club activists Fa'iz al-Khuri and Murad (Muhammad?) Rushdi; Gabriel Haddad, head of the gendarmerie (records indicate this payment was "for furniture"); various bedouin delegations visiting Damascus (for food and lodging); and newspaper proprietors, among others. Similar payments made the following month reached 22,378 P.E.—approximately one-tenth of projected government revenue.[72]

69. A complete account of ʿAli Rida al-Rikabi's trip is in Khalīl Mardam Bek, *Dimashq wal-Quds fī al-ʿishrīnāt*, 24–66.

70. *al-ʿĀṣima*, 5 April 1920, 5; MD 4H112/dossier 2b/68, "Renseignements d'officier liaison d'Alep," 10 June 1920; AD 2346/c1a/sous-dossier 19: Voyage Fayçal à Alep/73, "Renseignements d'officier liaison d'Alep," 15 July 1920; AD 2346/c1a/sous-dossier 19: Voyage Faysal à Alep/77, "Renseignements d'officier liaison d'Alep," 22 July 1920; Angelil, "L'occupation d'Homs."

71. DU SA 493/13/25–35, Shuqayr to Waters-Taylor, 3 September 1919.

72. DU SA 493/14/31–32; DU SA 493/13/4, Appendix to letter from Shuqayr

In spite of its efforts, however, the Arab government was able to maintain only a thin veneer of authority outside Damascus. The government apparatus that had been established to oversee the eastern zone was clumsy and inefficient: it actually consisted of a tangle of vaguely drawn and, at times, contradictory lines of authority connecting Allenby, Faysal, al-Rikabi, and the bureaucracy. Furthermore, the local governments that supervised the administration of most cities continued to be controlled by indigenous notables whose concerns and interests frequently clashed with those of the Arab government and its representatives sent from Damascus. This local urban leadership was jealous of the attention the Arab government showered on the capital city, fearful of the centralization policies planned by those whom it perceived to be upstarts and foreigners, and resentful of a government that not only arrogated to itself both domestic and foreign sources of revenue but seemed to match inefficiency with arrogance.[73] Relations between notables of Aleppo and the government in Damascus, aggravated by differences over issues of foreign policy and trade, were particularly tense. When the amir made his first trip north in 1918, he openly recalled the lack of assistance offered to the Arab Revolt by the inhabitants of the city, then dismissed the local administrative council (*majlis al-shūrā*) and appointed a governing committee composed of his supporters. Relations remained so strained that in the spring of 1920 a delegation of prominent Aleppans arrived in Damascus during the celebration of Faysal's coronation as king of Syria, reportedly demanding autonomy for their city and the surrounding countryside.[74]

Nevertheless, it might have been possible for the Arab government to circumvent or procure the endorsement of recalcitrant local leaders and to

---

to Waters-Taylor, 3 September 1919; DU SA 493/14/33; DU SA 493/13/5, Appendix to letter from Shuqayr to Waters-Taylor, 3 September 1919; DU SA 493/13/7, Appendix to letter from Shuqayr to Waters-Taylor, 3 September 1919; DU SA 493/9/19, "Statement of Estimated Expenditure Submitted to H.H. Emir Faisal on 5th June, 1919." The estimates for revenue include the monthly 150,000 P.E. stipend from the British government. It should also be noted that one British expert who studied the figures used the word *farcical* to describe Arab government revenue projections. FO 371/5032/990/93–97, "Report by Col. Waters-Taylor on his visit to Beirut, and interviews with General Gouraud and the Emir Feisal," 21 January 1920.

73. *Arab Bulletin*, 11 July 1918, 200; FO 371/3385/199351/16, Sykes to FO, 2 December 1918; FO 371/3386/208324, Sir L. Mallet, Minutes to Telegram 11457 and 11513, 18 December 1918; FO 371/4143/39115, Lt. Col. R. W. Graves, "Finance in OETA-East," 27 December 1918.

74. Kāmil Ghazzī, *Nahr al-dhahab fī tārīkh Ḥalab*, 3:655–656; USNA 59/890d.00/9/473, J. B. Jackson to U.S. Secretary of State, 13 March 1920.

manufacture popular consent over the long term had it acquired international support, maintained reliable access to economic resources, and presided over an economic recovery. It was, however, unable to do any of these things. From its inception, monetary and fiscal problems plagued the eastern zone. When entente forces entered Syria, a variety of coins and paper money was in circulation. To put an end to the monetary chaos, General Allenby mandated the use of the sterling-backed Egyptian pound as legal tender. It was a logical choice: the Egyptian-based British army occupying Syria was paid in the currency, and the alternative—maintaining Ottoman currency as legal tender—would have meant sanctioning the use of a currency issued by a government that no longer existed and backed by the worthless German mark. But Allenby's order created a host of unforeseen problems. Because the British authorities had initially restricted the circulation of Egyptian specie as a guard against inflation, it was scarce in areas outside Damascus and urban Palestine. Furthermore, Syrians were hardly enthusiastic about the new currency: many encountered difficulties converting from one system of valuation to another, and merchants trading with Anatolia and the coast feared being cut off from markets outside Syria.[75] To make matters worse, the local value of the Egyptian pound depreciated steadily for a year after the war before plummeting in the autumn of 1919.

Syrians thus continued to circulate Ottoman and foreign coins, appraising their worth on the basis of their metallic content. This proved to be impractical as well: relative currency values fluctuated wildly, often in response to decisions taken in London, Paris, Istanbul, and even Baghdad. When, for example, the British administration in Iraq declared the circulation of Turkish silver and nickel coinage illegal, Damascus was flooded with the coins, causing an abrupt depreciation that, according to one British observer, inflicted "great hardship to the population."[76]

Entente actions, bureaucratic shortcomings, and fiscal policies enacted by the Arab government also diminished government income. Not only had the Ottoman government already collected the taxes for the upcoming year by the time the Anglo-Arab army reached Damascus, but the new administration lacked sufficient authority in most areas of Syria to gather

75. FO 371/3383/169803, Adam Block and Mark Sykes, addendum to minutes for 17 October 1918; FO 371/3413/188081/Q.K.T. 4826, GHQ to WO, 10 November 1918; WO 106/189/75957, WO to GHQ, 7 March 1919; FO 371/4171/63664/395, India Office Bank to FO, 24 March 1919.

76. FO 371/4140/104076/E. A. 2588, GHQ to WO, 13 July 1919; AD 2347/12350/427, Adel Arslane [sic]to Cousse, 11 December 1919.

revenue. In addition, revenue agents of unquestioned competence and loyalty were uncommon. "I much regret that the accounts for June cannot possibly be forwarded to you by the middle of this month," Saʿid Shuqayr wrote to his British overseers in the summer of 1919,

> owing to the fact that accountants in Districts are very incapable and their accounts are deplorably behind hand. On my arrival here in May last, I found that neither the accounts for the past year (October to December) nor those for the first quarter of this year had been finally closed. . . . I may mention that some of the accountants have recently been discharged either for incapacity or corruption. They are being replaced by others, and it is hoped that in future the accounts will be kept in a better manner.[77]

Even *al-Kawkab,* a newspaper normally supportive of the Arab government, acknowledged that functionaries did "not have a command of writing in Arabic and are not even able to express their thoughts without error."[78] Furthermore, the government's revenue needs ran afoul of its strategy for securing popular support. Because the Arab government had initially sought to win over the Syrian population through tax relief, it abolished two of the most hated Ottoman taxes: *wīrkū al-ḥarb,* which, among other things, had increased taxes on salaries by 3 percent and taxes on real property by 25 percent, and the special taxes that had originally been imposed in 1911–1912 to supplement revenues. Finally, certain revenues, such as tithes for the sanjaks of Damascus, Aleppo, and Hama and the *aghnām* (tax on sheep) for Aleppo were unavailable to the Arab government since they had already been pledged to the Ottoman Public Debt Administration to repay debts incurred by the previous government.[79]

To make up for revenue shortfalls, the British extended the Arab government a monthly subsidy of 150,000 P.E. Because the subsidy provided Whitehall with the means to ensure both the financial solvency and unremitting loyalty of its wartime ally, British guarantees of a fixed sum payable in regular installments were perhaps an appropriate political solution to the Arab government's fiscal problems. However, these payments also created a debilitating economic problem: money injected directly into

77. DU SA 493/16/37/6/7762, Shuqayr, 7 July 1919.
78. *al-Kawkab,* 4 November 1919, 10.
79. DU SA 493/9/6, Proclamation of General Sir Edmund Allenby, 7 May 1918; FO 371/4143/39115, Lt. Col. R. W. Graves, "Finance in OETA-East"; MAE L:AH/vol. 3/98, Moulin, "Examen du budget de 1919. Zone Est," 7 February 1919; DU SA 493/6/71–2. "Revenues for 1919"; DU SA 493/6/35–41, Shuqayr, 15 January 1920.

the economy by the subsidy, augmented by sums spent by the British army of occupation, chased a limited amount of goods and consequently inflated prices. The prolongation of the entente embargo, restrictions on both interzonal trade and trade with Turkey, speculation, hoarding, and the insecurity of transportation, drove prices up even further.[80] In all, the inflation not only weakened the financial capabilities of the Arab government, but by presenting it with yet another seemingly insoluble problem that touched the day-to-day lives of those it governed, sapped its moral authority as well.

Faysal himself could spend little time in Syria dealing with either political or economic problems. On 11 November 1918, less than six weeks after the amir's arrival in Damascus, Sharif Husayn appointed his son as his emissary to the peace conference in Paris where the entente powers were deciding the fate of the former Ottoman territories. Faysal stayed in Europe five months. He returned to Damascus at the beginning of May 1919 to take charge of preparations for the arrival of the Inter-Allied Commission on Syria (hereafter, the King-Crane Commission), which had been appointed, at the insistence of President Woodrow Wilson, to "elucidate the state of opinion [in Syria] and the soil to be worked on by any mandatory"[81] and to make recommendations to the conference with regard to the future of Syria. In the aftermath of the ill-fated commission's visit, Faysal once again traveled to Europe, this time remaining four months. During Faysal's absences, Sharif Husayn delegated Faysal's twenty-one-year-old brother, Amir Zayd, to represent the family in Damascus. Zayd—described by British observers in terms like "soft in his ways and vague in his ideas," "malleable [and] much influenced by his surroundings," "very conscious of his own ignorance and overburdened by the anxieties of his present position," and "good material for the psychologist"—was such an uninspiring (and, according to several reports, debauched) ruler that the French liaison officer in Damascus advised the French government to stall

80. Russell, *First Modern Arab State,* 142–146; FO 371/3412/177154/3222, Clayton to FO, 22 October 1918; MAE L:SL/vol. 78/1586, Paul Cambon, 28 December 1918; *al-ʿĀṣima,* 26 April 1919, 7–8; FO 371/4143/104019, Major General Sir Walter Lawrence to Commander in Chief (Egypt), 13 May 1919; FO 371/4228/111406, Balfour to Curzon, 21 July 1919; FO 371/4228/120623/EA2612, GHQ to WO, 6 August 1919; FO 371/4228/156929/501, Meinertzhagen to FO, 25 November 1919; MD 4H114/2/261, Cousse to Gouraud, 3 April 1920; MD 4H112/2b/25, "Renseignements du 24 au 30 avril [1920]."

81. Hurewitz, *Middle East and North Africa,* 2:191. See also Arthur S. Link, ed., *The Papers of Woodrow Wilson,* 56:116.

negotiations with Faysal in Paris so that Syrians, increasingly exposed to Zayd, would come to loathe the entire Hashemite family.[82]

The announcement of the impending visit of the King-Crane Commission to the Middle East had repercussions for Syrian politics that neither the entente representatives meeting in Paris nor the Arab government in Damascus could have anticipated. Although nominally committed to "the establishment of national governments [in the Middle East] . . . deriving their authority from the initiative and free choice of the indigenous inhabitants,"[83] British and French representatives to the peace conference viewed the commission as little more than a nuisance and refused to appoint delegates to it or be bound by its findings. Even American support for the commission proved lackluster.[84] But whatever doubts Amir Faysal and his supporters may have privately held about the sincerity of the entente powers, they publicly grasped at this straw. In early June 1919, the amir convoked delegates to the Syrian General Congress and charged them with formulating a consensual list of demands to be presented to the American commission.[85] Soon afterward, the Arab government distributed *khuṭab* (sermons) to be read at Friday prayers and, in conjunction with political and cultural associations and government-sanctioned guilds, sponsored petition campaigns and mobilized demonstrations in support of the "Damascus Program" promulgated by the congress. It directed local political activists and quarter-based government functionaries (*makhātīr,* singular *mukhtār*) throughout Syria to compel homeowners and shopkeepers to placard their residences and storefronts with slogans demanding Syrian unity and absolute independence from the entente negotiators convened in Paris.[86] In

82. FO 371/2773/122968, Copy of report by Ronald Storrs, 10 June 1916; IO L/PS/10/802/11–13, Gertrude Bell, "Syria in October 1919," 15 November 1919. AD 2368/10/2, Rapports du capt. Pichon et du lt. col. Cousse 1919/66, Cousse to HC, 9 January 1919. According to another report, "Zayd displays no regret; without exaggeration, one hears of a thousand and one scandals concerning his private life, abominable orgies in Mazza, women tortured or killed, "licenses" demanded personally from certain merchants and exporters, etc. . . . He leaves Damascenes with the impression of a veritable savage." MAE 4H114/5/no no., Cousse to Toulat, 1 August 1920.

83. Hurewitz, *Middle East and North Africa,* 2:112.

84. See James L. Gelvin, "The Ironic Legacy of the King-Crane Commission," 13–14.

85. See Khoury, *Urban Notables,* 86–88; Yūsuf al-Ḥakīm, *Dhikrayāt,* 3:90–97; Safiuddin Joarder, *Syria Under the French Mandate: The Early Phase, 1920–1927,* 209–211.

86. MD L:SL/vol. 12/32–38, Cousse to HC, 6 April 1919; AD 2430/no no., Cousse to Dame, 18 April 1919; MAE L:AH/vol. 4/237–238, Picot to Pichon,

sum, while the entente powers had charged the commission with a simple fact-finding mission, its presence in Syria catalyzed a mobilization of the Syrian population that was unprecedented in scope.

The appointment of the King-Crane Commission had another unintended effect. The nationalist elites who prepared for the commission's arrival designed their demonstrations and propaganda campaigns for the purpose of presenting to an outside audience an image of a sophisticated nation eager and prepared for independence. But in the process of converting Syria into a large Potemkin village, they failed to integrate the majority of the population into their nationalist project. They never negotiated with the population about ideology or program, they never synthesized a political discourse that was compelling to non-elites, and they never established bonds with the population comparable to those established between nationalist elites and their future compatriots in other areas of the world. In short, the announcement of the formation of the King-Crane Commission and its subsequent visit to Syria initiated an unintended chain of events that culminated in the emergence of a popular nationalist movement dissociated from the direction of the Arab government and the nationalist elites. In this context, it is particularly ironic that the commission's report, finally published in 1922, never reached the peace conference.[87]

In September 1919, less than two months after the King-Crane Commission had left the Middle East, Amir Faysal received a second invitation to Paris. Concerned about tensions with France and excessive military expenditures, the British government had decided to withdraw its troops from Syria. According to the plan negotiated with its European ally, the British relinquished temporary control of the western zone (including the contested Biqaʿ Valley that lay between the eastern and western zones) to French military occupation and, pending the negotiation of a permanent arrangement between France and the Arab government, temporary control of the eastern zone to Faysal and his administration. The Anglo-French agreement (the so-called "September 15 Accord") precipitated what has been called the "Evacuation Crisis" by historians, the turning point in the history of Syria under the Arab government. The plan to substitute French

---

22 May 1919; MAE L:SL/vol. 14/897, Picot to MAE, 17 June 1919; MAE L:SL/vol. 44/3D, Minault (Latakia) to administrateur du vilayet de Beyrouth, 18 July 1919; MAE L:SL/vol. 43/39–41, "Renseignements d'agent," 10–20 July 1919; MD 7N4182/4/340, Picot to MAE, 21 July 1919; AD 2430/dossier confidentiel—départ/240, 11 August 1919. For texts of sermons distributed 11 and 18 April 1919, see AD 2343/286, Cousse to HC, 24 April 1919.

87. Russell, *First Modern Arab State*, 99.

troops for British in the Biqaʿ Valley in particular was a political disaster for Faysal, for it was widely perceived that, "popular will" to the contrary, the French would eventually extend their control over all Syria. The strategy of the Arab government to win independence for an undivided Syria by demonstrating to the entente powers that Syrians both desired and were prepared for independence was thus shown to be bankrupt. The political crisis in Damascus reached fever pitch in January 1920, after Faysal initialed a comprehensive agreement with President Clemenceau of France. The agreement not only limited the sovereignty of the Arab state, it confirmed separate administrations in the territories of the western and eastern zones. To many Syrians, the Faysal-Clemenceau Agreement put an official imprimatur on the division of Syria.[88]

The economic implications of the September 15 Accord were as profound as the political implications. Decisions made by Britain and France pushed the Arab government to the brink of insolvency and reduced its capacity to provide basic services. The inability of the government to ensure security of life and property, formulate fiscal policy, patrol its borders, or meet its payroll precipitated a sharp curtailment of economic activity. To make matters worse, the Arab government attempted to compensate for its financial shortfall by imposing a variety of exactments on the inhabitants of the zone, further increasing their immiserization and disaffection from the government. In short, with the onset of the "Evacuation Crisis," the already ailing economy of Faysali Syria went into a slide from which it never recovered.

According to the September 15 Accord, both France and Britain agreed to share responsibility for the payment of the monthly subsidy to the Arab government. Because the government was not eager either to be or to be perceived to be on the French payroll, however, it at first refused to acquiesce to the new arrangement.[89] The fact that both the British and the French used the subsidy to guarantee good behavior by the government in Damascus further compounded the government's economic distress. The British withheld their subsidy for September 1919 until the Arab government halted the drive to recruit twelve thousand volunteers for the Arab army, and for October and November 1919, pending successful completion of the evacuation of British troops. Later payments were delayed pending a British investigation into the "Dayr al-Zur incident" (an attack by Arab irregulars on the border town currently in eastern Syria in which the British

88. For the negotiations and terms of the settlement, see ibid., 93–131.
89. IO L/PS/10/802/P967, Waters-Taylor, 5 January 1920.

suspected Arab government collusion[90]) and other incidents perceived as emanating from the Faysali government and aimed at weakening the British position in the Middle East. As a result, the Arab government received the British share of the subsidy for the month of January 1920 in June of that year.[91]

To deal with the shortfall of revenue, the Arab government attempted to increase taxes and fees. It raised taxes on earnings, the use of roads, and stamps by 100 percent and taxes on real estate, sheep, and proceedings of the courts of justice by 50 percent. At the same time, it proposed levying special taxes on all towns and villages in which there were government possessions; imposing new taxes on matches, cigarettes, and playing cards; and increasing the *tamattuʿ* (professional tax) and the *badal* (fee paid in lieu of military service). To add to the burden, the government's plan to collect taxes at official currency rates greatly undervalued the actual market value of the Egyptian pound, thereby adding, in effect, a 28 percent surtax to the above rates. In some cases, the government added to the misery of taxpayers by demanding the payment of taxes in gold.[92]

In spring 1920, with the treasury still empty, the government floated a loan that further increased the financial obligations of many Syrians. Although participation in the loan was in theory voluntary, the Arab government required government functionaries to invest one month's salary. Others were similarly persuaded: while gendarmes and local *makhātīr* visited merchants, notables, and even foreign residents to "encourage" their participation in the loan, agents of the clandestine order "The Watchful Eye" extorted money from the wealthy. Although little is known for sure about this latter group, it probably included associates of the popular leader Kamil al-Qassab, whom the government had shrewdly selected to head the committee that marketed the loan in spite of his reputation for what might charitably be called "financial indiscretions."[93]

90. See Eliezer Tauber, "The Struggle for Dayr al-Zur: The Determination of Borders between Syria and Iraq," particularly 366–371.

91. FO 371/4183/132831/EA2697, GHQ to WO, 20 September 1919; FO 371/5149/E564/7, Meinertzhagen to FO, 24 February 1920; FO 371/5149/EA3084, GHQ to WO, 25 April 1920; FO 371/5036/E8177/7749/89, Faysal to Allenby, 21 June 1920.

92. *al-ʿĀṣima,* 29 January 1920, 2; *al-ʿĀṣima,* 2 February 1920, 4; *al-ʿĀṣima,* 26 April 1920, 4; WO 106/196/39–41, Shuqayr, "Memorandum Drafted by the Minister of Finance in Damascus re: The Financial Position of the Syrian Government for 1920," 20 May 1920; Russell, *First Modern Arab State,* 145.

93. MD 4H114/4/471, Cousse to Gouraud, 18 May 1920; MD 4H112/2b/162, Riza Sulh [sic] to gouverneur d'Alep, 2 June 1920; MD 4H112/2b/167, Fares

The deepening impoverishment of the Arab government during its second year casts doubt on the reliability of lists cataloguing governmental accomplishments that often appear in histories of the period.[94] While the pages of the official newspaper, *al-ʿĀṣima,* were replete with plans formulated by the Arab government for administrative reform and for the establishment, expansion, and/or support of social, cultural, and educational institutions, for example, it should not be surprising that little evidence exists to confirm that the government realized most of them or even that it had ever appropriated sufficient funds to initiate them. Thus, although it is not the purpose of this introduction either to celebrate or to denigrate the achievements of the Arab government, overwhelming evidence points to the fact that, perhaps inevitably (considering the economic and political context), failure attended the efforts of the Arab government more frequently than success.

The sometimes ineffective, sometimes reckless attempts by the Arab government to stave off insolvency merely exacerbated the overall economic problems of the eastern zone. As the economy went into a virtual free fall, the crisis touched Syrians of every class. Among the hardest hit were merchants of all types, from wealthy factors to small-scale retailers. By the early spring of 1920, trade between Damascus, Aleppo, and their hinterlands had come to a virtual standstill. Contemporary observers attributed the collapse of commerce to a number of factors: currency fluctuations, an 11 percent customs duty imposed on all goods entering Mesopotamia and Turkey from Syria, and raids by bedouin, whose spoliations had previously been held in check by bribes that the government could no longer afford. "The rock that the Arab Government has split on is the Beduin [sic]," Gertrude Bell later wrote, reflecting on reasons for the fall of the Arab government.

> No attempt was ever made to control them, they harmed the outlying cultivation and Nuri [al-Shaʿlan] took toll of all merchandize going out and coming in and even levied tolls on the donkey loads in the streets. . . .

Khoury [sic] to gouverneur d'Alep, 5 June 1920; MD 4H58/1, "Rapport hebdomadaire 383/2: 15 au 21 juin [1920]"; FO 861/69, Dr. J. Bauer to J. B. Jackson, 1 July 1920; MD 4H114/4/671, Cousse to Gouraud, 7 July 1920; MD 4H60/1, "Bulletin quotidien 1260," 19 July 1920.

94. These lists appear in Abdul-Karim Rafeq, "Arabism, Society, and Economy in Syria, 1918–1920," 16–17; Kasmieh, *al-Ḥukūma al-ʿarabiyya fī Dimashq,* 233–247; Yūsuf al-Ḥakīm, *Dhikrayāt,* 3:43–44.

> The depredations and arrogance of the Beduin are the chief grievances. It was said in Damascus that Nuri not Faisal was Amir.[95]

In addition, security on railroads in and around Damascus was so bad that, in an official complaint addressed to Amir Faysal, the commander of the French forces in the Levant, General Henri Gouraud, listed more than twenty incidents of robbery, hijacking, brigandage, and extortion that took place on or near the lines between 9 December 1919 and 9 January 1920.[96]

In an attempt to ameliorate the effects of the commercial breakdown, the Arab government established a ministry of supply, which assumed responsibility for provisioning cities, fixing prices, and "breaking the back" of speculators and hoarders. The government also promulgated laws forbidding the export of gold and grain outside the eastern zone. None of these measures proved to be enforceable, and merchants reportedly engaged in a host of illegal activities, from smuggling to the establishment of underground cartels, to evade them. Frequently, they were assisted in these activities by the popular committees, which used their leverage with merchants to minister to their constituencies and subsidize their movement. Thus, not only did the new regulations fail to achieve their objectives, they further alienated merchants from the Faysali government.[97]

In addition to its punitive regulations, the Arab government estranged merchants by its apparent inability to mount an effective response to French fiscal policies in the western zone. In January 1920, rumors began to spread among merchants in both zones that the French were planning to impose a new currency, the Syrian pound, in their zone. The possibility that a new currency would be circulated on the coast presented merchants in the eastern zone with a dilemma. If the Arab government refused to au-

95. FO 371/5040/E11756/152–153, "Note by Miss G. L. Bell, C.B.E.," 6 August 1920. See also MD 4H114/dossier 5/277, Cousse to GCC, 14 July 1920.

96. FO 371/4214/103277, Baghdad to IO, 26 June 1919; *Sūriyya al-jadīda*, 27 December 1919, 1; AD 2330/A1a, Gouraud, "Memorandum des principaux faits relevés depuis l'arrivée du général h.c. jusqu'à ce jour," 13 January 1920; WO 106/195/21, Wratislaw (Beirut) to FO, 4 March 1920; AD 2330/A1a/134, Roux (Baghdad) to GCC, 16 March 1920; FO 371/5034/E3182/FO41CPO31, Meinertzhagen, 31 March 1920; FO 371/5035/E5690/35, Wratislaw (Beirut) to FO, 13 May 1920.

97. *al-ʿĀṣima*, 15 December 1919, 3; *al-ʿĀṣima*, 12 January 1920, 2; *al-ʿĀṣima*, 1 March 1920, 2; *al-ʿĀṣima*, 3 May 1920, 2–3; MAE L:SL/vol. 64/731, Gouraud to MAE, 26 March 1920; *al-ʿĀṣima*, 26 April 1920, 7–8; FO 371/5037/E8350, Gertrude Bell, 29 May 1920; Russell, *First Modern Arab State*, 168–169; al-Rīmāwī, *al-Tajriba al-fayṣaliyya*, 41.

thorize the use of the Syrian pound in inland Syria, trade with the coast would collapse. If, on the other hand, the Arab government surrendered to French demands and allowed the Syrian pound to circulate as legal tender in both zones, Syrian merchants could expect a curtailment of their trade with Iraq, Egypt, and Palestine and a flood of French imports in inland Syria. Compounding the currency problem was the fact that the proposed Syrian pound would be linked to the notoriously unstable French franc, the value of which had consistently depreciated since the armistice. The thought that the Arab government would even consider the use of the currency horrified merchants who were already alarmed by the amir's reluctance to discuss either his previous dealings with Clemenceau or his plans for the future.[98] In contrast with the indecision of the government, the popular committees responded to the anxieties of those engaged in trade outside the eastern zone by organizing demonstrations and petition campaigns against the new currency.

Merchants were not the only group threatened by government policies and economic downturn. The economic collapse precipitated by the Evacuation Crisis also victimized civilian and military employees of the government. Not only were government employees forced to subsist on fixed salaries during a period of high inflation, salaries were frequently late or withheld. By June 1920, salaries for functionaries and gendarmes were two months in arrears, while salaries for military officers were regularly fifteen to twenty days late.[99] According to a British report on the state of the Arab army, issued in December 1919,

> The proportion of officers to men is one to three—in fact, they are all officers in some places. These worthies are derelict Turks mostly of the type that came up to apply for the levies and are refused—they wear gorgeous uniforms and decorations and draw handsome salaries on paper—the army has not actually touched any cash for the last two months, however, and they informed me that the Amir now says they will get their pay by taxation—the villagers don't seem very keen about this, though they probably lack the true national spirit—There are some six hun-

98. AD 2347/1, Le président de la chambre de commerce et d'industrie (Beyrouth) to Lt. Col. Nieger, 13 January 1920; AD 2347/3as/d2, "Extraits du bulletin de renseignements du 10 avril [1920]"; AD 2347/12, "Extraits du bulletin quotidien du 12 avril [1920]"; MAE L:SL/vol. 64/823–826, Gouraud to MAE, 14 April 1920; MD 4H58/1, "Rapport hebdomadaire: 27 avril au 3 mai [1920]."

99. MD 4H58/1, "Rapport hebdomadaire: 11–18 décembre [1919]"; IO L/PS/10/802/P967, Report of Waters-Taylor, 5 January 1920; WO 106/196/663G, GHQ to WO, 7 June 1920.

> dred of these beauties in Damascus, about eighty of whom are said to be Baghdadis.[100]

When the Arab government did manage to pay salaries to its employees, wages were low and often garnished for no apparent reason. By early 1920, soldiers whose pay had been reduced 75 percent before inflation were observed in the suqs of Damascus selling their equipment and uniforms in order to buy food. Other soldiers reacted to their impoverishment by desertion, and in some cases, mutiny.[101] Morale among government functionaries plummeted to such an extent that the government posted notices in *al-ʿĀṣima* reminding its employees of their hours of work and warning them against joining antigovernment organizations.[102]

The penury of government on all levels made life difficult and even desperate for much of the remainder of the urban population. For example, although the city of Damascus had an accumulated debt of 200,000 P.E., the municipal budget during the first year of Arab rule was a paltry 35,000 P.E.[103] As a result, the municipal government of Damascus, like the municipal governments of other financially strapped cities in Syria, neglected to provide basic services such as fresh drinking water, public lighting, and sanitation.[104] "Incessant rains have turned the streets into rivers," one Damascus newspaper, usually supportive of the Arab government, complained in January 1920. "The lack of income has prevented the municipal government from spending on necessary repair projects."[105] Another observer wrote at the end of 1919:

100. IO L/PS/11/169/P1512/1920, Major C. A. Boyle, 3 December 1919.

101. *al-ʿĀṣima*, 1 January 1920, 2; AD 2380/5/21/184, Cdt. Rouchdi to cdt. de la troisième brigade de cavalerie (Alep), 25 October 1919; MAE L:SL/vol. 19/1573, Gouraud to MAE, 30 November 1919; AD 2372/837, TEO (zone ouest) to cabinet politique, 20 April 1920; MD 4H58/1, "Rapport hebdomadaire: 20 au 26 avril [1920]"; MD 4H112/2b/51, "Renseignements," 25 May 1920; MAE L:SL/vol. 33, Gouraud to Millerand, 22 September 1920.

102. *al-ʿĀṣima*, 8 January 1920, 3.

103. MAE L:SL/vol. 64/3–39/"Note sur les finances municipales, les travaux urbains, et la nécessité d'un crédit communal," 8 January 1920. According to *al-Kawkab*, the budget for Damascus was 40,000 P.E. *al-Kawkab*, 27 January 1920, 11.

104. For information on Damascus, see *al-Kawkab*, 6 January 1920, 6. For Aleppo, see IO MSS EUR F152 (Frank Lugard Brayne Mss.)/18b. "Palestine and Syria Autumn 1918," 19–22 November 1918; IO MSS/EUR F152 (Frank Lugard Brayne Mss.)/20, 9 February 1919; Mardam Bek, *Dimashq wal-Quds fī al-ʿishrīnāt*, 44–45.

105. *al-Kawkab*, 6 January 1920, 10.

> The most salient feature [of Damascus] was that the town was many degrees dirtier than it had ever been in Turkish times. The bazaars were littered with vegetable and other refuse and secluded corners were no better than receptacles for filth of all descriptions.[106]

The increase in crimes against persons and property further indicates the deterioration of the quality of urban life. Reportedly, gun battles between armed gangs and police were a frequent occurrence on the streets of Damascus. Foreign observers noted that most residents of the capital refused to leave their homes after sundown; those who did venture out at night did so heavily armed.[107] The increase in violent acts committed on the streets of Damascus caused such alarm that in the autumn of 1919 Muslim notables of the city met with their non-Muslim counterparts to formulate a petition demanding the construction of police posts in strategic locations and the reinforcement of police patrols by armed civilians. Ironically, a French dispatch reporting an improvement in security was belied by a story in a progovernment newspaper published two months later reporting that the Damascus municipality was seriously considering permanently stationing a doctor at police headquarters to care for the unprecedented number of gunshot victims.[108] Foreign observers reported similar crime waves in Latakia, Duma, and Dayr al-Zur, while the American consul stationed in Aleppo complained in February 1920 that "families absent from their homes but a few hours return to find them pillaged even in the daytime."[109]

Further reducing the quality of urban life was the overcrowding that had begun during World War I and that nurtured higher levels of crime, unemployment, and intercommunal tension. This overcrowding not only

106. IO L/PS/10/802, Gertrude Bell, "Syria in October 1919," 15 November 1919.

107. USNA 59/867.00/1036/1717, Young (Damascus) to Wallace (Constantinople), 5 December 1919; FO 371/4186/162128/495, Telegram from acting Spanish consul (Damascus), forwarded by Spanish ambassador (London) to Curzon, 11 December 1919; USNA 867.00/1045/1825, Young (Damascus) to Secretary of State, 13 December 1919; *The Near East,* 8 April 1920, 495; FO 371/5037/E8350/4, "Note by Miss G. L. Bell C.B.E.," 29 May 1920; Howard N. Sachar, *The Emergence of the Middle East: 1914–1924,* 274.

108. AD 2344/c1/août–décembre 1919/362, Cousse to HC, 21 November 1919; *al-Kawkab,* 27 January 1920, 11.

109. USNA Aleppo Consulate RG84/121/800, J. B. Jackson to Adm. Mark Bristol (Constantinople), 9 February 1920; *The Near East,* 18 March 1920, 390; IO MSS Eur F152 (Frank Lugard Brayne Mss.)/20, F. B. Hanano (YMCA, Aleppo) to Brayne (?), 21 March 1920; *The Near East,* 8 April 1920, 495; FO 371/5076/E8007/74–79, "Note by Miss G. L. Bell—May 22, 1920."

continued throughout the Faysali period but was exacerbated by an influx of refugees from Anatolia, the Biqaʿ Valley, and the eastern frontier. Refugees entered Damascus, Aleppo, and other cities in the eastern zone in two waves. The first occurred during and immediately after the war. While this wave included approximately twenty-one thousand soldiers demobilized from the Ottoman army[110] and Arab war refugees, by far the largest component consisted of Armenians uprooted by the 1915 massacres. Aleppo and Damascus sheltered the largest number of Armenian refugees, approximately seventy thousand and thirty to thirty-five thousand respectively.[111] Most entered Syria with few or no possessions (one report filed at the close of the war estimated that 78 percent of Armenian refugees entering Syria were impoverished). In Homs, for example, the British counted two thousand destitute Armenian refugees. Because of their straitened circumstances, many depended on charity provided by the British army and the Arab government. At a time when the Arab government was facing insolvency, it was spending almost 45,000 P.E. on Armenian relief.[112]

The second wave of refugees began arriving in Syrian cities soon after the onset of the Evacuation Crisis. Most decamped from the Syrian countryside as the collapse of rural security made village life precarious. From Amman to Aleppo, from Tartus to Dayr al-Zur and Tadmur, an assortment of Circassians and ʿAnaza, Banu Sakhr, Shammar, Haddaydin, and al-Mawali tribesmen took advantage of weakened governmental authority to settle old scores and to enrich themselves by pillaging now defenseless hamlets—in the process sending thousands into flight.[113] Other refugees

110. FO 371/4163/14536/74070, DMI to GHQ, 17 January 1919.

111. According to reports, approximately sixty-one thousand of these Armenians were repatriated from Aleppo during the period 1 January to 20 July 1919. During this period, seventy-four thousand Armenians were repatriated from Syria and southern Turkey, leaving an additional seventy-two thousand who awaited resettlement. USNA Aleppo Consulate RG84/vol. 112/840.1/395, 23 August 1919.

112. FO 371/3058/137867, "Internal Conditions," 11 May 1917; WO 95/4372/C374, Sykes to OGS, 22 November 1918; FO 371/4143/32104/EA2135, GOC to WO, 22 January 1919; FO 371/4143/724011, Clayton to FO, 9 May 1919; FO 371/4143/104019, General Sir Walter Lawrence to Commander in Chief (Egypt), 13 May 1919; DU SA/493/6/46, Shuqayr to Faysal, 20 March 1920. In Aleppo, a British-run soup kitchen fed up to fifteen hundred daily and more than eight thousand Armenians in the city received other forms of assistance. In addition, a British-run orphanage housed almost two thousand Armenian children while more than four thousand Armenians lived in barracks housing. See Paul Monroe et al., *Reconstruction in the Near East.*

113. See FO 371/4178/7094/264–268, Hogarth to Chief Political Officer, EEF, 18 December 1918; FO 371/4214/103277/3814, Telegram from Baghdad to IO,

fled from the depredations of deserters from the Arab army and brigands. Inhabitants of the disputed Biqaʿ Valley were particularly affected by the militarization of the countryside. Not only did competition between the French and Arab governments create opportunities for intervillage and intercommunal animosities to resurface in a deadly fashion, but villagers often found themselves trapped between the French army and nationalist guerrillas in an ongoing border war. From 6 December 1919 to 6 January 1920, armed gangs crossed the frontier separating the eastern and western zones and pillaged thirty villages in the region of Marjʿayun in contemporary Lebanon. In response to this and similar raids, the French bombarded the valley from the sea and the air. According to an official complaint lodged by Amir Faysal with the British government, one such reprisal raid against the Jabal ʿAmil in the eastern zone in early 1920 left twenty thousand homeless, many of whom eventually sought refuge inland.[114]

As they had done in earlier times, the popular classes responded to what appeared to them to be unwarranted economic hardship and governmental abuse or callousness with acts of individual and collective resistance. Even though this period might be distinguished from earlier ones by an unprecedented level of organized political mobilization, the populace continued to resort to styles of protest that were spontaneous and ephemeral. Damascus, for example, experienced a strike wave during which railroad workers, printers, tram workers, glass and textile workers, employees of the electric company, and even independent artisans abandoned their places

---

26 June 1919; FO 371/4181/99833/512578, Col. French to WO, 7 July 1919; *The Near East,* 12 February 1920, 210; *The Near East,* 19 February 1920, 244; AD 2209/dossier: Bagdad jusqu'au 31 décembre 1920/47, Roux to GCC, 28 February 1920; FO 371/5034/E2539/18, British Consul General (Beirut) to Secretary of State, 17 March 1920; AD 2348/C15As/d1/9, Hussein Moudir (Meskine) to directeur général des télégraphes, 13 May 1920; AD 2348/c15as/d1/781, Gouverneur d'Alep to min. intérieur, Damas, 12 May 1920; IO L/PS/10/802/P5172/3–4, French report for the period May 25–31; FO 371/5188/E6197, Arabic Press Extracts for Week Ended May 31 1920; MD 4H114/4/491, Cousse to Gouraud, 3 June 1920; MD 4H58/2, "Rapport hebdomadaire 433/2: 29 juin à 5 juillet."

114. AD 2380/5/21/184, Rouchdi (cdt. de la 3ème div.) to cdt. de la 3ème brigade de cavalerie (Alep), 25 October 1919; AD 2330/A1a, Gouraud to Faysal, "Memorandum des principaux faits relevés depuis l'arrivée du général H.C. jusqu'à ce jour," 13 January 1920; FO 371/5035/5661/194–195, Faysal to Lloyd George, 1 June 1920; FO 371/5036/E7772/808, Shahbandar to Col. Easton (British liaison, Damascus), 5 June 1920. See also AD 2344/c1/août–décembre, 1919/149–150–151, 17 November 1919; FO 371/5035/E5690/35, Wratislaw to Secretary of State, 13 May 1920.

of work, demanding higher wages.[115] During the spring of 1920, bread riots erupted throughout the zone. In Hama, rioters chanting, "You offer grain to France while we starve," demanded that the government take action to lower the price of flour, break up monopolies, and prohibit the export of grain to the western zone. In Aleppo, protesters demanded that the government create a grain reserve modeled on the one created by the Beirut municipality.[116] Aleppo was also the scene of the bloodiest confrontation preceding the July insurrection. In February 1919, native-born rioters attacked the Armenian refugee community, leaving forty-eight dead and up to two hundred injured. Although subsequent accounts dispute the immediate spark that ignited the massacre, the conflagration was perhaps inevitable in spite of Aleppo's reputation for cosmopolitanism: the influx of refugees contributed to high rates of unemployment and overcrowding, and Aleppans reportedly resented the special treatment accorded the refugees by the entente powers, the Arab government, and private charities and feared the competition the refugees generated (one refugee camp alone housed four thousand looms).[117]

Without a doubt, however, the single most hated and provocative program initiated by the Faysali government—the program that sparked the most resistance—was conscription. Ironically, the conscription law, first enacted in December 1919 and further expanded and strengthened in May and June 1920,[118] was promulgated as a result of widespread alarm over French intentions and the increasingly popular demand for armed resistance. But Syrians quickly discerned the difference between voluntary participation in local militias and coerced service in an ill-equipped and ill-paid national army. In addition, because the leaders of the popular committees

115. *al-ʿĀṣima,* 16 June 1919, 1–2; *al-Kawkab,* 4 November 1919, 10; *al-ʿĀṣima,* 3 May 1920, 5–6.

116. *The Near East,* 8 April 1920, 495; MD 4H112/2b/23, "Renseignements," 29 April 1920; Russell, *First Modern Arab State,* 142–143; Kasmieh, *al-Ḥukūma al-ʿarabiyya fī Dimashq,* 231.

117. WO 106/189/30629/EA2269, GHQ to WO, 3 March 1919; AD 2342, "Rapport sur les troubles survenus le 28 février 1919 à Alep," 14 April 1919; MD 4H112, "Compte rendu du capitaine Gautherot sur la situation politique à Alep," 6 May 1920; FO 371/4143/104019, General Sir Walter Lawrence to Commander in Chief (Egypt), 13 May 1919; *Arab Bulletin* 89 (14 May 1918): 168–169; Kurd ʿAlī, *Khiṭaṭ al-Shām,* 3:163–165; Ghazzī, *Nahr al-dhahab fī tārīkh Ḥalab,* 716–718; Monroe, *Reconstruction in the Near East,* 12–13, 34–35.

118. *al-ʿĀṣima,* 25 December 1919, 3; *al-ʿĀṣima,* 29 April 1920, 4; *al-ʿĀṣima,* 20 May 1920, 1–2; *al-ʿĀṣima,* 24 May 1920, 1–2; MD 4H58/2, "Rapport hebdomadaire: 6 au 12 juillet [1920]."

rightly perceived that the Arab government intended to use the conscription law to co-opt the popular nationalist movement and to build an army that could crush its opposition, they obstructed its implementation.[119] The draft thus met with both individual and collective resistance throughout the eastern zone. Young men forged birth documents so they could prove that they were not draft-eligible; others fled town and even the country. Draft evasion occurred so frequently that the Arab government prohibited the emigration of young men of draft age from the eastern zone. Draftees, forced to join military units, deserted in droves; desertion was so rampant that Faysal himself later remarked that desertions from the army often outstripped enlistments. Anticonscription riots broke out in Darʿa, Hasbaya, and, of course, Damascus, where anonymous posters compared the government's policies to those of the Committee of Union and Progress. To quell the riots, the Arab government dispatched four hundred soldiers into the ever-troublesome Maydan.[120]

Clearly, over the course of 1920, the seemingly never-ending string of crises besetting Syria had all but collapsed the moral and political authority of Amir Faysal and the Arab government. As the arena for political activity increasingly shifted from the amir's palace to the streets, organizers for the popular committees moved in to fill the void left by the enfeebled government. As journalist Asʿad Daghir later wrote in his memoirs,

> In truth, the politics which followed in Syria was strange, inasmuch as the intellectuals, the leaders of public opinion, and the men of the government themselves stirred up, by all means possible, the excitement of the people and pushed it to the extreme. Then, all of a sudden, they retreated before the slightest obstacle which blocked their way. They abandoned the people who were perplexed, not knowing how to explain their position. On the one hand, they pressed for preparations to resist the French, and urged the population to resist [the enemy] by blocking their

119. *al-Kawkab*, 6 January 1920, 10; MD 4H114/2/38, Cousse to Gouraud, 18 January 1920.

120. *Sūriyya al-jadīda*, 27 December 1919, 2; AD 2375/chemise: division de la Syrie, 1919–1920/349/2, Lamothe to GCC (telephone message), 6 January 1920; AD 2375/chemise: division de la Syrie, 1919–1920/355/2, Arlabosse to GCC, 9 January 1920; *al-Difāʿ*, 13 January 1920, 2; WO 106/195/1845S, GHQ to DMI, 9 March 1920; WO 106/196, "GHQ Intelligence Survey," 15 May 1920; AD 2374/1032, "Rapport," 18 May 1920; AD 2358/dossier: renseignements politiques/444, Cousse to HC, 24 May 1920; IO L/PS/10/802/P5172, "French Report for the period May 25–31 [1920]"; MD 4H114/4/478, Cousse to Gouraud, 1 June 1920; MD 4H114/4/483, Cousse to Gouraud, 3 June 1920; MD 4H58/1, "Rapport hebdomadaire: 1 au 7 juin [1920]"; AD 2374/dossier: TEO zone ouest: adm., cabinet politique/1193/CP. "Zone est: situation générale," 15 June 1920.

> communications and setting up obstacles in their path. On the other hand, some of them adopted a policy of flattery and flexibility, and promised the French government that they would direct the country on a path which they had incited the country to oppose.
>
> This created a situation of enormous turmoil and squandered the trust which the people placed in their leaders. It made them openly accuse some of them of treachery so that gradually [their trust in them] was dissolved. The leaders to whom the people had entrusted the reins of government were not able to lead after the confidence [of the people] was torn away from them and they were scoffed at.[121]

Faysal recalled the Syrian Congress in early March. More a barometer than an architect of public opinion, the congress declared Syria independent on 8 March 1920. The entente powers naturally refused to recognize the validity of the declaration and, at the San Remo Conference convened two months later, awarded France the mandate for Syria. With the French army poised on the coast and a popular nationalism drawing extensive support at home, a clash became inevitable. On 14 July, General Henri Gouraud issued an ultimatum to the Arab government. Ten days later, French troops crossed the frontier, broke through Syrian defensive lines at Khan Maysalun, and occupied Damascus, ending the brief experiment in Arab rule and beginning a twenty-five-year period of French mandatory control of Syria.

121. Dāghir, *Mudhakkarātī*, 122.

Part One

THE STRUCTURE OF POLITICAL ORGANIZATION IN FAYSALI SYRIA

1 From "Patriotic Agitation" to the Advent of Mass Politics

As discussed in the Introduction, the economic and administrative transformation of the Ottoman Empire during the nineteenth century, although uneven in both distribution and effect, induced a correlated shift in social and political relations for a substantial number of inhabitants of the empire. Three aspects of this shift are particularly significant for understanding the emergence and evolutionary path of nationalism and mass politics in Syria. First, as alluded to above, the domain of formal politics expanded as the state took on new functions or as the state and institutions independent of the state wrestled for control of a variety of tasks that had never previously been in the hands of the former. As a result of this process, an increasing number of Syrians, mobilized by the state or its opponents and informed through new media outlets—the efficacy of which was ensured by enlarged urban concentrations, the restructuring of urban space, and the introduction of modern technologies for transportation and communication—began to contest a growing number of public issues.

At the same time, the expanding scope and scale of Ottoman economic integration and the structural effects of Ottoman administrative regeneration had a dual effect on the cultural cohesion of the empire. In the most abstract sense, the integration of economic activity, urban growth, intensification of government intrusiveness, and expansion of a modern public sphere resulted in an increased standardization of cultural norms and practices as large numbers of the Ottoman population were subjected to the leveling forces of market and state. This standardization broadened the domain receptive to what Benedict Anderson called the "cultural system" of nationalism.[1] But on another level this standardization was accompanied

1. Anderson, *Imagined Communities*, 12.

by a seemingly contrary process: Because the transformation of Ottoman society was uneven in both distribution and impact, it affected different social strata in different ways, in effect pitting those who successfully navigated the new social, economic, and political landscape against those who did not. As a result, late Ottoman culture, like the cultures of other empires and colonies on the periphery of Europe, bifurcated into separate and increasingly distinct subcultures that articulated variant responses to socioeconomic change. As will be seen below, each of these subcultures naturally structured itself through institutions and represented itself through paradigmatic activities that embodied its conception of the proper and veridical arrangement of society.

Concomitantly, the transformation of economic, administrative, and urban conditions rendered possible a contingent restructuring of relationships of power for many Syrians. More explicitly, during periods in which the needs and concerns of Syrians transcended and/or overtaxed the capabilities of narrowly circumscribed, vertical ties of personal dependency, the aforementioned changes made the reconstruction of relationships of power along horizontal, associational, and national lines practicable.

One such period commenced in the autumn of 1919. At that time, much of the population of urban Syria, unsettled by the devastating effects of World War I and partially mobilized by the Arab government and its allies through channels that circumvented (and thus undercut) the traditional notability and the customary ties that linked them with the urban masses, began confronting a new series of economic and political crises. Incapable of tempering the dislocations experienced by many Syrians, conventional bonds of clientage became increasingly hollow. Over the course of the next eight months, large numbers of Syrians availed themselves of a new form of political organization—the popular committee—that both institutionalized and broadened those horizontal, associational, and national ties that had never before been realized. Encountering a loss of social and symbolic capital, a number of established urban and rural leaders did likewise, in the process obscuring the revolutionary nature of these committees, which through their structure and program represented a new framework for social and political legitimacy.

The popular committees thus filled a void that neither the Arab government nor associated nationalist organizations such as al-Fatat and the Arab Club were structurally or ideologically capable of filling. The reasons for this incapacity on the part of these nationalist organizations and the innovative character of the popular committees is the subject of this and the following chapter.

"PATRIOTIC AGITATION"

So far, the discussion about nationalism has focused on the preconditions essential for its emergence. Although necessary, however, the diffusion of the structures and relations associated with "classical modernity" does not guarantee the appearance of nationalism among a population. Nationalisms require national movements; or, at the risk of belaboring the obvious, nationalism is impossible without nationalists.

The evolutionary path followed by the elite nationalist moment in the Arab Middle East was not unique to the region. Rather, this moment followed an evolutionary path similar to the one previously blazed by those "prenationalist" scholars and their "patriotic" successors studied by Miroslav Hroch who were responsible for the definition and articulation of nationalism among the "small nationalities" of Europe. According to Hroch, these late-arising (in the European context) nationalities—such as the Norwegian, the Flemish, and the Bohemian—might be differentiated from the European nationalities that had emerged earlier by the fact that they "were distinguished at the threshold of their independent existence by an incomplete social structure." In other words, however else they might have differed among themselves, because these nationalities had been subject nationalities, "[t]hey partially or entirely lacked 'their own' ruling class, and sometimes other classes and social groups were represented atypically."[2]

Hroch divides the history of the nationalist movements he studied into three phases, each characterized by a unique organizational structure, a targeted constituency, and a characteristic core leadership. The initial two phases of Hroch's model are particularly relevant for understanding the origins and practices of the organizations that are to be discussed in this chapter. The first, Phase A, actually antedates the emergence of the national movement. This phase is, according to Hroch, a period of cultural revival that "is marked by a passionate concern on the part of a group of individuals, usually intellectuals, for the study of the language, the culture, the history of the oppressed nationality."[3] In the Arab Middle East, this phase corresponds to the period during which the belletrists and scholars

2. Miroslav Hroch, *Social Preconditions of National Revival in Europe: A Comparative Analysis of the Social Composition of Patriotic Groups Among the Smaller European Nations*, 9.

3. Ibid., 22–23. Because my analysis of the origins of popular nationalism differs significantly from that of Hroch, I do not include here a discussion of what Hroch calls Phase C.

associated with the late-nineteenth-century *nahḍa* and *salafiyya* movements did their work both isolated from the majority of the population and, for the most part, oblivious to the potential political implications of their studies.

Phase B is, Hroch maintains,

> an epoch characterized by active patriotic agitation: the fermentation-process of national consciousness. . . . The driving force in this era of national agitation was a group of patriots who were already dissatisfied with the limitation of interest to the antiquities of the land, the language and the culture, and saw their mission as the spreading of national consciousness among the people.

According to Muhammad ʿIzzat Darwaza, who was both an early member of several nationalist groups and a prolific writer who divided the history of the Arab movement into phases similar to those delineated by Hroch, this phase lasted in the Arab Middle East from approximately 1908 to 1915. From 1908 through 1911, "enlightened [Arab] youth" focused their attention on local issues, such as the repeal of laws that mandated the official use of the Turkish language in the Arab provinces of the empire, the expansion of bureaucratic positions available to Syrians, and the reformulation of Arab/Ottoman identity. During the next four years, according to Darwaza, the Arab nationalist movement began to face issues that were broader in scope and, as a result, the movement began to divide along generational lines. On the one hand, Darwaza asserts, an "older" cohort preferred to work through public associations, such as the Ottoman Administrative Decentralization Party, which could appeal to a wider spectrum of the population. Ultimately, however, this strategy failed: although the party organized a conference of like-minded activists in Paris in 1913 to exact concessions from Istanbul, the Committee of Union and Progress, which ruled the Ottoman Empire, reneged on its promises to implement reform. As a result, the balance of power within the Arab nationalist movement shifted to a younger, more impatient generation. Working through secret societies such as al-Fatat and al-ʿAhd, these younger nationalists, like their scholarly predecessors, segregated themselves from the general population.[4]

Although the threat of repression was ever present to members of these secret societies, it was not the only reason for their decision to separate

4. The final period (1915–1920) was, according to Darwaza, a period of mass politics. Because of Darwaza's own political affiliations and biases, however, he places al-Fatat and its spin-off, the Arab Independence Party, in the center of the politics of this period, slighting the role of the popular committees. Muḥammad ʿIzzat Darwaza, *Ḥawla al-ḥaraka al-ʿarabiyya al-ḥadītha,* 1:21–79.

themselves from the majority of their compatriots. In his memoirs, Ahmad Qadri, a founding member of al-Fatat whose background was similar to that of Darwaza, complained that his countrymen themselves presented the major obstacle to nationalist organizing. Qadri divided potential recruits to the Arab cause into three occupational categories: merchants, who were "neither here nor there from the standpoint of politics and reform"; the educated classes—"children in the prime of youth who are not suited for politics"; and a category that consisted of military officers, employed bureaucrats, pensioners, and job seekers. Like the first two groups, those within this last category were also unorganizable: according to Qadri, the military officers had absolutely no experience in politics and tended to avoid it; pensioners "are like old ladies, for nothing satisfies them and no work appeals to them"; and sitting bureaucrats and job seekers wished only to retain or gain positions. As for those from different regions of the Arab world, Qadri maintained that Syrians and Iraqis had lived too long in submission to act in any way other than by "begging and resignation," and the organization of Gulf Arabs required extra effort because it had to be done without "cutting [the] ties [of their organizers] to civilization."

> Thus, it appears that in the capital under the present circumstances there is not an Arab we can depend on, or we could connect with, unless it be "so-and-so"; and all that "so-and-so" has told you is a mirage to which your thirsty brother would come and find that it does not exist at all.[5]

For Qadri and his associates, then, nationalist agitation was and would remain the province of a compact, professional, self-designated elite that possessed a unique and unifying social and cultural experience. This experience differentiated members of the elite from both their indifferent colleagues and, of course, the more benighted masses.

AL-FATAT IN FAYSALI SYRIA: CONSPIRATORS IN AN ERA OF MASS POLITICS

Al-Fatat was founded in 1909 or 1911 (depending on the source) by a small group of Arab students studying in Paris. Soon thereafter, they relocated its headquarters to Beirut.[6] Although the size of the organization did not

5. Aḥmad Qadrī, *Mudhakkarātī ʿan al-thawra al-ʿarabiyya al-kubrā,* 27. For more information on Qadri's life and activities, see MD 4H114/dossier 4/471, Cousse to Gouraud, 1 June 1920; Khālid al-ʿAẓm, *Mudhakkarāt Khālid al-ʿAẓm,* 1:94–95; Amīn Saʿīd, *Thawrāt al-ʿArab fī al-qarn al-ʿishrīn,* 99, 112, 259.

6. Darwaza, *Ḥawla al-ḥaraka al-ʿarabiyya al-ḥadītha,* 1:27; Qadrī, *Mudhakkarātī,* 12; Suhayla al-Rīmāwī, *Jamʿiyyat al-ʿarabiyya al-Fatāt al-sirriyya: Dirāsa*

exceed seventy members during the 1911–1918 period, al-Fatat has attracted the attention of historians primarily for two reasons. First, the membership of the organization, like the membership of affiliated groups, was heavily weighted toward scholars, journalists, and professionals—the type of people who write the memoirs, editorials, and local histories upon which many historians have relied. According to C. Ernest Dawn, who has analyzed the composition of the pre-1914 Arab movement, 67 percent of the members of al-Fatat, al-ʿAhd, and nonaffiliated "overt nationalists" whose backgrounds he could trace received "advanced" education, while 17 percent received "Western" education. Furthermore, 5 percent were scholars, 11 percent journalists, 22 percent professionals, and 30 percent military officers. Because membership in al-ʿAhd was limited to members of the military, it is probable that the vast majority of those whom Dawn classifies as scholars, journalists, and professionals were either unaffiliated or belonged to al-Fatat.[7]

The second reason for the posthumous renown of al-Fatat might be traced to the often fortuitous tactical choices made by the organization in its early days. Not only was al-Fatat the first prewar Arabist organization to call for the independence of the Arab provinces from the Ottoman Empire, but beginning in 1916, the organization linked its fate with that of the Hashemite family and the Arab Revolt. As a result, many members of the organization who had either remained in Syria or who had joined the Arab army or the Hijazi court during the war secured appointment in the Arab administration in postwar Syria. As the legend of Amir Faysal and the Arab Revolt grew during the postwar period, so did the mythology surrounding al-Fatat. Starting even before Antonius's assertion that "[n]o other society had played as determining a part in the history of the national movement [as al-Fatat]," writers have consistently characterized al-Fatat as "the most important" or "most influential" nationalist organization, in whose hands "actual political control during Faysal's short reign in Damascus lay."[8]

---

wathāʾiqiyya, 1909–1918, 65–69. The accounts of Darwaza and Qadri vary in details.

7. Dawn, *From Ottomanism to Arabism,* 177–178. The last statistic, that of the percentage of military officers in the prewar nationalist movement, is skewed by the fact that it is based on eleven subjects, ten of whom belonged to al-ʿAhd.

8. Antonius, *Arab Awakening,* 111; Russell, *First Modern Arab State,* 72; Kasmieh, *al-Ḥukūma al-ʿarabiyya fī Dimashq,* 20; Muhammad Y. Muslih, *The Origins of Palestinian Nationalism,* 120. Muslih makes this last statement about not only al-Fatat and its spin-off, the Arab Independence Party, but also, curiously, about the faction-ridden secret military society, al-ʿAhd. After the entrance of the

The problem with such assertions is twofold. First, they marginalize or ignore the influence of other organizations involved in "patriotic agitation," as well as other evolutionary paths for nationalism in Syria. One such path, which will be discussed in more detail in Chapter 3, linked the essentially autonomous activities of the wartime Syrian Union (*al-ittiḥād al-sūrī*), formed by Syrians living in Egypt, with the popular committees that began to dominate political activity in Syria starting in the autumn of 1919.[9] Second, the narratives that focus on the role of al-Fatat fail to take into account the changing nature of politics during the late Ottoman and early post-Ottoman periods, a change that shifted political influence away from self-styled "men of culture" (*mutanawwirūn*) and organizations structured exclusively for underground "patriotic agitation" or behind-the-scenes manipulation toward mass-based organizations.

Despite its early call for Arab independence, al-Fatat consistently avoided the potentially factious task of enunciating a clear ideological vision.[10] Even the decision to ally with the Hashemite-led rebellion, for example, was based more on political expedience and the vagaries of interfamilial politics in Damascus than on any ideological convergence linking the Syrians with the Meccans.[11] Amir Faysal first made contact with al-Fatat at the Damascus home of the Bakri family in 1915. Although the Bakris were relative upstarts among the notable families of the city, they had forged an alliance with the ʿAbid family at the end of the nineteenth century and had begun competing in local politics with the more established ʿAzms and Yusufs. During the struggle between Sultan ʿAbd al-Hamid II and the Committee of Union and Progress for control of the Ottoman Empire, the ʿAbids sided with the former while the ʿAzms and Yusufs backed the latter. Sharif Husayn, whose fear of the C.U.P.'s centralization policies also placed him in opposition to the committee, subsequently broke with ʿAbd al-Rahman al-

Arab army into Damascus, al-ʿAhd split into Syrian and Iraqi branches. The Iraqi branch, while actively involved in politics, focused its attention exclusively on the future of Iraq; the Syrian branch had no direct influence as an organization on politics during the Faysali period.

9. The Syrian Union was formed at the end of World War I from the remnants of the Ottoman Administrative Decentralization Party. Its executive committee included Rafiq al-ʿAzm, Khalid al-Hakim, Wahba ʿIssa, Michel Lutfallah, Kamil al-Qassab, Rashid Rida, Salim Sarkis, and ʿAbd al-Rahman Shahbandar. Darwaza, *Mudhakkarāt wa tasjīlāt*, 2:130–131. For its program (in Arabic and English), see FO 371/4178/16051, 10 January 1919.

10. al-Rīmāwī, *Jamʿiyyat al-ʿarabiyya al-Fatāt al-sirriyya*, 285.

11. For the ideological differences separating members of al-Fatat and Sharif Husayn, see Dawn, *From Ottomanism to Arabism*, 69–86.

Yusuf, *amīr al-ḥajj* (commander of the pilgrimage), and solicited the friendship of the Bakris, sealing the alliance by appointing Fawzi al-Bakri his personal bodyguard. Fawzi, along with his brothers Nasib and Sami, was an early member of al-Fatat. All three received sharifian patronage at the end of the war.[12]

The Bakri brothers were, of course, not the only members of al-Fatat to reap postwar benefits from the organization's wartime alliance with the Hashemites, nor did the good fortune of the Bakris and their colleagues escape the notice of ambitious Syrians, Palestinians, and Iraqis. With the elimination of Ottoman authority from Syria in September/October 1918, it became apparent that access to political power, jobs, and government funds depended upon membership in or affiliation with the organization, and Damascenes and recent arrivals in the capital sought to join al-Fatat en masse. As a result, al-Fatat rapidly changed from a secret society to a leading dispenser of political patronage as the stringent rules that had previously regulated recruitment were discarded.[13] Conversely, the leadership of the organization not only possessed the power to approve or disapprove contenders for even minor government posts, but it ensured that all who had important jobs in the government, such as cabinet-level positions, were members. In some cases, this stricture resulted in the near comic spectacle of appointees—such as the onetime foreign minister of the Arab government ʿAbd al-Rahman Shahbandar—being hastily sworn in to the organization after their appointments had already been announced.[14] Thus, according to Darwaza, the organization began to include

12. William Ochsenwald, "Ironic Origins: Arab Nationalism in the Hijaz, 1882–1914," 194–196; Schilcher, *Families in Politics*, 153, 160; Khoury, *Urban Notables*, 87; Antonius, *Arab Awakening*, 149, 188–91; al-ʿAẓm, *Mudhakkarāt Khālid al-ʿAẓm*, 1:90; al-Charkas, *al-Dalīl al-muṣawwar lil-bilād al-ʿarabiyya*, 1:66; Mary Wilson, "The Hashemites, the Arab Revolt, and Arab Nationalism," 207–208; FO 882/24/128–134, "Who's Who in Damascus," 14 May 1919. That the commitment of the younger Bakris (Nasib, Fawzi, Sami) to "Arab nationalism" was not firmly rooted in ideology is underscored by their subsequent activities. Although Nasib al-Bakri was *raʾīs al-diwān* (head of the chancellery) under Amir Faysal and has often been listed as the first president of al-Fatat's political arm, the Arab Independence Party, he later withdrew from the party to help found, along with his brothers Fawzi and Anwar, the Syrian nativist Syrian Patriotic Party. A marriage alliance was also attempted between the virulently anti-Hashemite Yusuf family and the Bakri family with the engagement of Sami al-Bakri to ʿAbd al-Rahman al-Yusuf's daughter in 1919. al-ʿAẓma, *Mirʾāt al-Shām*, 245; Muḥammad ʿIzzat Darwaza, *Mudhakkarāt*, 2:143–144.

13. Darwaza, *Mudhakkarāt*, 2:80, 111; Qadrī, *Mudhakkarātī*, 72.

14. Darwaza, *Mudhakkarāt*, 2:196.

> a large number driven by the desire [for jobs] . . and there was among them [those] who were vague in morals, spirit, heart, and patriotism, as well as opportunists. It can therefore be understood why many of them remained in their positions and complied with the French occupation.[15]

To deal with the new circumstances while retaining their prerogatives, the leaders of al-Fatat attempted to overhaul the structure of the organization. Initially, they divided the membership into two categories, *mu'assisūn* (those who had joined al-Fatat before the end of the war) and *muḥtasabūn* or *ʿādiyyūn* (new members). The former category of members met monthly to consult with, criticize, and if necessary elect a new administrative committee to set overall policy for the organization, relaying their decisions to the *muḥtasabūn* by means of a special representative.[16] Although designed to preserve "some dignity and importance and secrecy . . . for the organization," the two-tiered system was compromised by the fact that the leadership of al-Fatat formed a special committee to upgrade certain *muḥtasabūn* to the level of *mu'assisūn.* In addition to Shahbandar, the list of those whose status underwent transformation includes ʿAdil Arslan, political adviser to Amir Faysal; Wasfi al-Atasi and Subhi al-Tawil, members of the Syrian General Congress; General Yusuf al-ʿAzma; Muhammad al-Nahhas, director of revenues for the Arab government; Rashid Rida, onetime president of the Syrian General Congress; Sami al-Sarraj, editor of the Aleppan newspaper *al-ʿArab;* Saʿid al-Taliʿa, clerk of the Syrian General Congress; and Amin al-Tamimi, director of public security under the short-lived government of Saʿid al-Jaza'iri.[17]

As the membership of al-Fatat climbed to over two hundred, the leadership worried that the tenuous commitment and low quality of those who were joining would impede the ability of the organization to set the agenda for the Arab government. Therefore, on 5 February 1919, the administrative committee of al-Fatat commissioned the formation of a public political party, the Arab Independence Party (*ḥizb al-istiqlāl al-ʿarabī*) to absorb the new, lower-quality volunteers. According to its charter, the party was to act as a public front for the organization, "to raise the Arab nation to the level of advanced nations," and to spread propaganda calling for the unity of all Arab lands that had been under Ottoman authority.[18]

15. Darwaza, *Ḥawla al-ḥaraka al-ʿarabiyya al-ḥadītha,* 1:75–76.
16. Ibid., 1:78.
17. al-Rīmāwī, *Jamʿiyyat al-ʿarabiyya al-Fatāt al-sirriyya,* 89.
18. Darwaza, *Mudhakkarāt,* 2:141. See also Sulṭān, *Tārīkh Sūriyya 1918–1920,* 102; al-Rīmāwī, *Jamʿiyyat al-ʿarabiyya al-Fatāt al-sirriyya,* 97. Muhammad Muslih places the date at 17 December 1918. *Origins of Palestinian Nationalism,*

There was, however, a fundamental contradiction in the reasoning that underlay the establishment of the party. On the one hand, because the administrative committee viewed the party as a means of disseminating the propaganda of al-Fatat throughout Syria, the program of the party was supposed to reflect the positions taken by the committee. On the other hand, the administrative committee viewed the party as a place to dump all those who wanted access to patronage but who were not suited for the secret organization. Thus, although all members of the Arab Independence Party had, in theory, to undergo vetting through a process of nomination and selection before they could join, all members of al-Fatat, whether *mu'assisūn* or *muḥtasabūn* (who themselves were compelled to join the party) had the right to nominate new members. As a result, even many who had achieved notoriety for opposing the strategy and goals of al-Fatat enrolled in the party. They included Taj al-Din al-Hasani, ʿAbd al-Qadir al-Khatib, and Rashid Mardam Bek (all of whom subsequently affiliated with the Syrian Patriotic Party [*al-ḥizb al-waṭanī al-sūrī*], which was organized primarily to preserve government posts for native-born Syrians); Tawfiq al-Shamiyya (later, like ʿAbd al-Qadir al-Khatib, a member of the Higher National Committee); and Faris al-Khuri. The party leadership did balk, however, when the mainstays of the so-called "conservative" opposition, Muhammad Fawzi al-ʿAzm and ʿAbd al-Rahman al-Yusuf, demanded membership. At the suggestion of Amir Faysal, the two were invited to join an "advisory committee" that had no real function.[19]

Overall, the Arab Independence Party played a minimal role in Syrian politics during this period and, according to a British report, proved to be such a liability that Amir Faysal banned its participation in public activities soon after his return from Europe in the spring of 1919.[20] Thereafter, particularly during the period leading up to the arrival of the King-Crane Commission in Damascus, the Arab government relied on other organizations and institutions, especially those manned by the Arab Club and loyal government functionaries, to disseminate propaganda and mobilize the population.

---

132. Sources dispute the names of those who were commissioned by the administrative committee to found the party. The individuals whose names are mentioned most often are Tawfiq al-Natur (one of the original founders of al-Fatat in Paris and editor of the newspaper *al-Fajr*) and/or Nasib al-Bakri, assisted by Muhammad ʿIzzat Darwaza and/or Saʿid al-Ghaz. See al-ʿAẓma, *Mir'āt al-Shām*, 245; Qadrī, *Mudhakkarātī*, 82; Darwaza, *Mudhakkarāt*, 2:142.

19. Darwaza, *Mudhakkarāt*, 2:142; Dāghir, *Mudhakkarātī*, 110.

20. FO 371/4181/89850/117–120/24, Clayton to Curzon, 17 June 1919.

Al-Fatat's difficulties, however, went beyond structural problems. Factionalism, which had remained latent within an organization whose members had been united merely by their opposition to certain aspects of Ottoman rule, began to emerge after the war as new and divisive issues—policy toward the entente powers, the borders of a projected Arab state, defense, localist loyalties, and so on—rent the organization. Because al-Fatat had no mechanism with which to enforce discipline, members often ignored or attempted to sabotage decisions with which they disagreed.[21] Both Yasin al-Hashimi (president of the war council who was associated with a hard-line military policy) and ʿAli Rida al-Rikabi (who, as military governor, advocated a more conciliatory policy toward the entente powers) attempted to use their membership in the administrative committee of al-Fatat and Faysal's inner circle to impose their political agendas on the organization. At various times, each sought to outmaneuver the other by stacking the administrative committee in his favor. Others organized or affiliated with outside organizations that enjoyed a broader base of support or advocated goals that were more clearly defined than those advocated by al-Fatat. Overall, of seventy-five prominent members of al-Fatat during the Faysali period—those who had the status of *muʾassisūn,* were members of the administrative committee, or both—5 percent were also or became members of the Syrian Patriotic Party, 7 percent were members of the Syrian Union, 7 percent were prominent members of the Iraqi branch of al-ʿAhd, 8 percent were members of the Committee of National Defense, and 12 percent were members of the Higher National Committee.[22]

The direct meddling of outsiders in the internal affairs of al-Fatat also exacerbated the factionalism within the organization. Almost immediately after the establishment of the Arab government in Damascus, the generally anti-sharifian Syrian Union, many of whose members espoused republican sympathies, infiltrated its partisans into al-Fatat in an attempt to influence appointments and policies. The French did likewise, although their motives were more clearly disruptive.[23] For its part, the Arab government—and Amir Faysal personally—lobbied and browbeat individual members of the organization and manipulated internal elections to enlist support for

21. Darwaza, *Ḥawla al-ḥaraka al-ʿarabiyya al-ḥadītha,* 1:81–88.

22. Some members of al-Fatat (such as Kamil al-Qassab) belonged to more than one other party. Although there is some evidence to indicate that the Higher National Committee had been established by al-Fatat, the committee reorganized and adopted policies at odds with al-Fatat within three months of its founding.

23. Darwaza, *Ḥawla al-ḥaraka al-ʿarabiyya al-ḥadītha,* 1:81–88, 91; AD 2429/131, Mercier(?) to Picot, 13 December 1918.

the policies of the government. The most potent weapon in the government's arsenal was, of course, financial; not only did the government suborn individual members, it financed the day-to-day activities of the organization as well. As a result, according to Amin Saʿid, when the French entered Damascus, they found sixteen thousand P.E. in the treasury of al-Fatat.[24]

As the internal cohesion of the organization began to dissolve, members abandoned all attempts to unite on issues of strategy. Darwaza reports that al-Fatat split into three factions around the time of the visit of the King-Crane Commission to Syria. The first faction, known as the dissenters (*rāfiḍūn*), included Darwaza, Saʿid Haydar, Ahmad Muraywid, Rafiq al-Tamimi, Khalid al-Hakim, Kamil al-Qassab, and Ibrahim al-Qasim. Members of this faction denounced both Britain and France for their plans to implement the Sykes-Picot Agreement and the Balfour Declaration and refused to support either nation as mandatory power. Many later affiliated with the popular committees. The second faction included Amir Faysal, his brother Zayd, and others who preferred the British to the French but nevertheless agreed that the Sykes-Picot Agreement had to be modified in light of the victory of the Arab army. The final faction was made up of those who held out hope for an American mandate.[25] This hope was, of course, dashed by the unwillingness of the United States to assume responsibility for Syria and by the September 15 Accord between Britain and France.

When Faysal returned to Syria from Europe in January 1920 having negotiated a provisional agreement with the French, the breach between the remaining factions in al-Fatat became unbridgeable. To gain the organization's approval for the Faysal-Clemenceau Agreement, the amir and ʿAli Rida al-Rikabi tried to manipulate the elections for a new administrative committee.[26] While their maneuverings infuriated all the *rāfiḍūn*, no one reacted more angrily than Kamil al-Qassab, the leader of the Higher National Committee. Accusing the administrative committee of "slackness" and "neglect of the national interest," al-Qassab severed the ties that had linked his organization with al-Fatat. At the same time, in an effort to take advantage of what Ahmad Qadri called the "cleavage [that] was opened up

24. Darwaza, *Mudhakkarāt*, 2:164, 180–181; Darwaza, *Ḥawla al-ḥaraka al-ʿarabiyya al-ḥadītha*, 1:74, 80; Amīn Saʿīd, *al-Thawra al-ʿarabiyya al-kubrā: Tārīkh mufaṣṣal jāmiʿ lil-qaḍiyya al-ʿarabiyya fī rubʿ qarn*, 2:36, 126. While Saʿid Shuqayr's records show no direct payments to al-Fatat, they do indicate that large and unexplained payments were made to members of the administrative committee such as Yasin al-Hashimi and Nasib al-Bakri.

25. Darwaza, *Mudhakkarāt*, 2:76–77, 81–82.

26. Saʿīd, *al-Thawra al-ʿarabiyya al-kubrā*, 2:126.

between al-Fatat and the popular nationalist formations," a group of Syrian notables both inside and outside al-Fatat established the Syrian Patriotic Party as an alternative to both the Arab Independence Party and the politics of the street. Although the size of the Syrian Patriotic Party remained small, its advocacy of a separate state of "Syria within its natural boundaries" added another voice to a demand associated with al-Qassab's popular committees.[27]

Contemporary observers outside al-Fatat were oblivious to both the structural shortcomings that limited the organization's efficacy and the increasingly disruptive disputes over strategy that divided its members. As a result, they promoted an image of al-Fatat that wildly overstated its capabilities. "[T]he educated and upper class Moslems . . . have discovered the political power they possess over the mass of ignorant Moslems," William Yale, the technical adviser to the King-Crane Commission, wrote upon the completion of his tour of Syria. "It is this group which form the back bone of the Young Arab Party, [and] it is in their hands that the real power lies. . . ."[28] But in light of the organization's internal problems, its penchant for backroom political dealings, and its aversion to organizing the non-"enlightened" population for active participation in politics, it should not be surprising that the "real power" attributed to al-Fatat never extended much beyond government circles. The organization's list of candidates to represent

27. Qadrī, *Mudhakkarātī*, 172–173; al-ʿAẓma, *Mirʾāt al-Shām*, 245; Darwaza, *Mudhakkarāt*, 2:143–144; Saʿīd, *al-Thawra al-ʿarabiyya al-kubrā*, 2:42. The exact history of the Syrian Patriotic Party is confusing. While most sources indicate it was created in January 1920, others indicate either that it was founded in June 1920 or that it was created in January, became dormant, then recreated in June. Although most Arabic sources (and indeed, the charter of the organization itself) indicate that the party was, except for its staunch nativism, fully within the mainstream of the Arab nationalist tendency, French sources from the period indicate that the party was pro-French at a time when it joined in an alliance with the "extremist" Higher National Committee. In this context, the assertion of Muhammad Harb Farzat that there were two parties with identical names has credibility. The first was founded in January 1920, with the characteristics outlined above. The second, founded in June 1920 (by, according to Farzat, Muhammad Kurd ʿAli), was also a party of notables and was pro-French, or at least sought to reach a compromise with the French during the final days of the Faysali regime. See Muḥammad Ḥarb Farzat, *al-Ḥayā al-ḥizbiyya fī Sūriyya: Dirāsa tārīkhiyya li-nashʾat al-aḥzāb al-siyāsiyya wa taṭawwurihā bayna 1908–1955*, 77. For an alternative view, see Russell, *First Modern Arab State*, 147, 185; al-Rīmāwī, *al-Tajriba al-fayṣaliyya*, 98.

28. Yale Papers, Boston University, "A Report on Syria, Palestine and Mount Lebanon for the American Commissioners, prepared by Captain William Yale, Technical Advisor to the American Section of the International Commission on Mandates in Turkey," 24.

Damascus in the Syrian General Congress was soundly defeated in the elections held in June 1919 by a list compiled by Muhammad Fawzi al-ʿAzm, head of the powerful ʿAzm family and "dean" of the traditional Damascus landowning notability.[29] At around the same time, key elements of the platform ratified by the Arab Independence Party suffered critical setbacks: not only did the popular demand for "complete independence for Syria within its natural boundaries" overwhelm the demand for a pan-Arab union (including the Hijaz) endorsed by the party, but events overtook the party's support for an American or British mandate. Tellingly, after the onset of the Evacuation Crisis, neither al-Fatat nor the Arab Independence Party sponsored or even participated in the huge demonstrations mounted in the Syrian capital. In sum, as the arena for Syrian politics increasingly widened, both groups were eclipsed by a style of politics they were incapable of directing or controlling.

THE ARAB CLUB

The Arab Club (*al-nādī al-ʿarabī*) shared important characteristics with al-Fatat. Both al-Fatat and the Arab Club of Damascus initially drew most of their primary and secondary leadership from similar layers of the population: members of the middle strata and the second tier of Damascus notability.[30] Furthermore, not only were the original members of both organi-

29. According to Khalid al-ʿAzm, Jamil Mardam Bek and Muhammad ʿIzzat Darwaza told Muhammad Fawzi al-ʿAzm that they represented a group of young men called *al-rijāl al-ghuyyab* ("hidden men," a term Darwaza uses in his memoirs to describe the inner circle of al-Fatat) who had decided to nominate al-ʿAzm as a representative to the Syrian General Congress. To demonstrate who really wielded power in Damascus, al-ʿAzm put together his own electoral list that included himself, ʿAbd al-Rahman al-Yusuf, Taj al-Din al-Hasani, ʿAbd al-Qadir al-Khatib, Shaykh Muhammad al-Mujtahid, Fawzi al-Bakri, Ahmad al-Qudamani, George Harfush, Yusuf Linyado, and ʿIzzat al-Shawi. (After the death of al-ʿAzm, Musallim al-Husni took his seat in the congress.) Of the above, seven became prominent members of the Syrian Patriotic Party. This list won in its entirety in spite of the fact that the opposing list supported Amir Faysal and was endorsed by ʿAli Rida al-Rikabi. Muhammad Fawzi al-ʿAzm later defeated Hashim al-Atasi, the candidate of the *rijāl al-ghuyyab* in elections held to determine the president of the Syrian General Congress. al-ʿAẓm, *Mudhakkarāt Khālid al-ʿAẓm,* 1:94–95.

30. Philip Khoury divides the political leadership of Damascus in the early twentieth century into two categories: a group of approximately twelve families at the pinnacle of society (families such as the ʿAzms, ʿAbids, Yusufs, etc.) and a group of approximately fifty families of lesser prominence. The first group was more powerful because of its ability to monopolize the highest administrative positions and because of its greater landed wealth. According to Khoury, most prewar activists were associated with the second tier. *Urban Notables,* 44–45.

zations very much aware of the social and cultural differences that separated them from the majority of their compatriots, but their privileged access to the Arab government served to reinforce their view of politics as the domain of conspiracy and manipulation. As discussed above, the *mu'assisūn* of al-Fatat attempted to differentiate between the roles they accorded themselves, the *muḥtasabūn*, and the members of the mass Arab Independence Party. Similarly, since the purpose of the Arab Club was to engage the "enlightened" elements of society (the self-styled *mutanawwirūn*) in politics on the side of the Arab government, the club's leadership viewed politics as the instrument through which a small elite might impose its values and goals, along with their supporting institutions, on an otherwise backward and passive population. The Arab Club designed its activities according to this dichotomous view of the Syrian population: it hosted tea parties and receptions to which only local *mutanawwirūn* and their guests were invited, it planned lectures "for the advancement of the nation," it sponsored didactic theatrical productions to inculcate "nationalist values" among the population, and it initiated petition campaigns and literally staged demonstrations to display the genuine "will of the nation" to Syrians and foreign observers alike.

On the other hand, because of its hybrid structure, the Arab Club might also be regarded as a transitional link connecting the earlier conspiratorial form of nationalist organization as represented by al-Fatat with the popular committees. In many ways the Arab Club more closely resembled the Arab Independence Party than it resembled al-Fatat. While both the Arab Club and the Arab Independence Party shared a similar structure and followed the prescriptions of an inbred and secretive group of political activists, both encouraged, and even at times demanded, public participation in their activities.[31] Furthermore, the Arab Club not only had the same relationship with the Arab government that the Arab Independence Party had with al-Fatat, but its function—to propagandize for the values of the institution that spawned it and to define and delimit direct popular participation in government and politics—were analogous to those of the party. Thus, because part of its purpose was to mediate between an elite national-

31. Not surprisingly, three members of the first executive committee of the Arab Independence Party—Fawzi al-Bakri, Salim ʿAbd al-Rahman al-Hajj Ibrahim, Muhammad ʿIzzat Darwaza—were also on the executive committee of the Arab Club. In addition, Tawfiq al-Natur, who was, according to Ahmad Qadri, the individual commissioned by al-Fatat to establish the party, also served on the executive committee of the Arab club. Darwaza, *Mudhakkarāt*, 2:142; Qadrī, *Mudhakkarātī*, 82; AD 2430/dossier confidentiel—départ/161s, 21 February 1919.

ist leadership and the public, the Arab Club, like the Arab Independence Party, began to attract, in the words of a British observer, "all the young hotheads in Syria."[32]

Some of these hotheads who now sought to participate in nationalist politics came from backgrounds similar to those of individuals who had joined the closed prewar or wartime secret societies. Unwilling to participate earlier, or deterred by youthfulness or fear, they waited until the establishment of the Arab government to engage in political activity. Others came from social layers that had not previously played a role in nationalist politics. Both groups of political novices experimented with innovative techniques of mobilization, such as the deployment of flying squads to disseminate propaganda in coffeehouses and other local venues and the organization of neighborhood-based militias. The spread of Arab Club chapters throughout Syria thus had the unintended effect of opening up the ranks of the nationalist leadership and broadening the popular base of organized nationalist politics.

THE ARAB CLUB OF DAMASCUS

The Arab Club was originally modeled on another cultural reformist organization, the Literary Society (*al-muntadā al-adabī*), which had been active in Istanbul from 1909 until 1915 and which Darwaza characterized as "one of the most important manifestations of the Arabist movement and its sustenance" during the immediate prewar period.[33] The first members of the society were expatriate Arab students who had created the organization to strengthen ties among themselves and to discuss cultural and historical matters. Among the founders were ʿAbd al-Karim al-Khalil (often cited as the chief architect of the society), Rafiq Rizq Sallum and ʿAbd al-Hamid al-Zahrawi (from Homs), Jamil al-Husayni (from Jerusalem), ʿIsam Basisu (from Gaza), Yusuf Haydar (from Baʿalbek), ʿIzzat al-ʿAzma (from Baghdad), and Shukri al-ʿAsali (from Damascus). They were later joined by Thabit ʿAbd al-Nur, ʿAli ʿAziz, ʿAdil Arslan, Jaʿfar al-ʿAskari, Tawfiq al-Bisat, ʿAbdallah al-Damluji, Khalid al-Hakim, Saʿid Haydar, ʿAbd al-Wahhab al-Inklizi, Salim al-Jazaʾiri, Sayf al-Din al-Khatib, Yusuf Mukhaybar Sulayman, ʿAbd al-Rahman Shahbandar, Ramadan Shallash, Najib

32. FO 882/24/100/6890, Director, Arab Bureau to Major G. W. Courtney, 11 May 1920.

33. Farzat, *al-Ḥayā al-ḥizbiyya fī Sūriyya*, 65; Darwaza, *Ḥawla al-ḥaraka al-ʿarabiyya al-ḥadītha*, 1:23–24, 91.

Shuqayr, Shukri al-Quwwatli, Rushdi al-Shamʿa, and ʿArif al-Shihabi. The society sponsored meetings and lectures attended by the Arab representatives to the Ottoman Parliament, students, politicians, and bureaucrats, and also published a magazine in its own name.[34]

Initially, the members of the Literary Society eschewed nationalist politics. Indeed, the founder and first president of the organization, ʿAbd al-Karim al-Khalil, along with several of his associates who later returned with him to Damascus during World War I, had been at one time both a supporter and a confidant of the notorious governor of Syria, Jamal Pasha (nicknamed *al-saffāḥ*, "the butcher"). According to Asʿad Daghir, it was through al-Khalil that Jamal Pasha first learned of the existence of the Arab movement that he later sought to eradicate.[35] But as the attitude of the Committee of Union and Progress toward the Arabist movement began to harden on the eve of the war, members of the society could not help but be drawn into the political debate. Even then, however, the political posture of the organization differed from that of al-Fatat, and many participants in the society, opposed to an Arab independence movement that they felt would weaken the Ottoman Empire and expose it to European aggression, became spokesmen for a moderate Islamic modernism.[36] In his memoirs, Daghir recalled some of the issues raised during the organization's internal debates as follows:

TAWFIQ AL-BISAT:	Do we want an Islamic federation? Why do we [then] attempt to disseminate the idea of Arabism?
ʿABD AL-KARIM AL-KHALIL:	The idea of an Islamic federation leads to weakness more than to strength. By rejecting the West it is not able to provide the East with power.
JALAL AL-BUKHARI:	How would it be possible to reconcile our embrace of Islamicism with our rising against the nation of the caliphate?

In spite of their differences, however, the Literary Society shared members with al-Fatat. While the Literary Society was still in Istanbul and al-

34. Qadrī, *Mudhakkarātī*, 11; Dāghir, *Mudhakkarātī*, 35; Darwaza, *Ḥawla al-ḥaraka al-ʿarabiyya al-ḥadītha*, 1:23–24.

35. Dāghir, *Mudhakkarātī*, 86.

36. Ibid., 86. See also Darwaza, *Ḥawla al-ḥaraka al-ʿarabiyya al-ḥadītha*, 1:23–24; Tawfīq Birrū, "al-Muntadā al-adabī wa dawruhu fī al-niḍāl al-ʿarabī," 35–44.

Fatat in Paris, for example, the latter organization inducted Sayf al-Din al-Khatib, Yusuf Mukhaybar Sulayman, and Rafiq Rizq Sallum, all members of the Literary Society, who acted as intermediaries between the two organizations.[37]

More important for subsequent events than the link with al-Fatat was the link connecting the Literary Society with the British and, through the British, the Arab Revolt. In October 1916, the British Arab Bureau began financing an Egyptian-based newspaper, *al-Kawkab,* to promote the activities of the society (and later the Arab Club as well) in those areas of Palestine that had been detached from Ottoman control and were subsequently under British occupation. It appears that the motivation of the British Arabists was twofold. First, members of the Arab Bureau sought to use *al-Kawkab* to spread a "moderate," pro-British Arab nationalism, a nationalism that would seek accommodation with, rather than rejection of, the West. Second, the bureau sought to promote the Islamic modernist doctrines that circulated among the members of the Literary Society. These doctrines, which also informed the editorial policy of *al-Kawkab,* were not only congruent with the nationalism sanctioned by the bureau, they situated that nationalism within a more comprehensive conceptual framework. In addition, members of the Arab Bureau believed that through the endorsement of Islamic modernism they could placate two different sets of critics. On the one hand, the bureau hoped to allay the suspicions of traditionalists who considered the Arab Revolt to be little more than a plot by the West against Islam in general and the caliphate in particular. On the other hand, the bureau needed to calm the fears of those Palestinians and Syrians who loathed the politics of the sharif of Mecca, which they claimed was based on a conservative interpretation of Islamic law inappropriate for the Levant.[38]

The British approved first the appointment of ʿAbd al-Rahman Shahbandar, then Shaykh Muhammad al-Qalqili, as editors of *al-Kawkab.* Dr. Shahbandar, a graduate of the American University in Beirut, was a member of the Syrian Union and a signatory of the famous "Declaration

37. Qadrī, *Mudhakkarātī,* 12–13.

38. DU Wingate Files 143/2/167 (AB202), Arbur (Cairo) to Sirdar (Khartoum), 13 November 1916; FO 371/2781, "Report of the Arab Bureau for November 1916," 31 October 1916; AD 2326/dossier du Hedjaz, Extraits de la lettre 94M de M. Bensaci, envoye du gouvernement de la république à la Mecque, 16 May 1919; FO 371/4206/139468, "Note on the Accounts of the Arab Bureau," 17 September 1919.

of the Seven" of June 1918, a document submitted by Syrian exiles in Egypt to the British government requesting a clarification of British war aims.[39] He also enjoyed close relations with David Hogarth, director of the British Arab Bureau, and later served as liaison between Faysal and the British government. Like Shahbandar, Shaykh al-Qalqili spent the war in Egypt and was close enough to Syrian Union circles to undertake a secret trip to Beirut on their behalf immediately before the war.[40]

The British invaded southern Palestine in January 1917. As British troops moved north, they directly and indirectly (i.e., through Faysal and al-Fatat) underwrote the formation of political clubs modeled on the Literary Society. These clubs would later form the core of Arab Club affiliates in the region. At the same time, they picked up Palestinian camp followers who would later play important roles in the Arab Club and, frequently, the Arab government as well. Among them were Salim ʿAbd al-Rahman al-Hajj Ibrahim from Tulkarm, who would later lead the Arab Club of Damascus; Muhammad ʿAli Bey al-Tamimi from Nablus, who became the chief of police of Damascus under Faysal; Subhi al-Khadra from Safed, who became chief of the gendarmerie under Faysal; and Muhammad ʿIzzat Darwaza from Nablus.[41]

The Arab Club of Damascus was founded soon after sharifian troops entered the city, purportedly to facilitate the integration of new arrivals to

39. In an attempt to consolidate British control over all members of the nationalist movement, even those suspicious of or hostile to the Arab Revolt, Osmond Walrond, a member of the British Arab Bureau stationed in Cairo, had asked the Syrian nationalist societies in Egypt to select seven representatives who would present the concerns of the exiles to the British. See FO 371/4217/69267, "Note by the Arab Bureau, Cairo," 6 May 1919; Fromkin, *A Peace to End All Peace*, 331. For the British response, see Hurewitz, *Middle East and North Africa*, 2:110–112.

40. Khoury, *Syria and the French Mandate*, 121; Antonius, *Arab Awakening*, 433; MAE L:SL/vol. 8/64–70, Lutfallah to Pichon, 23 January 1919; FO 371/3397/83621, "Arab Bureau Report for March 1918," 1 April 1918; al-Rīmāwī, *Jamʿiyyat al-ʿarabiyya al-Fatāt al-sirriyya*, 223. Before the war, Rashid Rida and Rafiq al-ʿAzm, both Egyptian-based members of the Ottoman Administrative Decentralization Party and later the Syrian Union, sent Shaykh al-Qalqili to Beirut to determine the possibility of a revolt against the Ottomans launched from Syria.

41. Anne Mosely Lesch, *Arab Politics in Palestine, 1917–1939: The Frustration of a Nationalist Movement*, 83; al-ʿAẓma, *Mirʾāt al-Shām*, 244; Darwaza, *Ḥawla al-ḥaraka al-ʿarabiyya al-ḥadītha*, 1:74; Yehoshua Porath, *The Emergence of the Palestinian-Arab National Movement, 1918–1929*, 77. Because of his focus on Palestine and reliance on materials from the Zionist Archives, however, Porath, like Muhammad Muslih, probably overstates the importance of the Palestinian connection in the formation and activities of the Arab Club of Damascus.

the capital and to disseminate pro-sharifian and nationalist propaganda.[42] Although the military governor, ʿAli Rida al-Rikabi, became the titular head of the organization, a president and executive committee managed its day-to-day affairs. An analysis of the backgrounds of twenty-four of the most prominent members of the Arab Club of Damascus—the founders of the club and members of the executive committee as of February 1919—reveals a group of individuals who came from a milieu similar to the one that produced the dominant personalities of the secret societies.[43] Included among them were representatives of some of the most prominent families in Syria, including the ʿAzms, the Muʾayyads, the Mardam Beks, the Bakris (all of Damascus), and the Haydars (of Baʿalbek), as well as professionals such as ʿUmar Shakir (an engineer), Muhammad ʿAli al-Tamimi (a lawyer), Thabit ʿAbd al-Nur (a belletrist), Khayr al-Din al-Zirikli (a poet and journalist), Tawfiq al-Natur (a lawyer and newspaper editor), and Muhammad ʿIzzat Darwaza.

Amir Faysal himself selected the first president of the organization, Shaykh ʿAbd al-Qadir al-Muzaffar. Al-Muzaffar had been mufti of the Eighth Ottoman Army based in Nablus and Balqaʾ. When the commander of the army, Jamal Pasha al-Mersini (al-Saghir), gained appointment as the last Ottoman governor of Syria in the closing days of the war, al-Muzaffar traveled with him to Damascus.[44] Although he owed his appointment as president of the Arab Club to the fact that he was a popular *khaṭīb*, al-Muzaffar's nationalist and intellectual credentials were weak. He was, according to a later British assessment,

> From Jerusalem, strong anti-Zionist and pro-Arabist propagandist. Under the Turks he preached against British and Sherif, but now curses Turks and praises the Sherif. A typical example of the unprincipled time-server so numerous in the Arab independence party, and a thoroughly "bad lot."[45]

42. Sulṭān, *Tārīkh Sūriyya 1918–1920*, 107; al-ʿAẓma, *Mirʾāt al-Shām*, 244. According to Sultan, the founding date of the Arab Club of Damascus was 18 November 1918.

43. AD 2430/dossier confidentiel—départ/161s, 21 February 1919; Porath, *Emergence of the Palestinian-Arab National Movement*, 77. In fact, nine of the twenty-four—Fawzi al-Bakri, Nasib al-Bakri, Muhammad ʿIzzat Darwaza, Salim ʿAbd al-Rahman al-Hajj Ibrahim, Ibrahim Hashim, Muʿin al-Madi, Ahmad Muraywid, Tawfiq al-Natur, and Muhammad ʿAli al-Tamimi—had joined al-Fatat before or during the war. Thabit ʿAbd al-Nur and Yusuf Haydar had also been members of the original Literary Society.

44. al-ʿAẓma, *Mirʾāt al-Shām*, 244; Darwaza, *Mudhakkarāt*, 2:146; AD 2371, Gouraud to Cousse, 10 February 1920.

45. FO 882/24/128–34, "Who's Who in Damascus," 14 May 1919.

Al-Muzaffar was, however, not the only leader of the Arab Club who had been a relative latecomer to the politics of Arab nationalism. Of the fifteen members of the executive committee of the club, for example, only five—Ibrahim Hashim, Fawzi al-Bakri, Nasib al-Bakri, Muʿin al-Madi, and Ahmad Muraywid—had been members of al-Fatat or any other prewar nationalist group. Furthermore, four others—Sami al-ʿAzm, Yusuf Haydar, Rida Mardam Bek, and Khayr al-Din al-Zirikli—joined al-Fatat only after the sharifian occupation of Damascus. The fact that so many of the leaders of the club who supervised its daily activities were political neophytes affected the efficacy of the Arab Club: the political and personal wrangling that divided the leadership and spread amongst the rank and file of the organization originated, in part, from the inexperience of the leadership in the conduct of political and administrative operations and from a deficiency of the sort of bonding that comes from the continuous threat of persecution.

The British and Arab governments had intended for the Arab Club to remain above politics. Indeed, a sign that read, "It is forbidden to discuss politics," had initially been posted on a wall in the Arab Club building. But such a policy was doomed from the start, and one can only imagine the exasperation of Amir Faysal when, in a speech delivered before the club in January 1920, he called attention to the fact that the sign had been removed.[46] The Arab Club, after all, had originally been established to propagandize for the values that underlay Arabism and, by extension, the Arab government that was the self-professed embodiment of Arabism. As a result, not only did government functionaries participate in the Arab Club (and vice versa), but the government, both directly and indirectly, continued to finance the activities of the club well into the Faysali period, as the records kept by Saʿid Shuqayr attest.[47] In exchange, the Arab Club shared with the Arab government responsibility for providing certain public services normally retained under the exclusive control of the state, such as the organization of an auxiliary Damascus police force that was in direct contact with *makhātīr* and the leaders of the quarters, and the reorganization

46. Qadrī, *Mudhakkarātī*, 163.

47. Shuqayr's records include the following expenditures for the period October 1918 through 31 July 1919:

1. Under the heading "Secret Service" (total expenditures: 104,170 P.E.): 500 P.E. to ʿAbd al-Qadir al-Muzaffar.
2. Under the heading "Donations" (total expenditures: 46,645 P.E.): 50 P.E. to Arab Club member Yusuf Istifan in September 1919; 200 P.E. to Haddad Pasha, club member and head of public security in January and June 1919; 350 P.E. to club member Thabit ʿAbd al-Nur; 265 P.E. directly to the Arab Club in April and July 1919; 100 P.E. to the

of artisanal guilds and education.[48] Furthermore, the Arab Club played a major role in organizing for the Arab government petition campaigns and demonstrations that were staged to display to the entente representatives in Damascus and Paris the unity of the Syrian population, its faith in Amir Faysal and the Arab government, and the fitness of Syrians for independence.

The plan to keep the Arab Club above politics was undercut by the fact that the Arab government was not a neutral observer in the struggle for political authority in post-Ottoman Syria; rather, it was one contender among several. Furthermore, because the competition to define the very substance of Arab nationalism paralleled the battle for political authority, discussions and lectures about Western-style progress, the essential nature of Arab culture and the foundations for Arab unity, the common roots of the three monotheistic religions, and the benefits that could be derived from individual economic initiative were hardly free of normative connotations. Indeed, they represented the very essence of political debate during the Faysali period. Far from being the spokesman for "the nation," therefore, the Arab Club necessarily became embroiled in the very disputes that not only divided nationalists from nonnationalists, but divided those within the nationalist tendency as well.

In mid-December 1918, while Faysal was in Europe, members of the Arab Club of Damascus held a series of meetings in an attempt to fashion a political program. According to French sources, the meetings included

---

Literary Society in June 1919; and 1,117 P.E. to "36 members of the Arab Club" in July 1919.

3. Under the heading "Irregular Payments" (total expenditures: 68,902 P.E.): 50 P.E. to the Arab Club of Beirut; 150 P.E. to the Arab Club of Damascus; 60 P.E. to Salim ʿAbd al-Rahman al-Hajj Ibrahim; 100 P.E. to the Literary Society of Palestine.

4. Under the heading "Extraordinary Payments": 600 P.E. to ʿAbd al-Qadir al-Muzaffar; 100 P.E. to Muʿin al-Madi and Saʿid Taliʿa.

Given that a few expenditures within each category are itemized, the above accounts reveal merely the minimum payments disbursed to the identified individuals and groups. DU SA 493/13/25–35, Shuqayr to Waters-Taylor; DU SA 493/13/1–6, Appendices to letter from Shuqayr to Waters-Taylor; DU SA 493/14/31–38; DU SA494/2. See also al-ʿAẓma, *Mirʾāt al-Shām*, 244; Darwaza, *Mudhakkarāt*, 2:72.

48. Muṣṭafā Balāwī, "al-Aḥzāb al-siyāsiyya fī Sūriyya (1920–1939)," 26; FO 371/4181/89850/24, Clayton to Curzon, 17 June 1919. The participation by the Arab Club in the organization of an auxiliary Damascus police force was likely related to the membership of the Damascus police chief, Muhammad ʿAli al-Tamimi and the commander of the gendarmerie, Subhi al-Khadra, in the club.

approximately thirty Muslims and five Christians, including ʿAdil Arslan, Sami al-ʿAzm, Muhammad al-Tamimi, Sami Mardam Bek, Naji Bey al-Suwaydi, Saʿid Haydar, Asʿad Haydar, Ismaʿil Shihabi, Fuʾad Shihabi, Amin Bey Hashimi, Rashid al-Taliʿa, Shukri al-Quwwatli, Shakir al-Hanbali, ʿAbd al-Qadir al-Muzaffar, Nasib al-Bakri, Faris al-Khuri, Nicolas Shaghuri, Khalil Maʿtuq, ʿIzzat Shawi, and Joseph Saba. The discussions were intense. Both Maʿtuq and Shawi, who were Catholics, opposed any connection linking Syria with Sharif Husayn or the Hijaz and argued in favor of a French protectorate.[49] Al-Muzaffar and al-Suwaydi, on the other hand, presented the case for independence guaranteed by the British alone. While al-Suwaydi, an Iraqi, sought the creation of a pan-Arab state that would include both Iraq and the Hijaz under Sharif Husayn, al-Bakri, seeking a compromise in which all religious questions would be set aside, urged the club to organize for the independence of Syria within its natural boundaries (i.e., present day Syria, Lebanon, Palestine, and parts of Iraq).

Overall, then, although they shared a common worldview and vision for the future, the leaders of the Arab Club initially divided ranks on the specifics of political strategy and, concomitantly, on the boundaries that would encompass the future Arab or Syrian state. Accordingly, while some supported the establishment of a pan-Arab federation that would include Syria, Palestine, Iraq, and the Arabian peninsula under the authority of Sharif Husayn, others insisted on a complete separation of Syria from the Hijaz and the rest of Arabia. While members of the former group offered assurances that they did not support the creation of an Arab caliphate under the sharif, haggling reportedly continued over other issues: borders; whether Britain, France, or the four entente nations (Britain, France, the United States, and Italy) acting in concert should guide Syria toward independence; and whether the selected Western nation or nations would merely provide technical assistance or would be allowed to assume a more intrusive supervisory role.[50]

The acrimony within the Arab Club increased, however, as those whom

49. The three seemed to be repeating the argument made earlier in the month by representatives of the "Circle of Young Catholics." The attempt made by the Arab Club to incorporate the circle failed because the latter group objected to the club's professed loyalty to Sharif Husayn and to its pro-British, anti-French stance. AD 2429/dossier 1918/115, Mercier to HC, 9 December 1918.

50. AD 2429/144, Mercier to HC, 16 December 1918; AD 2429/161, Mercier to HC, 26 December 1918.

both the government and foreign observers regarded as "extremists"[51] fought to assume control of the organization's policy and tactics. Some insurgent members, banding together informally, disrupted Arab Club events. In March 1919, for example, "a gang of young men of the Arab Club" led by Sa'ad al-Din al-Mu'ayyad, a member of the executive committee of the Arab Club, and Fa'iz al-Khuri, Faris al-Khuri's younger brother, disrupted a fundraising event for the *Alliance israélite* hosted by 'Ali Rida al-Rikabi and Amir Zayd. According to a French report, the group interrupted the

> gathering which they judged did not conform to their reasonable doctrines . . . [T]he incident is insignificant in itself, but it indicates the state of affairs created, little by little, by a small band which has taken over the club and which intends to direct the affairs of Syria to its liking . . .[52]

Dissident members of the Arab Club did not merely confine their contention to activities that took place within private meetings, however. Because the Arab government promoted the club as a means to bridge the gap that separated the government from the indigenous population, and because the government had thus entrusted the club with the task of ordering and mobilizing the population, internal fissures traversed the walls of the clubhouse as club members took their disagreements with the organization or with the Arab government to the streets. One Arab Club member, playwright and newspaper editor Ma'ruf al-Arna'ut, for example, was

51. The term *extremist* was widely used in British, American, and in particular, French dispatches (especially those of the French liaison officer stationed in Damascus, Lt. Col. Cousse) in a variety of contexts, and its meaning changed accordingly. It was commonly applied to those individuals or political tendencies that were unwilling to compromise with the entente powers on any of several issues (the division of Syria, the nature of Syrian sovereignty, the powers to be granted to or the identity of the mandatory government), had a propensity for violence, and/or encouraged the participation of non-elites in nationalist politics. The term was also used to designate those organizations or individuals who were considered to be nativist in general and Muslim/anti-Christian in particular. The terms *fanatic, bolshevik, Young Arab* (i.e., a participant in an alleged conspiracy led by al-Fatat), and *pan-Islamic* were frequently used (again, in particular by French observers) as synonyms for extremist. See: MAE L:SL/vol. 12/32–38, Cousse to Gouraud, 6 April 1919; WO 106/191/MI2B, "Report from GHQ-EEF," 22 April 1919; FO 371/4181/89850, Clayton to Curzon, "Report by British Liaison Officer (Cornwallis) on Political Situation in Arabia," 17 June 1919; AD 2358/dossier: mystification chérifienne, Gautherot, 13 September 1919; MD 4H58/1, "Rapport hebdomadaire: 9 au 16 février 1920"; FO 371/5035/E4858, Wratislaw to FO, 15 May 1920; MD 4H114/4/594, Cousse to Gouraud, 24 June 1920.

52. MAE L:AH/vol. 4/66–67, Cousse to Gouraud, 21 March 1919.

so successful in pioneering innovative theatrical techniques for spreading news and "extremist" and "anti-Christian" political propaganda from coffeehouse to coffeehouse that British authorities demanded his expulsion from Damascus and later arrested him for committing the same transgressions in Aleppo.[53]

The activities of al-Arna'ut and others might be seen as an important step in the process through which the Arab government and the Arab Club forfeited control of political debate and the streets to the popular committees that emerged after the first year of Faysali rule. While the young "hotheads" who began to fill the ranks of the Arab Club of Damascus or who acted independently also took advantage of the newly politicized public spaces, they brought with them a radically different political agenda and, increasingly, organic linkages with the Damascene population. Loosely affiliated club members such as Rida al-Hariri, Abu Muhammad Hasan al-Kharrat (a *qabaḍāy* [quarter thug] from the quarter of Shaghur who would later play a prominent role in the Great Revolt of 1925[54]), Shukri Khusari, Hasan Maʿruf, Dib Saʿid and his brothers, Amin Trabulsi, Mustafa al-Zaghat, and Khalil Zirabli spread their brand of Arab nationalism in the suqs of Hamidiyya and Ma'dhanat al-Shahm, and in the neighborhoods of Shaghur, Bab Sarija, and Suwayqa.[55] "No grandiloquent speeches, however; no flashy gatherings," complained one French observer.

> To the contrary, a quantity of private meetings where . . . the same agents call on brave Syrians to sacrifice themselves for the cause of complete independence without protection or supervision. The lies about us mount in their wake. Rather the Chinese than the French, desecrators of the true religion and violators of women. In the cafés, the well-rehearsed storytellers weave the theme of independence and Islam. Karakuz [himself] has become an ardent patriot at the simple invitation of the Arab Club.[56]

Thus, during Amir Faysal's initial sojourn in Europe (he arrived back in Damascus at the beginning of May 1919), the battle for control of the Arab Club seesawed back and forth between supporters of the Arab government and their opponents among the so-called "extremist" wing of the organi-

53. MAE L:SL/vol. 12/32–38, Cousse to HC, 6 April 1919; AD 2430/dossier confidentiel—départ/634, Cousse to HC, 24 October 1919.

54. Khoury, *Syria and the French Mandate,* 174–176.

55. Interview with Abu Ribah al-Jaza'iri, 15 November 1989; MAE L:SL/vol. 12/32–38, Cousse to HC, 6 April 1919; AD 2430/dossier confidentiel—départ/945, Lt. Col. F.L.O. (DCPO Damas), 26 September 1919.

56. AD 2430, Cousse to Dame, 18 April 1919. Karakuz was a figure in the popular shadow plays staged in cafés and coffeehouses.

zation. Upon the amir's return, he responded to British and French complaints about the Arab Club by overseeing, with the assistance of his military adviser, Nuri al-Saʿid, the club's reorganization. Faysal later explained his motivations in a speech before the Arab Club of Aleppo:

> I must repeat that our first task after the [King-Crane] Commission departs, and it will not be a far-reaching task, is to see that our gatherings are scientific and cultural, not political. I shall encourage all my countrymen who are trying to establish learned societies; I shall be happy to see my name registered among theirs.
>
> You would like me to say more about politics, but I think I have said enough. I am talking now about learning. I want this club, before which I have the honor to stand, to be a servant of knowledge and a source of culture. These people may well contemplate their future with satisfaction.
>
> We must be brothers and permit no parties to divide us or influence our future. He who suffers an injury at the hands of anyone is to bear it patiently and notify a responsible official of what took place. Perhaps there are deceivers who want you to quarrel among yourselves, as has happened in the past, so that they can besmirch our reputation before the world and say we do not deserve self-rule. I warn you of the consequences of these things—God grant that you not hear or see them.[57]

Although tempted to ban the organization entirely, both the entente powers and Amir Faysal were satisfied with its reorganization. While the British in particular sensed that the organization "provided a safety valve and its abolition would merely lead to underground and possibly dangerous conspiracies," Faysal feared that dismantling the club would provoke the creation of an organized opposition party.[58] The amir therefore stacked the committees of the Arab Club with allies of the Arab government, in the process replacing Shaykh ʿAbd al-Qadir al-Muzaffar with the seemingly more trustworthy Salim ʿAbd al-Rahman al-Hajj Ibrahim. Like al-Muzaffar, al-Hajj Ibrahim was a Palestinian; unlike the former Arab Club president, he had been a member of al-Fatat during World War I, during which time he had worked on behalf of the sharifian cause.[59]

However, because the activities of the club and its dissident members

57. Quoted in Abu Khaldun Satiʿ al-Husri, *The Day of Maysalun: A Page from the Modern History of the Arabs*, 112–114; *al-ʿĀṣima* 35, n.d., 3.

58. FO 371/4181/89850/24, Clayton to Curzon, "Report by British Liaison Officer (Cornwallis) on Political Situation in Arabia," 17 June 1919; FO 882/24/100/6890, Director Arab Bureau to Major G. W. Courtney, 11 May 1920.

59. Saʿīd, *Thawrāt al-ʿArab*, 258–259; Darwaza, *Ḥawla al-ḥaraka al-ʿarabiyya al-ḥadītha*, 1:27. Unfortunately, detailed information about the daily administration of the Arab Club, particularly in the wake of its reorganization, is spotty:

had, deliberately as well as inadvertently, expanded not only the number of Syrians mobilized for political action but the scope of their political activities, the organization could not merely function as "a servant of knowledge and a source of culture." Some organizers, whose endeavors were sanctioned by the newly reconstituted leadership of the Arab Club, extended their activities beyond the controlled mobilization of the population and, seeking the endorsement of public opinion, engaged the dissidents in public debate. Soon after the reorganization of the Arab Club, for example, the executive committee authorized the dissemination of pro-sharifian, proentente leaflets throughout Damascus, signed "The Sword, The Fire, and The Ardor of Youth." One representative tract reads as follows:

> There are among you certain individuals lacking morality who have sold their honor to those who would place on our necks the yoke of colonialism. These individuals have spread false rumors and relate gossip to win over the representatives of certain powers, hoping by these base intrigues to bring about their desires.
>
> They have published, and continue to publish that France will occupy Syria. They ignore their own faults by doing this, for noble France, which has fought with the allies for the deliverance of nations and the independence of peoples, will ignore their base behavior.
>
> To these individuals who seek the gold which would be their reward, we say that Britain and France have, by their own free will, given their assent to the independence of Syria. Shame on these impostors! Our compatriots who ignore these lies know that Syria will be free!
>
> Greetings to those who follow the truth.[60]

Both the idiom and bizarre logic of this tract reveal the extent to which the

---

records of meetings are rare and the records that do exist come mostly from French archives. Although the French had an efficient network of spies, and even managed to place the secretary of the Damascus Arab Club's Bureau of Recruitment, Yusuf Sayufi, on their payroll, the information passed on was haphazard and naturally skewed to reflect French concerns. For example, while definitive information about the selection of the president of the Arab Club of Damascus does not exist, it appears that after al-Muzaffar the presidency changed hands more than once, probably reflecting the variable relationship between the Arab government and the club, on the one hand, and members of the executive committee, on the other. Both Sami al-ʿAzm and Fawzi al-Bakri are variously cited in documents as Arab Club presidents. See FO 882/24/128–34, "Who's Who in Damascus," 14 May 1919; AD 2324/dossier a-1: politique, 25 June 1919; MD 7N4182/4/340, Picot to MAE, 21 July 1919; AD 2430/696, Sayufi to Cousse, 22 August 1919.

60. MAE L:AH/vol. 4/48 (in Arabic and French); AD 2430/dossier confidentiel—départ, Cousse to HC, 17 May 1919.

opponents of the Arab government, including Arab Club dissidents, had, as early as the spring of 1919, begun to define and eventually dominate the terms of political debate. For example, club members Khayr al-Din al-Zirikli, Tawfiq al-Muffarij, and Habib Kahala—editors, respectively, of the newspapers *al-Mufīd* and *al-Muʾayyad, Harmūn,* and *Sūriyya al-jadīda*—continued their dissident activities by organizing secret anti-sharifian groups such as "Black Hand" and the ominously named "Inescapable Fate" (*al-qaḍāʾ al-mubram*). Among the posted broadsheets of the former group that appeared during the same period was one condemning Faysal for dividing the Muslim world in the face of Western imperialism. It also compared the spinelessness of the Arab government with the resolution of the Kemalists fighting the French in Anatolia:

> Woe unto him who has sold the fatherland! Awaken, O Syrians, and be vigilant! Your fatherland has been sold and you must take revenge on those who have sold it![61]

Although the Arab Club continued to organize demonstrations and engage in propaganda activities to promote the policies of the Arab government even after the onset of the Evacuation Crisis and the initialing of the Faysal-Clemenceau Agreement, the government's authority continued to wane as its strategy for achieving independence for a united Syria through diplomacy unraveled and the economy of Syria foundered. The enfeeblement of governmental authority naturally devalued the political capital of its allies among the *mutanawwirūn* of the Arab Club. As the issue of defense began to dominate political discussion, as the logic of military preparedness animated the construction of popularly based organizations that were compatible with mass mobilization, and as those popularly based organizations increasingly took control of the nationalist agenda, the Arab Club goal of defining the contours of the nation and molding public opinion to match those contours proved ever more elusive.

THE ARAB CLUB OUTSIDE DAMASCUS

During the summer and autumn of 1918, the future leaders of the Arab government and their allies not only consolidated branches of the Arab Club throughout Palestine and in Damascus but organized or encouraged the organization of new affiliates in Aleppo, Homs, and Hama. Over the

61. AD 2343/c1: janvier-juillet 1919, Cousse, n.d.; AD 2324/dossier a-1: politique, 25 June 1919.

next year, Arab Club organizers founded chapters throughout the territory of Syria and beyond, from al-Salt in the south to Istanbul in the north, where members of the Syrian diaspora still lived.[62] In most cases, large, centrally located chapters organized and/or maintained the subsidiaries established in their environs. The Arab Club of Damascus took responsibility for supervising affiliates in surrounding villages; the Arab Club of Aleppo organized satellite chapters to the east in al-Furat, Baghdad, and Mosul; and the Arab Club of Nablus transmitted funds and instructions from the Damascus headquarters to other Palestinian branches, including the sizable chapter based in Jerusalem.[63]

The Arab Club branches throughout the region were linked to the central branch located in Damascus. The local chapters recognized the Arab Club in the capital as *primus inter pares* and, on occasion, took part in regionwide political campaigns organized by the Arab Club of Damascus. Nevertheless, each of the largest branches maintained an independence that ensured that cooperation would remain, at best, sporadic. In the spring of 1919, for example, ʿAbd al-Qadir al-Muzaffar, representing the Arab Club of Damascus, toured Palestine to persuade local Arab Club leaders to coordinate their upcoming testimony before the King-Crane Commission and to endorse the Damascus chapter's call for British aid and technical assistance for Syria. Although Amir Faysal himself favored al-Muzaffar's position, and although, according to Darwaza, al-Muzaffar offered bribes to the Palestinian leadership for their support, the local organizations rebuffed his overtures.[64]

Only after the reorganization of the Arab Club in Damascus on the eve of the Evacuation Crisis—the period during which rumors of the entente "betrayal" proliferated and the organization of neighborhood militias began in earnest—does it appear that the Damascus club, probably in response to popular agitation, attempted to exert tighter control over its affiliates. At the beginning of September 1919, an article in *al-ʿĀṣima* announced plans for an upcoming meeting to be held in Damascus to draw up general rules for all clubs. One month later, representatives from Arab Club affiliates met in the capital and agreed to publish a magazine, *al-*

62. *al-Kawkab*, 29 July 1919, 9–10; FO 371/5168/E6631, "Weekly Summary of Intelligence Reports Issued by M.I.1C, Constantinople Branch, for Week Ending 20th May 1920."

63. Balāwī, "Al-Aḥzāb al-siyāsiyya fī Sūriyya," 26; AD 2358/dossier: emir Fayçal, "Mystification chérifienne," 13 September 1919; Darwaza, *Mudhakkarāt*, 2:25–26; Muslih, *Origins of Palestinian Nationalism*, 167–168.

64. Darwaza, *Mudhakkarāt*, 2:59.

Andiya (*Clubs*), and to found in every Syrian city Arab Club "squads" (*arhāṭ al-nādī al-ʿarabī*) staffed by members of the Damascus club to oversee volunteers performing "benevolent acts." There is no evidence to indicate that these plans ever came to fruition. Indeed, if the Arab government and the leadership of the Arab Club of Damascus proposed the creation of the squads to distract Syrians from military activities by engaging them in the moral equivalent of war, their plan failed, and soon thereafter the Arab Club of Damascus itself contacted clubs in Homs, Hama, and Aleppo "inviting volunteers to join immediately troops at the frontier."[65]

For the most part, then, both the activities and structure of Arab Club affiliates outside Damascus reflected local concerns and conditions. The influence of indigenous patterns of political and social organization on individual chapters of the Arab Club was perhaps most evident in Palestine, where clubs in Nablus and Jerusalem, for example, not only differed in significant ways from clubs in cities outside Palestine, but from each other as well.

A fairly homogeneous merchant elite, linked by commercial ties with other cities in the Levant, played an important role in Nablus society.[66] The coalition of individuals who founded and maintained control of the city's Arab Club thus resembled, in terms of occupation and social background, the coalition of middle strata and landowning activists who formed the backbone of the Damascus and Aleppo clubs: Hafiz Kanʿan was a physician and early member of al-Fatat; al-Hajj Tawfiq Hammad was a landowner, former deputy in the Ottoman Parliament, and president of the local Muslim-Christian Association; and Muhammad ʿIzzat Darwaza was trained as a bureaucrat but had spent much of his life as a political activist. In contrast, the more insular elites of Jerusalem were less dependent on trade and industry, less connected to broader Syrian issues, and more liable to adopt organizational strategies described by the "politics of notables" model that reflected the high level of interfamilial competition. The Arab Club of Jerusalem, led by al-Hajj Amin al-Husayni, Hilmi al-Husayni, Ibrahim al-Husayni, Jamil al-Husayni, Shaykh Hasan Abu Suʿud (the Shafiʿi mufti of Jerusalem), and, ex officio, Shaykh Muhammad Salih, head of the Arab Club's Rawdat al-Maʿarif School, became little more than a tool of the pow-

65. *al-Kawkab*, 28 October 1919, 9; *al-ʿĀṣima*, 4 September 1919, 3; MD 4H114/1, Cousse to Gouraud, 29 November 1919.

66. Muslih, *Origins of Palestinian Nationalism*, 98–100. See also Beshara Doumani, *Rediscovering Palestine: Merchants and Peasants in Jabal Nablus, 1700–1900*.

erful Husayni family. Thus, while the Nablus organizers consciously sought to transcend religious and clan loyalties by building coalitions with other nationalist political organizations such as al-Fatat and the Muslim-Christian Associations, the Arab Club of Jerusalem remained locked in permanent contention with the Jerusalem chapter of the Literary Society, which was dominated by the rival Nashashibi clan.[67]

What little documentation exists about the day-to-day activities of the two Arab Clubs seems to confirm these underlying differences. While both chapters encouraged many of the same endeavors, the Nablus chapter seemed to concentrate on promoting activities that paralleled those undertaken by the Arab Club in the Syrian capital. Like the Arab Club of Damascus, for example, the Nablus chapter organized charities, lectures, and benefit theater parties to which local *mutanawwirūn* were invited.[68] The Jerusalem chapter, on the other hand, animated no doubt by interelite rivalries that put a premium on militancy, focused on anti-Zionist activities. According to one British observer, the chapter armed its members with small arms, prepared lists of names and addresses of local Zionists and their supporters, organized loyalists in Amman, trained and appointed agents to collect information about Zionist activities, infiltrated and propagandized among the police and gendarmerie, and "[taught] . . . pan-Arab ideals to children, especially those in Residieh and Raudat el-Maarif [sic] Schools."[69]

As with the Arab Clubs of Palestine, the Arab government initially encouraged and even facilitated the formation of the largest and most influential club outside the capital[70]—the Arab Club of Aleppo. Nevertheless, as

67. Darwaza, *Mudhakkarāt*, 2:20–26; Porath, *Emergence of the Palestinian-Arab National Movement*, 76. A British observer described the Jerusalem Arab Club/Literary Society rivalry as follows: "Nearly all the important members [of the Arab Club of Jerusalem] belong to the Husseini family, many of whom are not on good terms with the leading lights in the Muntada el Adabi. The aim of the Nadi el Arabi is about the same as that of the Muntada, but the members of the Nadi are not so radical. That is, they are not so strong on Arab independence, but are just as much opposed to Zionism and Jewish immigration." FO 371/4182/125609/M56, J. N. Camp (Jerusalem) to CPO (Cairo), "Arab Movement and Zionism," 24 October 1919.

68. These activities were regularly reported in *al-Kawkab*. See, for example, *al-Kawkab*, 31 December 1918, 10–11; 14 January 1920, 12.

69. FO 371/4182/125609/M56, J. N. Camp (Jerusalem) to CPO (Cairo), "Arab Movement and Zionism," 24 October 1919.

70. See, for example, MAE L:SL/vol. 10/151Y154, "Rapport du capitaine Pichon, officier français de liaison à Alep sur la société de Nadi-el-arabi," 4 March 1919.

with the Arab Clubs of Palestine, over the course of the twenty-two-month Faysali period, local conditions were more important than directives from Damascus in shaping both the club's composition and its activities.

Many of the difficulties faced by Aleppans in the immediate aftermath of the war have already been discussed in the Introduction. As a commercial center oriented toward Anatolia and the Iraqi hinterland, Aleppo's economy had not only suffered severe dislocations during World War I, but commercial conditions continued to deteriorate even after the installation of the Arab government in Damascus. Not only had the Ottoman army confiscated merchants' goods and pack animals necessary for overland trade during the war, for example, but it had destroyed important rail links connecting the city with outside markets to prevent them from falling into the hands of the advancing Anglo-Arab army. Other rail links fell into a state of disrepair during the postwar period. Trade also suffered as the depredations of bedouin and *chete* (bands of Turkish irregulars) virtually guaranteed that Aleppo's hinterland would remain inaccessible to merchants and travelers. Finally, customs barriers imposed in the postwar period restricted trade with Turkey, Iraq, and commercially vital coastal cities.[71]

An interview that Gertrude Bell conducted with Ihsan al-Jabiri in October 1919 reveals the relationship connecting the economic anxieties of Aleppan elites and their political predilections. Al-Jabiri, scion of a prominent landowning family, Arab Club member, and onetime president of the Aleppo municipality, embodied all the contradictions inherent in the nationalist tendency in Aleppo. On the one hand, he was a member of al-Fatat (joining after the war) who attended Amir Faysal as chamberlain. At the behest of the Arab government, he participated in the "Committee of Arabian Brotherhood," an organization set up after the February 1919 massacre of Armenians to promote intercommunal harmony and to demonstrate to the entente powers that the massacre was an aberration and did not reflect the true level of civilization in Syria. On the other hand, al-Jabiri had not only served in the Ottoman government, returning to Syria several months after the conclusion of hostilities, but like many Aleppans from his social milieu, continued to harbor pro-Turkish sentiments in

71. See FO 371/3412/187713/184, Clayton to FO, 14 November 1918; FO 371/4214/103277, Baghdad to IO, 26 June 1919; FO 371/4237/137623, "Middle East Political Situation: Notes by Col. Brayne, P.O., Aleppo," 1 August 1919; FO 371/4228/120623/EA26121, GHQ (Egypt) to WO, 6 August 1919; Khoury, *Syria and the French Mandate*, 17.

the postwar period.[72] In the interview, al-Jabiri expressed concern about Aleppo's access to the port of Alexandretta, the future of the Baghdad railway, and the "disastrous" economic implications of the proposed severance of Syria from Iraq. According to Bell, "The settlement which he would prefer[,] and his opinion was echoed by several others, ulama and ashraf . . . would be a nominal Turkish suzereignty [sic] over all Arab provinces, combined with decentralized Arab administration under British protection."[73] French sources also suggest that al-Jabiri's concerns about the economic consequences of the division of Syria were not unique: one month before the French occupation of inland Syria, for example, "un grand nombre" of merchants reputedly prepared a petition for the French high commissioner in Beirut requesting that Alexandretta, Aleppo, and Cilicia be united under French control.[74]

But economics was not the sole reason for the estrangement of Aleppans from the Arab government and for the feeling among some observers that, in the immediate aftermath of the war, the city probably contained more partisans of the Turks than of the sharifians.[75] Some of the pro-Turkish sentiment can be attributed to cultural affinities that connected Aleppans with their neighbors to the north. In addition, the successful anti-French resistance launched by the Kemalists—an energetic resistance that contrasted sharply with the hesitant diplomatic strategy pursued by the Arab government—and the gainful opportunities offered by participation in raids launched by Turkish partisans also bolstered the pro-Turkish ardor in the city. Furthermore, while many, fairly or unfairly, ascribed the deterioration of urban conditions in Aleppo to the indifference of the Arab government or to its policies, others chafed at the fact that choice government posts—both in Aleppo and in Damascus—seemed to be reserved for Iraqis and Palestinians who had participated in the Arab Revolt or who had shown themselves loyal to the regime. Whether or not they were "convinced that the 'bedouins' [i.e., the sharifians] are too inferior to impose themselves on

72. Darwaza, *Ḥawla al-ḥaraka al-ʿarabiyya al-ḥadītha,* 1:77–78; Joarder, *Syria Under the French Mandate,* 207–209; MAE L:SL/vol. 25/285–290, Extrait du journal Difah, 9 March 1920; MD 4H112/2A/38/R, "Renseignements," 20 February 1920; USNA 59/890d.00/9/473, Jackson (Aleppo) to Sec. of State, 13 March 1920; AD 409/dossiers de principe: Congrès syriens 1920–1938, 21 December 1929.

73. IO L/PS/10/802, Gertrude Bell, "Syria in October 1919," 15 November 1919.

74. MD 4H114/4/562, Cousse to Gouraud, 16 June 1920.

75. IO Curzon Papers 112/265, Notes in Curzon's hand, 27(?) November 1918.

the Aleppan aristocracy," as one French observer reported, many elites in the city reacted bitterly to rule from Damascus.[76]

The history of the Arab Club of Aleppo must be placed within this context. Sharif Nasr, nephew of Amir Faysal, entered Aleppo at the head of the Arab army on the night of 23 October 1918. According to historian Kamil Ghazzi, a little over a week and a half later a group of "Arab youths" took over the former headquarters of the local Committee of Union and Progress, renamed it "*nādī al-ʿarab*," and began issuing a newspaper, *al-ʿArab*.[77] Whatever the identity of these youths, an Arab Club leadership soon emerged from the ranks of some of the most prominent families and politicians of the city. The first president of the Arab Club of Aleppo was Masʿud al-Kawakibi, a member of a highly regarded religious family.[78] Assisting him was al-Hajj Najib al-Baqi, scion to a wealthy and influential local family, who became the first secretary of the chapter. Rashid al-Taliʿa (governor of the province of Aleppo), Ibrahim Hananu (president of the provincial council), Rushdi Bey al-Safadi (commander of the Arab army in Aleppo), Nabih al-ʿAzma (the chief of police of Aleppo and brother of Yusuf al-ʿAzma, the hero of Maysalun), Tahir al-Kayyali (a member of the most prominent landowning family in the city), and Sami al-Sarraj all assumed influential positions in the administration of the club.[79]

Initially, the activities of the Arab Club of Aleppo differed little from activities that the *mutanawwirūn* planned for the Arab Club of Damascus. It thus arranged the greeting for Faysal during the amir's first trip to the north, hosted receptions for ʿAli Rida al-Rikabi and François Georges-Picot, and

76. MAE L:SL/vol. 13/171–81, Pilley to Picot, 22 May 1919; AD 2358/dossier: emir Fayçal, Gautherot, "Mystification chérifienne: Récit d'un témoin oculaire," 13 September 1919; MD 4H112/2A, Agent 1, 2 February 1920; FO 371/5129/E5005, "Precis of an Interview with Mr. Sassoun Hezkail," 10 March 1920; MD 4H112, "Compte rendu du capitaine Gautherot sur la situation politique à Alep," 6 May 1920.

77. Ghazzī, *Nahr al-dhahab fī tārīkh Ḥalab*, 3:654.

78. Mardam Bek, *Dimashq wal-Quds fī al-ʿishrīnāt*, 47, 52.

79. Sami al-Sarraj, who acted as intermediary between the Arab Clubs of Damascus and Aleppo, was, according to a French source, also a member of the "Circle of Sacrifice," a terrorist cell whose sole purpose was the "elimination" of anyone who advocated pro-French policies. See MAE L:SL/vol. 10/151–154, "Rapport du capitaine Pichon, officier français de liaison à Alep, sur la société de Nadi-el-arabi," 4 March 1919; AD 2342, "Rapport sur les troubles survenus le 28 février 1919 à Alep," 14 April 1919; MD 4H112/1, "Compte rendu du capitaine Gautherot sur la situation politique à Alep," 6 May 1920; Khoury, *Syria and the French Mandate*, 422; Darwaza, *Ḥawla al-ḥaraka al-ʿarabiyya al-ḥadītha*, 1:77–78.

organized petition campaigns in the city and its environs supporting the appointment of Faysal as the Syrian representative to the Paris conference.[80] But while the founders and leaders of the Arab Club of Aleppo belonged to the same occupational and estate categories as the founders and leaders of the Arab Club of Damascus, and while some remained loyal to the policies of the Arab government, others within the club were not so inclined. As a result, the autumn 1919 crisis, which diminished the authority and credibility of the Arab government, cleaved the Arab Club of Damascus, and flustered many of that club's supporters, encouraged a group of merchants and notables within the Arab Club of Aleppo to forge new alliances and undertake unconventional forms of political activity.

Thus, in the aftermath of the Evacuation Crisis, members of the Arab Club of Aleppo, acting in conjunction with *comitajis* (members of partisan gangs) operating in the area and with members of the local committee of national defense, established their own political order in Aleppo and its environs. As will be detailed in the next chapter, Ibrahim Hananu, working through the Aleppo committee of national defense, became a principal organizer of the northern Syria military campaign against the French, a campaign that lasted through 1921. During the early phases of this insurrection, al-Hajj Najib al-Baqi acted as intermediary between Hananu and the local committee, collecting and distributing money and weapons for guerrilla activities. Rashid al-Tali'a and Rushdi Bey al-Safadi likewise supported the activities of the Aleppo committee of national defense. While president of the Arab Club of Aleppo, al-Safadi not only aligned the club with the committee but personally participated in the organization of neighborhood militias. Tahir al-Kayyali, who became president of the club after al-Safadi, was also a member of the local committee of national defense and served as the chief of a pro-Kemalist guerrilla band that centered its activities in nearby Idlib. Other members of the Kayyali family—Dr. 'Abd al-Rahman al-Kayyali, 'Abd al-Wahhab al-Kayyali, Shaykh Kamil al-Kayyali, Muhammad Darwish al-Kayyali, Sami al-Kayyali—were, like Tahir al-Kayyali, members of the Arab Club, the committee of national defense, or both.[81] In sum, a group of the city's most prestigious citizens, animated by the gen-

80. Ghazzī, *Nahr al-dhahab fī tārīkh Ḥalab*, 654–656; Mardam Bek, *Dimashq wal-Quds fī al-'ishrīnāt*, 47, 52; Adham al-Jundī, *Tārīkh al-thawrāt al-sūriyya fī 'ahd al-intidāb al-faransī*, 63.

81. al-Jundī, *Tārīkh al-thawrāt al-sūriyya*, 63, 116; Darwaza, *Ḥawla al-ḥaraka al-'arabiyya al-ḥadītha*, 1:77–78; Darwaza, *Mudhakkarāt*, 2:148–149; al-Amīr Muṣṭafā al-Shihābī, *Muḥāḍarāt fī al-isti'mār*, 2:96; Qadrī, *Mudhakkarātī*, 133; Khoury, *Syria and the French Mandate*, 10; AD 2429/144, Mercier to HC,

eral crisis of autumn 1919 and by local concerns, transformed the Arab Club of Aleppo into a centerpiece of a regionwide nexus of armed bands and popular political associations.

Although the Arab Club of Aleppo forged its political alliances under conditions that were unique, the club's reorientation betrays the more general direction taken by Syrian politics during this period. For almost a year after the end of World War I, nationalist elites, working both through the Arab government and through organizations such as the Arab Club, had arrogated political power to themselves. In exchange, they professed an ability to create effective institutions of governance, guide the nation to independence, and guarantee security and prosperity. By the autumn of 1919, they had realized none of these goals. Instead, they had unintentionally accomplished something very different: as a result of the mobilizations sponsored by the Arab government and the Arab Club, the nationalist elites had expanded the public's expectations of politics as well as the public's participation in political activity. As a result, they now found themselves forced to contend with new claimants for political leadership and new forms of political organization.

16 December 1918; AD 2429/161, Mercier to HC, 26 December 1918; AD 2375, Cousse to HC, 19 October 1919; FO 371/4186/163275/139–141, Meinertzhagen to Curzon, 19 December 1919; MD 4H112/2A/38R, "Renseignements," 20 February 1920; FO 882/23/221–223, Military Intelligence Division Commander (Aleppo), "Personalities: Arab Government of Syria," March 1920; MD 4H112/2B/2, Rapport politique (période du 16 au 30 avril 1920); AD 2346/c1a, 25 May 1920; MD L:SL/vol. 33, Gouraud to Millerand, "Note au sujet des rapports entre le haut-commissionaire de la République Française en Syrie-Cilicie et l'emir Fayçal," 22 September 1920.

2 The Popular Committees

The unilateral decision by the British government to withdraw its forces from Syria and the subsequent Anglo-French accord marked both a symbolic and a real turning point in the history of Faysali Syria. Because both the decision and the accord were reached without consulting the Arab government, it was apparent that the latter's strategy of winning independence by demonstrating to the entente powers that Syria was already prepared for independence had failed. The Arab government and its supporters in al-Fatat and the Arab Club now found themselves on the defensive, facing not only a reinvigorated opposition led by political elites but also a population whose partial mobilization they had authorized but now were unable to control.

In the wake of the withdrawal decision, the British government reduced by half the stipend it had been paying to the Arab government and then withheld or delayed monthly payments to punish the Arab government for a variety of transgressions. As a result of British parsimony, the Arab government was no longer able to buy off its political rivals. Worse still, the government could no longer afford to pay "protection" money to bedouin to assure their support and good behavior. The collapse of security in the countryside spilled over into urban areas, further exacerbating already difficult economic conditions. The economy of inland Syria went into a free fall, taking along with it both the power of, and much of the remaining approbation for, the Arab government.

As refugees from the Biqaʿ Valley and other zones of conflict entered the already crowded popular quarters of Damascus and other cities of Syria, as peasants sought asylum from the pillaging of gangs that seemed to raid with impunity, and as Syria lurched from one economic and political crisis to another, the pace of the ongoing breakdown of traditional patterns of political and social organization accelerated. While, depending on the circumstances, the emergent new patterns of political and social organization either subsumed previously held relationships within a new framework or bypassed them altogether, they had the overall effect of enabling Syrians to cope more effectively with their changed conditions.

Soon after the onset of the Evacuation Crisis, a diverse group of Syrians began constructing an interlocking set of committees that, while ostensibly founded to organize the defense of Syria or to assume functions abandoned by the Arab government, might be seen as the institutionalized expression of these new patterns of political and social organization. Although the original initiative that led to the founding of these new organizations came in part from a small number of political activists who belonged to prominent families, had participated in the activities of al-Fatat or the Syrian Union, or both, leadership did not remain exclusively in their hands. Instead, a new type of local leadership emerged, often chosen through elections in which large numbers of adult male Syrians participated. Because responsibility for the organization and activities of local committees devolved downward, small merchants, ulama, merchant ulama, *qabaḍāyāt*, recent immigrants to cities, and others who had previously been excluded from nationalist politics or whose participation had been superficial now assumed a central role in public life. They distributed emergency relief, manned patrols for local protection, outfitted and trained militias for national defense, secured provisions for their quarters and cities, assessed and collected taxes, and, in some cases, dispensed justice and enacted legislation. Furthermore, because they brought values and symbols apposite to the milieu from which they came, their participation in political activity transformed the character of nationalism in Syria.

THE ORIGINS OF THE POPULAR COMMITTEES

The British and French governments ratified the agreement that outlined the terms of the British withdrawal from Syria on 15 September 1919. Immediately thereafter, Yasin al-Hashimi, the president of the war council of the Arab government, called for the enlistment of twelve thousand volunteers to defend Syria.[1] While patriotism may have been one factor influencing al-Hashimi, it was certainly not the only one. A professional soldier from a lower-middle-class Iraqi family and an early supporter of al-Fatat, al-Hashimi had nevertheless refused command of the Arab army during

1. AD2430/dossier confidentiel—départ/263, Cousse to HC, 15 September 1919.

World War I and remained in Ottoman service. Distrustful of the British and the Hashemites and disdainful of the Arab Revolt, he had reportedly believed that Arab officers in the Ottoman army should spearhead any uprising against the Turks. After the war, al-Hashimi received his commission from the Arab government and subsequently did everything possible to consolidate the Arab military forces under his sole command. "His Turkish training has stamped him Turkish, the military Teutonized Turk, not the Effendi," complained an observer in a profile written at the instruction of the British government. "Intensely ambitious he aims at personal aggrandisement and is not really in sympathy with the Syrians or Prince Feisal." Arguing that the sharifian forces were ill-disciplined and that their mission had ended with the conquest of Damascus, al-Hashimi ordered them disbanded, on occasion forcibly disarming units personally loyal to Amir Faysal.[2]

Frequently in conflict with the other members of the inner circle of the Arab government, al-Hashimi took advantage of the absence of Faysal (the amir had been out of the country a mere three days when the enlistment of volunteers began) and the youth and naiveté of Faysal's surrogate, Amir Zayd, to institute a new military structure, a committee of national defense (*lajnat al-difāʿ al-waṭanī*). According to al-Hashimi's plan, local notables, working through "commissions of recruitment," were to enlist volunteers in a military force that would be under the supervision of the committee and, by extension, be loyal to al-Hashimi alone.[3] British pressure forced the Arab government to disavow the committee of national defense within a week. "'The Committee of National Defense' and its public activities have no official sanction," read an announcement in the government journal *al-ʿĀṣima*, "and no compulsory military service exists."[4] The Arab government dismantled the committee, and two months later the British kidnapped al-Hashimi and exiled him to Palestine.

2. FO 882/23/221–223, "Personalities: Arab Government of Syria," Military Intelligence, March 1920; FO 882/24/128–134, "Who's Who in Damascus," 14 May 1919; MAE L:SL/vol. 15/324, Picot to Pichon, 18 July 1919; Saʿīd, *Thawrāt al-ʿarab fī al-qarn al-ʿishrīn*, 258; al-ʿAjlūnī, *Dhikrayāt*, 72–73, 83; Qadrī, *Mudhakkarātī*, 81.

3. Richard Meinertzhagen, *Middle East Diary, 1917–1956*, 48. al-Ḥaffār, "al-Ḥukūmāt allatī taʿāqabat" 1(15 tishrīn al-thānī 1372): 10; AD 2430/dossier confidentiel—départ/263, Cousse to HC, 15 September 1919; IO L/PS/10/801/P6132/450, Meinertzhagen to FO, 23 September 1919. This committee of national defense should not be confused with the other organization of the same name, founded later and affiliated with the Higher National Committee.

4. *al-ʿĀṣima*, 22 September 1919, 3.

The dissolution of al-Hashimi's committee of national defense did not affect the drive for volunteers. Even before the September 15 Accord, opponents of the Arab government's policy of negotiation and compromise with the entente powers had begun recruiting military units. After the signing of the accord, the recruitment expanded as a variety of political associations and urban and rural notables scrambled to form volunteer companies. The Arab Club of Damascus, for example, commissioned Fakhri al-Barudi, a wartime member of al-Fatat, and Nasib al-Bakri to organize and equip volunteer units. On paper, al-Bakri's regiment comprised approximately three hundred men, of which about one-third were cavalry.[5]

In part, fear motivated the notables who enlisted volunteer detachments: as some notables armed their clients, prudence required that others respond in kind, particularly as formal structures that should have guaranteed both urban and rural security collapsed. According to an American diplomat stationed in Aleppo,

> the condition locally and throughout the surrounding country grows more grave daily. Aleppo has become the rendezvous of the chiefs of the hundreds of villages of the entire territory hereabouts, who, together with practically all the important landed proprietors of Aleppo, are arming the peasantry with modern rifles and ammunition. Each chief regards his neighbor and even his own men with a certain suspicion.[6]

In addition to fear, however, affiliation with and support for volunteer units took on the trappings of a status symbol. A report in *al-ʿĀṣima* about a regiment recruited by the Arab Club from among its members ended by explaining, with a touch of irony, that "a large number of esteemed ulama, writers, and sons of notables [of the regiment] are awaiting the finishing touches by their tailors on the details of their military uniforms."[7] According to another report in the same journal, Khalid al-ʿAzm, son of the conservative landowner Muhammad Fawzi al-ʿAzm (whose attitude toward Amir Faysal and al-Fatat was recounted in the previous chapter), regularly donned a military uniform before stepping out in the evenings. The excitement even swept up the impressionable amir Zayd, who joined a regi-

5. AD 2344/c1/août-décembre 1919/305–306, Cousse to Picot, 31 October 1919; AD 2430, Letter from Cousse, 1 November 1919; AD 2344/c1/310, Cousse to Picot, 3 November 1919; AD 2325/a1, "Journaux de l'intérieur" (extract from *al-Urdunn* 47), TEO zone ouest—Bureau de la presse, 24 November 1919; AD 2334/dossier E/1/50/S.R., TEO zone ouest, 9 December 1919.

6. USNA Aleppo Consulate RG84/vol. 121/800, Jesse Jackson (Aleppo) to Mark Bristol (Constantinople), 9 February 1920.

7. *al-ʿĀṣima,* 15 September 1919, 4. See also *al-ʿĀṣima,* 4 September 1919, 3.

ment organized by the Arab Club "as a soldier" and donated twenty-five uniforms to his unit.[8]

These regiments could hardly be considered "popular militias," nor could their establishment be considered an indication of the emergence of a popular political movement per se. Although both notables working alone or through organizations such as the Arab Club and military officers loyal to al-Hashimi recruited volunteers from among the lower classes, each militia remained autonomous and acted independently, like the army of a feudal baron. While the excitement aroused by agitation and recruitment for defense stimulated the process of mobilization, the autonomy and vertical structure of each militia frustrated the emergence of an institutional framework that might have promoted a broader set of loyalties. That framework did take shape through the efforts of individuals such as Kamil al-Qassab, the founder of the Higher National Committee, who envisioned a national movement that was radically different from that supported by the Arab government and its allies.

Kamil al-Qassab, like many other activists associated with the Higher National Committee, came from a modest background. His father, a merchant from Homs, moved to Damascus before the birth of his son and died when Kamil al-Qassab was seven. His mother (whose maiden name he took as his own when he was a youth) was a member of the Karim family of the ʿUqayba quarter of Damascus, a family that included not only merchants but *qabaḍāyāt*.[9] Al-Qassab received a traditional education in his quarter, then, at age twenty-five, completed his education at al-Azhar in Egypt, where he studied with, among others, the Islamic modernist *ʿālim* Muhammad ʿAbduh. Upon his return to Damascus, he founded a school,

8. *al-ʿĀṣima*, 15 September 1919, 4; Yūsuf al-Ḥakīm, *Dhikrayāt*, 3:123.

9. Interview with ʿAdnan al-Khatib, 8 November 1989; Interview with Shaykhs Muhammad Murad al-Tabbaʿ, ʿAbd al-Ghani Daqqar, and Yasin ʿUrufa, 2 January 1990; Interview with Shaykh Yasin ʿUrufa, 4 January 1990; Samīḥ Ḥamūda, *al-Waʿī wal-thawra: dirāsa fī ḥayāt wa jihād al-Shaykh ʿIzz al-Dīn al-Qassām, 1868–1935*, 119–120. Part of al-Qassab's appeal was his lower-middle-class origins, from which arose legends about the shaykh's earthiness. One story about al-Qassab was related to me during several interviews. According to the story, after al-Qassab returned to Syria following the imposition of the French mandate and the declaration of a general amnesty, he was riding in a railway car with a French officer and his family. The officer offered al-Qassab some wine, which the shaykh refused. Later the officer noticed that al-Qassab was eating grapes and asked him why he partook of the fruit and not its product. Al-Qassab pointed to the officer's companions and asked him if they were his wife and daughter. When the officer confirmed this, al-Qassab asked him why, using the same logic, he slept only with the mother and not the daughter as well.

the Madrasa al-ʿUthmaniyya (later the Madrasa al-Kamiliyya) in Hayy Buzuriyya.[10]

According to Ahmad Hilmi al-ʿAllaf, a former student at the Madrasa al-ʿUthmaniyya, the curriculum and pedagogy offered at the school reflected an idiosyncratic amalgam of traditionalist and modern influences. On the one hand, the school had a reputation for attracting instructors of high quality and for offering instruction in nontraditional subjects, such as theater, mathematics, and geography. On the other hand, the school continued to emphasize traditional subjects, such as grammar and *ṣarf* (Arabic inflection), in what al-ʿAllaf calls "the old and sterile manner" of memorization and repetition. Al-Qassab taught *ṣarf* himself ("He had us memorize in the form, 'Know that there are thirty-five gates of inflection . . . .' and in this manner to the end without understanding") and was noted for the harsh punishments he inflicted on ill-prepared or ill-disciplined students:

> For [the student] who did not master his lessons word-for-word, there was a bamboo cane tucked under his [al-Qassab's] arm. He listened to each student in the class one-by-one. The student read what was demanded, and looked at the eyes of Shaykh Kamil which exuded malice and anger, at his glowering face, at the stick under his arm, and at the grammar book in his hand. He followed what we read, and if we made a mistake or hesitated or stopped, the cane arose with a complete motion . . .
>
> It is worth noting that Shaykh Kamil did not land these blows to guide the student; rather these blows were the result of strife between him and his wife or someone else. He rounded out his struggle with the erring student, showering him with blows until he was on the brink of shattering him, and sometimes it was not sufficient to strike the legs without [first] anointing them with water. He struck them with all his might, sometimes as many as twenty blows.[11]

Because, according to al-ʿAllaf, corporal punishment was not commonly practiced in schools during this period, he suggests that its use in the Madrasa al-ʿUthmaniyya may have been responsible for the high rate of turnover among instructors and for the deterioration of the school's repu-

10. Muḥammad Muṭīʿ al-Ḥāfiẓ and Nizār Abāẓa, *Tārīkh ʿulamāʾ Dimashq fī al-qarn al-rābiʿ ʿashar al-hijrī*, 657; Khayr al-Dīn al-Ziriklī, *al-Aʿlām: qāmūsa tarājim li-ashhar al-rijāl wal-nisāʾ min al-ʿArab wal-mustaʿribīn wal-mustashriqīn* (n.p., 1984), 13.

11. al-ʿAllāf, *Dimashq fī maṭlaʿ al-qarn al-ʿishrīn*, 202.

tation. Al-ʿAllaf, like many other students, departed the *madrasa*, enrolling in a government-sponsored school that he claimed was less old-fashioned.[12]

Kamil al-Qassab joined al-Fatat when the organization moved from Paris to Beirut in 1913. During the war, he undertook two missions for the society. In 1915, al-Fatat sent him to Egypt to ascertain the political opinions of Syrians in exile there and to determine British attitudes toward the nationalist movement. Arrested in Alexandria, al-Qassab obtained his release as a result of the entreaties made on his behalf by Rashid Rida and Rafiq al-ʿAzm, two members of the Ottoman Administrative Decentralization Party.[13] Later that year, al-Qassab once again traveled on behalf of al-Fatat, this time to the Hijaz, where he served as the envoy to Sharif Husayn. He remained with the sharif until the beginning of 1918, giving him enough time to form an opinion of the Hijazi leadership and of the Arab Revolt that he carried back to Syria when he returned there after the war. As later reported by journalist and political gadfly Muhibb al-Din al-Khatib:

> Muhibb al-Din al-Khatib and Shaykh Kamil al-Qassab wanted all the best for King Husayn and his sons, on the condition that they would want all the best for the nation which they would lead. But King Husayn

12. At the school, al-Qassab fostered a network of instructors who later played diverse roles in nationalist politics. Rashid Baqdunis, instructor of mathematics, later became a member of the Syrian branch of al-ʿAhd. Dr. Asʿad al-Hakim, a physician and instructor in theater, joined al-Fatat after the organization moved from Paris to Beirut. After the war, he became a member of the executive committee of the Higher National Committee and founding member of the Democratic Party (*al-ḥizb al-dimuqrāṭī*), the political arm of the Higher National Committee. ʿAbd al-Wahhab al-Inklizi and Amir ʿArif al-Shihabi were instructors in geography and Arab history, respectively. The former was a founding member of the Literary Society in Istanbul, the latter a member of al-Fatat. Jamal Pasha hanged both during World War I. Other instructors included Salim al-Jundi (grammar) who was one of the initial contributors to the national board of the Arab Independence Party, ʿAbd al-Rahman Shahbandar (oratory) and Khayr al-Din al-Zirikli (Arabic composition). See al-ʿAllāf, *Dimashq fī maṭlaʿ al-qarn al-ʿishrīn*, 203; Darwaza, *Mudhakkarāt*, 2:130–131; 139; Dāghir, *Mudhakarrātī*, 35; Interview with Shaykh Ahmad al-Qasimi, 6 November 1989; *al-ʿĀṣima*, 10 March 1919, 4; *al-ʿĀṣima*, 7 November 1919, 5; *al-Kināna*, 26 June 1920, 2; AD 2323/A-1/91, M. P. Lefévre-Pontalis to Picot, 26 November 1918; AD 2430/dossier confidentiel—départ/161s, Cousse to HC, 21 February 1919; FO 371/4217/69267, Note by Arab Bureau, Cairo, 6 May 1919; FO 371/4183/136154, Lutfallah to Lloyd George, 16 September 1919; FO 882/24/209–210, Major G. W. Courtney, 21 May 1920.

13. Saʿīd, *Thawrāt al-ʿArab*, 38–39; Qadrī, *Mudhakkarātī*, 37; Khoury, *Urban Notables*, 64. After his return from Egypt, al-Qassab was arrested by Jamal Pasha. Arguing that he had gone to Egypt to purchase school supplies, he was released.

> and his sons lived and died with the beliefs of the age of feudalism, that the nation is the domain of the king.[14]

There is evidence that, unbeknownst to British authorities and the sharifian administration in the Hijaz, al-Qassab organized for an independent political committee while in Mecca. A petition signed by a dozen Syrians based in the city (most of whom were former officers in the Ottoman army) and addressed to al-Qassab reads as follows:

> To al-Qassab (15 July 1918): We, the Syrians in Mecca, wish to inform your national committee [*lajna qawmiyya*] that we support it, its principles, and its activities, and that we have been following [it] for many years. [Our] country has offered up the flower of its youth and the best of its men as precious victims [to these principles] in the nooses and in front of the trenches. These principles, which we shall support as long as we live, are the struggle for the independence of our Arab country, its unity, and its governance by civil structures based on freedom, equality, and brotherhood between all its sons regardless of personal or religious beliefs. We shall support every action that you do in fulfillment of these principles with all our might. We hope that God will enable you and us to succeed in our goal of advancing the fatherland and the happiness of its sons.[15]

While it is possible that the signatories are referring to al-Fatat or al-ʿAhd, the existence of an independent "national committee" for Syrian exiles in the Hijaz is not implausible, given al-Qassab's misgivings about the Arab

14. Saʿīd, *Thawrāt al-ʿArab*, 56, 241–243; al-Ḥāfiẓ and Abāẓa, *Tārīkh ʿulamāʾ Dimashq*, 659; Fāʾiz al-Ghuṣayn, *Mudhakkarātī ʿan al-thawra*, 213; Muḥibb al-Dīn al-Khaṭīb, autobiographical manuscript kept in the Salafiyya Library in Cairo and in Markaz al-wathāʾiq al-tārīkhiyya in Damascus, 43. See also al-Khatib's autobiographical series in *al-Thaqāfa* (Algiers), serialized between January 1972 (1:6) and December/January 1973 (3:18). Muhibb al-Din al-Khatib was an enigmatic figure: he edited Sharif Husayn's newspaper, *al-Qibla*, at a time when he was, according to his later writings, already disillusioned with the Arab Revolt, and he edited and wrote for the Arab government newspaper *al-ʿĀṣima* while working as secretary for the Higher National Committee. In part, his seemingly contradictory political activities and ideas replicated the contradictions inherent in *salafism*, which sought to balance Enlightenment ideals and Islamic authenticity. Although his actual views may never be known, his writings nevertheless provide valuable information about contemporary debates, and historians owe him a debt of gratitude for conserving documents relating to the early nationalist movement. For an alternative view of al-Khatib's nationalist activities, see Muslih, "Rise of Local Nationalism," 174–175.

15. Document contained in SL:LW.

Revolt and his concerns about the relationship that had developed between British officials and exiled nationalists in Egypt. It would not have been out of character for al-Qassab, who used his time abroad to establish connections between his Syrian-based networks and diaspora Syrians, to have founded such a committee.[16] Nor would the establishment of such a committee have been ineffective: the disillusionment al-Qassab felt toward the sharifians was not unique, and while some Syrians had preferred to sit out the war in Egypt rather than join Faysal's Arab army, others followed in the footsteps of al-Qassab and abandoned the sharifian cause before the occupation of Damascus.

At times, the British treated the activities of the expatriate Syrian nationalists as a nuisance; at other times, as a threat to the horse they backed. They thus adopted a two-pronged strategy toward the expatriates: if they could not co-opt them (as they attempted to do by encouraging the establishment of the committee that drafted the "Declaration of the Seven"), at least they could prevent the Egyptian-based nationalists from establishing contact with their compatriots in Syria. As late as mid-December 1918, the U.S. military attaché in Cairo complained that the British not only censored private correspondence entering Egypt from Syria and Palestine, but that they refused permission for newspapers printed in Damascus and Beirut to be imported and circulated in the Egyptian capital.

> The Syrian leaders in Egypt have been kept in complete ignorance of the state of affairs in Syria. Neither the French nor the British have informed these prominent Syrians of the fact that a Cherifean Government has actually been established throughout Syria, with the exception of the Lebanon and the coast! This appears to be a deliberate means of keeping the Syrians muzzled, so that they cannot make their voices heard at Paris in the Peace Conference.
>
> Dr. Nimr, the Editor of *el-Mokattam* says that he has requested time and time again permission to publish editorials and articles expressing the desires of the Syrians concerning the future of their country. He was informed by the censor that he could say anything he pleased about Syria and the Syrian question, but he was not to write anything that touched on Great Britain, France, or the Cherif of Mecca, or their interests in Syria![17]

16. MAE L:SL/vol. 7/179, Service des informations de la marine dans le Levant à marine, Paris, 24 December 1918; FO 882/24/85–90, Walrond to Cornwallis, 13 January 1919.

17. USNA 165/2075–108/173, U.S. Military Attaché (Cairo), "Facts in Connection with the Syrian Question Which Have Recently Been Learned," 16 December 1918. According to Rashid Rida, the British in Egypt censored news from Syria un-

The British blockade not only prevented news of Syria from reaching Egypt; the British government also deliberately obstructed the departure of Syrian nationalists based in Egypt who wished to return home. As a result, al-Qassab, who had traveled to Egypt after his sojourn in the Hijaz, was forced to remain there until April 1919.[18]

Overall, Kamil al-Qassab's life was filled with an array of seeming inconsistencies. His background and early education were modest, his lineage on his mother's side a bit disreputable, and he commanded the loyalty of quarter-based *qabaḍāyāt* and petit-bourgeois merchants and ulama. Nevertheless, he hobnobbed with nationalists from more distinguished backgrounds who championed an ideology that reflected their status as "rising elites." He studied with the leading Islamic modernist of his times, Muhammad ʿAbduh, and supported the activities of al-Fatat even before its postwar expansion. Yet he led a traditionalist social movement that rejected the side of ʿAbduh's teachings that inspired other nationalist activists to espouse modernist apologetics and to embrace ideals borrowed from Europe.

In part, these incongruities might be attributed to the fact that the disparate influences that shaped al-Qassab's life and informed his worldview placed him at the juncture of the cultural divide described in the Introduction. Although al-Qassab and a select number of his colleagues in the popular committees had been habituated to the culture and idiom of the nationalist elites, constraints imposed by their experiences and the ambiguity and precariousness of their social position militated against their assimilation into the world of those elites and disposed them instead to assume a mediatory role between the cultural divisions. Thus, while selectively extracting language and symbols from the polemics of the nationalist elites, they simultaneously repudiated as alien many of the ideological precepts that the nationalist elites had used to sustain those polemics. Through this process of selection and recontextualization, al-Qassab and his colleagues articulated a nationalism that ostensibly reaffirmed "traditional values" yet did so within the institutional and discursive framework of a modern national movement.

---

til the departure of the King-Crane Commission in the summer of 1919. *al-Manār,* June 1920, 428–429.

18. In addition to al-Qassab, those who had to wait several months before they received travel permits to Syria from Egypt included Asʿad Daghir (who received permission to return to Damascus in late December 1918), Fawzi al-Bakri, ʿAbd al-Rahman Shahbandar, Khalid al-ʿAzm, and Rashid Rida (who was not permitted to return home until the late summer of 1919). Dāghir, *Mudhakkarātī,* 100–101, 106; *al-Manār,* June 1920, 428–429; Yūsuf al-Ḥakīm, *Dhikrayāt,* 3:83.

THE HIGHER NATIONAL COMMITTEE

Like much of the information concerning the popular committees, data on the origins of the Higher National Committee, particularly the role that other political organizations played in its founding, are both meager and contradictory. Several sources attest to the fact that the committee began as a project of al-Fatat, of its offshoot, the Arab Independence Party, or of both. Ahmad Qadri, a member of al-Fatat during the prewar period and later Amir Faysal's personal physician, claimed that he suggested the formation of the committee to prevent Faysal from succumbing to pressure from those who encouraged the amir to come to terms with the French. "When I noticed that all who were in the retinue of the amir encouraged him to ratify the treaty with Clemenceau," Qadri explained,

> I wrote to the central committee of al-Fatat in Damascus with the purpose of resisting this idea and benefiting from Shaykh Kamil al-Qassab's impetuosity and expertise in influencing the minds of the masses (*jamāhīr*) to refuse the treaty. Al-Qassab carried out the request, and on 27 November he attended a meeting in [the] Qanawat [quarter of Damascus] at the home of the Barudi family. There he delivered an enthusiastic speech in which he demanded complete independence, and he called on all attendees at the meeting to sign a covenant refusing any agreement that impinged on the sovereignty of the nation and its independence. The attendees did not leave until they signed. Thus, al-Qassab had the first word in the Higher National Committee.[19]

In contrast, Muhibb al-Din al-Khatib, who in his writings overlooks divisions among nationalists, presents what is probably a similarly mythologized version of the founding of the Higher National Committee. When Faysal left for Europe, al-Khatib recalled many years later, the amir turned to al-Qassab and told him, "I expect you and your patriotic brothers to establish a popular movement that will arm the nation and to transform Damascus and other cities of Syria into a military barracks and the nation into an armed camp."[20]

Differences aside, both accounts concur that the Higher National Committee was founded as a response to the new political atmosphere that enveloped Syria in the wake of the Evacuation Crisis. Facing mounting popu-

19. Qadri, *Mudhakkarātī,* 149–150. See also Dāghir, *Mudhakkarātī,* 107; Kasmieh, *al-Ḥukūma al-ʿarabiyya fī Dimashq,* 144–145.

20. Muḥibb al-Dīn al-Khaṭīb, "Mudhakkarāt Muḥibb al-Dīn al-Khaṭīb," *al-Thaqāfa* (Algiers) 3 (June–July 1973): 92; al-Rīmāwī, *Jamʿiyyat al-ʿarabiyya al-Fatāt al-sirriyya,* 104.

lar outrage against the actions of Britain and France, the established political organizations looked for ways to channel popular passions and gain control over the movement advocating defense. Although the exact role of these organizations is obscure, it is clear from the records of the Higher National Committee that beginning in late October, notables who had been organizing militias in their respective quarters began holding meetings to coordinate their activities.[21] The minutes of one of these meetings, probably held on the eve of the formation of the Higher National Committee, reveal both the names of those involved in formulating the final plans for the committee and their concerns. In the minutes, participants are divided into two categories, one unlabeled and one labeled "*aʿyān*" (notables). Among the legible names on the first list are those of "Shaykh Kamil" (al-Qassab), Zayn Murtada (a member of a distinguished Shiʿi family), Yasin Diab (a prominent merchant), Asʿad Daghir (the representative of the executive committee of the Arab Independence Party), Father Mikhail Shahada, and Muhammad Hamdi Safarjalani (an *ʿālim*). The names of "Fawzi Bey" (al-Bakri?), Ahmad Effendi al-Husayni (a member of al-Fatat and later the Syrian Patriotic Party), Tawfiq Bey al-Shamiyya, Salim Bey al-Anhuri (a Christian merchant), Saʿid Agha Mahayini (a merchant with *qabaḍāy* connections), and Fakhri Bey (al-Barudi?) appear on the second list. It is interesting to note that even at this early stage of organizational development, the list of names associated with the Higher National Committee contains a much higher percentage of individuals from the occupational categories of *ʿālim* and merchant than, for example, might be found among the *muʾassisūn* of al-Fatat or the founders of the Arab Club of Damascus.

The minutes read as follows:

> After reading the minutes from the last meeting and approving them, the list of regulations was read, those attending discussed the name of the group, and it was decided by a majority to be the National Committee [*al-lajna al-waṭaniyya*].
>
> Item #1: Ten [attendees] suggested adding a sentence about all parts of Syria.
>
> Zionism [*qawmiyya yahūdiyya*]: it was decided to add the sentence "Resisting every principle leading to the establishment of a nationalism [*qawmiyya*] that threatens the political existence of the country and Syrian unity."
>
> Ten suggested adding a paragraph indicating that our work is tied to all other similar activities taking place in the rest of the Arab nation [*al-bilād al-ʿarabiyya*], but the majority vetoed that.

21. Saʿīd, *al-Thawra al-ʿarabiyya al-kubrā*, 2:101–103.

Suggestion put forward by Shaykh Kamil regarding electing al-Hajj ʿIssa Diab.[22]

Two items on the agenda of these minutes are of particular interest. First, it appears that, in contrast to the speculation of some historians, anti-Zionism did not become a component of Syrian nationalism merely because Palestinians played an important role in nationalist organizations such as the Arab Club. As might be expected, the significance of the struggle against "all nationalisms but Arab nationalism" (as the confrontation with Zionism was euphemistically labeled[23]) was critical for both distinguishing the boundaries and elucidating the very nature of the Syrian national community. Second, these minutes reveal that at least some of the founders of the Higher National Committee always planned to sever the bonds that connected the committee with other political organizations and to construct a completely autonomous organization. This is especially significant because the committee, as originally constituted, was little more than a loosely constructed coalition to which Damascus-based political parties and associations sent representatives. Initially, for example, Muhammad ʿIzzat Darwaza, Saʿid Haydar, and Tawfiq al-Shamiyya represented the interests of the Arab Independence Party in the committee, while Hasan al-Hakim, Husni al-Barazi, Mustafa Wasfi, and Muhyi al-Din Sadiq represented those of al-ʿAhd.[24]

According to several accounts, the Higher National Committee sponsored elections on Saturday, 1 November 1919, for the purpose of choosing four representatives to the committee from each of forty-eight neighborhoods (*aḥyāʾ*) of Damascus. Four days later, the representatives convened at the home of Ahmad al-Hasibi, brother-in-law of ʿAli Rida al-Rikabi and president of the municipality of Damascus, to select one elector from each neighborhood who would be eligible to vote for the twenty-seven leaders of the committee.[25] From mid-November through the beginning of Febru-

22. These minutes are contained in SL:LW.

23. See, for example, *al-ʿĀṣima,* 17 November 1919, 3–4.

24. Darwaza, *Mudhakkarāt,* 2:154–155; Dāghir, *Mudhakkarātī,* 107; Saʿīd, *al-Thawra al-ʿarabiyya al-kubrā,* 2:103–105.

25. Saʿīd, *al-Thawra al-ʿarabiyya al-kubrā,* 2:101–3; Kasmieh, *al-Ḥukūma al-ʿarabiyya fī Dimashq,* 144; *al-ʿĀṣima,* 4 November 1919, 5; SL:LW, "Niẓām al-lajna al-waṭaniyya al-ʿulyā fī al-ʿāṣima al-sūriyya," 17 November 1919. The text of the charter of the Higher National Committee has been reprinted in Iḥsān ʿAskar, *Nashʾat al-ṣiḥāfa al-sūriyya: ʿArḍ lil-qawmiyya fī ṭawr al-nashʾa min al-ʿahd al-ʿuthmānī ḥattā qiyām al-dawla al-ʿarabiyya,* 500–506. (Note: The actual publication date of the above-cited issue of *al-ʿĀṣima* was probably 6 November 1919.) One undated document in the archives of the Salafiyya Library lists the districts

ary 1920, representatives from each *thuman* (one of originally eight, then nine administrative districts of the city), and three officers—a secretary, an accountant, and a treasurer—supervised the activities of the committee. No permanent president presided over these meetings. Instead, according to the charter, those in attendance were to select one of their number to officiate at each meeting. Thus, although Kamil al-Qassab would soon emerge as the preeminent leader of the organization, his official status, like that of his colleagues Salih al-Kalfundi and Muhibb al-Din al-Khatib, was initially that of representative from the Qaymariyya quarter.[26]

The charter of the Higher National Committee sanctioned suffrage for all (implicitly, adult male) residents of Damascus in the election of local representatives to the committee. As organizing for the committee spread from Damascus to other cities and towns as far away as Amman, so did the committee's electoral activities. These elections were not artifice. Unlike the petition campaigns organized by the Arab Club to impress upon a foreign audience the image of popular support for the Arab government and its policies, the Higher National Committee not only derived its legitimacy from the elections, but elections were the means through which the committee attempted to redefine the Syrian national community. "Every individual of the nation is legally bound to the national committee by virtue of the national interest, because the nation was never unanimously involved in anything like this task, because its goals have been set by unanimous consent, and because representatives have been chosen in a serious and orderly manner," the committee's charter declared. "As a result of this legal tie between the Higher [National] Committee and individuals, all citizens of the nation are electors of the Higher [National] Committee and support its stated goals."[27]

Both the organizers of the Higher National Committee and the committee's constituents thus took elections quite seriously. In one district,

---

and the names of forty-one representatives in attendance at one meeting of the Higher National Committee. Representatives from al-Akrad, Muhajirin, and Suq al-Maydan were absent, some districts sent more than one representative, and other districts shared representatives. Interestingly, the list includes at least one Jewish representative (Yusuf ʿArari) from *ḥārat al-yahūd* and at least one Christian representative (Tawfiq al-Shamiyya) from the quarter of Bab Tuma.

26. SL:LW, al-Qassab et al. to al-Rikabi, 13 November 1919; SL:LW, "Niẓām al-lijān al-waṭaniyya al-farʿiyya fī bilād Sūriyya," 17 November 1919. The text of the charter of the branch committees has also been reprinted in ʿAskar, *Nashʾat al-ṣiḥāfa al-sūriyya*, 507–513.

27. SL:LW, "Niẓām al-lajna al-waṭaniyya al-ʿulyā fī al-ʿāṣima al-sūriyya," 17 November 1919.

Qaymariyya, the branch committee publicly cited the use of a secret ballot in the election of representatives to the Higher National Committee to demonstrate the authenticity of the electoral process.[28] In other cases, the names of those nominated and elected appeared in sympathetic newspapers.[29] Much of the "Lajna Waṭaniyya" file in the Salafiyya Library in Cairo, the main repository for materials on the popular committees, is made up of reports of local election results that were validated by the electors themselves. These electors signed affidavits such as the following:

> We, the people [*ahālī*] of the neighborhood of Ma'dhanat al-Shahm, among us effendis, merchants, youths and old men, have re-elected Sayyid Talʿat Effendi Jabiri as our representative to the national committee. He was, is, and will be trustworthy. We give our signatures as an official memo to be acted upon.

Approximately one hundred signatures accompanied this affidavit.[30] Other affidavits that have been preserved include those from winners of elections who attested to their right to act as representatives of their neighborhoods, as well as from representatives apparently elected without their knowledge who were claiming an inability to serve, usually for health reasons. One of the more intriguing of these letters came from the journalist Muhammad Kurd ʿAli, editor of the newspaper *al-Muqtabas* and later one of the founders of the (pro-French) Syrian Patriotic Party. His letter, the text of which lends credence to a British observation that he was "an unprincipled . . . charlatan," reads as follows:

> I received the news of the decision of the national committee regarding my election to be a member. I am thankful that you have given consideration to this invalid, and from the depths of my heart I would have loved to respond positively to this request had it not been for the fact that my

28. In this case, Shaykh Musa Tawil was elected. SL:LW, Secretary of branch committee of Qaymariyya to the president and members of the [Higher] National Committee, 16 December 1919.

29. SL:LW. One letter, addressed to Muhibb al-Din al-Khatib, reads as follows: "I am writing to request the names of those who were elected during the meeting of the committee yesterday and were nominated to be members of the Higher [National] Committee so that I can print them on the pages of *al-Mufīd*. And if it pleases you, please add the names of Saʿid Effendi al-Malih and Kamil Effendi Iyas, for this is what some members wish to see."

30. Interestingly, the signatures following this affidavit are divided into two categories: members (approximately one-fifth of the signatures) and nonmembers. SL:LW, 17 December 1919.

> health has deteriorated recently. Please accept my apologies for not standing up to this responsibility. May God grant the committee success.[31]

Kurd ʿAli passed away in 1953.

On the basis of these elections, the Higher National Committee, its branches, and the affiliated committees of national defense claimed the right to act as the true representatives of the Syrian people. "Committees of national defense, which are tied to the national committee in the capital, have been created in all of Syria," *al-Kawkab* reported.

> The method of creation of these committees is by true, lawful election, so that they legitimately represent the nation. . . . The committee takes the place of the Syrian Congress in its services, nay, we can say that its services are more comprehensive because of the existence of permanent branches throughout all parts of Syria, from Aleppo to Karak.[32]

This assertion was not, of course, undisputed. Amir Faysal used a variety of means—petition campaigns, ceremonies in which prominent notables, clerics, and tribal leaders pledged homage (*mubāyaʿa*), and so on—to validate his right to act as the sole representative of the Syrian people. Likewise, the Syrian General Congress, which also based its claim to represent Syria on the election of its members, might also have challenged the pretensions of the Higher National Committee had it not been prorogued by Amir Zayd at the beginning of December 1919.[33] But because the Higher National Committee, like the Syrian General Congress before it, could not sponsor elections in the territories administered by the British or the French—that is, in Palestine or the territory that is present-day Lebanon—the committee's political opponents disputed its assertion that it alone truly represented "Syria within its natural boundaries" and that its authority therefore superseded that of the congress. "It was not long before we heard that the [Higher National] Committee called only some notables from some cities of the eastern zone and that it passed over the representatives of the coast and Palestine," protested an editorialist in *Sūriyya al-jadīda*. "How do we explain the fact that deputies from the coast were not invited

31. SL:LW, Muhammad Kurd ʿAli to [Higher] National Committee, 7 December 1919; FO 882/24, "Who's Who in Damascus," 14 May 1919.

32. *al-Kawkab*, 6 January 1920, 10. For the founding of one such committee in Nabk, see SL:LD, Catholic metropolitan, mufti, president of the municipality et al. to Kamil al-Qassab, 18 December 1919.

33. By the time the congress reconvened in early March, the Higher National Committee was strong enough to define the nationalist agenda. See Russell, *First Modern Arab State*, 114, 132.

to participate in the committee in spite of the fact that the entire movement is calling for the inclusion of the coast in the Syrian kingdom . . . ?"[34] To circumvent questions raised by the absence of Palestinian representation in the committee and to assure its influence in Palestine, the Higher National Committee, working with other groups and congressional deputies in Damascus, formed the Palestine Congress and immediately pushed through resolutions that declared Palestine an inseparable part of Syria and condemned Zionism and Zionist immigration.[35]

The elections held by the popular committees both expedited and validated the appearance of a new breed of nationalist activist in Damascus as well as in other parts of Syria. These activists differed significantly from those who had originally organized al-Fatat or the Arab Club. Based on electoral lists found in the Salafiyya Library and on other written sources, an analysis of forty-five secondary leaders of the popular committees in Damascus whose backgrounds can be traced—directors of branch committees, representatives from the branch committees to the Higher National Committee, and organizers who worked in tandem with the various committees—reveals a group one-third of which was composed of merchants and another third of ulama. About one-third of the latter category also engaged in commerce. In contrast to the previously cited organizations, only one-quarter of the secondary leaders of the popular committees were government employees, and only about one-tenth had received professional training.

Electoral activity, the diffusion of the principle of representation, and the often widespread participation in activities sponsored by the Higher National Committee and its branches thus signaled the emergence of new relationships of power among urban Syrians and heralded the appearance of a different type of local political leadership in Syria. Nevertheless, the popular committees did not ignore or even directly challenge previously existing political and social arrangements. As will be seen below, the Higher National Committee, its branches, and the affiliated committees of national defense absorbed both existing and emerging structures of power within a single framework. This temporary coexistence of new and old was not unique. Eric Hobsbawm describes a similar situation in late-nineteenth-century Europe with the emergence of the "mass parties-cum-move-

34. *Sūriyya al-jadīda,* 27 December 1919, 1.

35. AD 2372/dossier: propagande anti-française/5–8, 3 March 1920; FO 371/5034/E2915/2/44, CPO, EEF to Curzon, 27 March 1920; Russell, *First Modern Arab State,* 132–133.

ments" discussed in the Introduction. For Hobsbawm, what was significant about these movements was not the complete disappearance of the patron or *cacique*, but rather the transformation of his role as he was incorporated within a larger political machine. This increasingly "made the notable, or at least . . . saved him from isolation and political impotence, rather than the other way round." Hobsbawm adds,

> Older elites transforming themselves to fit in with democracy might well develop various combinations between the politics of local patronage and influence and those of democracy. And, indeed, the last decades of the old century and the first of the new were filled with complex conflicts between old-style 'notability' and the new political operators, local bosses or other key elements controlling the local party fortunes.[36]

The Higher National Committee and its affiliates recast traditional structures of power in four ways. First, they asserted the prerogatives of representative bodies on all levels, in the process diminishing the precedence of those who stood outside the electoral process. Second, the presence of the popular committees incited competition for positions of power between members of established families and those who were political upstarts and subalterns. Third, the committees, acting in the name of the "nation," weakened the power and prestige of the urban notability by taking control of resources and carrying out functions previously entrusted to or appropriated by them. Finally, the committees diminished the salience of traditional neighborhood power brokers by sponsoring elections for a political leadership whose purview extended beyond the confines of their urban quarter to the nation as a whole. Overall, by subsuming customary structures of power within a larger framework, the popular committees enervated those structures and accelerated their breakdown.

The Higher National Committee maintained a continuous presence in the neighborhoods of Damascus through the branch committees (*lijān farʿiyya*). As outlined by their charter, these committees were to include six to twelve men elected from each neighborhood who would act as mediators between the population and the Higher National Committee. On the one hand, the branch committees were charged with enforcing the policies of the Higher National Committee: each branch was to elect a "supervisory committee" (*lajna taftīshiyya*) to "oversee the people of the neighborhood or town, to guide them in the path of the general interest, to urge them to meet the goals of the national committee, and to instill in them a spirit of

36. Hobsbawm, *Age of Empire*, 94.

harmony and order." On the other hand, the branch committees were responsible for transmitting the concerns of the population to the Higher National Committee. This was to take place at monthly general meetings to which all residents of the neighborhood (or village) were invited. In addition, each branch committee was to keep informed of the policies of the Higher National Committee by sending four members to observe the twice-monthly meetings of the parent organization.[37]

While it is uncertain that the branch committees fully complied with the organizational directives of the Higher National Committee, reports confirm that the committees did establish a presence throughout the region. As a result of local initiative, branch committees appeared in Damascus quarters such as the Maydan, Shaghur, Ma'dhanat al-Shahm, and Bab al-Jabiya, in Homs and Hama, and as far away as Jenin in Palestine and Amman and ʿAjlun in present-day Jordan.[38] The Ma'dhanat al-Shahm branch committee, seeking recognition from the Higher National Committee, sent the following telegram describing its founding and adjuring the approval of the committee:

> To the office of the national committee: May God grant you success.
>
> We want you to know that a group of people of Ma'dhanat al-Shahm have designated an area for offices in their neighborhood, have begun meetings in order to discuss national issues in their capacity as a branch of your committee, [and have begun] securing patriotic contributions from the people of the neighborhood and recording the names of volunteers to defend our beloved fatherland. And in order that we obtain the legal status that would give us the right to meet to discuss volunteering and contributing, we have circulated this petition to be approved.
>
> We hope that God grants you success.[39]

For the most part, however, it is likely that local committees of national defense assumed the role of the branch committees outside Damascus. The activities of these committees overlapped with those undertaken by the branch committees and, depending on location, included administrative

37. SL:LW, "Niẓām al-lijān al-waṭaniyya al-farʿiyya fī bilād Sūriyya," 17 November 1919.

38. Saʿīd, *al-Thawra al-ʿarabiyya al-kubrā,* 2:101–103; *al-ʿĀṣima,* 18 December 1919, 3–4; SL:LW, Letter to the national committee from Bab al-Jabiya, 21 December 1919; SL:LW, Letter to Muhibb al-Din [al-Khatib], 22 jumādā al-ūlā; SL:LW, Saʿid al-Halawa et al. to Presidency, Higher National Committee, 16 December 1919; SL:LW, Saʿid Khayr et al. to Presidency, Higher National Committee, 3 March 1920; MD 4H114/4/539, Cousse to Gouraud, 13 June 1920.

39. SL:LW, 26 November 1919.

tasks, refugee and poor relief, and, as in the case of the branch organization of Ma'dhanat al-Shahm, the assessment and collection of "contributions." Most important, it was incumbent on the local committees of national defense to (in the words of *al-Kawkab*) "organize and prepare the movement for defense so that it might appear before the world with a powerful, firm visage; to collect supplies and money in reasonable ways for support of the volunteers and their families; to buy whatever provisions, ammunition, and clothing they need; and to unify the patriotic movement and all great works and march side by side with the government for the good and happiness of the country."[40]

Although eyewitness accounts attest to the fact that the meetings in the neighborhoods of Damascus often attracted hundreds of participants,[41] no record of the day-to-day functioning of these local organizations, or the loyalty they engendered, exist. It appears that, after an initial burst of popular enthusiasm, support for the activities of the Higher National Committee and its branches fluctuated as political events unfolded. Records from December 1919, for example, show a disappointing turnout for military exercises sponsored by the Higher National Committee in Damascus: while the committee had planned to recruit a one-thousand-man militia from its followers in Damascus, the local branch committees pledged only 527 volunteers. Of these, little more than half showed up for early-morning drill.[42] While these statistics must, of course, be taken with a grain of salt—they do not, for example, take into account either the logistical difficulties that practitioners of professions and merchants must have faced when asked to attend early-morning drill across town or the notorious antipathy of the Damascene population toward any activity resembling compulsory military service—they do support the observation made by a reporter for *al-Kawkab*, a newspaper generally unsympathetic to the committee, that

> the national committee continues its work and continues to spread branches throughout the region, but I cannot deny that the great concern we witnessed weeks ago has all but dissipated. Perhaps this partial standstill arose from the desire to delay until it could be learned what

40. *al-Kawkab*, 6 January 1920, 10.
41. See, for example, Darwaza, *Mudhakkarāt*, 2:154.
42. See letters sent from commander of the civil guard of Damascus (qā'id al-liwā' al-mulkī[?] bi-Dimashq) to the presidency of the national committee, 8 December 1919, 10 December 1919, 13 December 1919, 19–20 December 1919 in SL:LW.

> Amir Faysal wants after his arrival. For this reason, there might be some excuse . . . [43]

The polarization of politics that took place after the initialing of the Faysal-Clemenceau Agreement and the amir's return from Europe in January 1920—a polarization that seems to have shattered the momentary political calm in Syria—prompted a reinvigoration of the Higher National Committee as well as its restructuring. Faysal, reacting to the explosive conditions in the capital that his provisional agreement with Clemenceau had triggered, attempted to undercut the reemergent popularity of the Higher National Committee by splitting and co-opting the opposition to the agreement. He disciplined those officers in the Arab army who had participated in training the volunteer militias, organized a party of the loyal opposition, and plotted the exile of popular leaders such as Kamil al-Qassab.[44] The leadership of the Higher National Committee reacted by rationalizing the structure and strengthening the oppositional role of their organization.

The first general conference of representatives to the Higher National Committee from the eastern zone convened during the third week of January to plan the centralization and coordination of activities such as fundraising.[45] On 1 February the assembled delegates chose the first administrative committee (*al-lajna al-idāriyya*) of the Higher National Committee, which was intended to have broad supervisory powers over all national committee activities. The idea for an administrative committee had been circulating among the leadership of the national committee for several months. In December 1919, ʿUmar Shakir, a member of both the Higher

43. *al-Kawkab*, 13 January 1920, 12. Although few residents of the Maydan and Shaghur participated in these military exercises, others volunteered to prepare the drill ground and pitch tents for those who did. See Saʿīd, *al-Thawra al-ʿarabiyya al-kubrā*, 2:101–103.

44. MD 4H114/1/434, Cousse to Gouraud, 28 December 1919; MD 4H114/2/no no., Cousse to Gouraud, 1 January 1920; MD 4H114/2/38, Cousse to Gouraud, 18 January 1920; AD 2375/chemise: division de la Syrie, 1919–1920/406/2, Record of telephone message from Arlabosse to GCDS, 19 January 1920; AD 2347/serie: c admin. personnel/dossier b/65, Cousse to HC, 20 January 1920; FO 371/5032/E990/93–97, "Report by Col. Waters-Taylor on his visit to Beirut, and Interviews with General Gouraud and the Emir Feisal," 21 January 1920; Saʿīd, *Thawrāt al-ʿArab*, 62.

45. In addition, ʿAbd al-Rahman Shahbandar, who was present at the session, proposed sending a photographer to the villages that the French destroyed and to offer the photographs as documentation to the "high international examiners" if needed. *al-Kawkab*, 27 January 1920, 11.

National Committee and the Arab Club of Damascus, had suggested the creation of an administrative council

> whose only function would be to execute the decisions of the committee and to organize its activities and the activities of its branches. [The administrative council] would have seven members in addition to the secretary, accountant, and treasurer. Its job would be the preparation of the important points of the agenda for meetings. It would [also] have the right to convene the national committee for meetings when it deems it necessary.

At the same time, Shakir also proposed the formation of an information bureau (*lajnat al-istikhbārāt*) that would not only disseminate propaganda and marching orders but would "punish those who spread treachery."[46] A week after the formation of the first administrative committee, al-Qassab published a declaration announcing that the Higher National Committee was above all parties and would not be subservient to any outside group.[47]

Records indicate the election of two administrative committees, the first in February 1920 and the second in June. The membership of the two administrative committees remained fairly stable: six members of the eleven- and twelve-man committees served from February 1920 until the imposition of the French mandate. Besides Kamil al-Qassab, members included four merchants (Ahmad Diab, who dealt in textiles and rice; Asʿad al-Muhayini and ʿAbd al-Qadir al-Sukkar, Maydanis who traded in grain; and Shukri al-Tabbaʿ, who dealt in tobacco and other commodities), three merchant ulama (ʿId al-Halabi, ʿAbd al-Qadir al-Khatib, ʿAbdallah al-Kuzbari), two other ulama (Muhammad al-Taji, imam and *khaṭīb* at Jamiʿ al-Jisr; Nasib al-Hamza, former president of the Damascus municipality and landowner), four politically experienced professionals and military officers

46. SL:LW, Shakir to presidency of the Higher National Committee, 2 December 1919. An unsigned letter in the same file, dated 30 rabīʿ al-awwal and addressed to the members of the national committee, urged the formation of "an administrative committee that continuously meets and is responsible to the committee, so that the committee will be able to study every matter presented to it according to an agenda that prioritizes matters and expedites its work." See also FO 371/4183/136154, Lotfallah [sic] to Lloyd George, 16 September 1919; AD 2430/dossier confidentiel—départ/325, Cousse to HC, 10 November 1919; Saʿīd, *al-Thawra al-ʿarabiyya al-kubrā*, 101–103; al-Ḥaffār, "al-Ḥukūmāt allatī taʿāqabat," 1 (tishrīn al-thānī 1372): 10.

47. Farzat, *al-Ḥayā al-ḥizbiyya fī Sūriyya*, 73–74. Farzat claims that the purpose of al-Qassab's declaration was to justify an alliance with the socially conservative Democratic Party.

(As'ad al-Hakim, a physician; Khalid al-Hakim, an engineer; As'ad al-Maliki, a former officer in the Ottoman army; 'Awni al-Qudamani, a former major in the Ottoman army and member of the Ottoman parliament), and three politicians or experienced political agitators (Jamil Mardam Bek; his cousin, Sami Mardam Bek, a former member of the Ottoman parliament, the Damascus court of appeals and, during the Faysali period, the Damascus administrative council; Muhammad al-Nahhas, former Damascus subdirector of *wīrkū* and director of revenues for the Arab government).[48]

Some of the members of the administrative committee thus had professional or familial backgrounds that resembled those of nationalists who had participated in the prewar secret societies or who had founded the Arab Club of Damascus. Indeed, al-Qassab, As'ad and Khalid al-Hakim, and Jamil Mardam Bek had been among the early members of al-Fatat. Nevertheless, like the secondary leadership of the popular committees in Damascus, the administrative committee's overall composition differed significantly from the nationalist groupings discussed earlier. Six of the seventeen committee members had received training and/or employment as ulama, seven

48. All biographical data on the administrative committee of the Higher National Committee have been obtained from the following sources: Interview with Shaykh Ahmad al-Qasimi, 6 November 1989; Interview with Abu Ribah al-Jaza'iri, 15 November 1989; Interview with Shaykh 'Abd al-Rizaq al-Halabi, 3 January 1990; Interview with Shaykh Yasin 'Urufa, 4 January 1990; *al-'Āṣima*, 6 May 1920, 5; *al-Kināna*, 26 June 1920, 2; DU SA/493/7/33; AD 2323/a-1/91, M.P. Lefévre-Pontalis to Picot, 26 November 1918; MAE L:SL/vol. 8/64–70, Lutfallah to Pichon, 23 January 1919; AD 2367/10/1/146, Cousse to HC, 14 February 1919; MAE L:SL/vol. 12/32–38, Cousse to HC, 6 April 1919; FO 371/4217/69267, Note by Arab Bureau, Cairo, 6 May 1919; FO 882/24/128–134, "Who's Who in Damascus," 14 May 1919; FO 371/4183/136154, Lotfallah [sic] to Lloyd George, 16 September 1919; AD 2430/dossier confidentiel—départ/634, Cousse to HC, 24 October 1919; FO 882/24/209–210, G. W. Courtney, 21 May 1920; AD 2347/500, Cousse to HC, 5 June 1920; MD 4H60/1, "Bulletin quotidien 1260," 19 July 1920; FO 317/5040/E13211/1171, Ernest Scott to Curzon, 18 October 1920; al-Ḥuṣnī, *Kitāb muntakhabāt al-tawārīkh li-Dimashq*, 2:829, 871–872, 873, 876, 883, 910; al-'Allāf, *Dimashq fī maṭla' al-qarn al-'ishrīn*, 203; Darwaza, *Ḥawla al-ḥaraka al-'arabiyya al-ḥadītha*, 1:27, 77–78; Ẓāfir al-Qāsimī, *Maktab 'Anbar: ṣuwar wa dhikrayāt min ḥayatina al-thaqāfiyya wal-siyāsiyya wal-ijtimā'iyya*, 23; Dāghir, *Mudhakkarātī*, 106; Darwaza, *Mudhakkarāt*, 2:76–77, 81–82, 110–111, 130–131, 142–144, 188; al-Ghuṣayn, *Mudhakkarātī 'an al-thawra*, 38; al-Jundī, *Tārīkh al-thawrāt al-sūriyya*, 172; Khoury, *Urban Notables*, 34, 41, 44, 63, 66–67, 73, 114, 130, notes 60–61; Sa'īd, *al-Thawra al-'arabiyya al-kubrā*, 2:101–103; al-Ḥaffār, "al-Ḥukūmāt allatī ta'āqabat 1(3 shawwāl 1372):19, (tishrīn al-thānī 1372): 10; al-Ḥāfiẓ and Abāẓa, *Tārīkh 'ulamā' Dimashq*, 460–464; al-'Aẓm, *Mudhakkarāt Khālid al-'Aẓm*, 1:94–95; Yūsuf al-Ḥakīm, *Dhikrayāt*, 3:19; Schilcher, *Families in Politics*, 214.

worked as merchants at some time during their careers, and four (al-Qassab, al-Muhayini, al-Sukkar, al-Tabbaʿ) had *qabaḍāy* connections. Although four members of the administrative committee had participated in prewar Arabist political formations, several others had been vocal opponents of Arabism. Sami Mardam Bek, whom Jamal Pasha had nominated to represent Damascus in the Ottoman parliament, had attacked the Ottoman Administrative Decentralization Party on behalf of the Committee of Union and Progress, as did Nasib al-Hamza. ʿAwni al-Qudamani, also a vocal supporter of the C.U.P., took his seat in the Ottoman parliament after winning the uncontested election of April 1914. Others played a role in the short-lived attempt to establish an indigenous government before the entrance of Arab troops into Damascus in October 1918: in addition to the previously mentioned role played by ʿAbd al-Qadir al-Khatib in Saʿid al-Jazaʾiri's post-Ottoman government, both the Muhayini and the Sukkar families recruited volunteer units of the "civil guard" in the Maydan to maintain order on behalf of the Jazaʾiri government. Interestingly, *pace* those who have found the exclusive roots of "Arab nationalism" in the *salafiyya* movement, ʿAbd al-Qadir al-Khatib was a well-known opponent of salafism who had once denounced Rashid Rida as a proponent of "Wahhabism."[49]

That at least some members of the administrative committee should have supported the attempt to establish an indigenous government in Damascus is not surprising. Unlike the geographically diverse leadership of al-Fatat and the Arab Club of Damascus, all members of the administrative committee were Damascenes. Their suspicion and resentment of outsiders—whether those outsiders were the Iraqis, Palestinians, and Hijazis who joined the Arab administration or the entente powers that seemed determined to partition Syria—was demonstrated by the fact that three members (al-Qassab, Khalid al-Hakim, and Sami Mardam Bek) had belonged to the Syrian Union, which, from its base in Egypt, never relinquished its mistrust of Amir Faysal and the Arab Revolt, and five members (al-Hamza, al-Khatib, al-Qudamani, and both Mardam Beks) simultaneously belonged to the Higher National Committee and the nativist Syrian Patriotic Party. According to some reports, as a result of the common disaffection from the sharifians felt by leaders of both the Higher National Committee and the Syrian Patriotic Party, the two parties confederated in

49. See David Dean Commins, "Religious Reformers and Arabists in Damascus, 1885–1914," 414.

the early summer of 1920 to form the Democratic Party.[50] Named after the committee-linked bloc in the Syrian General Congress, the party's program counterposed a traditionalist social agenda and an organic view of Syrian society to the foreign political and ideological domination that they believed accompanied sharifian rule.

One further difference distinguished the members of the administrative committee of the Higher National Committee from the majority of the prewar Arabists and the self-described *mutanawwirūn* allied to the Arab government: their age. Although the birth dates of only five of the leaders of the administrative committee can be determined with certainty—'Id al-Halabi (1863), 'Abd al-Qadir al-Khatib (1874), Jamil Mardam Bek (1869), Kamil al-Qassab (1873), and Shukri al-Tabba' (1865)—these individuals were members of a political generation that predated that of the nationalists who belonged to either of the two aforementioned categories. While the median birth year for the five members of the administrative committee was 1869, statistics compiled by C. Ernest Dawn indicate that the median birth years for the total field of "Pre-1914 Nationalists" and "1919–1920 Nationalists" were 1886.5 and 1883 respectively.[51] As will be seen in Part II, the self-identified *mutanawwirūn* themselves made an issue of generational sodality by highlighting and reifying the experiential dissimilarities between the two political generations in their discourse, particularly through their routine juxtaposition of "youth" with "old age" and "progress" with "stagnation."

The distinctive backgrounds and extensive experience of the members of the administrative committee were, in part, a blessing for the Higher National Committee, for they often ensured the success of projects initiated by the committee. Both Ahmad Diab and Shukri al-Tabba' capitalized on the commercial ties they had nurtured over the years to run guns for the committee; Ahmad Diab and his cousin Yasin Diab used their contacts to supply the capital with imported foodstuffs as well.[52] Shukri al-Tabba' organized a unit of fifty men from among his retainers in Qanawat to wage "jihad" against the French. 'Abd al-Qadir al-Sukkar, who owned ovens in the Maydan and reportedly distributed bread to the poor of his district, mobilized the personal following that he had attracted on the eve of the

50. The founding of the party has been dated as early as April and as late as mid-July 1920. MD 4H114/5/700, Cousse to Gouraud, 16 July 1920; FO 371/5188/E4829/36, "Arabic Press Abstracts for Week Ending May 3," 28 April 1920.

51. See Dawn, *From Ottomanism to Arabism*, 176.

52. SL:LW, Ahmad Diab to Higher National Committee, 19 December 1919.

Battle of Maysalun. ʿId al-Halabi, a merchant and an *ʿālim*, maintained contacts in both worlds: as a dealer in cloth in Suq al-Hamidiyya, the central market of Damascus, al-Halabi served the Higher National Committee as "commercial delegate," mediating between the committee and other merchants to assure their financial support and their compliance with the price-fixing arrangements initiated by the committee. In addition, as a representative of a distinguished scholarly family of the Qaymariyya quarter, he remained in constant contact with other ulama who participated in politics, such as Taj al-Din al-Hasani and ʿAbd al-Qadir al-Khatib.

Nevertheless, the ability of the administrative committee to exert control over the day-to-day activities of local branches of the Higher National Committee seems to have been minimal. From newspaper accounts and records of the organization, it appears that the administrative committee served more as window dressing than as a true executive body. Furthermore, the authority of the administrative committee did not go unchallenged. Members of branch committees questioned the activities and even the personal probity of leaders of the organization. ʿAbd al-Qadir al-Khatib, whom the British once characterized as a "time-serving and fanatical humbug," was the target of similar vituperation in leaflets distributed by an organization affiliated with the Higher National Committee, and members of local affiliates even called Kamil al-Qassab to task publicly for his alleged misappropriation of funds—allegations that may have been initiated by the Arab government or the French.[53]

In spite of the resources available to various members of the administrative committee, and in spite of the allegations of corruption, power within the committee after its reorganization seems to have remained in the hands of Kamil al-Qassab, who worked through a few of his closest associates, such as ʿId al-Halabi. Much of the correspondence to the Higher National Committee from members, sympathizers, branch organizations, and even the Arab government was addressed either to "the presidency of the national committee" or to al-Qassab personally. No other individual

53. FO 882/24/128–134, "Who's Who in Damascus," 14 May 1919; MD 4H114/4, Leaflet signed "The Eye That Watches," 6 July 1920; MD 4H114/4/241, Cousse to Gouraud, 14 June 1920; FO 371/5038/E9625, Lt. Col. Easton, "Haut Comité National, Damascus," 23 June 1920; *al-Kināna*, 26 June 1920, 2; MD 4H114/4/613, Cousse to Gouraud, 28 June 1920; AD 2372/no no., "Note du colonel Cousse du 1er juillet 1920: Damas." Whatever their validity in this case, allegations of corruption were commonly used during this period to smear political rivals. Amir Faysal himself, for example, attempted to use them against the popular Yasin al-Hashimi. See FO 371/5032/EA2989, GHQ (Egypt) to WO, 4 February 1920.

within the committee commanded like authority or inspired comparable loyalty: even after ʿAwni al-Qudamani had publicly charged him with corruption in June 1920—an accusation that forced al-Qassab to submit his resignation as president of the Higher National Committee—the charismatic shaykh reemerged as leader a short time later, outpolling all other candidates in elections for the administrative committee.[54] The singular devotion that al-Qassab elicited from the petit-bourgeois merchants and ulama of Damascus who comprised much of the secondary leadership of the organization is illustrated by a story related about Shaykh Kamal al-Khatib. On the eve of the French invasion

> the ulama and *khuṭabāʾ* [preachers] went to the minbars urging the people to jihad against the French, and [Kamal al-Khatib] was among the most enthusiastic. And on the day he spoke, a questioner asked, "What have you prepared for jihad; will you fight with weapons or is it sufficient to fight with speeches?" These words stirred him, and he bought . . . an Ottoman rifle and ten rounds of ammunition. . . . He attached the rifle and bullets to the front of his shop and he prepared for battle. During this time, Shaykh Kamil al-Qassab was riding through the streets and suqs of the city, inciting the people to fight the French. . . . When [al-Qassab] saw him, he called him to him and said to him, "Where are you, Shaykh Kamal?" And Shaykh Kamal indicated that he was ready, pointing to his gun.[55]

Kamal al-Khatib died shortly after these events at the Battle of Maysalun.

It would, of course, be simplistic to ascribe the popular approbation for the Higher National Committee and its branches merely to the personal attributes of Kamil al-Qassab. In part, the committees commanded popular support because they integrated a variety of preexisting, informal networks that bound together individuals within their quarters and villages into a formal structure that was congruent with daily practice. For example, large numbers of men from the same extended families were active in the popular committees; in Damascus alone, at least four members of the Hakim family (Asʿad, Hashim, Hasan, Khalid), five members of the Halabi family

54. In the elections for the administrative committee held on 24 June 1920, al-Qassab received the most votes (47), followed by ʿAwni al-Qudamani and Shukri al-Tabbaʿ (46 each), Khalid al-Hakim (45), ʿAbd al-Qadir al-Sukkar (43), ʿAbdallah al-Kuzbari (39), Muhammad al-Taji (38), ʿId al-Halabi (35), Ahmad Diab (33), Sami Mardam Bek (30), Asʿad al-Hakim (29). *al-Kināna,* 26 June 1920, 2; MD 4H114/4/493, Cousse to Gouraud, 4 June 1920.

55. al-Ḥāfiẓ and Abāẓa, *Tārīkh ʿulamāʾ Dimashq,* 381–382. See also Naṣūḥ Bābīl, *Ṣiḥāfa wa siyāsa: Sūriyya fī al-qarn al-ʿishrīn,* 18.

(ʿAbdallah, Hashim, ʿId, Kamal, Nazih), nine members of the Khatib family (ʿAbd al-Qadir, ʿAbd al-Rahman, ʿAbd al-Razzaq, Hasan, Khalid, Muhammad Rida, Muhibb al-Din, Salah al-Din, Zaki), and five members of the Qudamani family (Ahmad, ʿAwni, Muhammad, Rida, Subhi) held positions in the primary or secondary leadership of the Higher National Committee. In addition, more than one member of the ʿAqil, Diab, Khayr, Laham, Mardam Bek, Mosuli, Muhayini, Muhayri, Qabbani, Samman, Shaykh al-Ard, and Sibaʿi families are listed in committee documents as second-level leaders. The family networks provided a crucial, if informal, bond among the primary and secondary leadership of the committees. In one of his autobiographical sketches, Muhibb al-Din al-Khatib described how these family ties facilitated the committee-directed mobilization during the days before the French occupation of Damascus:

> The neighborhood in which the author of these memoirs lived was Qaymariyya, which bordered on Christian neighborhoods. Fearing communal strife during the period of chaos [July 1920], he collected a very large number of relatives belonging to the Khatib family, especially the ulama among them, and armed them with rifles. . . . The shaykhs of the Khatib family, many of whom were included among the members of the Higher National Committee . . . were stationed at various points on the streets and in the Christian neighborhoods, preserving the peace and terrifying anyone who appeared to be looking for trouble.[56]

Consanguinity overlapped with and reinforced other bonds that united neighborhood residents with each other and with the committees. The role played by the so-called "merchant ulama" in organizing for the committees offers perhaps the most conspicuous example of how the Higher National Committee and its affiliates profited from the interaction among familial, occupational, and market bonds. The merchant ulama were mainly retail traders who dealt in commodities such as textiles. Although beneficiaries of a religious education, they often lacked the proper family connections that would ensure regular appointment as *khuṭabāʾ*, imams, or muftis. They thus either alternated intervals of their lives in which they engaged in study, employment as religious functionaries, or teaching with intervals in which they engaged in commerce, or they divided their days between suq and mosque.[57] Because the merchant ulama came from petit-bourgeois

56. Unpublished autobiographical manuscript found in Markaz al-wathāʾiq al-tārīkhiyya (Damascus) and the Salafiyya Library, 47–48.

57. Interview with Shaykh Ahmad al-Qasimi, 6 November 1989; Interview with Ihsan Haqqi, 10 November 1989; Interview with Shaykhs al-Tabbaʿ, Daqqar,

backgrounds, from prominent families that had fallen on hard times, or from poorer branches of otherwise prominent families, they stayed behind in the crowded quarters of Damascus at a time when their social betters among the landowner-bureaucrats were increasingly moving out. They thus continued to construct their worldview according to the contours of their quarter, their local market, and their traditional education.[58]

The Khatib family provides a typical example. Although this family had been prominent in Damascene affairs since the early nineteenth century, committee activists came from a branch of the family tree that hardly ranked at the apex of society. The Khatibs who filled out the ranks of the secondary leadership of the Higher National Committee and elicited the deference of their neighbors did not derive their status by fostering ties of personal dependency. Instead, the source of their authority was more prosaic: because at least five members of the Khatib family were ulama who simultaneously engaged in petty commerce in Suq al-Buzuriyya and Suq al-Qalbaqjiyya, they were known to and respected by a wide circle of Damascenes with whom they were in daily contact.[59]

The presence of overlapping and often interrelated networks of merchants, merchant ulama, and ulama is perhaps the most important reason why suqs and mosques throughout Damascus became hotbeds of political organizing during the Faysali period. In Suq al-Qalbaqjiyya, the Khatibs mingled with other merchant ulama such as Najib Kiwan and Taha Kiwan. As in the case of the Khatibs, nationalist politics was a family affair for the Kiwans: Yasin Kiwan, working with Shaykh Hamdi al-Juwajani, organized militia units that fought at Maysalun, and both he and ʿAbd al-Qadir Kiwan, who had once been imam at the Umayyad Mosque, died in the battle. Similarly, in Suq Midhat Pasha, the politically active shaykh Mahmud Abu Shammat and his ten sons rubbed elbows with merchant ulama from the Tabbaʿ family.[60]

Other ulama from the same social milieu joined the popular militias and/or used their positions to mobilize those around them. Shaykhs Saʿid al-Barhani of Jamiʿ al-Tuba, Muhammad al-Fahl of the Madrasat al-

---

and ʿUrufa, 2 January 1990; Interview with Shaykh Yasin ʿUrufa, 4 January 1990; al-Ḥāfiẓ and Abāẓa, *Tārīkh ʿulamāʾ Dimashq*, 535.

58. Khoury, *Syria and the French Mandate*, 296–297.

59. Interview with Shaykh Yasin ʿUrufa, 4 January 1990; Schilcher, *Families in Politics*, 191–193; al-Ḥāfiẓ and Abāẓa, *Tārīkh ʿulamāʾ Dimashq*, 535.

60. Interview with Shaykh Ahmad al-Qasimi, 6 November 1989; Interview with Shaykhs al-Tabbaʿ, Daqqar, ʿUrufa, 2 January 1990; Interview with Shaykh Yasin ʿUrufa, 4 January 1990; al-Ḥāfiẓ and Abāẓa, *Tārīkh ʿulamāʾ Dimashq*, 384, 386, 535.

Qalbaqjiyya, and Muhammad al-ʿAshmar, a *qabaḍāy* leader with forty to fifty men under him,[61] all fought at Maysalun, as did ʿAbd al-Hamid Karim, a policeman turned *ʿālim* and relative of Kamil al-Qassab. When the French forced al-Qassab into exile after the battle, Karim took charge of the Madrasa al-Kamiliyya. Tawfiq al-Darra, a merchant and former mufti of the Fifth Ottoman Army who preached jihad on the eve of the French invasion, died in the battle. ʿAli Daqqar of the Masjid al-Sadat and Masjid Sinan Pasha was more fortunate: having survived the Battle of Maysalun, he toured the Syrian countryside with the doyen of Damascus ulama, Shaykh Badr al-Din al-Hasani, preaching resistance to French rule.[62] These ulama possessed a moral authority that inspired their neighbors and associates and made their connection with the popular committees especially valuable. Thus, Muhammad al-Sharif al-Yaʿqubi, who founded religious schools for North African expatriates and children of merchants, led a contingent of his students at Maysalun, and when, on the eve of the French invasion of inland Syria, a branch of the "Organization of Religious Scholars" (*munaẓẓamat ʿulamāʾ al-dīn*) of Damascus met in the nearby village of Duma and called for jihad against the advancing enemy, five hundred volunteers reportedly converged on Damascus in response.[63]

A significant group of wealthier merchants, including the Muhayinis and Sukkars whose livelihood depended upon trade in cereals, shared essential traits with the merchant ulama and ulama; as a result, their participation in the activities of the Higher National Committee was in a way both inevitable and invaluable. As Philip Khoury has noted, one characteristic that united the wealthy "Muslim commercial bourgeoisie" of Damascus with merchants further down the social ladder was the experience of a "traditional" quarter-based education. This naturally differentiated them from those in the nationalist movement who had received advanced train-

61. According to Shaykh Ahmad al-Qasimi, al-ʿAshmar's credentials as an *ʿālim* did not go unchallenged. Interview, 6 November 1989.

62. Interview with Shaykh Ahmad al-Qasimi, 6 November 1989; Interview with Ihsan Haqqi, 10 November 1989; Interview with Abu Ribah al-Jazaʾiri, 15 November 1989; Interview with Shaykhs al-Tabbaʿ, Daqqar, ʿUrufa, 2 January 1990; Interview with Shaykh Yasin ʿUrufa, 4 January 1990; Interview with Muhammad Rida al-Khatib, 6 January 1990; Muḥī al-Dīn al-Safarjalānī, *Fājiʿat Maysalūn wal-baṭal al-ʿaẓīm Yūsuf al-ʿAẓma*, 340; al-Ḥāfiẓ and Abāẓa, *Tārīkh ʿulamāʾ Dimashq*, 409, 420, 535, 540–542, 579–585, 588, 794–802, 878–891, 917, 963; al-Jundī, *Tārīkh al-thawrāt al-sūriyya*, 170.

63. al-Ḥāfiẓ and Abāẓa, *Tārīkh ʿulamāʾ Dimashq*, 579–585; al-Jundī, *Tārīkh al-thawrāt al-sūriyya*, 160.

ing in Western or Ottoman professional schools.[64] Because they thus not only shared popular prejudices but were forced, by virtue of their social standing, to strike a balance between the exigencies of the market and the demands of their local constituents, they remained responsive to popular impulses—as their response to the calls for defense demonstrated. Furthermore, through both familial and occupational ties and status-based obligations, they were connected to a nexus of social relationships that included their poorer brethren—networks that facilitated popular mobilization.

The Higher National Committee looked on the commercial classes as a natural constituency for other reasons as well. As described in the Introduction, all categories of merchants, from the petit-bourgeois merchant *ʿālim* who participated in the retail trade to those involved in long-distance or large-scale commercial enterprises, had ample justification for resenting the sharifian regime and anticipating the worst from the entente powers. Their hostility was not unrequited: the Arab government blamed the merchants for the financial predicament of the eastern zone and attempted to deal with them by confiscating their goods, restricting the trade in luxury items, and promulgating draconian commercial codes to prevent hoarding, end monopolies, and reduce prices. The posture of the Higher National Committee toward the commercial classes differed dramatically. Partly because of the inclusion of merchants among its leaders, partly because the successful implementation of committee policies required the cooperation and financial contributions of merchants, the Higher National Committee actively solicited the support of merchants by establishing a commercial division to work with them, sanctioning monopolies set up by committee-affiliated traders and organizing a political campaign against the potentially devastating French monetary and trade policies.[65]

Associational and familial bonds that linked merchants, merchant ulama, and ulama also linked these groups with the local *qabaḍāyāt* upon whom the Higher National Committee depended to mobilize the urban population. Usually recruited from lower- and lower-middle-class families, the *qabaḍāyāt* derived the prestige they enjoyed in their communities from two sources: the services they provided and a self-aggrandizing mythology.

64. Khoury, *Syria and the French Mandate*, 209.

65. For activities of the Higher National Committee aimed at merchants, see SL:LW, Letter, 20 November 1919; MD 4H114/2/155, Cousse to Gouraud, 9 April 1920; MD 4H114/2/157, Cousse to Gouraud, 10 April 1920; AD 2347/12, "Extraits du bulletin quotidien du 12 avril 1920"; MAE L:SL/vol. 64/823/6, 824/6, Gouraud to MAE, 14 April 1920.

Since government in early-twentieth-century Damascus rarely provided effective police protection, the twenty to forty *qabaḍāyāt* in each quarter patrolled the streets at night and guarded the shops of those merchants who paid the legendary "thousand lira." Providing protection for the community from criminals or bands of troublemakers from other quarters bolstered their image as defenders of the weak against the depredations of outsiders and the powerful and ensured a close relationship with those engaged in commerce.[66]

What differentiated *qabaḍāyāt* from *zuʿrān* (common criminals) was the mythology with which the former were associated. Like members of the ancient *futūwa* brotherhoods on which they may have been modeled, the *qabaḍāyāt* swore to uphold a chivalric code that included not only physical protection for the weak but also protection of the poor against the rapacity of the rich. For example, they ensured a "just price" for grain and bread and oversaw the distribution of welfare to the needy of the quarter. The activities of the *qabaḍāyāt* thus overlapped with those of the other group knowledgeable about and responsible for juridical and ethical behavior, the local ulama. *Qabaḍāyāt* used local mosques for meetings and ceremonies and, theoretically at least, were responsible for fulfilling the behests of the ulama. Thus, there was a functional as well as a familial connection among merchant, *ʿālim*, and *qabaḍāy*. As far as the popular committees were concerned, the cooperation of *qabaḍāyāt* was a prerequisite for closing down a quarter or local suq for demonstrations, recruiting volunteer militias, preventing the penetration of quarters by military police and other agents of the government, and collecting the "donations" they required to continue their operations.[67]

While the association between merchant and *qabaḍāy* might have been mutually beneficial, it was not frictionless. To the contrary, it was sustained as much through the extortion of protection payments and the threat of violence as through elective or familial ties. The Higher National Committee profited from the reputation and talents of the *qabaḍāyāt* in their fundrais-

66. Michael Johnson, "Political Bosses and Their Gangs: Zuʿama and Qabadayat in the Sunni Muslim Quarters of Beirut," 207–224 (particularly 211); al-ʿAllāf, *Dimashq fī maṭlaʿ al-qarn al-ʿishrīn*, 41; Interview with Abu Ribah al-Jazaʾiri, 15 November 1989.

67. Interview with Fakhri Nuri al-Kaylani, 8 November 1989; Interview with Abu Ribah al-Jazaʾiri, 15 November 1989; Interview with Shaykhs al-Tabbaʿ, Daqqar, ʿUrufa, 2 January 1990; Interview with Shaykh Yasin ʿUrufa, 4 January 1990; al-ʿAllāf, *Dimashq fī maṭlaʿ al-qarn al-ʿishrīn*, 244–245; Khoury, *Syria and the French Mandate*, 302–303, 316–317.

ing. Although the charters of the Higher National Committee and the branch committees stipulated that the primary source of revenue for the organization be contributions, and although rooms were set aside in mosques for representatives of the committees to collect a "participation fee" (*ishtirāk*), expenditures soon exceeded income.[68] As a result, the committee authorized local agents to collect a tax assessed at the rate of 2 percent of an individual's wealth. Collecting the assessment proved to be difficult, however: the committee imposed the levy unevenly and collected it, according to a British report, "largely by threats and blackmail . . . from the wealthy merchants and landlords of the neighborhood."[69]

Both the Higher National Committee in Damascus and its affiliates outside the capital relied on a combination of additional fundraising strategies as well. Foreign observers cited rumors of speculation in grain and gunrunning, as well as financing from Kemalists who hoped that the Syrians would use their subsidies to open up a second front against the French.[70] Overall, it appears that the Higher National Committee permitted its affiliates considerable freedom to experiment with a variety of approaches to fundraising. The committee chapter established in ʿAjlun, for example, "assessed contributions" at the rate of 50 percent of the *wīrkū* collected from the villages in the region. The ʿAjlun committee also claimed to have collected 30,000 *qurūsh* (piasters) from (government?) employees and to have received contributions of 350 *majīdī*s (silver coins worth 20 *qurūsh*) and 30,000 *qurūsh* collected by the local women's association and from lo-

68. SL:LW, "Niẓām al-lijān al-waṭaniyya al-farʿiyya fī bilād Sūriyya," 17 November 1919; SL:LW, "Niẓām al-lajna al-waṭaniyya al-ʿulyā fī al-ʿāṣima al-sūriyya," 17 November 1919; Interview with ʿAdnan al-Khatib, 8 November 1989. According to the first document, 10 percent of the revenues of the branch committees would go to the Higher National Committee, which would in turn redistribute it as necessary. Under extraordinary circumstances, all locally collected revenues would go to the Higher National Committee.

69. The report added that "the wealthier elements of Damascus formed a Young Men's Party in order to stop the Committee's extortions, and have been fairly successful." FO 371/5038/E9625, "Haut Comité National, Damascus," 23 June 1920; Saʿīd, *al-Thawra al-ʿarabiyya al-kubrā,* 2:101–103.

70. See MAE L:SL/vol. 121, "Rapport de renseignements hebdomadaire 7," 10–17 November 1919; MD 4H114/4/483, Cousse to Gouraud, 3 June 1919; MD 4H114/4/493, Cousse to Gouraud, 4 June 1919; AD 2211/693–94/6, Gouraud to Diplomatie Paris, 3 March 1920; AD 2345, Leaflet, "Le Cri du Droit," 5 March 1920; AD 2345/C1A5/221, Cousse to HC, 15 March 1920. According to French sources, Tawfiq (Chewfik) al-Sharkas (al-Masri), an agent for Mustafa Kemal in Syria, solicited contributions for the Higher National Committee and the Democratic Party, citing the need for an Arab-Turkish pan-Islamic alliance against the "colonizer."

cal notables, respectively. Having accumulated the equivalent of 600,000 *qurūsh* to equip and feed a militia, the ʿAjlun committee began enlisting volunteers and registering all men between the ages of twenty and forty. "The payment was uninterrupted," the *qāʾimmaqām* (governor) of the district wrote to the editors of *al-ʿĀṣima* with more than a touch of hyperbole, "and the bulk of the population was filled with patriotic fervor. People declared that, whenever necessary, they would offer themselves and their money."[71]

The Higher National Committee also demanded remuneration from the Arab government on the grounds that the committee provided such public services as defense and relief that the Arab government should have, but did not, provide. Soon after the reorganization of the committee, al-Qassab demanded that the government turn over the entire proceeds of the *badal* "to aid in recruitment and to augment the well-being of those soldiers already serving." When Faysal refused, al-Qassab demanded, again unsuccessfully, 5 percent of the revenue that the Arab government obtained from the *wīrkū*.[72] He may have been more successful in his subsequent solicitations: on the eve of the French invasion, the French liaison officer in Damascus reported that the committee had received credits worth 20,000 P.E. from the ministry of defense, half of which was intended for the establishment of militias and half for discretionary spending.[73]

Al-Qassab's contention that the Higher National Committee, its affiliates, and the committees of national defense provided essential services for the government or commanded the authority of a government was not mere bravado: both members of the government and much of the population looked to the committees not only to deliver services but to mediate between the state and the citizenry. When Hama was flooded with refugees from a nearby village that had been burned by the French, the interior ministry called on the Higher National Committee to provide them with temporary shelter and food.[74] At the request of residents of the capital, the Higher National Committee intervened with the municipal government to demand adequate supplies of rice at low prices, and then, relying on networks of merchants based in both Syria and abroad, the committee obtained authorization from the government to import the rice and other

71. *al-ʿĀṣima*, 18 December 1919, 3–4.
72. MD 4H114/2/132, Cousse to Gouraud, 19 February 1920.
73. MD 4H114/4/241, Cousse to Gouraud, 14 June 1920.
74. SL:LW, Advisor to the ministry of the interior to al-Qassab, 18 April 1920.

grains (at a profit) from Egypt.[75] Likewise, in June 1920, *al-Kināna* reported that "many people [in Damascus] had come to [al-Qassab] complaining about the present city administration, so he went to the government and demanded that it consider their demands."[76] Ultimately, the Arab government was itself forced to acknowledge the influence of the Higher National Committee: to ensure popular support for the national loan, the Arab government appointed al-Qassab to head the nine-man committee overseeing the government's public relations campaign. One result of the campaign was the appearance of full-page advertisements such as the following in the newspapers of Damascus during the summer of 1920:

> You want a government of defense, independence and freedom, the respect of foreigners? You want to be master in your country and in your homes? Participate in the Syrian National Loan—for independence is taken by force, not given as a gift![77]

The raison d'être of the Higher National Committee was, however, defense, and the formation of the one-thousand-man militia to defend Damascus represented only one small aspect of the committee's efforts. In addition to its support for the activities of the committees of national defense (which will be discussed in the next section), the Higher National Committee promoted the organization of guerrilla bands, mobilized *chete* and tribes for the nationalist cause, and provided assistance to a variety of military and quasimilitary formations for the ongoing campaign against the French.

Because of the collapse of rural security and the economy of the eastern zone, guerrilla bands proliferated during the second year of the Arab government. The activities of marauding bedouin and *chete* threw much of the countryside into chaos and generated what might be termed an autogenous economy of looting: with the destruction of their homes and harvests and with commercial activity at a standstill, peasants, refugees, and deserters from the Ottoman and Arab armies avoided starvation by joining armed

75. The formal request calling for the intervention of the Higher National Committee was made by Yasin Diab, a brother of Ahmad Diab of the administrative committee and member of the Damascus chamber of commerce, who acted on behalf of the petitioners. SL:LW, Yasin Diab to [Higher] National Committee, 19 December 1919; MD 4H114/4/493, Cousse to HC, 4 June 1920. See also Kasmieh, *al-Ḥukūma al-ʿarabiyya fī Dimashq*, 231–232.

76. *al-Kināna*, 26 June 1920, 2.

77. *al-Kināna*, 1 June 1920, 4. See also AD 2347/500, Cousse to HC, 5 June 1920.

bands and plundering the homes and harvests of their neighbors. These, in turn, had few options but likewise to live by despoiling the countryside, thus continuing the cycle. The Higher National Committee offered money and arms to guerrilla leaders to enlist those who fled their homes, particularly those who sought refuge in the overcrowded cities of Syria.[78] According to an informant interviewed by Gertrude Bell, "all the peasants from the villages round Aleppo, Urfa, Ain Tab, Killis, Birijik, Marash, Ras al-Ain, Jarablus, etc. come in to Aleppo and enrol themselves as Chattah, receiving arms and ammunition from Damascus. . . . Kan al-safarbaaliq ahsan bi kathir [the period of the *seferberlik* was much better]."[79]

A variety of tribal, sectarian, and rural leaders also threw in their lot with the Higher National Committee. From Qunaytra, overlooking the Golan Heights, Mahmud Faʿur of the Fadl tribe directed the activities of a force that combined almost two thousand tribal horsemen and infantry with four hundred Maydani volunteers.[80] Ahmad Muraywid, a member of the *rāfiḍūn* faction of al-Fatat and representative to the Syrian General Congress, resigned his seat and returned home to Qatana to organize a band of seventy volunteer horsemen. In conjunction with Kurdish, Circassian, and tribal levies (including about one thousand from Faʿur's al-Fadl), Muraywid's cavalry battled French troops in Marjʿayun, Rashaya, Shtura, and Muʿallaqa in present-day Lebanon.[81] Kamil al-Asʿad, a member of one

78. SL:LW, ʿUmar Shakir to LW, 2 December 1919; SL:LW, Qāʾid fawj al-mill(?) Dimashq to the presidency of LW, 15 December 1919; SL:LW, Fawzi and Nasib al-Bakri to LW, 19 December 1919; SL:LW, Letter to LW, n.d.; SL:LW, Raʾīs al-baladiyya [Duma] to LW, n.d.; MD 4H58/dossier 1, "Rapport hebdomadaire," 26 janvier au 2 février 1920; MD 4H58/dossier 1, "Rapport hebdomadaire" 23 au 29 mars 1920; USNA 59/890d.00/17/507, Jackson (Aleppo) to Adm. Bristol (Constantinople), 19 May 1920; MD 4H114/dossier 4/483, Cousse to Gouraud, 3 June 1920.

79. FO 371/5076/E8007/74–79, "Note by Miss G. L. Bell," 22 May 1920.

80. MD 4H114/2, "Tribus de la Syrie intérieur," 16 December 1919; MD 20N171/2, "Rapport hebdomadaire 18–25 janvier 1920"; AD 2375/chemise: division de la Syrie, 1919–20/442/2, Arlabosse to général commandant division de la Syrie (telephone message), 27 January 1920; MD 4H114/4/491, Cousse to Gouraud, 3 June 1920; FO 371/50337/E9014, "Extracts from French Report for Week 8th to 14th June 1920"; MD 4H114/4, Cousse, "Renseignements," 13 July 1920; MD 4H114/8, Arlabosse to Catroux, 13 October 1920; FO 317/5040/E13211/1171, Report by Col. G. L. Easton, sent by Ernest Scott (Acting High Commissioner, Ramleh) to Curzon, 18 October 1920; Aḥmad Waṣfī Zakariyyā, *ʿAshāʾir al-Shām*, 396.

81. AD 2375/dossier: Division de la Syrie/259, Arlabosse to général commandant en chef l'AFL, 18 December 1920; MD 4H114/2/12, Cousse to Gouraud, 6 January 1920; FO 371/5188/E4829/36, Arabic Press Abstracts for Week Ending May 3 (1920); MD 4H114/4/491, Cousse to Gouraud, 3 June 1920; MD 4H114/4/

of the six large *muqāṭaʿjī* (feudal landholding) families of south Lebanon and leader of up to forty thousand Mutawallis (a Syrian Shiʿi sect), led two to six thousand followers against the purportedly pro-French Christian village of ʿAyn Ibl, a town close to the Palestinian border, inflicting from fifty to eighty casualties.[82]

While these groups lived in close proximity to the frontier zone separating the eastern and western zones, the committee looked beyond the borders of the territory under the jurisdiction of the Arab government as well. Committee activists planned organizing tours of Palestine, Jordan, and the coastal region and drew up lists of sympathetic leaders residing there, noting the number of armed supporters they could assemble. One committee member, complaining that "those Palestinians here [in Damascus] do not represent [their] country," submitted an itinerary for a thirty-two day organizing tour through Palestine. Beginning in Qunaytra, the proposed tour included stops in Jisr Banat Yacub, Tabariyya, Nazareth, Safed, Haifa, Tulkarm, Nablus, Jerusalem, Ramleh, Gaza, Jabal Khalil, Beersheba, al-Salt, Ghur, Balqa', and Amman. The trip, he asserted, would enable the committee to secure the loyalty of listed "*umarā*' and *wujahā*'" (tribal chiefs and notables), who would "ignite the country" by mustering nearly one hundred thousand fighters for the Higher National Committee. Ultimately, it appears that the committee authorized a scaled-down version of this mission. Another activist offered to travel through Lebanon to urge local leaders to "begin forming bands of guerrillas [*ʿiṣābāt*] from among their men. [These leaders] will have absolute power to undertake the patriotic revolution [*al-thawra al-waṭaniyya*] and to light its fires in western Syria against foreign occupation." He accompanied his proposal with a list that included the names of forty prominent individuals who he asserted could raise thirty thousand men.[83]

---

no no., "Renseignements," Cousse, 13 July 1920; MD 4H114/8, Arlabosse to Catroux, 13 October 1920; Darwaza, *Mudhakkarāt,* 2:76–77, 81–82; al-Jundī, *Tārīkh al-thawrāt al-sūriyya,* 157, 394.

82. *al-Kawkab,* 6 January 1920, 5; AD 2375/chemise: division de la Syrie, 1919–1920/406/2, Arlabosse to général commandant division de la Syrie (telephone message), 19 January 1920; *The Near East,* 19 February 1920, 244; FO 371/5120/E6193, Military Governor Safed to Military Governor Galilee, "Attack on Ain Ibl," 11 May 1920; IO L/PS/10/802/P4953/40, Wratislaw (Beirut) to FO, 25 May 1920; Meir Zamir, *The Formation of Modern Lebanon,* 85–86.

83. SL:LW, Author unknown, n.d.; SL:LW, "Palestinian Qahtani" to presidency LW, 15 December 1919; SL:LD, "aḥad al-waṭaniyyīn" (one of the patriots), 20 November 1919.

Patriotism aside, a number of factors motivated the tribal and guerrilla leaders who organized, joined, or worked in conjunction with the Higher National Committee and the committees of national defense. For some, the lack of government control over the countryside provided the opportunity to settle old scores or simply to loot. During the attack on ʿAyn Ibl by Kamil al-Asʿad's Mutawallis, for example, "their women came to urge them on and [help] to carry away the loot, including furniture, window frames, brooms, and even wood." For others, such as the sedentary Fadl tribe, the militarization of the countryside foreclosed other options. Still others resented governmental interference or feared the social and economic consequences of French or British domination. For example, according to one observer, the Alawite leader Salih al-ʿAli began his insurrection—the first mounted against the French—after the French offered discounted lands to villagers who collaborated with them.[84]

For its part, the Higher National Committee attained more from the mobilization of the countryside than just opportunities to harass the French. Once local leaders had performed an "heroic" raid, either on French outposts or on their (often Christian) neighbors, committee leaders invited them to meetings in Damascus, presented them at demonstrations, or took them on tour, in the process encouraging urban fantasies of the martial abilities of the legendary bedouin horde.[85] After the French had presented their first ultimatum to the Arab government in July 1920, for example, Kamil al-Qassab addressed a rally of the Democratic Party, declaring in part

> [Gouraud] has stipulated the surrender of the leaders of the country who mobilized the movement for defense of your honor and your country. Should we surrender the Dandashi amirs, Amir Mahmud, Kamil al-Asʿad, Shaykh Salih al-ʿAli and other leaders?
>
> I bring you great news: I have learned from one of the leaders, a reliable source, that Shaykh Salih al-ʿAli has collected a group of three thousand who have sworn an oath of allegiance to your party, the Democratic Party, and he said to me that he will obey the council of the Democratic Party in Damascus.
>
> O brothers! Our forefathers were not cowards. They waged war against their powerful enemies with hearts filled with faith and deep-rooted belief. Let us emulate our forefathers and mix our blood with tears in the earth which we inherited from them. . . . Know that your

84. Qadrī, *Mudhakkarātī*, 133. See also WO95/4373/EA2613, Egypforce (Cairo) to Troopers (London), 6 August 1919.

85. *al-ʿĀṣima*, 25 March 1920, 5; FO 371/5188/E4829/36, "Arabic Press Abstracts for Week Ending May 3 1920"; MD 4H112/2b, "Habib Bey Estephane."

party is the strongest party in Syria, for the Dandashis and Hawranis, and the Druze of the Hawran, and the Alawites have entered your Democratic Party. Be a single arm, and cut the arm which seeks to do you harm, and keep the peace with all who desire our happiness and advancement.[86]

The Higher National Committee thus exploited its association with bedouin and guerrilla fighters for the benefit of the urban shopkeepers and lower classes that were its principal constituency. In the process of celebrating small raids as great military victories, the propaganda of the committee and its affiliates fostered the impression that any French move into the eastern zone would lead inevitably to their defeat at the hands of a host of noble Arab warriors.[87]

COMMITTEES OF NATIONAL DEFENSE

In addition to providing support for *chete* and tribes, the Higher National Committee worked in tandem with local committees of national defense. While the original purpose of these committees was military, the exigencies of mobilization forced them to assume numerous other functions as well. For this reason, the spread of local committees of national defense had wide-ranging and often unforeseen consequences. The committees linked local leaders with each other and with a national political machine,[88] politicized the bonds connecting town and countryside, expanded the reach of a popular nationalist idiom, and in some cases fostered the emergence of a new local leadership and new institutions of governance.

While the Higher National Committee encouraged the spread of these committees (although most appear to have been founded by local groups acting on their own) and provided various types of assistance for their day-to-day operations, the exact relationship between the committees and the Higher National Committee is obscure. One leaflet preserved in the French consular archives alludes to the "Congress of Committees of National Defense," but no mention of the body is to be found in the Salafiyya

86. *al-Kināna,* 15 July 1920, 3.

87. See AD 2375/chemise: division de la Syrie, 1919–1920/406/2, Arlabosse to général commandant division de la Syrie (telephone message), 19 January 1920; MD 4H112/2b, "Habib Bey Estephane"; *al-ʿĀṣima,* 27 November 1919, 6; *al-ʿĀṣima,* 25 March 1920, 5.

88. According to a telegram sent to Kamil al-Qassab from dignitaries in the region between Homs and Damascus, for example, prominent residents of Dayr al-ʿAtiya, Yabrud, al-Nabk, and Kara banded together to found a regional committee of national defense in December 1919. SL:LD, Letter to al-Qassab, 18 December 1919.

Library. It is probable that if such a congress existed it was neither formal nor permanent.[89] A document preserved in the library does, however, spell out the relationship between the Higher National Committee and an "Administrative Committee of the Committee of National Defense." The document ascribes five functions to the administrative committee:

1. To execute decisions of the Higher National Committee, to set the agenda for the general membership meetings, and to convene extraordinary meetings.
2. To supervise the work of tributary committees and negotiate with them on matters that concern the Higher National Committee.
3. To file daily reports about the work of the tributary committees with regard to defense.
4. To negotiate with committees outside the capital and to coordinate their activities.
5. To correspond with local leaders about issues of national defense, coordinate their activities, provide them with information, transmit news of their activities abroad, and apprise the Higher National Committee of local developments.[90]

It is clear from this document and other records that in spite of continuous personal, telegraphic, and telephonic communication with Damascus, the local committees enjoyed a great deal of autonomy. According to one account, local committees even disputed important matters of policy with the Higher National Committee, such as the proper response to the final French ultimatum to the Arab government.[91]

It should not be surprising, then, that local committees of national defense, like the local branches of the Arab Club discussed in Chapter 1, commonly replicated in microcosm regional political and social structures. For example, the Baʿalbek Committee of National Defense in the northern Biqaʿ Valley was dominated by members of the Sulayman branch of the Haydar family, the most powerful Mutawalli landowning family in the area. The political leadership of the committee, comprising Tawfiq Bey Sulayman, his two sons (Farid and Mustafa), and Dr. Muhammad Haydar, supervised the distribution of weapons and money and the organization of anti-French demonstrations in villages surrounding Baʿalbek. They also

89. AD 2372/dossier: propagande anti-française, 17 January 1920.

90. SL:LD, "Purpose of the Administrative Committee of the Committee of National Defense," n.d.

91. Jamīl Ibrāhīm Pāshā, *Niḍāl al-aḥrār fī sabīl al-istiqlāl,* 20.

oversaw relations with the Higher National Committee in Damascus, which supplied the committee of national defense with military advisers, financial assistance, and logistical supplies. The preeminent position of the Sulayman/Haydars facilitated their local fundraising efforts: the family not only "solicited contributions" from other local notables and from their retainers, they appropriated a share of the loot acquired in raids conducted against neighboring villages and against the railroad that cut through the Biqaʿ Valley. These latter raids were a particularly lucrative source of revenue for the committee. "Every day hundreds of peasants invade the trains," one French observer complained, "attracted by the lure of spoils."[92]

Yusuf Mukhaybar Sulayman, who had received training as an attorney and had participated in the activities of the Literary Society before the war, directed the military campaigns of the committee. Drawing the core of his guerrilla band from among family retainers and dependents who resided in his home village of Bayt Naʾil, it included, according to French sources, "those of middle income, unemployed artisans, peasants from the countryside, and professional brigands." The Baʿalbek committee spearheaded the military campaign against the French in the valley, the scene of some of the bloodiest fighting during this period. Beginning with what a British observer described as "an unimportant fracas" near the town of Rayaq in early December 1919, the confrontations escalated after rebels forcibly removed the French liaison officer from Baʿalbek. Throughout the remainder of the month, French troops sought to reassert their control in the valley by occupying Muʿallaqa, Rayaq, and Baʿalbek, suffering "considerable casualties" at the hands of "so-called brigands who no doubt are working under the extremist party in Damascus."[93]

The committees of national defense thus benefited from the ties that bound rural and urban notables with those who worked their lands, borrowed their money, and in general were dependent on the resources provided by others. Sometimes the networks of retainers and clients supervised by urban-based notables stretched far into the countryside. Each of the wealthiest families of Homs, for example, owned from forty-five to

92. MAE L:SL/vol. 33/167, "Rapport du lt. Sol, sur l'ensemble des faits qui se sont déroulés dans la région de Baalbeck, entre le départ des troupes anglaises et l'occupation de la ville par les troupes françaises," 6 January 1920; AD 2375/chemise: division de la Syrie, 1919–1920/361/2, Arlabosse to G.C.C., 11 January 1920; AD 2375/chemise: division de la Syrie, 1919–1920/361A, Col. Sousselier to GCC, 7 February 1920.

93. FO 371/4186/174490, Meinertzhagen to GHQ, EEF, 13 January 1920. For an alternative description of events, see *al-Kawkab*, 6 January 1920, 4–5.

sixty villages located on the surrounding plain, villages that were in part inhabited by settled bedouin.[94] Although called, disparagingly, *fallāḥīn* (peasants) by their nomadic and seminomadic kinfolk, the cultivators were not the only tribespeople who maintained close relations with prominent urban families. City dwellers acted as bankers and merchants for tribal leaders, sometimes reinforcing their economic relationships through ties of marriage. Such a combination of bonds linked the powerful Atasi and Rifaʿi families of Homs with, respectively, the Banu Khalid and the Ahsana tribes, and linked the Durubi family, also of Homs, with the Wild ʿAli, the ʿUqaydat, and the Mawali.[95] Representatives from the Atasi and Durubi families were prominent in the Homs committee of national defense: ʿUmar al-Atasi and Muhyi al-Din al-Durubi each served as president of the committee, and ʿUmar and Wasfi al-Atasi received subsidies from Damascus that they used to administer the activities of the committee.[96] Along with the "*atasiyyūn*" and "*rifaʿiyyūn*," tribal levies not only fought against the French in the December 1919 battle for Tall Kalkh in the Biqaʿ Valley, but, after the Homs committee of national defense began preparations to resist the invading French army in July 1920, bedouin from as far away as Tadmur—variously estimated to have numbered between fifteen hundred and six thousand—descended on the city in a period of two days.[97]

94. According to a French report, for example, the Jindalis and Jundis numbered "about sixty families which maintain their numerous peasants in [a state of] absolute obedience." Gharib, Saʿdallah, Saʿd al-Din, and Salih Jindali were all prominent members in the Homs committee of national defense. SL:LD, Muhyi al-Din al-Durubi et al. to Committee of National Defense, Damascus, 21 November 1919; AD 2372/dossier: affaires militaires et politiques, J. Jacottet, "Renseignements sur les villes de Homs, de Hama, et les régions qui en dépendent," 10 July 1920. See also Iḥsān Hindī, *Kifāḥ al-shaʿb al-ʿarabī al-sūrī, 1908–1948*, 89.

95. AD 2372/dossier: affaires militaires et politiques, J. Jacottet, "Renseignements sur les villes de Homs, de Hama, et les régions qui en dépendent," 10 July 1920; AD 4H114/2/n.d., "Tribus de la Syrie intérieure." For more information about these tribes, see Zakariyyā, *ʿAshāʾir al-Shām*, 404–409, 434–442, 444–449, 499–500, 507–521.

96. SL:LD, Muhyi al-Din al-Durubi et al. to Committee of National Defense, Damascus, 21 November 1919; AD 2375/chemise: division de la Syrie 1919–1920/384/2, Arlabosse to GCC, 15 January 1919; MD 4H112/1/84/6, Gouraud to Lt. Dejean, 19–24 February 1920; AD 2372/dossier: affaires militaires et politiques /no no., "Renseignements sur les villes de Homs, de Hama et les régions qui en dépendent," 10 July 1920.

97. *al-Kawkab*, 6 January 1920, 5; MD 4H58/1, "Rapport hebdomadaire: 24 février au 1 mars 1920"; MD 4H60/1, "Bulletin quotidien 1266," 21 July 1920; Angelil, "L'occupation d'Homs."

Not only were the committees of national defense able to call upon an extensive network of tribal levies and retainers, they also periodically bolstered their forces by working in concert with each other. Members of the most prominent landowning family of Tall Kalkh, the Dandashi clan, founded a committee of national defense after residents of the town resisted French attempts to establish a military presence there. As the fighting in the town escalated, the committees of national defense of Homs and Tripoli sent reinforcements that fought alongside a contingent sent from Damascus led by the Druze chieftain, Sultan al-Atrash.[98] In a like manner, Salih al-ʿAli not only led his followers in attacks against the French depot in Tartus and against Christian villages in the area, but with the assistance of the committees of national defense in Homs and Hama and the Higher National Committee in Damascus, established a camp in the town of al-Qadmus in western Syria to train volunteer fighters.[99]

The Aleppo committee of national defense provides an unusually well-documented picture of the distribution of power among urban-based notables, the local committee of national defense, and tribal and guerrilla bands. The committee originated as the result of the efforts of a group of prominent Aleppans who described themselves as *anṣār* (partisans) of Mustafa Kemal and who were motivated by a combination of pro-Turkish sentiments, distrust of Anglo-French intentions, and alienation from Damascus.[100] In August 1919—a month before the onset of the Evacuation Crisis and three months before the organization of the Higher National Committee—the *anṣār* began plotting a Syria-based military campaign against the French that would coordinate its operations with those undertaken by the Turkish nationalist movement. Although this group met throughout

98. *al-Kawkab*, 6 January 1920, 5; MD 4H114/4/no no., "Renseignements," Cousse, 13 July 1920; Darwaza, *Mudhakkarāt*, 2:160; Hindī, *Kifāḥ al-shaʿb al-ʿarabī al-sūrī*, 89; Khoury, *Syria and the French Mandate*, 9; Saʿīd, *al-Thawra al-ʿarabiyya al-kubrā*, 2:111; Zakariyyā, *ʿAshāʾir al-Shām*, 477–478, 485–487.

99. MD 4H58/1, "Rapport hebdomadaire: 24 février au 1 mars 1920"; FO 371/5034/E2539/18, British Consul General (Beirut) to Secretary of State, 17 March 1920; MD 4H58/1/"Rapport hebdomadaire: 23 au 29 mars 1920"; MD 4H58/1, "Rapport hebdomadaire: 20 au 26 avril 1920"; MD 4H58/2, "Rapport hebdomadaire: 13–19 juillet 1920"; MD 4H60/1/1327/cp., "Bulletin quotidien," 12 August 1920; Hindī, *Kifāḥ al-shaʿb al-ʿarabī al-sūrī*, 56–57.

100. Among them were Jamil Ibrahim Pasha, Shakir Shaʿbani, al-Hajj Fath al-Marʿashli, Mustafa Barmada, Badr al-Din al-Naʿsani, Fuʾad al-ʿAdli, Qasim al-Sibaʿi, ʿAbd al-Qadir al-Kikhya, and Fuʾad al-Mudarris.

August, it was able to accomplish little more than founding a newspaper and holding receptions for other notables of the city.[101]

With the onset of the Evacuation Crisis, the circle of those who responded to *anṣār* propaganda expanded as Aleppans reacted to the British withdrawal in much the same manner as did Damascenes. At the urging of Rushdi al-Safadi, the divisional commander of the Arab army stationed in Aleppo who was also a member of the local Arab Club and a close associate of Yasin al-Hashimi, a number of notables began organizing volunteer militias throughout the quarters and public areas of the city. Each organizer received the rank of major and was instructed to appoint his own captains and lieutenants.[102] In the Qasila district, for example, Ahmad Kadru al-Masri organized a 680-man militia to help maintain order in the city and, working alongside al-Hajj Najib al-Baqi of the local Arab Club, was instrumental in mobilizing the resources of his quarter to provide logistical support for the Hananu Revolt.[103] In Bab al-Nayrab, a quarter of twelve thousand inhabitants that resembled the Maydan in Damascus, Kanju Hamada and ʿAbd al-Fath al-Baytar, both heads of distinguished families, along with members of the equally prominent Barri family and several lesser lights, established a militia composed of a machine-gun unit, infantry, and cavalry. Previously, the inhabitants of this district, like the inhabitants of the Maydan, had strenuously resisted the conscription policy of the Arab government. "If the enemy ever arrives, they know they can hold their own without having to deck out their sons in some uniform that

101. IO L/PS/10/802, Gertrude Bell, "Syria in October 1919," 15 November 1919; MD 4H112/2a/38r, "Renseignements," 20 February 1920; USNA 59/890d.00/8/468, Jackson to Secretary of State, 13 March 1920; MD 4H112/2b/2, "Rapport politique: période du 16 au 30 avril 1920"; MD 4H112/2b/51, "Renseignements," 25 May 1920; al-Jundī, *Tārīkh al-thawrāt al-sūriyya*, 62–63, 74; Ibrāhīm Pāshā, *Niḍāl al-aḥrār* 3, 6, 11–14; Ghazzī, *Nahr al-dhahab fī tārīkh Ḥalab*, 2:136–137, 156, 177, 215, 275, 335; Khoury, *Syria and the French Mandate*, 10, 113.

102. MD 4H112/1/84/6, Gouraud to lt. Dejean, February 1920. For a list of quarter commanders, see MAE L:SL/vol. 33/120–121, Gouraud, "Note au sujet des rapports entre le haut commissionaire de la République Française en Syrie-Cilicie et l'emir Fayçal," 22 September 1920. Al-Safadi would later write to the ministry of war, "Although the volunteers report on time to the drill grounds, we should not count on the collaboration of twenty percent of them in time of crisis, because, for the most part, they are proprietors, men of affairs, or people who can be recognized through their families."

103. MAE L:SL/vol. 33/119, Gouraud, "Note au sujet des rapports entre le haut commissionaire de la République Française en Syrie-Cilicie et l'emir Fayçal," 22 September 1920; Ibrāhīm Pāshā, *Niḍāl al-aḥrār*, 6; al-Jundī, *Tārīkh al-thawrāt al-sūriyya*, 62.

would not make them more patriotic or more courageous," the French liaison officer stationed in the city reported to his superiors in Paris. "Moreover, they realize that the recruitment is most simply a way to try to replenish the empty coffers of the treasury of Damascus from which the officers will not receive salaries and soldiers will not be supplied." Nevertheless, residents of the quarter enlisted in the volunteer units that subsequently formed the core of the four thousand insurgents who, on 21 July 1920, attacked the Aleppo citadel.[104]

In early November, militia leaders, leaders of the Arab Club, *anṣār,* and local and provincial administrators merged the militias into a citywide committee of national defense. A list of committee participants reads like a "Who's Who" of Aleppo. The committee included leaders of government (Ihsan al-Jabiri, the president of the municipality; Fakhir al-Jabiri, a member of the administrative council; Gharib al-Mudarris, the local tax administrator; and Shafiq Bey, director of the land registry), Arab Club activists (ʿAbd al-Rahman al-Kayyali, ʿAbd al-Wahhab Tlas, and Subhi Barakat), *anṣār* (Fuʾad al-ʿAdli and Fath al-Marʿashli), and militia leaders (Rida al-Rifaʿi and Sadiq al-Rifaʿi). In addition, Munib al-Natur, editor of *al-Rāya,* and ʿAbd al-Qadir al-Jasmati and al-Hajj Ahmad Muyassar, two wealthy merchants, joined the committee.[105] Thus constituted, the Aleppo committee of national defense sponsored twice-weekly drills under the supervision of officers in the regular army and held armed demonstrations for both militias and tribal levies every Thursday afternoon in the center of the city.[106]

A variety of factors might have induced some of the most distinguished citizens of Aleppo to participate in the founding of the committee. Some were undoubtedly motivated by the chance to participate in an organization that promised to provide an access to power in unsettled times. Others may have been attracted by nationalist sentiment or, conversely, by the hope that their presence on the committee might moderate nationalist goals. In

104. *al-ʿĀṣima,* 13 November 1919, 6; MD 4H112/2b/55, "Renseignements," 29 May 1920; MAE L:SL/vol. 33/119, Gouraud, "Note au sujet des rapports entre le haut commissionaire de la République Française en Syrie-Cilicie et l'emir Fayçal," 22 September 1920; Ghazzī, *Nahr al-dhahab fī tārīkh Ḥalab,* 2:356, 372. Kersante, "Syrie: L'occupation d'Alep," 172.

105. MD 4H112/2A/38R, "Renseignements," 20 February 1920. The report includes the names of the following additional members of the Arab Club who were in contact with the *"comitajis"*: Ibrahim Hananu, Tawfiq al-Bissar, Sanussi Bey, Sami al-Sarraj, Sami al-Kayyali, Ghalib Bey (Zadih?), and Shaykh Nur al-Jisri.

106. MAE L:SL/vol. 33/120–21, Gouraud, "Note au sujet des rapports entre le haut commissionaire de la République Française en Syrie-Cilicie et l'emir Fayçal," 22 September 1920.

the case of the Jabiris, for example, interfamilial rivalry probably played a role as well: the Jabiris were locked in competition with the wealthy and powerful Shaʿbanis, who were involved in pro-Kemalist agitation. If nothing else, participation in the committee enabled the Jabiris to display their nationalist credentials. It is also possible that less distinguished committee activists solicited the support of the city's grandees and placed them in positions of rank to broaden the organization's appeal, legitimacy, and fundraising base.

By the spring of 1920, however, a group of influential Aleppan families, including the Jabiris, began to distance themselves from the organization, which had increasingly taken on a populist coloration. Not only did ʿAbd al-Hamid al-Jabiri resign as president of the committee, but the Jabiris and their allies sent petitions complaining about the activities of the organization to the governor of Aleppo and to the Syrian General Congress.[107] In their stead, a new group of leaders emerged, including Fath al-Marʿashli, one of the original *anṣār* who had personally negotiated with Mustafa Kemal; Sadiq Shahin al-Khattam, who was, according to reports, particularly adept at procuring money from merchants; and Rida al-Rifaʿi, who, along with Kamil al-Qassab, ʿAbdullah Kuzbari, the Hakims, ʿId al-Halabi, Shukri al-Tabbaʿ, and a handful of others, founded the Democratic Party.[108]

The two most important issues that split the committee were fundraising and support for the guerrilla bands. As economic conditions deteriorated, voluntary donations to the committee fell precipitously. Concurrently, the Kemalists agreed to an armistice with the French and suspended financial support for their allies to the south. To finance its military operations and to sustain payments to the families of full-time guerrillas, the committee increasingly relied on extortion, forced taxation, the licensing of monopolies (such as those for rice and other cereals), and arms smuggling (from which, it was reported, al-Marʿashli reaped a considerable profit).[109]

107. MD 4H112/2b/2, "Rapport politique: période du 16 au 30 avril 1920"; MD 4H112/2b/26, "Renseignements," to Trenga, 1 May 1920; MD 4H112/2b/31, "Renseignments," to Trenga, 5 May 1920; MD 4H114/4, Cousse to Gouraud, 14 May 1920.

108. MD 4H112/2a/38r, "Renseignements," 20 February 1920; MD 4H112/2b/2, "Rapport politique: période du 16 au 30 avril 1920; FO 882/24/209–210, Major G. W. Courtney, 21 May 1920; Khoury, *Syria and the French Mandate,* 10.

109. Ibrāhīm Pāshā, *Niḍāl al-aḥrār,* 6. See also MD 4H112/2b/51, "Renseignements," 25 May 1920; MAE/vol. 33/125–126, Gouraud, "Note au sujet des rapports entre le haut commissionaire de la République Française en Syrie-Cilicie et l'emir Fayçal," 22 September 1920.

One particularly ominous fundraising appeal, signed by al-Marʿashli, al-Rifaʿi, and al-Khattam, began by stating,

> We do not demand either alms or charity for which you will be rewarded. Rather we invite you to do your duty for the defense of the homeland.

and ended with the warning,

> If you respond to our appeal, you will have done your duty. If you refuse, we will not refrain from monitoring your actions.[110]

Adding to the dissension were complaints from large landowners about guerrilla depredations. The promotion of guerrilla activities was the most important function of the Aleppo committee of national defense. The organization solicited recruits for the guerrilla bands at demonstrations, political meetings, theaters, and movie houses, and sent money and supplies to guerrilla leaders and their followers. According to one French source, the committee provided new *chete* members with five gold pounds, a rifle, one hundred rounds of ammunition, and, in some cases, a horse. The committee also coordinated guerrilla raids and furnished safe houses for fighters visiting in the city.[111]

Perhaps the most effective of the committee-affiliated guerrilla leaders was Ibrahim Hananu. Hananu was the son of a wealthy rural notable who had held a variety of governmental positions in Aleppo. Elected as a representative to the Syrian General Congress from his home village of Kafr Takharim, Ibrahim Hananu resigned his seat and returned home to join the military campaign against the French. At first, he organized logistical support for the operations of Subhi Barakat, the guerrilla leader active in the area around Antioch. With the backing of the committee of national defense of Aleppo, however, Hananu soon assumed command of his own network of guerrillas.[112] Committee support proved crucial to Hananu's campaign: not only did the committee provide Hananu with weapons and financial assistance, it also promoted his activities among local ulama, persuading them to endorse his campaign by calling for jihad against the French. The committee also enlisted the help of the leader of the Second

110. MD 4H112/2b/2, "Rapport politique: période du 16 au 30 avril 1920"; MD 4H112/2b/51, "Renseignements," 25 May 1920; MD 4H114/4/483, Cousse to Gouraud, 3 June 1920; al-Jundī, *Tārīkh al-thawrāt al-sūriyya,* 76, 80.

111. USNA 59/890d.00/17/507, Jackson to Bristol, 19 May 1920; MD 4H112/2a/38r, "Renseignements," 20 February 1920.

112. al-Jundī, *Tārīkh al-thawrāt al-sūriyya,* 74–76; Hindī, *Kifāḥ al-shaʿb al-ʿarabī al-sūrī,* 70.

Division of the Arab army, Ibrahim al-Shaghuri. With al-Shaghuri's assistance, Hananu initially supervised the deployment of four squads, each consisting of ten *mujāhidūn* (fighters), from his base in Kafr Takharim. By April 1920, military successes swelled the number of *mujāhidūn* under Hananu's direct authority to approximately four hundred.

Hananu was a highly successful military leader, coordinating units of guerrillas whose size frequently ranged from three to six hundred men. Nevertheless, the "Hananu Revolt" is most notable for institutions constructed to administer liberated territory and to ensure the rebellion would remain self-sustaining. The *mujāhidūn* began by reorganizing the government of the village of Armanaz, working through the previous municipal president to impose new taxes on landowners, farmers, and owners of livestock to support their activities. From Armanaz, the area of their administrative and financial authority spread as far as the regional center of Harim. At the height of his organizing, Hananu coordinated the activities of guerrillas and municipalities as far as Idlib, Kafr Takharim, Jisr Shaghur, and Harim. While municipal governments in territory occupied by Hananu's forces remained in the hands of local officials, they were reconstituted to ensure compatibility with the military needs and social convictions of the rebels. On the regional level, a legislative committee (*lajna tashrīʿiyya*) based in Kafr Takharim collected money and weapons from local sources for the *mujāhidūn,* while a revolutionary council (*majlis al-thawra*), whose authority superseded that of the local courts, oversaw judicial affairs. In effect, Hananu's guerrillas established an independent state that stretched from Aleppo west to the Mediterranean Sea.[113]

The final mobilization undertaken by the committee of national defense of Aleppo occurred on the eve of the French invasion, when Arab Club and committee leaders such as Rashid al-Taliʿa, Nabih al-ʿAzma, Munib al-Natur, and Sami al-Sarraj, working alongside officers of the regular Arab army, organized the defense of the city.[114] Under the supervision of committee leaders and military officers, volunteers dug trenches to guard the approaches to the city and assaulted and captured the Baghdad Railway Station and the citadel. A full-page proclamation in Munib al-Natur's *al-Rāya,*

113. al-Jundī, *Tārīkh al-thawrāt al-sūriyya,* 62–63, 74–79; Ibrāhīm Pāshā, *Niḍāl al-aḥrār,* 6, 70.

114. As district governor of Hama, al-Taliʿa had channeled assistance to Salih al-ʿAli. According to one source, it was al-Taliʿa who persuaded Hananu to undertake his rebellion. See al-Jundī, *Tārīkh al-thawrāt al-sūriyya,* 62–63; Qadrī, *Mudhakkarātī,* 133; Hindī, *Kifāḥ al-shaʿb al-ʿarabī al-sūrī,* 70.

entitled "To Defense, to Defense," reproduced the text of the telegram sent from the Arab government to the municipal government of Aleppo:

> The traitorous French have crossed over the zone where they should have stopped, and are marching on the capital. An order of H.M. the King has been issued urging you to prepare all means you possibly can for the defense and to call all the nation to sacrifice to the last drop of their blood. . . . Relying on God and on the spirit of the prophet . . . defense has been decreed. The country is calling you and the religion is inviting all of you to do your duty.

Printed on a single page, the paper was distributed throughout Aleppo as a broadsheet; slogans shouted by the insurgents who attacked the Aleppo Citadel echoed its phrases.[115]

In spite of these preparations, however, Aleppan resistance to the French invasion was short-lived. The approximately three thousand tribesmen who had entered the city inspired as much fear among the citizenry as did the approaching French. By the time the French neared the city, Aleppans had ceded control of the streets to these outsiders: the suqs were closed, and Aleppans began to react to the shortages that threatened. The explosion at an arms depot that killed between five and six hundred civilians on the evening of 21 July drained the energy of the population and dissipated their enthusiasm for war as well: volunteers who had been mobilized by the committee now abandoned defensive positions and collected at the site to search for victims. At the same time, leaders of the committee of national defense fled the city in face of the French advance, relinquishing their recently assumed authority to a small group of civilian and military officials. With the encouragement and assistance of the American consul, the new authority organized armed patrols to maintain order and prepared a peaceable surrender of the city to the French. On 23 July, the French army entered the city without resistance.

POPULAR POLITICS AND POLITICAL AUTHORITY

With the arrival of French troops and the flight of popular leaders who feared arrest or worse, most overt resistance ended in the very cities where the Higher National Committee, the branch committees of the Higher National Committee, and the committees of national defense had focused

115. USNA 890d.00/34, Jackson (Aleppo) to Bristol (Constantinople), 21 July 1920; FO 371/5039/E10316/38, J. B. Jackson, 30 July 1920; Kersante, "Syrie: L'occupation d'Alep."

their activities. The desultory armed resistance that continued in the quarters of the Maydan in Damascus and Bab al-Nayrab in Aleppo seems to belie accounts that describe the passions generated a short time before by the popular committees. For foreign observers, the collapse of resistance came as no surprise: even before the French invasion of inland Syria, their reports had described periods—the first half of January 1920 (before the return of Faysal to Damascus and the reorganization of the Higher National Committee) and the second half of May 1920 (in the immediate aftermath of the San Remo agreement)—during which much of the urban population seemingly met the activities of the popular committees with indifference.[116] How, then, is the contemporary observer to understand the significance of the popular committees?

The dismemberment of the Ottoman Empire in the wake of World War I eliminated the overarching political structure that had loosely linked an emergent stratum of Westernizing elites with much of the remainder of the population. As a result, the two-year interregnum that separated the end of the war and the French invasion of inland Syria was a period of intense competition during which contrasting visions for the Syrian future vied directly against each other.

With adequate resources and time, it might have been possible for the Arab government and its allies among the nationalist elites gradually to enlist the support of the remainder of the population. However, the British decision to reduce its subsidy to the Arab government by half and to withdraw its forces from Syria undercut both the economic and the political capabilities of the Arab government and its allies and generated a crisis from which they never recovered. Its foreign policy in shambles, unable to guarantee a stable economy, provide a modicum of security, or enunciate a vision of the Syrian future that had resonance for most of the population, the government, along with its allies, alienated not only the indigenous notables whom they had attempted to bypass, co-opt, or coerce, but merchants, artisans, popular ulama and *qabaḍāyāt*. These groupings formed the backbone of the popular committees.

The emergence of the committees attests to the efficacy of the processes that had transformed the Ottoman Empire during the nineteenth century.

116. See MD 4H114/2/no no., Cousse to Gouraud, 1 January 1920; *al-Kawkab*, 13 January 1920, 12; MD 4H114/2/28, Cousse to Gouraud, 14 January 1920; AD 2374/dossier: TEO zone ouest: adm., cabinet politique/1032/cp., 18 May 1920; MD 4H114/4/451, Cousse to Gouraud, 25 May 1920; MD 4H114/4/459, Cousse to Gouraud, 27 May 1920; Russell, *First Modern Arab State*, 147, 180.

These processes rendered many Syrians capable of "imagining" a national community, and they looked to the popular committees to effect it. But the "imagining" of a national community has implications for the structuring of relationships of power, and the popular committees provided an alternative to the customary structures that had proven to be ill-suited to the circumstances many inhabitants of early-twentieth-century Syria faced. Although the popular committees frequently took advantage of localized networks of patrons and clients, they also subverted these networks by organizing on an extralocal scale, by rationalizing lines of political authority, and by bypassing them to provide services for their constituents. Functions once entrusted to the local notability now became responsibilities diffused through a more broadly defined political sphere, clients became members of "the nation," and the delivery of services became inextricably entwined with an ideology that was informed by popular symbols and popular notions of equity.

Part Two

NATIONALIST COMMUNITIES OF DISCOURSE

3 The Symbolic Component of Rival Nationalist Discursive Fields

On 27 January 1920, the newspaper *al-Kawkab* printed the following report of a demonstration held in Damascus to celebrate the return of Amir Faysal from Europe:

> While His Highness Amir Faysal was in the saray today, he met well-wishers who had organized a great demonstration in which 120,000 participated, demanding unity and complete independence. His Highness announced that he was firmly committed to unity and that he would accept nothing but complete independence. He praised military conscription for the preservation of order. . . . The entire city was locked up tight so that all might participate in the demonstration, and enthusiasm was great.[1]

This was the sort of report a reader of *al-Kawkab* might have expected to read. As discussed in Chapter 1, *al-Kawkab* was launched by the British Arab Bureau "to support [the] Arab movement and further good relations between England and the Arabs."[2] The newspaper thus regularly and favorably reported on the Arab Revolt, on the wartime and postwar activities of its leader, Amir Faysal, and on the activities of the pro-Faysali Palestinian and Syrian literary associations and political clubs, such as the Literary Society and the Arab Club.

The same reader might have been perplexed, however, by the article printed directly below the first, an article written by Kamil al-Qassab that presented a different picture of the same demonstration:

> A great, patriotic demonstration took place today, bringing together more than one hundred thousand people from all *ṭabaqāt*. Appearing among them were the conference of the committees of Syrian national

1. *al-Kawkab*, 27 January 1920, 5.
2. DU, Wingate Files 143/2/167 (AB202), Arbur (Cairo) to Sirdar (Khartoum), 13 November 1916.

> defense, the political parties, the ulama, the notables, the municipal council, civilian and military employees, farmers, doctors, pharmacists, journalists, the Arab clubs, the Imperial Schools of Law and Medicine, the normal school for secondary-level teachers, the Amiriyya and public schools, members of all religious sects, merchants, artisans, guilds, leaders of the quarters and neighboring villages.
>
> The demonstration presented a declaration of the nation calling for complete independence, the unity of Syria, and the amir's support for military service, which the nation planned to use as shield. The people assembled before the government headquarters, orators spoke, and the amir came down and spoke with them, saying that he did not strive and will not strive for anything other than complete independence, and that there was nothing which separated him from the nation—that there was, fundamentally, agreement for an independent, indivisible Syria. He praised the nation for demanding conscription.

Two contradictory tendencies become apparent when the first article is compared with the second. On the one hand, both articles use many of the same phrases and emphasize many of the same phenomena: slogans calling for "complete independence" and "unity"; the demand for conscription; the description of the excitement and large size of the crowd. On the other hand, there are significant differences between the two articles. Most obviously, the center of attention of the first article is Amir Faysal; the crowd of "well-wishers" exists in relation to him and is the passive recipient of his largesse. To al-Qassab, it is the crowd—"the nation"—that is active; Faysal is a foil who must respond to its will. But in addition to the shift in focus, there are more subtle differences between the two articles. For example, the author of the first article would probably not divide the crowd, or, for that matter, Syrian society, into *ṭabaqāt;* nor would he be likely to separate the nation from the ruling institution.

The differences between the two articles underscore an issue raised in the Introduction: the tendency, on the part of historians who work within an idealist framework, to emphasize unity and downplay diversity when writing about the evolution of nationalist sentiment in the modern Middle East. Even the use of the term *Arab nationalism* to denote what is to be studied noticeably restricts the frame of reference. "Scholarly studies on the origins and ideas of Arab nationalism abound," one scholar wrote in the early 1990s.

> Few works, however, explore the rise of local nationalism (*waṭaniyya*) and the internal Arab conditions that made it strike root in the Arab East after World War I. This study will attempt to fill the gap. It is an analysis

> of the Arab factors that *contributed to the weakening of the framework of Arab nationalism in Syria, and consequently helped usher in to existence the forces of territorial nationalism.*[3] [Italics mine.]

Yet evidence from the immediate post-Ottoman period does not justify the historical privileging of an "Arab" identity over others, or for viewing those other identities as an unnatural truncation of a "true" Arab one. Fewer than one-third of the leaflets and posters that were distributed or displayed in Damascus from October 1918 through July 1920 and that can be found in various archives in Europe and the Middle East or in contemporaneously published newspapers were addressed to "Arabs." Others were addressed to "Syrians" or employed multiple or more ambiguous salutations ("Citizens," "Fellow Citizens"). For the inhabitants of Syria, an "Arab" identity not only represented one possible identity among several, but as will be seen below, signaled an affinity with a select group of attitudes toward intercommunal relations, the nature of the bonds uniting members of the community, the relationship between the government and the "nation," the role of the sharifian family in Syria's future, relations with the Hijaz, Turkey, and Iraq, and a variety of other issues.

Furthermore, by privileging "Arab nationalism," historians are privileging a select group of intellectuals and activists, political associations, and institutions that did not necessarily represent the aspirations of a majority of those involved in nationalist politics, much less a majority of Syrians, during the Faysali period. While some within the nationalist camp—members of the Arab government allied with Amir Faysal, the Hijazis, Palestinians, and Iraqis who had entered Damascus with the Arab army, self-described intellectuals and professionals from the Muslim and minority communities whose experiences differentiated them from the majority of the Syrian population—might have rooted their nationalism in philosophic musings or, more prosaically, in political expediency or the wartime promise of self-determination made by the entente powers, others—including many non-elite Muslim Syrians and their advocates in the popular committees such as Kamil al-Qassab—rooted their national aspirations in a very different set of experiences and conventions.

Thus, in post-Ottoman Syria, the nationalist field included a disparate collection of activists, organizations, and constituencies that expressed their nationalisms through discourses that were likewise disparate.[4] Had the

3. Muhammad Muslih, "Rise of Local Nationalism," 167.

4. For a definition of the analogous "political field," see Victor Turner, "Hidalgo: History as Social Drama," 127.

Ottoman Empire been homogeneous, had class and sectarian differences not existed, and had the effects of expanding market relations and the efficacy of Ottoman administrative reforms been uniform and coincident, historians might be justified in assuming a unitary ideological response to changing conditions. This, however, was obviously not the case. The twin processes acted unevenly, affecting different regions and social strata both asynchronously and unequally. As a result, while all nationalist discourses reflected the global processes at work in the Middle East, both the extent to which and the manner in which they did so were dissimilar. In addition, because of the weakness of both the Ottoman government and the Arab government of Amir Faysal, and because of the range of the economic and political transformation, no single dominant nationalist discourse could be either coaxed or coerced.

This is not to say that components of political discourse did not become the common property of many or all nationalist groupings in post-World War I Syria. A diverse assortment of nationalist organizations, even those that appealed to or attempted to mobilize very different constituencies, shared a number of slogans ("We demand complete independence,"), physical symbols (the Arab flag, Amir Faysal), vocabulary (the word *ṭāmiʿūn* [coveters] to describe imperialists), and metaphors. No nationalist organization remained unaffected by the activities of the others: while, for example, Kamil al-Qassab and his colleagues took advantage of their intermediary position to reconcile the idiom of nationalism with popular symbols and discursive practices, the nationalist elites were not entirely unaware of the constraints on their organizing posed by those symbols and practices either.

The charged political atmosphere of postwar Syria facilitated the interchange among nationalist groups as well. The Arab government and various political associations organized demonstrations (such as the one described in the above-cited newspaper accounts) in which tens of thousands took part. The government invented new secular patriotic holidays marking the anniversary of the entrance of the Arab army into World War I on the side of the entente powers, mourning the Arab "martyrs" executed by Jamal Pasha, and celebrating Independence Day. Political posters not only festooned the walls of buildings in cities from Aleppo to Amman but could be seen adorning structures in many villages. Activists reconceptualized popular cultural activities and rewrote plays, historical accounts, and *karakūz* shadow plays to incorporate nationalist messages. Schools inculcated the tenets of patriotism and herded students to demonstrations. The Arab government, its allies in extragovernmental organizations, and the popular committees closed down suqs on national holidays and designated days of protest, circulated petitions with the aid of *makhātīr, qabaḍāyāt,* and police, and extorted donations from wealthy merchants for the National Loan. In short, a new *political* public was both created and mobilized.

In spite of these commonalities, however, competing nationalist organizations clearly did articulate alternative visions for the nation and for the future. As a result, the early post-Ottoman period—the period during which varieties of nationalism became the ideological construct through which large segments of the population of Syria expressed their notion of community—was a period of intense competition between rival "communities of discourse."

In general, communities of discourse possess three interrelated attributes. First, individuals within each community participate in and interact through common institutions and consentient social practices. These institutions and practices substantiate the proper ordering of societal relations as it is apprehended by community members and as it is articulated through a shared ideology. Conversely, institutionalization assures the autonomy of the community of discourse and its component discursive field: through institutions, individuals within the community remain in constant contact, both reinforcing and reenacting their commitment to the community through, for example, shared propaganda and rituals. Second, although contemporaneous but competing communities of discourse frequently utilize identical symbols, members of each community derive congruent and community-distinct meanings from the most important symbols (such as "key symbols," discussed below) and symbolic actions (such as the "rites of violence" identified by Natalie Zemon Davis, or E. P. Thompson's "countertheater"). Finally, community members share a discrete discursive field—the "space" that encompasses, arranges, and integrates the community's preeminent symbols. Because the discursive field acts to circumscribe the range of possible meanings that can be derived from the symbols it encloses, it shapes the categories and demarcates the boundaries that guide and enframe the thoughts, activities, and discussions of those within the community.[5]

5. Robert Wuthnow, *Communities of Discourse: Ideology and Social Structure in the Reformation, the Enlightenment, and European Socialism,* 13–15, 553, 555; François Furet, *Interpreting the French Revolution,* 37–38, 52, 130, 173–176; Cornelius Castoriadis, *The Imaginary Institution of Society,* 124; Clifford Geertz, "After the Revolution: The Fate of Nationalism in New States," 249–254; Natalie Zemon Davis, "The Rites of Violence: Religious Riot in Sixteenth-Century France"; E. P. Thompson, *Customs in Common: Studies in Traditional Popular Culture,* 64–

The Arab government, al-Fatat (during much of the Faysali period), and the Arab clubs in which the influence of the *mutanawwirūn* was dominant, on the one hand, and the popular committees and their allies, on the other, embodied two distinct institutional frameworks that sustained competing communities of discourse in post-Ottoman Syria. Because the composition and structure of these political associations were the subject of Part I, only the symbols and discursive fields that distinguished these two discursive communities will be compared in this and the following chapter.

The fundamentally binary division of the nationalist tendency in Syria during the immediate post-Ottoman period that is presented here and in subsequent chapters rests upon two assumptions discussed in the Introduction. First, it assumes that factors external to the peculiarities of nationalist ideologies themselves play an important role in the success or failure of nationalist movements. Thus, although other nationalist discursive communities emerged after the dismemberment of the Ottoman Empire, the access to resources such as manpower, media, and political structures enjoyed by the two communities examined below enabled them to marginalize or integrate their indigenous competitors and thus to dominate the nationalist field.[6] Second, although fictive boundaries of identity are ordinarily "soft"—that is, relatively flexible, nonexclusive, and unselfconscious—they become reified during periods of mobilization and crisis, when individuals and the communities of which they are part directly confront their counterparts as "the other." As should now be evident, the twenty-two months that followed the end of World War I, particularly the interval that extended from January through July 1920, constituted such a period.

69. While my debt to Robert Wuthnow's *Communities of Discourse* will, over the course of Part II, become obvious, I have taken the liberty of modifying Wuthnow's framework of analysis.

6. Post-Ottoman Syrian society, like all societies, was made up of smaller, often overlapping groups that engaged in distinctive activities and fretted over particular "focal concerns." See John Clark et al., "Sub Cultures, Cultures, Class," 56. While disparate responses to the spread of market relations and modern state institutions delineated the principal fault line that divided Syrian society, other factors—regional, generational, experiential, religious, "class," and professional—cannot be entirely discounted. For example, the community of discourse sustained by the popular committees contained several subcommunities and local variants. Among these might be included a Palestinian variant, in which anti-Zionism played an axial role, and an Aleppan variant, which treated Turkish/Arab ethnic and linguistic differentiation with relative indifference.

KEY SYMBOLS AND SLOGANS

Before an analysis of the symbols that dominated nationalist discourse during the Faysali period can be undertaken, it is first necessary to define the two categories of symbols that will be discussed in this chapter: "key symbols" and slogans. Nels Johnson, applying the work of anthropologist Sherry B. Ortner to his study of Palestinian nationalism, defines key symbols as "those [symbols] which dominate a conceptual system by virtue of their relatively great capacity either to summarize or to elaborate a social order."[7] According to Ortner, key symbols are "signaled by more than one of [the following] indicators":

1. The natives tell us that X is culturally important.
2. The natives seem positively or negatively aroused by X, rather than indifferent.
3. X comes up in many different contexts. . . .
4. There is greater cultural elaboration surrounding X, e.g., elaboration of vocabulary, or elaboration of details of X's nature, compared with similar phenomenon in the culture.
5. There are greater cultural restrictions surrounding X, either in sheer number of rules, or severity of sanctions regarding its use.[8]

The symbols analyzed in this chapter display some or all of these attributes.

Ortner does not limit her discussion of key symbols to those that are contained in written and oral communication, however; as she demonstrates, physical artifacts may act as key symbols as well. Although this chapter will focus on written and spoken symbols, objects also exhibited the characteristics of key symbols during the Faysali period. Clothing was one such object. Because of regional variations in dress, clothing initially served as a geographic marker. But because of regional stereotypes, geography was not dissociated from other connotations. Even before the entente troops occupied Damascus in October 1918, a split had emerged between native Syrians who had remained at home during the war, on the one hand, and the Hijazi and Iraqi officers who had participated in the Arab Revolt, on the other. The Hijazis in particular were held up to scorn for their lack of sophistication, and by November 1918, Damascenes were already

7. Nels Johnson, *Islam and the Politics of Meaning in Palestinian Nationalism*, 66.
8. Sherry B. Ortner, "On Key Symbols."

calling them, contemptuously, "bedouins" (*badw*).[9] Because they were subjected to public derision, members of the Arab army gave up wearing the previously favored kaffiyeh (cloth headdress) and donned a European-style helmet that became known as the *fayṣaliyya.* One young eyewitness described the transformation of Faysal himself as follows:

> When I arrived home I told my grandfather what I had seen on [the day of the king's visit to Homs in the spring of 1920], that the king had been more splendid on the day of his previous visit. Then, when the king had been an amir, he wore a flowing white Arab cloak [*faḍfāḍ*], on top of which was a fine, soft black aba (which was wrinkled), a slender white kaffiyeh bound by a black ʿ*iqāl.* This made him look like a pure bedouin. As for today, he wore a military uniform. On his shoulders and breast were epaulets and medals, and he was crowned by the cap [*sidāra*] of an officer (now called a *fayṣaliyya*). He gave no impression other than that he was an important officer.[10]

Faysal's younger brother and cousin, Zayd and Nasr, also adopted European dress "in response to hints."[11] By means of their sartorial transformation, Hijazis were, in effect, announcing that they held the same "civilized" aspirations as did the more urbane *mutanawwirūn* of Damascus.

As early as May 1919, however, British observers in the Syrian capital reported a movement aimed at discouraging the wearing of European-style clothes in public.[12] During and after the autumn 1919 Evacuation Crisis, as it became increasingly apparent that the entente powers were planning to divide Syria "within its natural boundaries" and place both the coastal and eastern zones under a French mandate, popular sentiment in Damascus turned particularly anti-Western. Lower-class youths, responding to patriotic fervor and emboldened, as a result of their empowerment through the popular committees, to display their class resentments publicly, insulted and even attacked women who wore European-style clothes in public. In response, the Arab government issued a proclamation that not only threatened the attackers with punishments but warned women that trained gov-

9. IO L/PS/11/140 P497/1918 (P1171), Sir Mark Sykes, "Appreciation of the Situation in Syria, Palestine, and Lesser Armenia," 15 November 1918; FO 371/4178/7094, Hogarth to CPO, EEF, 18 December 1918; AD 2358/dossier: emir Fayçal, "Mystification chérifienne," 13 September 1919; MD 4H112/1, "Compte rendu du capitaine Gautherot sur la situation politique à Alep," 6 May 1920.

10. Riḍā Ṣāfī, ʿ*Alā janāḥ al-dhikrā,* 1:234.

11. IO L/PS/11/140P497/1918 (P1171), Sir Mark Sykes, "Appreciation of the Situation in Syria, Palestine, and Lesser Armenia," 15 November 1918.

12. FO 371/4149/114964, Civil Commission Baghdad, "Confidential Report for Week Ending 31/5/19."

ernment functionaries would henceforth patrol the streets and admonish the guardians of every woman "who transcends the limits in her adornment and who departs from custom."[13] Thus, over the course of the Faysali period, clothing was transformed from a geographic to a political marker, and clothes took on the role of what Ortner calls a "summarizing symbol": a symbol that is "seen as summing up, expressing, representing for the participants in an emotionally powerful and relatively undifferentiated way, what the system means to them."[14]

The other category of symbols to be discussed in this chapter, slogans, bears a twofold relationship with key symbols: slogans might contain key symbols, or themselves become key symbols.[15] In their mobilization efforts, the Arab government, its allies, and rival political groups such as the popular committees attempted to appeal to as broad a range of the public as possible by inventing and disseminating slogans. While some proved to be popular, others failed for a variety of reasons. The Arab government actively discouraged the dissemination of some slogans, such as those accusing the government of betrayal or those with anti-Zionist messages.[16] Other slogans lacked the symbolic richness that would have enabled them to appeal to many constituencies simultaneously. Effective slogans drove out ineffective ones and, in a process similar to natural selection, political factions that did not or could not represent themselves or their program through effective slogans and key symbols could not gain or maintain popular support. As a result, those factions that could represent their programs compellingly supplanted those that could not.[17] Slogans might thus be situated at the juncture connecting popular aspirations with the organizational requirements of political enterprises.

The discussion of representative symbols and slogans that follows is based upon a variety of sources, including propaganda brochures, transcriptions of speeches, copies of broadsheets and graffiti, collections of poetry,

13. *al-ʿĀṣima,* 29 April 1920, 4.

14. Ortner, "On Key Symbols," 1339.

15. For slogans acting in the latter role, see George Rudé, *The Crowd in History: A Study of Popular Disturbances in France and England, 1730–1848,* 245. According to Harold D. Lasswell, slogans might be defined as "synoptic statements submitted to the public for guidance," which "[mediate] between the single word and the full-length propositions of law or philosophy," and which "gain meaning by repetition and context." "The Language of Power," 17.

16. For the attitude of the Arab government to anti-Zionist propaganda, see MAE L:SL/vol. 12/32–38, Cousse to HC, 6 April 1919.

17. For a parallel analysis of the "natural selection" of rumors, see Tamotsu Shibutani, *Improvised News: A Sociological Study of Rumor,* 176–182.

accounts of slogans chanted in demonstrations or shouted in riots, newspaper articles and editorials, telegrams, and memoirs. A collection of approximately fifty original leaflets, gathered from various archives, has been particularly valuable for this study. Since the leaflets were all intended for roughly the same purpose and thus were bound by the same conventions, and since the diplomats, travelers, and spies who gathered them recorded the dates and circumstances of their distribution, they provide a practical means to ascertain and evaluate the evolution of symbolic usages situated within a consistent and singularly purposive medium.[18]

FROM THE "DAMASCUS PROTOCOL" TO "COMPLETE INDEPENDENCE FOR SYRIA..."

In May 1915, before the commencement of the Arab Revolt, Amir Faysal arrived in Damascus for the second time in two months to meet with those leaders of al-Fatat and al-ʿAhd who had evaded discovery by Jamal Pasha. According to Antonius, they presented the amir with a draft of the so-called "Damascus Protocol," a document that outlined the terms that the British would have to meet before the secret societies would offer their assistance to the entente cause.[19] The following July, Amir ʿAbdallah, the second son of Sharif Husayn of Mecca, sent a letter on behalf of his father to Ronald Storrs, the oriental secretary at the British residency in Cairo, opening negotiations that would culminate in the Arab Revolt. In the letter, ʿAbdallah requested that the British approve the creation of an Arab caliphate and recognize the "independence of the Arab countries" within boundaries delimited in the north by Mersina and Adana up to the thirty-seventh parallel, in the east by the Persian border, in the south by the Indian Ocean (excluding Aden), and in the west by the Red Sea and the Mediterranean. These boundaries were identical to those demanded by the secret societies in their protocol.[20]

Approximately four years later, immediately before and during the visit of the King-Crane Commission to Damascus, the capital was flooded with

18. Unless otherwise indicated, all citations are from the original Arabic. I have tried to render quotations in language that adheres as closely as possible to the original.

19. For a critical assessment of the story of the Damascus Protocol contained in Antonius's *The Arab Awakening,* see Liora Lukitz, "The Antonius Papers and The Arab Awakening, Over Fifty Years On."

20. Hurewitz, *Middle East and North Africa,* 2:47–48; Antonius, *Arab Awakening,* 157; Fromkin, *A Peace to End All Peace,* 175.

thousands of leaflets.[21] Among them was one entitled "Independence or Death!" that contained the following paragraphs:

> All oppressed nations today demand their independence and freedom, and sacrifice their blood and money for this purpose. Does it not behoove us that we, the Syrian Arab community, unite as a single bloc to demand complete independence, free from any blemish of protection or tutelage? The hand of God is with the community. (Protection and mandate are synonyms, and are the precursors to annexation.)
>
> We do not deny what the allies have done to help us to achieve our purposes, but is it just and equitable that we give them our countries in return for this aid? Is it reasonable and proper that we place our country under the yoke of protection or mandate to one of them? No—certainly not. . . .
>
> All parts of Syria—its south, its north, its west, affix their hopes in you, as does Palestine (southern Syria), the first to be consulted by the commission, which demanded complete independence with no division of Syria and refused all protection, tutelage, or mandate. No doubt the other parts of Syria will be no less patriotic and zealous than the people of Palestine who surprised the commission by their unity and the agreement of their opinions. Should we not also unite our opinions and our hearts to eradicate disgrace and colonialism from this fatherland and refuse all protection, tutelage, and mandate, or anything else intended to enslave us? Thus, we must demand:
>
> 1. Complete independence for the country of Syria and for the other liberated Arab lands, such as Iraq.
> 2. Refusal of all protection, tutelage, mandate, or their like. We protest strongly Article 22 of the Charter of the League of Nations.
> 3. The complete unity of all parts of Syria (from the Taurus Mountains in the north, the Khabur and Euphrates in the east, the Arabian Desert and Mada'in Salih in the south, the Red Sea and the Aqaba-Rafah line, and the Mediterranean Sea in the West). We refuse completely all Zionist immigration.
> 4. History cannot deny the level that our great dynasties, such as the Umayyad and Abbasid, achieved by their complete independence. Inasmuch as we need specialists in some matters, we will purchase their services with our money as is done in the most civilized country.

This leaflet—typical of those distributed throughout Syria in the spring and summer of 1919—demonstrates just how far the debate about independence had progressed in four years. Although addressed to "Arabs,

21. A large selection of these leaflets can be found in MAE L:SL/vol. 15/340/92–95, Picot to Pichon, 21 July, 1919; MD 7N4182/4/340, Picot to MAE, 21 July, 1919.

Muslims, Christians, and Jews," and signed "An Arab Patriot," and although demanding independence for "the country of Syria and for the other liberated Arab lands, such as Iraq," the leaflet clearly regards both its author and audience as members of a distinct "*Syrian* Arab" collectivity (*maʿshar, jamāʿa*) composed of the residents of the territory that lies within the so-called "natural boundaries" of Syria. Furthermore, the author of the leaflet substitutes several variations of the awkward but nonetheless more explicit and popular slogan "We demand complete independence for Syria within its natural boundaries, no protection, no tutelage, and no mandate [*lā ḥimāya, lā wiṣāya, wa lā intidāb*]" for the more nebulous appeal for "independence for the Arab countries" included in both the Damascus Protocol and ʿAbdallah's letter.

A clearer understanding of the evolution of the terms of nationalist debate can be attained from the sample leaflets. From October 1918 through April 1919, 55 percent of the leaflets that can be found in French, British, Syrian, and American archives or that were reproduced in contemporaneous Syrian newspapers were addressed to Arabs, while 16 percent were addressed to Syrians. In addition, 16 percent called for Arab unity, 9 percent for "complete independence," and none mentioned the natural boundaries of Syria. During the next five months, on the other hand, only 5 percent were addressed to Arabs while 23 percent were addressed to Syrians,[22] none called for Arab unity, 45 percent mentioned the natural boundaries of Syria, and 68 percent included the demand for "complete independence" (*istiqlāl tāmm*).

According to French sources, the slogan "We demand complete independence," alone or accompanied by one or both of the provisions outlined in the above-cited leaflet ("for Syria in its natural boundaries," "no protection, no tutelage, no mandate") had, by the time of the arrival of the King-Crane Commission in Damascus in the summer of 1919, achieved a ubiquity in nationalist leaflets, graffiti, and broadsheets that had no parallel during the Faysali period.[23] This occurred in spite of the fact that the slogan included pronouncements on two subjects—the nature of independence and the delineation of the boundaries of the nation—that had been the focus of contentious debate both during the war and for the first months of the post-Ottoman period. It also occurred without the assistance

22. Twenty-three percent were addressed to citizens, countrymen, and so on, while the remainder contained no salutation.

23. MAE L:SL/vol. 15/340/92–95, Picot to Pichon, 21 July 1919.

of the popular committees—the principal institutional proponent of the slogan—whose formation was still several months in the future.

While the rapid spread of the slogan encumbers the recovery of its origins and history, it does not entirely frustrate it. To the contrary, the genealogy of the slogan can still be determined in two ways. First, the slogan contains elements—the use of the words *istiqlāl tāmm* to denote complete independence and the phrase *lā ḥimāya, lā wiṣāya, wa lā intidāb* to express the absolute repudiation of entente control—that are so distinctive that they can be traced back to their initial articulation with some precision. Second, because the slogan was commonly embedded within or accompanied other texts, its constituent words and phrases were often expressly defined. This makes it possible to link those words and phrases to specific nationalist organizations, organizers, or political initiatives. For example, the enumeration of a particular set of geographic references in the above-cited leaflet connects the slogan with earlier efforts to determine the outer reaches of the national community. Overall, then, it is possible to reconstruct the history of the demand for "complete independence for Syria . . ." as follows:

As discussed in the preceding chapters, the Arab Revolt and its supporters represented one among several groups that composed the Syrian/Arab nationalist movement during World War I. In point of fact, support for the Arab Revolt among a large faction of the politically active Syrian exile community in Egypt, for example, was grudging at best. This faction questioned the motivation that drove both the British and the sharifians to conclude their alliance, doubted the ability of the Meccans to guide a modern nationalist movement, and/or feared that linking the movement to the proponents of an Arab or Hashemite caliphate would alienate the Christian population of Lebanon and Syria. "There is no doubt a very real fear amongst Syrians of finding themselves under a government in which [the] patriarchalism of Mecca is predominant," Gilbert Clayton, the chief political officer attached to the British army wrote to Sir Mark Sykes of the War Office.

> They realize that reactionary principles from which [the] Sharif of Mecca cannot break loose are incompatible with progress on modern lines. Increased touch between Syrian intellectuals both Christian and Moslem and Mecca accentuates rather than diminishes this feeling by disclosing [the] ineptitude and inertia of [the] Sharifian government.[24]

24. FO 371/3054/227658, Clayton to Sykes, 28 November 1917.

In addition, the unique status of Syrian exiles in Egypt may have contributed to their notion of themselves as distinctly Syrian and, as a result, may have dissuaded many of their number from supporting the Arab Revolt and the promise of "Arab" independence. While many exiles held privileged positions in Egyptian society, they nevertheless remained unassimilated. They were also politically isolated: because the Egyptian experience of occupation by a European power forced native nationalists to confront problems that differed from those challenging nationalists in other parts of the Ottoman Empire, the Egyptian nationalist movement evolved separately from the national movements emerging to the north and, for the most part, remained indifferent to appeals to a common Arab identity. Excluded from Egyptian nationalist politics and regarded with suspicion by their Egyptian counterparts for their "Syrianness," many Syrian nationalist exiles thus turned attribution into communal self-definition.[25]

Direct evidence pointing to entente duplicity further fueled the misgivings the nationalist exiles felt toward the Arab Revolt. In early 1918, the newly installed Bolshevik government in Russia published the texts of the secret agreements concluded by the entente powers. Likewise, the text of the Balfour Declaration, which had been publicly issued and announced in the *Times* (London), was widely known.[26] In response to these revelations, Syrian nationalist activists in Egypt issued the "Declaration of the Seven" and organized the Syrian Union from, among others, the ranks of the declaration's signatories and remnants of the Ottoman Administrative Decentralization Party.[27]

In an article published in June 1919 in the Egyptian periodical *al-Manār,* Rashid Rida described the debate over program that raged among the founders of the union.[28] The nationalist exiles differed on several interconnected issues, including the boundaries of the nation for which the exiles should organize and the future relationship between Syria and the rest of the Arab world, particularly the Hijaz. Britain's equivocation about

25. See Thomas Philipp, *The Syrians in Egypt, 1725–1975,* 114.
26. See Rashīd Riḍā, *Mukhtārāt siyāsiyya min majallat "al-Manār,"* 241; Hurewitz, *Middle East and North Africa,* 2:102, 110; Fromkin, *A Peace to End All Peace,* 297–299.
27. Founding members included Rafiq al-ʿAzm, Khalid al-Hakim, Wahba ʿIssa, Michel Lutfallah, Kamil al-Qassab, Rashid Rida, Salim Sarkis, ʿAbd al-Rahman Shahbandar, Iskandar ʿAmmun, Haqqi al-ʿAzm, and Muhibb al-Din al-Khatib. Darwaza, *Mudhakkarāt,* 130–131; Zeine, *Struggle for Arab Independence,* 22; FO 371/4178/16051, 10 January 1919.
28. See Riḍā, *Mukhtārāt siyāsiyya,* 245–247.

its postwar plans, however, triggered the most divisive debates among the unionists. For example, the British reply to the "Declaration of the Seven" was a masterpiece of ambiguity: while the British pledged "complete and sovereign independence" for those "areas in Arabia which were free and independent before the war" and "areas emancipated from Turkish control by the action of the Arabs themselves during the present war," they were vague about their plans for other territories.[29] Uncertain about British intentions and thus unable to formulate a coherent reply, the Syrian Union divided into two factions, the so-called *iḥtilāliyyūn* and the *istiqlāliyyūn.* The former group comprised those who were willing to support the temporary occupation of Syria by one of the entente powers in exchange for financial and technical assistance—the "civilizing" mission later enunciated in Article 22 of the Covenant of the League of Nations. In contrast, the *istiqlāliyyūn* demanded immediate (*ḥālī*) and complete (*tāmm, nājiz*) independence for Syria.[30]

The program upon which the union eventually settled reveals the outcome of the struggle between the two factions. As in the leaflet cited above, article one of the program of the Syrian Union defines Syria as an integral unit that lies between the Taurus Mountains in the north, the Khabur and Euphrates rivers in the east, the Arabian desert, Mada'in Salih, and the Red Sea in the south, and the line that connects the towns of Aqaba and Rafah with the Mediterranean Sea in the west. According to article two, "Syria will enjoy complete independence [*istiqlāl tāmm*]" guaranteed by the League of Nations. Finally, article fourteen proclaims, "in the case that the Arab nation comes to realize its national unity, Syria will join this union only on the condition that this undermines neither Syrian national unity nor the form of the Syrian government in any manner."[31]

At least two of the founders of the Syrian Union left records of the positions they had adopted during the discussions about the program. While Rashid Rida hints that he agreed with those who sought to curtail the role

29. In those territories that, having been under Ottoman authority, were occupied by entente forces during the war, the declaration pledged that "the future government . . . should be based upon the principle of consent of the governed"; in those areas "still under Turkish control, . . . it is the wish and desire of His Majesty's Government that the oppressed peoples of these areas should obtain their freedom and independence . . . " See Hurewitz, *Middle East and North Africa,* 2:111–112.

30. Riḍā, *Mukhtārāt siyāsiyya,* 247.

31. Most of the remaining articles deal with issues of local government, minority rights, and so on. FO 371/4178/16051, "Program of the Syrian Union" (in Arabic and French), 10 January 1919.

of the entente powers in postwar Arab affairs and that he harbored suspicions about the sharifians and about the sharifian-British connection, he professes to have initially opposed severing the ties directly binding Syria with the Hijaz and Iraq. What persuaded him to compromise, he wrote, was his realization that a choice had to be made between Syrian Christian participation in the Syrian Union (several Christians were among the founders of the organization) and Syrian integration into a state that included the Hijaz. Defending his willingness to compromise, he maintains that he concluded that a loose confederation of Arab territories—the solution endorsed by the union—would not hinder Syria and the Hijaz from providing each other with assistance in their common struggle for independence.[32]

Muhibb al-Din al-Khatib, on the other hand, refused to consider relinquishing his hostile stance toward the sharifians and Syrian/Hijazi integration. In an interview conducted by the French representative to Mecca in the spring of 1919, al-Khatib equated the Syrian struggle against sharifian pretensions with its struggle against an entente mandate:

> Syria must have, I promise, its natural boundaries and will be an independent Arab state, in every meaning of the word. We do not want to have any contact with the Hijazi element, and on this point I share entirely the opinion of my compatriots. Syrians now must unite their efforts and struggle for a single purpose: the independence of their homeland. They must equally struggle, on the one hand, against the claims of certain nations who want to place Syria under their tutelage, and, on the other hand, against the active desire of the king, who is searching for a way to apply the Qur'an as the law of Syria. If the king persists in his idea, we will be finished, [and we will] detach ourselves entirely from him.[33]

The Syrian Union began circulating its program soon after it was ratified. Nevertheless, deciding the agenda for an organization of exiles is a far cry from winning widespread support in Syria for that agenda. As described above, not only did the Arab government initially promote a program that was very different from that endorsed by the Syrian Union—the program for *Arab* unity enunciated by Amir Faysal at the Paris peace conference on 29 January and 6 February 1919[34]—but the government had

32. Riḍā, *Mukhtārāt siyāsiyya,* 247.

33. AD 2326/dossier du Hedjaz, "Extraits de la lettre 94M de M. Bensaci, envoyé du gouvernement de la république à la Mecque," 16 May 1919.

34. See, inter alia, Ḥasan al-Ḥakīm, *al-Wathā'iq al-tārīkhiyya al-muta'alliqa bil-qaḍiyya al-sūriyya fī al-'ahdayn al-'arabī al-fayṣalī wal-intidābī al-faransī, 1915–1946,* 43–44; Antonius, *Arab Awakening,* 286–287.

access to British financial resources to assist in its dissemination. In contrast, the British authorities in Egypt, aware of the program of the Syrian Union and of the group's plans for organizing in Syria, attempted to undermine its activities by censoring communications between Egypt and Syria and by delaying the repatriation of many politically active exiles.[35] How, then, did the program of the Syrian Union come so swiftly to dominate the political debate in Faysali Syria?

The expressly worded slogan calling for complete independence (*istiqlāl tāmm*) for Syria within its natural boundaries won widespread support in Syria for three reasons. First, in spite of measures taken by the British to quarantine both Syrian Union activists and propaganda, the union was nevertheless able to launch what proved to be an effective organizing campaign for its program in Syria. While evidence detailing the activities of those Syrian Union organizers who successfully entered Syria is sketchy, it does indicate that the exiles regarded the dissemination of the program of the union as a matter of urgency and that they were assisted in their efforts by activists who had remained in Syria during the war years. According to Rashid Rida, even before the formal creation of the union a cadre of organizers, including officers of the Arab army [and al-Qassab and al-Khatib?], traveled between Egypt, the Hijaz, and Syria and "instructed others to keep the word going."

> As a result, many among the Syrian population came to know the truth, and their most fervent hope was for complete independence. [They directed] their pessimism and their ambivalence to the connection between Syria and the Arab government, so that no one who came to know the truth was in support of the connection.[36]

At the close of the war, the Syrian Union planned to deploy a number of organizers to Syria: Khalid al-Hakim to Homs and Hama; Rashid Rida to Latakia and Tripoli; Hasan Khalid to Aleppo and Dayr al-Zur; Mukhtar al-Sulh to Beirut; Hasan Hamada to the Hawran; Rafiq al-ʿAzm, Kamil al-Qassab, and ʿAbd al-Rahman Shahbandar to Damascus; and Wahba al-ʿIssa, Shibli al-Jamal, al-ʿAzm, and Shahbandar to Palestine. While this plan ultimately miscarried, other organizers did make it to Syria, including Michel Lutfallah and his brother Georges, who traveled under the pretext of organizing famine relief. Starting with 2,000 P.E. in seed money from

35. FO 882/24/85–90, Walrond to Cornwallis, 13 January 1919.
36. Riḍā, *Mukhtārāt siyāsiyya,* 245.

Georges, the Lutfallahs subsidized administrative, translation, and transcription activities in Syria, and reportedly spent large sums for telegrams soliciting assistance from Syrian émigrés in Europe and the Americas.[37] Among the materials disseminated by the brothers and their associates in Syria were items sent from Egypt by Iskandar ʿAmmun, a former vice president of the Ottoman Administrative Decentralization Party and one of the founders of the Syrian Union. In January 1919, for example, a French informant reported that ʿAmmun was shipping "several thousand" items to Syria, including a copy of a provocative report issued in 1915 by Etienne Flandin, a member of the French senatorial committee for the defense of French interests abroad. Because it included phrases such as "Syria would be a splendid colony for France" and "Can we abandon an invaluable means [i.e., Syria] to penetrate the lands that are at the heart of Islam?," the report ended up serving the interests of ʿAmmun and the union rather than those of the *parti colonial*.[38]

Once in Syria, organizers for the Syrian Union worked alongside resident nationalists who were unaffiliated with the union. According to a British report, one group of Damascus-based nationalists adopted as their own the call for independence for Syria within its natural boundaries and distributed propaganda that reproduced the precise boundaries delineated in the charter of the union. Coordinating their activities with their counterparts in Beirut, this group sent organizers to Aleppo, Homs, Hama, and Latakia to proselytize for their program. "Saayda [sic] and Nablus were being canvassed by agents who travel by donkey or cart," the report added, "and they are . . . working south into Palestine."[39]

In addition to direct Syrian Union organizing, the popularity of the slogan calling for complete independence for Syria within its natural boundaries might be attributed to the emotive power of its message. To be successful, the nationalist reinterpretation of history must have resonance with a population, and while nationalists have ample leeway in constructing their narratives, they cannot weave those narratives entirely from whole cloth. Ultimately, then, the demand for *Syrian* independence succeeded because Syrians found it compelling, and at least for the brief dura-

37. Ibid., 249; FO 882/24/85–90, Walrond to Cornwallis, 13 January 1919; MD 16N/3202/book 19/599, Feer to MAE, 23 April 1919; AD 2209/145, Cousse to Picot, 28 April 1919.
38. MAE L:SL/vol. 8/230, Cousse to HC, 14 January 1919.
39. FO 882/24/85–90, Walrond to Cornwallis, 13 January 1919.

tion of the Faysali period, most apparently found it more compelling than the pan-Arab vision initially advocated by the sharifians.

The notion of Syria as an integral unit can be traced as far back as the Middle Ages.[40] Although the Ottomans divided the territory into separate administrative units, thereby effacing Syria (within its natural boundaries) as a political marker, over the course of the Ottoman period Greater Syria continued to function as a socio-economic space, reinforced through, for example, market, migratory, and even—among elites—matrimonial practices. In times of crisis or famine, for example, peasants and tribesmen from the Hawran regularly migrated north to Damascus or west to Palestine, while under the same conditions Palestinian peasants and tribesmen migrated in the opposite direction. From the eighteenth century onward a regional division of labor (with attendant labor exchanges and crop specializations) integrated the area stretching from Aleppo in the north through Mt. Lebanon and Palestine in the south. Trade networks traversed the area, linking merchants from Beirut, Jaffa, Nablus, Damascus, and Aleppo. A rail system, completed in the last decade of the nineteenth century, connected coastal cities with cities in the interior and cities in the interior with their hinterlands, in the process creating what one scholar has called an "emergent national political economy."[41]

The economic and social linkages that bound the inhabitants of the region to one another, along with cultural habituation to the signifier "Syria," simultaneously inspired and authenticated the nationalist appropriation of terms like *Syria* and *Syrian-Arab*. By the turn of the century, the terms began to appear in a variety of nationalist texts, including the declaration of the 1913 Arab Congress in Paris (at which Syrians from the Ottoman Administrative Decentralization Party—including, among others, Iskandar ʿAmmun—played a critical role) and the program of the Syrian Union.[42]

40. See Dominique Chevallier, "Consciences syriennes et représentations cartographiques à la fin du XIXe siècle et au début du XXe siècle," 2.

41. L. S. Schilcher, "The Impact of the Railways on the Grain Trade of Southern Syria, 1890–1925." See also Doumani, *Rediscovering Palestine*, 56, 74–76; Faruk Tabak, "Agrarian Fluctuations and Modes of Labor Control in the Western Arc of the Fertile Crescent, *c.* 1700–1850," 146–152; Gad G. Gilbar, "Changing Patterns of Economic Ties: The Syrian and Iraqi Provinces in the 18th and 19th Centuries."

42. See, inter alia, Muḥibb al-Dīn al-Khaṭīb, *al-Muʾtamar al-ʿarabī al-awwal;* Antonius, *Arab Awakening*, 115; Ahmed Turabein, "ʿAbd al-Hamid al-Zahrawi: The Career and Thought of an Arab Nationalist," 102; James Jankowski, "Egypt and Early Arab Nationalism, 1908–1922," 246; Chevallier, "Consciences syriennes," 4.

It is not being argued here that the idea of Syria within its natural boundaries had a more legitimate claim to popular sentiment than other national representations or that such sentiment was primordial or immutable or even exclusive. Nor is it being argued that popular support for the integrity of Syria within its natural boundaries resulted inevitably from the aforementioned processes of reinforcement. Rather, the argument here is that the concept of Syria as a distinct geographic unit was readily accessible during this period, and that contingent political events and the organizing efforts of activists associated with the Syrian Union and the popular committees—organizing efforts that included the dissemination of a comprehensive discursive field that imbued "Syria within its natural boundaries" with new meaning and distinction—accorded this national representation primacy within the nationalist tendency.

The pervasiveness of the slogan demanding complete independence for Syria within its natural boundaries might finally be attributed, ironically, to the activities of Amir Faysal and the Arab government. The political position of the amir at the close of the war was hardly enviable. On the one hand, the organizing of Syrian Union activists and their confederates in Syria and the popular response to their program threatened to create rifts within the nationalist tendency that the amir feared would weaken his position both at home and abroad. On the other hand, a variety of external factors—British vacillations, French ambitions in Syria and British ambitions in Iraq and Palestine, public and secret arrangements made between the two European governments, and constraints imposed by his ambiguous status at the conference—limited the options available to the amir for containing domestic disaffection. As a result, Faysal had to walk a tightrope, voicing agreement with popular sentiment for the sake of unifying the national movement or allaying doubts about his independence and sincerity while simultaneously engaging in face-saving and practicable diplomacy. Not surprisingly, he met the challenge with an approach that mixed equivocation, compromise, and obfuscation.[43]

43. According to a report filed by Major Kinahan Cornwallis, British liaison officer, on the eve of the arrival of the King-Crane Commission in Syria, "Feisal has taken the whole of the political campaign into his own hands, and has already sent instructions to all parts of the country. These instructions will be communicated to the people by Government officials, who, no doubt, will be used for political purposes much more openly than before. The people have been told to ask for complete independence for Syria, and, at the same time, to express a hope that it will be granted to other Arab countries. By this compromise Feisal has reconciled the 'Ittihad es-Suri,' which thinks only of Syria, with the pan-Arab empire enthusiasts

Ostensibly, Faysal adopted the call for "complete independence" as his own months before he accepted a compromise formula on the issue of Arab unity. While the popularity of the expression "complete independence" (*istiqlāl tāmm*) certainly contributed to his sanctioning its use and aligning himself with its advocates, two other factors influenced his decision to embrace the slogan: his initial faith in the British and their wartime commitments to his father, and his desire to establish his nationalist credentials by portraying the realization of "complete independence" as a legacy exclusively attributable to the Arab Revolt. Consequently, not only did the amir announce in his first declaration to the Syrian people (5 October 1918) the formation of an "Arab constitutional government in Syria [that is] completely independent" (*mustaqilla istiqlālān muṭlaqān lā shā'iba fīhi*), but during the first year of his government—even after he had decided to back a British mandate for Syria—he endorsed the dissemination of the slogan.[44]

Thus encouraged, government on all levels, as well as allied political organizations, adopted and spread the call for "complete independence." Shortly before Faysal's first departure for Europe in November 1918, for example, the French liaison officer in Damascus complained to his superiors that ʿAbd al-Qadir al-Muzaffar of the Arab Club of Damascus, with the complicity of the amir, organized daily demonstrations in honor of "the liberator of Syria and champion of complete Arab independence without supervision."[45] In April 1919, less than a week after the appointment of Henry Churchill King and Charles R. Crane to lead the interallied commission of inquiry, another French diplomat stationed in the capital reported that gangs of youths, possibly connected to the Arab Club, were painting "Complete Arab Independence" on walls throughout the city, and merchants "were advised to make signs imprinted with the same slogan and place them in their shop windows."[46] The following month, the municipal government of Damascus instructed the guilds that were to partic-

represented in the 'Istiklal el-Arabi.'" FO 371/4181/89850/24, Clayton to Curzon: "Report by British Liaison Officer (Cornwallis) on Political Situation in Arabia," 17 June 1919.

44. Ḥasan al-Ḥakīm, *al-Wathā'iq al-tārīkhiyya*, 35; AD 2324/379, Cousse to HC, 16 June 1919; FO 371/4181/89850/24, Clayton to Curzon, "Report by British Liaison Officer (Cornwallis) on Political Situation in Arabia," 17 June 1919. See also comments by Cornwallis in Sulaymān Mūsā, *al-Murāsalāt al-tārīkhiyya*, 2:78.

45. MAE L:SL/vol. 5/58–61, Mercier to HC, 20 November 1918.

46. MAE L:SL/vol. 12/32–38, Cousse to HC, 6 April 1919.

ipate in an Arab government-sanctioned demonstration to welcome Faysal home after his sojourn in Europe to paint or embroider signs reading, "Long live Arab independence," and to chant, "Long live the amir and complete Arab independence."[47] Little wonder, then, that shortly thereafter, when Faysal, chastened by events in Paris, solicited the help of Muhammad Fawzi al-ʿAzm in convincing the Syrian people of the need for accepting a British mandate, the old man placed the blame for stirring up popular sentiment for "complete independence" squarely on Faysal's shoulders.[48]

Not surprisingly, considering the difficult position in which Faysal had been placed, the concept of "complete independence" accommodated greater flexibility for the amir than it did for either Syrian Union activists or for most of the rest of the population. On the day the French representative in Damascus wrote of demonstrations honoring "the liberator of Syria and champion of complete Arab independence without supervision," for example, the amir sent a telegram to his father in which he reconciled "complete independence" with what he called a "definitive link" (*irtibāṭ nihāʾī*) with the British:

> I shall authorize a definitive alliance [*al-taḥāluf al-nihāʾī*] between England and the Arabs on the condition that no foreign power but England have relations with religious minorities. In exchange for this we shall grant the English the [right to] use everything of benefit to them. We shall request from [England] everything we lack in the way of administrators, advisers, money, and weapons on the condition that we do not forfeit one iota of our independence, and that we be a nation that rules itself by itself. Then I shall grant whatever they wish, on any terms they find acceptable.[49]

Underlying Faysal's generous offer that, in effect, would have placed the Arabs under a British protectorate, was the fear of French ambitions in the Middle East and the assumption that British and Arab interests converged to prevent the realization of those ambitions:

> I refused all help offered to me from France because I saw their desire to occupy the country. The link with the British must be a definitive link, for the Arabs have no life except through their integrity and love. I do not know if they do what they do from expedience or sincerity. Never-

47. MAE L:AH/vol. 4/237–238, Picot to Pichon, 25 May 1919.
48. al-ʿAẓm, *Mudhakkarāt*, 96.
49. Mūsā, *al-Murāsalāt al-tārīkhiyya*, 1:244–245.

theless, we will abide by their policy because our interest is connected to theirs.

By means of this formula—"complete independence" under a virtual protectorate—Faysal hoped to balance the demands of his constituents at home with the conditions imposed by the entente powers at the bargaining table in Paris.

Entente recognition of "complete independence" was not the only demand Faysal presented to the assembled diplomats. In his first address to the conference, delivered on 29 January 1919, for example, Faysal offered a further elaboration of his views, declaring that, on behalf of his father and as leader of the Arab Revolt, he sought the recognition of the independence of all Arabic-speakers in Asia from the Alexandretta-Diyarbakr line in the north to the Indian Ocean in the south, excluding the Hijaz and Aden.[50] One week later, Faysal reiterated these demands and, apparently trusting in promises made by the entente powers in the "Declaration to the Seven" and in the Anglo-French Declaration of 7 November 1918, as well as in Woodrow Wilson's assertion that self-determination was "an imperative principle of action which statesmen will henceforth ignore at their peril,"[51] proposed the formation of a commission that would ascertain the will of the Arab inhabitants of the former Ottoman Empire.

Faysal's call for entente recognition of an Arab nation based on the principle of self-determination flew in the face of diplomatic realities. To begin with, Faysal's role at the conference was itself disputed, and in the wake of French resistance to his claim to represent all Arabs, the amir's status was reduced to that of the representative of the king of the Hijaz. Furthermore, not only was the French government unwilling to abandon the principles underlying the Sykes-Picot Agreement, but shortly after the entente representatives to the conference had convened in Paris, they accepted in principle the establishment of the mandates system. By the spring of 1919, with other options foreclosed, the amir left the conference and returned to Damascus, resigned to making the best of a bad situation by abandoning both his insistence on the recognition of a single Arab nation and his resistance to the imposition of a mandate.[52]

50. Ḥasan al-Ḥakīm, *al-Wathā'iq al-tārīkhiyya,* 43–44.
51. Ray Stannard Baker and William E. Dodd, eds., *Public Papers of Woodrow Wilson,* 5:180.
52. al-ʿAẓm, *Mudhakkarāt,* 95; Antonius, *Arab Awakening,* 286; Stephen Hemsley Longrigg, *Syria and Lebanon under French Mandate,* 71; Russell, *First Modern Arab State,* 36. According to Antonius, Faysal knew of the discussions be-

The shift in Faysal's position with regard to the establishment of an Arab state that incorporated Syria can be seen by comparing two statements made by the amir before and after his first trip to Europe. A month after he had entered Damascus in October 1918, Faysal issued a statement that addressed Syrian fears about Hijazi domination of a pan-Arab state:

> The Arabs are not a homogeneous people with respect to region. The Aleppan differs from the Hijazi and the Syrian differs from the Yemeni. My father divided the country into regions. In each region special laws that correspond to the conditions and advancement of the local population will be applied.[53]

After his sojourn in Paris, Faysal spoke of a different type of "decentralized" Arab nation, one that more closely approximated the proposals advocated by the Syrian Union and the author of the above-cited leaflet. One speech, reprinted in part in *al-ʿĀṣima* and widely circulated in that form, stated

> Syria, the Hijaz, and Iraq are divisions of [the] Arab [nation], and all the inhabitants therein want their independence. Najd and other areas which are on an equal footing with the Hijaz are subject to the Hijaz; as for Syria, it is necessary that it be independent within its natural boundaries. The same with Iraq, and it is necessary to establish in Iraq a government that is separate from the government of Syria and the rest of the Arab lands.[54]

To ensure that the meaning of Faysal's statement was clear to its readers, the newspaper appended, "From this decree it appears that His Highness the amir approved the founding of independent governments in Syria and Iraq united with an independent Hijaz in foreign policy and domestic economic policy." In June of 1919, the Arab government distributed tracts throughout Damascus and other cities of the eastern zone that not only reiterated the amir's call for "complete independence for Syria within its nat-

---

tween France and Britain that led to the 20 March 1919 revision of the Sykes-Picot Agreement. The entente representatives approved the Charter of the League of Nations, which authorized the mandates system, on 28 April 1919, shortly after Faysal departed for Syria.

53. Abū Khaldūn Sātiʿ al-Ḥuṣrī, *Yawm Maysalūn*, 198.

54. *al-ʿĀṣima*, 12 May 1919, 1–2. Slightly different renderings of the same speech exist in the following: Sulṭān, *Tārīkh Sūriyya 1918–1920*, 431–442; AD 2343, "Annexe au journal 'Hermon' 35," 7 May 1919; FO 371/4181/89850/24, Clayton to Curzon: "Report by British Liaison Officer (Cornwallis) on Political Situation in Arabia," 17 May 1919.

ural boundaries" but expressed his "hope for the independence of other territories."[55]

Similarly, in the spring of 1919, shifting diplomatic circumstances, coupled with the persistent fear of France, prompted Faysal to advocate "complete independence for Syria" under a British mandate.[56] Months before, at the peace conference, Woodrow Wilson had advocated an international commission to assist the entente powers in determining the future of Syria. However, the commission as established differed in two significant ways from the commission embraced by Faysal. First, neither France nor Britain participated in the activities of the commission, thus rendering the validity of its findings uncertain. In addition, rather than delegating the commission to determine whether or not the mandates system should be applied in Syria, Wilson charged the commission with "elucidat[ing] the state of opinion and the soil to be worked on by any mandatory." Once the commissioners had been chosen, Wilson's instructions were even more blunt. "It is the purpose of the Conference," he wrote, "to separate from the Turkish Empire certain areas comprising, for example, Palestine and Syria, Mesopotamia, Armenia, Cilicia, and perhaps additional areas in Asia Minor, and to put the development of their people under the guidance of Governments which are to act as Mandatories of the League of Nations."[57] By accepting the role of the commission and the principle of a mandates system, the Arab government was easily put on the defensive by those who, while willing to accept advisers from abroad, portrayed the mandates system as little more than a fig leaf behind which the European powers concealed imperialist ambitions. As the poet Khayr al-Din al-Zirikli wrote at the time,

55. AD 2324/379, Cousse to HC, 16 June 1919; FO 371/4181/89850/24, Clayton to Curzon, "Report by British Liaison Officer (Cornwallis) on Political Situation in Arabia," 17 June 1919.

56. See, inter alia, al-ʿAẓm, *Mudhakkarāt*, 96; Yūsuf al-Ḥakīm, *Dhikrayāt*, 3:80; Russell, *First Modern Arab State*, 86–87. According to a British report, Michel Lutfallah claimed that Faysal was prepared to accept not only a British mandate but "to progress via Mandate to the status of a self-governing dominion within the British Empire." The same report also states that Lutfallah told a British representative that the Syrian Union was also willing to accept autonomy within the British Empire, but was opposed for tactical reasons to the imposition of a mandate. FO 371/4182/125032/CPO, "Report on a conversation in Cairo with Michel Bey Lotfullah on his return from Syria August 5th 1919."

57. Albert H. Lybyer Papers (R.S. 15/13/22), University of Illinois at Urbana-Champaign, "Instructions for Commissioners from the Peace Conference," 25 March 1919. See also "Condensation of Instructions," 1 May 1919; "Supplementary Instructions," 1 May 1919, also contained among the Lybyer Papers.

The enemy have cloaked themselves in hypocrisy, and enfolded it in rancor and hatred.
They took an oath of loyalty and they were disloyal, and from among them you have trusted some as allies who were treacherous. . . .
What is amiss with those who have carried the scales of guidance on their arms, that they have failed to discern the truth?
If they do not help those who need help and bring success to those who deserve it, then let them break the scales.[58]

Or, in the words of the leaflet reproduced above, "Protection and mandate are synonyms, and are the precursors to annexation."

Faysal's willingness to accept a British mandate polarized the nationalist movement. As described in the previous section, the administrative committee of al-Fatat split into three groups, with the so-called *rāfiḍūn* rejecting supervision by any mandatory. According to one account, Kamil al-Qassab, perhaps the most vocal of the *rāfiḍūn,* appended the words "no protection, no tutelage, no mandate" (*lā ḥimāya, lā wiṣāya, wa lā intidāb*) to the slogan calling for "complete independence for Syria within its natural boundaries" to prevent any further slippage in the meaning of "complete independence."[59] On the eve of the arrival of the commission, the Arab government deemed demonstrations held in Damascus to protest Faysal's position so dangerous that it banned further public gatherings and ordered the placement of machine-gun nests on the streets.[60]

In the wake of this crisis, Faysal backed away from his advocacy of a British mandate, first testifying in favor of a "limited mandate" before the King-Crane Commission, then renouncing the idea altogether at a banquet organized by Michel Lutfallah for that purpose.[61] In the meantime, however, the Syrian General Congress had formulated a program to present to the commission that, in fact, integrated many of the claims and much of the language that had been introduced into the nationalist debate by the Syrian

58. Khayr al-Dīn al-Ziriklī, *Dīwān al-Ziriklī: al-Aʿmāl al-shiʿriyya al-kāmila,* 24–25.

59. al-Amīn, *Dhikrayāt,* 27. The dissemination of the slogan was rapid: it appears in approximately 40 percent of the sample leaflets dated within three months of its introduction.

60. *al-ʿĀṣima,* 24 July 1919, 5; FO 371/4182/125032/CPO, "Report on a conversation in Cairo with Michel Bey Lotfullah on his return from Syria August 5th 1919." The report attributes the demonstrations to the Arab Independence Party.

61. Russell, *First Modern Arab State,* 90; FO 371/4182/125032/CPO, "Report on a conversation in Cairo with Michel Bey Lotfullah on his return from Syria August 5th 1919."

Union. Since, as can be determined from the minutes of its deliberations and from its resolutions, the congress was more reactive than active, the Damascus Program provides a useful (although, of course, imprecise) barometer by which to gauge public opinion in Syria. The program is particularly telling because the range of opinion represented in the congress extended beyond the nationalist field: the nonnationalist Muhammad Fawzi al-ʿAzm, for example, was not only the dean of the Damascus delegation, but reportedly played a significant role in drafting and forcing passage of the program.[62]

The Damascus Program denied the applicability of Article 22 of the Charter of the League of Nations to Syria by stating that "the Arab people living in the Syrian nation are a people that is no less advanced intellectually than other advanced peoples . . . [such as] the Serbs, Greeks, and Romanians at the beginning of their independence." In addition, it included the following demands: complete independence (*al-tāmm al-nājiz*) for Syria, defined as the territory bounded in the north by the Taurus Mountains, in the south by the Rafah-Aqaba line (by way of al-Jawf), in the east by the Euphrates and Khabur rivers and a line stretching from Albukamal to al-Jawf, and in the west by the Mediterranean Sea; independence "without protection or tutelage" (*bidūn ḥimāya wa lā wiṣāya*); a "broadly decentralized" government in Syria, with Amir Faysal as king; nonrecognition of the claims of both the French and the Zionists; and complete independence (*istiqlāl tāmm*) for Iraq. Finally, the document recommended that if the entente powers insisted on furnishing assistance to Syria, Syria would accept technical and economic assistance from the United States on the condition that such aid did not impinge on the "complete political independence" (*istiqlāl siyāsī tāmm*) and unity of Syria and that it did not continue for more than twenty years. If the United States proved unable to furnish such assistance, Syria would accept it from Great Britain, subject to the same conditions.[63]

Thus, although hailed by one historian as "a skillful blend of views,"[64] the program that Antonius calls with typical embellishment "the authoritative statement of the Arab attitude towards the issues of the day"[65] in fact demonstrates the extent to which the center of the nationalist debate had

62. al-ʿAẓm, *Mudhakkarāt,* 95–97.
63. For the complete text of the Damascus Program, see Ḥasan al-Ḥakīm, *al-Wathā'iq al-tārīkhiyya,* 85–88.
64. Russell, *First Modern Arab State,* 89.
65. Antonius, *Arab Awakening,* 293

already shifted and narrowed during the year that preceded the formation of the popular committees.

THE ARAB REVOLT, SYRIAN REVOLUTIONARIES, AND "THE MARTYRS"

Faysal's first declaration to the Syrian people, cited above, contains a peculiar locution: by announcing that "an Arab constitutional government [that is] completely independent has been formed in Syria," Faysal was, in effect, asserting that with the entry of the Arab army into Damascus, the struggle to realize Arab independence had come to an end. The amir premised his pronouncement on the pledges contained within the "Declaration to the Seven," in which the British promised "complete and sovereign independence" to the inhabitants of territories liberated by "the action of the Arabs themselves." It was Faysal's stated contention—whether accurate or not—that by being the first to enter Damascus, "the Arabs" had met the conditions for independence stipulated in the document.[66] Thus, as Faysal declared in his 29 January 1919 speech at the Paris peace conference, the only task that remained for the entente representatives was the official recognition of a fait accompli.

Faysal's adherence to the terms of the "Declaration to the Seven" at the conference was a logical diplomatic strategy, considering the lengths to which the British had gone to ensure that the Arab army received credit for entering Damascus before any other military force[67] and the amir's belief, described above, that when it came to Arab-British relations, "our interest is connected to theirs." But Faysal's claims cannot be entirely attributed to the exigencies of diplomacy, for the amir and his allies continued to insist to Arab audiences that "complete independence" had been won even after it had become apparent that the entente powers, including Britain, thought otherwise.[68] For Faysal and his supporters both inside and outside the government, maintaining the fiction that Arab independence had been attained on 1 October 1918 was of critical importance, for by so doing they en-

66. For an overview of the controversy about the liberation of Damascus, see Kedourie, "The Capture of Damascus, 1 October 1918."

67. Ibid., 51.

68. Such a claim was made in the sermons provided by the Arab government for delivery in the mosques of Damascus on 11 and 18 April 1919. Interestingly, the sermons interspersed the admonition to Syrians to "safeguard your independence" with the contradictory charge to "demand and persevere in your demand for independence." AD 2343/286, Cousse to HC, 24 April 1919 (Arabic and French).

hanced the stature of the military campaign that had fought to win that independence. The Arab Revolt against Ottoman rule—the sole foundation upon which the sharifians based their claim to preeminence within the nationalist tendency and their right to rule in Damascus—thus became the axial symbol of sharifian legitimacy.

With so much depending on the widespread recognition of and approbation for the symbol among the population, the Arab government and its allies engaged in an energetic campaign to disseminate the legend of the Arab Revolt and its heroes throughout Syria. "If the devoted Syrian claims to be grateful, he will prove it by his respect for the liberator of the Syrians from the Turkish yoke," proclaimed a sign surreptitiously hung on the gates of a park in Beirut. "This liberator is our beloved Amir Faysal. The man of honor cannot but wish for his well-being."[69] Thabit ʿAbd al-Nur, one of the original founders of the Literary Society in Istanbul, traveled from Aqaba to Amman distributing postcards depicting an unidentified sharifian officer (who closely resembled Amir Faysal) brandishing the sharifian flag. Two legends adorned the card: "Greetings from the *fidāʾiyyīn* [those who sacrifice themselves] to the liberated Arabs" and "It [the flag] waves in his hand."[70] In Tulkarm (Palestine), a local nationalist club staged a benefit production of a play, *The Battle of Tafila,* in which club members reenacted the battle between the Arab army led by Amir Zayd and the Turks.[71] The government even established a holiday, *ʿīd al-thawra* (Day of the Revolt) in April 1920 to commemorate the exploits of the Arab army and—a year and a half after the establishment of the Arab government—to celebrate "the completion of the fourth year of the revolt."[72]

British military leaders in Syria, concerned about both internal and external challenges to sharifian rule, also encouraged the propagation of the myth of the Arab Revolt. On the eve of Faysal's first trip to Europe, the French liaison officer in Damascus telegraphed his superiors criticizing the British for spreading propaganda "to establish the legend of the liberation of all the Arab territories, including Palestine and Syria, by the army of Amir Faysal alone." He bemoaned the fact that the "myth" of the Arab Revolt was being fed by self-serving newspaper interviews given by leaders

69. AD 2372/297/bureau b., 13 March 1919.
70. MAE L:SL/vol. 3/3, Durieux (délégué du haut commissariat de France à Jerusalem) to capt. Coulandre (Beirut), 28 October 1918.
71. *al-Kawkab,* 7 October 1919, 12.
72. *al-ʿĀṣima,* 29 April 1920, 4.

of the revolt, and that the publication of a telegram sent by the commander of the entente forces, General Sir Edmund Allenby, to Faysal lauding the latter's "brilliant victories" had spread the amir's fame as far as Europe.[73]

In one sense, the efforts of the Arab government and others were not inefficacious: all nationalist factions, even those that included individuals who had deliberately avoided participation in the Arab Revolt or had abandoned Sharif Husayn during the war because they loathed his policies or feared his foreign connections, felt compelled to pay homage to, or at least acknowledge, the Arab Revolt. In Palestine and Lebanon—territories that Britain and France had effectively detached from inland Syria and placed under direct control—the symbol of the revolt, and through it the elevation of Sharif Husayn and Amir Faysal to an iconic stature, often assumed connotations of anti-imperialism. When the French forbade *khuṭabāʾ* (preachers) in the coastal zone from delivering sermons in the name of Sharif Husayn during Friday prayers, for example, and in one case exiled the popular *khaṭīb* who disobeyed this ordinance, protests erupted in Beirut that spread throughout both zones.[74]

But the meaning of the Arab Revolt was more nuanced in the eastern zone where it was too closely associated with sharifian legitimation to connote mere anti-imperialism. Once again, this might be attributed to the effectiveness of Arab government propaganda: since the Arab government and allied associations furnished authorized exegeses of the revolt through oratory, strategically placed newspaper articles, and dramatic reenactments, the symbol mostly escaped autonomous and eclectic reinterpretation. Nevertheless, because reinterpretation of the symbol did occur—most often through its recontextualization in non- or anti-sharifian texts—the

73. MAE L:SL/vol. 5/58–61, Mercier to HC, 20 November 1918.

74. MD 7N4182/4, M. X. de Laforcarde to Pichon, 19 August 1919; MD 4H114/2, Toulat to Gouraud, 10 April 1920; MD 4H112/2b/215.

Translation of article from *al-Rāya:* "Manifestation de protestation contre les actes du gouvernement du littoral," 14 April 1920. The French eventually restored the shaykh, Muhammad al-Makkawi, to his position as *khaṭīb* of the Majidiyya Mosque. Interestingly, subsequent developments soured the shaykh on the amir. According to a French report, on 22 July 1920, immediately before the fall of Damascus, members of his congregation asked al-Makkawi if he intended to mention Faysal's name before his *khuṭba* (sermon). His reply included a phrase popularized by the popular committees when they warned of Faysal's willingness to reach a compromise with the entente powers: "God damn him, he's sold us [out]." The next day, the French surveyed the mosques of Beirut to determine whose name would be mentioned at the beginning of the sermons; Makkawi planned to mention no one at all. MD 4H60/1, "Bulletin quotidien," 24 July 1920.

evocation of the revolt was not confined to the discursive community that included the sharifians and their supporters.

Amir Faysal himself enunciated perhaps the most comprehensive elaboration offered by the sharifians of the meaning of the Arab Revolt in a speech delivered to Syrian notables on 5 May 1919. Because of the significance of the meeting—Faysal had called it so that those in attendance and, by proxy, those whom they represented, might authorize him to continue "direct[ing] the external and internal policies of the government"—the Arab government not only circulated Faysal's remarks widely (in one case granting a subvention to a newspaper to distribute complimentary copies of a special edition in which the speech was reprinted) but included in its transcription interjections of support for Faysal from the audience.[75]

Faysal's speech, fundamentally a vindication of sharifian claims, skillfully blended two themes. First, Faysal asserted that the Hijazis deserved the continued trust and fidelity of the Arabs because, by rebelling against Ottoman authority while "most notables" had remained quiescent or had accused them of treason, they alone had demonstrated a true understanding of international affairs. As a result of their prescience, the Hijazis in general and Sharif Husayn in particular had preserved at least a portion of the Ottoman Empire from inevitable defeat and dismemberment:

> My father rose in revolt during the great international conflict after he had seen that the Turks were being carried along by the German current and they were conveying the Ottoman nation to disaster. He saw that if the Arabs remained in the war with the Turks in alliance with the Germans they would end up in the same way. He saw that the Arab nation, which had wished for release from the yoke of despotism, was eager for a revival of its past history and hoping for an escape from the snares of its enemy.[76]

As a second theme, Faysal situated the Arab Revolt within the context of a broader Arab national movement that included Syrians. Although he conceded that Syrians were the first to formulate the doctrine of Arabism, he credited Hijazis and the Arab Revolt with translating inchoate ideas into action. The Arab Revolt was therefore the sine qua non of Arab independence, and as Arab deliverers, the sharifians merited a paramount place within the nationalist pantheon:

75. *al-ʿĀṣima* 24 (n.d.); AD 2343/"Annexe au journal 'Hermon' 35," 7 May 1919; FO 371/4181/89850/24, Clayton to Curzon, 17 June 1919.
76. Ḥasan al-Ḥakīm, *al-Wathāʾiq al-tārīkhiyya*, 50–51.

> There is no doubt that, first, my father, then materially, the Hijazis who participated, are responsible for the movement—that is, the Arab revolutionary movement. As for the Syrians, they are conceptually responsible because they inspired the Hijazis with the desire to launch the movement. Praise God, the glory that first belonged to the Hijazis is everyone's glory. Because this revolt was a nationalist revolt, we could not have made it without the support of the entire nation. . . .
>
> After I arrived in Damascus and met with those who advocated revolt, I returned to the Hijaz and told my father how they rose to the occasion and supported him. But for reasons you all know—the pressure the Turks put on them—circumstances did not permit the Syrians to support the Hijazis. Nevertheless, history will immortalize their acts and inscribe in golden letters the names of those Syrians who were martyred during this period. My father launched the revolt against the Turks without regard for the consequences to the Hijaz and the Hijazis. He was not certain of the outcome, for God does not reveal these things. The Turks, however, evacuated all Syria.

At the very moment that Faysal was engaged in his celebration of the Arab Revolt before select notables of Syria, however, a variety of nationalist groups distributed leaflets in the streets of Damascus that only infrequently and incidentally alluded either to the Arab Revolt or to the "Declaration to the Seven." In place of the Arab Revolt, the authors of these leaflets based their demand for Syrian independence on historical precedent and/or the right to self-determination. "Oh people: our fathers and forefathers had freed the country by shedding their blood and sacrificing their lives," read one leaflet. "Our fathers and forefathers were not colonized, but were free Arabs who loathed oppression and were contemptuous of enslavement."[77]

Government officials found perhaps an even greater reluctance to embrace the legend of the Arab Revolt among nationalists in Aleppo, where the allure of a myth that cast Hijazi protagonists against Ottoman oppressors ran afoul of the pronounced pro-Turkish sentiment. Visiting members of the Arab government acknowledged that Aleppans provided a particularly skeptical audience. When Faysal first traveled to the city in November 1918, for example, he attempted to address this skepticism by conceding that the location of Aleppo "at the tip of Arab territory" had distanced its inhabitants from the Arab Revolt and had made the "simpleminded"

77. These sentences come from one among a set of original leaflets in MAE L:SL/vol. 43, The sentiment is repeated in other leaflets.

among them predisposed to believe the anti-sharifian propaganda disseminated by the Ottomans.[78]

It should not be surprising, therefore, that in a speech celebrating the proclamation of independence and the coronation of Faysal as king of Syria, ʿAbd al-Rahman al-Kayyali, one-time president of the Arab Club of Aleppo and member of the local committee of national defense, made only brief allusion to the Arab Revolt. Instead, he focused on the collective suffering endured by Syrians throughout history, particularly during World War I, as the foundation for Syrian independence. For al-Kayyali, the struggle against the Ottomans was not a unique and defining event in Syrian history but was rather one episode in a broader conflict that had pitted the inhabitants of Syria—"the talisman of conquerors . . . [whose] soil became the graveyard for soldiers and the cause of their ruin"—against "pharaohs and Persians and caesars and Tatar sultans and Turks and French and British princes who found here their graves rather than the bridge to the East." As for Faysal, al-Kayyali credited the new king as a warrior—albeit "in the light of [the Syrians'] sun"—upon whom Syrians had chosen to bestow a throne not because of his leadership of the revolt but because they "believed him to be fit and qualified, constant in trust, loyalty, determination, energy, knowledge, of noble descent, and virtuous." Ironically inverting the Arab Revolt legend, al-Kayyali shifted the obligation for maintaining Syria's independence away from Faysal to the Syrians themselves, proclaiming, "we are his [Faysal's] soldiers, his sword, and his arm."[79]

Al-Kayyali's speech is but one example of Syrians appropriating a collectively borne responsibility for their own liberation. A similar act of appropriation is illustrated by the struggle between sharifians and non- or anti-sharifians to impart meaning to the words *thawra* (revolution) and *thāʾir/thuwwār* (revolutionary/revolutionaries). *Thawra* was the most common of several words (including *inqilāb* and *nahḍa*) that orators and journalists used to describe the Arab Revolt.[80] In his presentation of

78. al-Ḥuṣrī, *Yawm Maysalūn*, 196; Ghazzī, *Nahr al-dhahab fī tārīkh Ḥalab*, 656. See also ʿAli Rida al-Rikabi's farewell remarks to the inhabitants of Aleppo in Mardam Bek, *Dimashq wal-Quds fī al-ʿishrīnāt*, 59.

79. AD 2346/c1a, "Remembrance of Syrian Independence Day: A Collection of Speeches and Poems Delivered on the Occasion of Independence Day," collected and published by the Arab Club of Aleppo (in Arabic), n.d., 8–12.

80. For use of the word *inqilāb*, see, for example, the speech delivered by Khalil al-Sakakini before the Arab Club of Damascus and excerpted in *al-ʿĀṣima*, 22 August 1919, 4; for *nahḍa*, see speech of Wadi Effendi al-Bustani delivered before the Literary Society of Jerusalem and excerpted in *al-Kawkab*, 27 May 1919, 9.

5 May 1919, for example, Faysal himself used the terms *thawra, thuwwār, al-ḥaraka al-thawriyya* (the revolutionary movement), and so on, no less than nine times to describe the revolt or its participants. But even though the term was widely promoted through government channels, its meaning began to change as other groupings, including the popular committees, their journalist sympathizers, and bands of irregulars who were raiding into French and British occupied areas, arrogated it for themselves. By ensconcing their activities beneath the mantle of *thawra,* these groups and their supporters sought a legitimacy that their opponents hoped to deny them and that the acts of brigandage, raiding, and extortion that they frequently undertook or supported seemed to belie.

The expansion of the number of referents denoted by the term ran counter to sharifian attempts to assert that the Arab Revolt had been a unique event, and it thus worked to erode the symbolic underpinning of sharifian legitimacy, particularly in the context of widespread disillusionment with the sharifians for acquiescing first to a British mandate, then to the January 1920 Faysal-Clemenceau Agreement. For example, while the 13 January 1920 issue of *al-Difāʿ*, a publication associated with the popular committees, slyly raised doubts about the credibility of the amir in a front-page article entitled, "Did the Amir Agree with France on Its Mandate for Syria? Is It Possible?" ("We know, as does everyone else in the country, that His Highness Amir Faysal could not contract with the French government in our name on a matter for which we did not delegate him"), the newspaper lashed out at the French news agency Havas for calling "our revolutionaries [*thuwwār*], thieves [*luṣūṣ*]." Likewise, the newspaper consistently employed the terms *thāʾir/thuwwār* in news accounts about the activities of anti-French guerrillas.[81] As a result of such popularization, even the normally pro-sharifian Arab Independence Party adopted the

81. For example, the same issue of *al-Difāʿ* included the following:

Page 2. In an article entitled "How the Foreigners Portray the Actions of Our Revolutionaries," the newspaper used the word *thuwwārinā* (our revolutionaries).

Page 3. The article "On the Iskanderun Front" contained the following lines: "It appears that the blaze of revolution (*thawra*) has spread north and now engulfs all districts of the western zone. The news arrived yesterday notifying us that a band of revolutionaries [*thāʾirīn*] attacked a French convoy . . . "

Page 3. "On the Marjʿayun Front": "We learned that volunteers are still arriving from many areas on horseback and foot to join the revolutionaries [*thāʾirīn*] to water the soil of the fatherland with their blood."

In addition, the newspaper reprinted a story about Ramadan Shallash that originally appeared in *al-Kawkab,* 6 January 1920, under the title, "*al-Thāʾir al-jadīd*" ("The New Revolutionary"). *al-Difāʿ*, 13 January 1920.

nomenclature of the popular committees, calling the activities of the guerrilla bands "nothing but a people's revolution" (*thawrat al-shaʿb*).[82]

But the popular committees and their sympathizers did not limit their use of the term *thawra* to guerrilla activities aimed against the British and the French. In the aftermath of the Evacuation Crisis, as the outlines of entente plans for Syria began to emerge clearly, the committees employed the term to denote activities undertaken against those such as Amir Faysal, his government, and his supporters, who they felt were prepared to compromise the nation's interests from expediency or treachery. In November 1919, for example, the Higher National Committee distributed the following leaflet entitled "Treason and Outrage" in the streets of Damascus:

> Since our allies have betrayed us and mocked us, there is nothing left for us to do but to knock at the gate of revolution [*thawra*] from which fires will burn and flames climb to the sky. Citizens: Prepare for the revolution. Revolution, revolution if they betray us. Revolution, revolution if they do not keep their promises. Down with traitors! Down with renegades! The fire will burn their [unclear]. Down with them on that terrible day.[83]

Surprisingly, Faysal and his brother Zayd also adopted this usage of the word *thawra* in their correspondence. While Faysal was out of the country, Zayd warned of impending revolution against the sharifians in telegram after telegram to his brothers and father: "I cannot stop the revolution," "the revolution is at the gates," he wrote, pleading for their assistance.[84] Learning of the attack on Dayr al-Zur, Faysal wrote that people like Ramadan Shallash, were "*thuwwār* who deserve the stick."[85]

The discursive community that included the popular committees and their allies thus grudgingly accepted the symbol of sharifian legitimacy—the Arab Revolt—but invested it with meanings other than those its promoters originally intended by incorporating it within a different discursive field. A similar phenomenon took place with another key symbol that the Arab government and its supporters had encouraged and used to validate their position atop Syrian society: the "martyrs"—those inhabitants of present-day Syria and Lebanon who were executed for political crimes during World War I by Jamal Pasha (the Elder), the penultimate Ottoman governor of Syria and commander of the Ottoman Fourth Army.

82. *al-ʿĀṣima*, 22 December 1919, 2.
83. AD 2344/325 (original leaflet enclosed), Cousse to Picot, 8 November 1918.
84. Mūsā, *al-Murāsalāt al-tārīkhiyya*, 2:205, 224, 232, 234, 235, 236; FO 371/4185/154755, Zayd to Faysal, 17 November 1919.
85. *al-Kawkab*, 6 January 1920, 5.

Over the years, the myth that the executions ordered by Jamal Pasha delineated a critical boundary in the history of the evolution of the "Arab movement" has become commonplace among historians of "Arab nationalism"; the executions, after all, performed at the very time Amir Faysal was visiting Damascus, reportedly convinced the amir of the necessity of launching the Arab Revolt and Damascenes of the necessity of removing the yoke of Turkish tyranny. As rendered by George Antonius, in the wake of the executions,

> A shudder shook the country. No one, even among those who knew the savagery latent in Jemal's nature, had expected such severity. The sentences were all the more appalling as they had fallen on innocent and guilty alike, since many of the victims were known to have kept aloof from anything approaching treason. On the population at large the immediate effect was one of terror. The few leaders who had remained undetected were horror-stricken: not in their wildest moments of apprehension had they imagined such a toll of their confederates; and, realising their own powerlessness, they turned with heavy hearts to the contemplation of their strangled liberties and to the task of securing freedom, no longer for its own sake alone but as a means to vengeance as well. Faisal was deeply affected. . . . Whatever doubts may have lingered in his mind as to the wisdom of breaking with the Turks were now swept away in a passionate revulsion of feeling, and the cry which escaped him on hearing the news of the executions became the battle-cry of the Arab Revolt.[86]

Unmentioned in this and similar accounts, however, is the fact that even after the executions, Jamal Pasha was frequently feted and celebrated by Damascenes, many of whom would later figure prominently in nationalist activities. Even the post-1918 embodiment of Arab nationalism, Khayr al-Din al-Zirikli, wrote a paean to the Ottoman governor that included the lines

> Bow your heads and avert your glances,
> This is a likeness which comforts distress.[87]

The initial attempts to create meaning from the executions ordered by Jamal Pasha were made by those who had participated in the Arab Revolt and their supporters who worked with the Arab government. Within a week of the British/sharifian entrance into Damascus, representatives of the Arab army in Beirut held a ceremony to celebrate the unity of the two zones. The central drama of the ceremony was the raising of the Arab flag

86. Antonius, *Arab Awakening,* 190.
87. al-ʿAẓm, *Mudhakkarāt,* 1:69–70.

over the city by the sister of Muhammad and Mahmud al-Mahmasani, two of the "martyrs" hanged by Jamal Pasha.[88] One of the first public observances organized by the Faysali government in Damascus was a memorial service to commemorate the martyrs, held on 19 October 1918, just three weeks after the amir entered Damascus at the head of the Arab army. Simultaneously, al-Fatat sent representatives from Damascus to Beirut to oversee a similar ceremony there.[89] The families of the martyrs received stipends from the government, their children attended special schools administered by the Arab government, and they were the focus of attention during the national commemorations organized in their honor.[90]

Perhaps the most extravagant of the commemorations "dedicated to eulogizing the blessed memory of the martyrs" was held on 6 May 1920. The ceremonies took place in the "martyrs' squares" of Damascus and other cities, where the Arab government had ordered poles decorated with wreaths of flowers and inscribed with the martyrs' names to be erected. Next to the poles, the ritual planners ordered the placement of platforms from which dignitaries might deliver their eulogies. According to the detailed instructions provided by *al-ʿĀṣima,* the ceremony was to consist of the following sequences:

> The commemoration will begin with the singing of the song of the martyrs, followed by eulogies to the martyrs of the nation. After this all will go to the graves of the Muslims and Christians where they will place wreaths of flowers on the graves of the martyrs; a delegation will be organized to visit their families. Committees outside Damascus will join in this by sending telegrams of condolence to them.
>
> In the evening the Arab Club has organized memorial gatherings. On the next day [Friday] the story of the noble birth of their spirits will be read, and our Christian brothers will consecrate the spirits of those executed from among their brothers. On this occasion the Commission

88. USNA 59/867.00/955, "Report of Elias Khouri, First Dragoman of Beirut Consulate," 8 September 1919; IO MSS EUR 152 (Frank Lugard Brayne Mss.)/18b, "Palestine and Syria Autumn 1918," 7 October 1918.

89. AD 2429/9, HC Beyrouth, 21 October 1918; FO 371/3412/177154/3222, Clayton to FO, 22 October 1918.

90. For attempts by the state to "invent tradition" around the symbol of the martyrs, and for the celebration of the families of the martyrs, see FO 371/3412/177154/3222, Clayton to FO, 22 October 1918; DU SA 493/15/5, n.d.; *al-Kawkab,* 3 December 1918, 8; USNA 59/867.00/955, "Report of Elias Khouri, 1st Dragoman of Beirut Consulate," 8 September 1919; *al-ʿĀṣima,* 4 May 1920, 5; MD 4H112/2B, Notebook entitled "Habib Bey Estephane," n.d. (entry for 6 May 1920); USNA DC/vol. 24/845, Al-Muzaffar to U.S. consul, 4 May 1920; MD 4H114/4/374, Cousse to Gouraud, 7 May 1920; *L'Asie Francaise,* 15 June 1920, 4.

> of Commemoration—representing the commemorators—will issue a faithful proclamation that supports the demands of the nation for unity and independence, the demands for which the sons of the nation sacrificed themselves.[91]

Both King Faysal and Amir Zayd attended the ceremonies in Damascus.[92]

In return for its honors and expenditures, the Arab government and its supporters derived reciprocal benefit from the state-sponsored hagiolatry. According to Arab government propaganda, the Turks had executed the martyrs because of their nationalist activities; the martyrs were thus part of the same struggle as those who had participated in the Arab Revolt, and the celebration of their memory was a celebration of the ties that bound Hijazis, Iraqis, and Syrians, "the martyrs of the scaffolds and trenches," in a common purpose "in the shade of His beloved Highness [Amir Faysal]."[93] For al-Fatat, the memory of the martyrs allowed the increasingly bureaucratic organization to retain its revolutionary mantle: the symbol of the martyrs legitimated the privileged position of an organization whose raison d'être had become the distribution of patronage. Furthermore, since the martyrs had come from both the Christian and the Muslim communities, their placement in the nationalist pantheon served to extol the virtues of intercommunal cooperation (as rendered in the slogan "Religion belongs to the individual, the nation to all"), as well as to prove to the entente powers that Arabs had outgrown religious fanaticism and were thus ready for independence.[94]

Although the mobilization and propaganda activities of the Arab government generated the same wide acceptance for the symbol of the martyrs as they did for the Arab Revolt, the symbol connoted a different set of meanings within the community of discourse associated with the popular committees. As a result, even those within the nationalist field who professed political positions that were diametrically opposed to those of the Arab government—such as those who decried the interference by non-Syrians (particularly the French and Hijazis) in Syrian affairs, the aspirations of the *mutanawwirūn* to create a replica of a European nation state in

91. *al-ʿĀṣima*, 3 May 1920, 5.
92. *al-ʿĀṣima*, 6 May 1920, 6.
93. *al-ʿĀṣima*, 29 April 1920, 4.
94. For warnings by Syrians against religious fanaticism, see MAE L:SL/vol. 6/20–21, Mercier to Picot, 10 December 1918; AD 2372/dossier: propagande anti-française/219/41/Bureau b5/d, 19 December 1918. For martyrs as exemplars of Muslim/Christian cooperation, see MD 4H58/1, "Rapport hebdomadaire: 27 avril au 3 mai 1920."

Syria, and the Arab government's tactic of compromise with and appeasement of the entente powers—invoked the "spirit of the martyrs" to enlist support for their own brand of nationalism.

In the Independence Day speech cited above, for example, ʿAbd al-Rahman al-Kayyali called on his audience to "Remember your yesterday!"

> [Remember] who was dwelling here and who was hanged and jailed and exiled without limit, not by law but merely because of your nationality. Do not forget those oppressors and the crying of orphans and the bereaved which still echoes in the ears . . . [T]he ghosts of those who died, sacrificed to hunger, disease, war, hanging, and exile are still in front of your eyes, pointing to what must be done to purify this soil and calm these spirits.

Others speaking the same day echoed similar sentiments:

> If the West imagined the silence of Syrians after they sacrificed the cheap and the expensive, the new and the inherited, and after they shed the blood of their devoted brothers and sacrificed their own children, yielding to ignominy and submitting to imperialism, then what they imagined will be calamitous [for them]. The Syrian could not refrain from announcing his independence which he bought with the blood of his children when he heard with composure, judgment, reason, and reflection the decision of the peace conference.[95]

In both speeches, the martyrs served the purpose of metonymy, symbolizing the martyrdom of the entire Syrian nation during the war.

For still others, particularly those in the popular committees and guerrilla bands who advocated armed resistance to entente plans, the lesson of the martyrs was not that Syria deserved independence because of their martyrdom; rather than victims to be mourned, the martyrs were exemplars of revolutionary struggle. In May 1920, on the day set aside by the Arab government to commemorate the martyrs, the newspaper *al-Kināna,* which frequently spoke in the name of the popular committees, published the following appeal:

> The Cry of the Arab Fatherland
>
> Syrian people! Remember that on this day you lost the noblest of your liberal sons who gave their lives to place you by the side of the great and

95. Speech of Tahir al-Kayyali in AD 2346/c1a, "Remembrance of Syrian Independence Day," 26. Felix Faris, another speaker, also cited the passion of the martyrs. Ibid., 12.

free nations. They devoted themselves to this noble end and they call to you to remember them, and with them their principles. . . .

Syrian nation! If the memory of your noble sons moves you and you weep for them precious tears, know that you cannot pay them their due unless you follow in their steps and are molded in their mold. The [French] government, which is eager to colonize you, usurp your wealth, and kill nationality in the souls of your sons, does not desire to grant you your manifest right. Rise like one man to defend that independence and Syrian unity without which there is no right. They desire to enslave the sons of the nation. They desire to make Palestine a national home for the Jews! They have driven a deadly thorn into the body of our nation which breaks our unity and destroys our national spirit, our freedom, our prosperity, and our souls. They desire to give the foreigner control over us so that discord is sown amongst us, our race and language are impaired, and in the future soldiers will be taken from us to fight for the foreigner.

Your noble ancestors appeal to you to preserve their heritage, and defend and fight for their honor. He who loves his life shall be humiliated.[96]

This article was published almost three months after al-Kayyali had delivered his speech. By this time, the entente powers had signed the San Remo Agreement dividing Syria into separate mandated territories, thereby proving that it was too late to expect that the powers would be moved by either the sacrifices endured by the Syrians during the war or by demonstrations that the level of civilization in Syria met entente criteria for "complete independence." Furthermore, by this time the British government had reduced its subsidy to the Arab government, crippling the latter's capacity to repress its rivals and disseminate sustentative propaganda. Under these circumstances, it was perhaps inevitable that the meanings previously assigned by the Arab government to the symbol of the martyrs would lack credibility for many Syrians.

It is interesting to note that the symbol of the martyrs retained its emotive force (and for succeeding governments, its utility) even after the dissolution of the Faysali state. In the wake of the French invasion of inland Syria, nationalist historians amalgamated the story of Faysal's expulsion from Damascus and the story of the martyrs within the trope of Arab victimization at the hands of outsiders (Turks, Westerners, Zionists). As a result, the passion of the martyrs, as recounted in textbooks and popular his-

96. FO 371/5188/E6132/39, "Arabic Press Extracts for Week Ending May 24 1920." For similar usage, see MD 4H112/2b, Notebook entitled "Habib Bey Estephane," n.d.; MD 4H114/4/374, Cousse to Gouraud, 7 May 1920.

tories and as commemorated in ritual, still serves as a key evidentiary component in the widely celebrated contemporary Arab national myth.[97]

"RELIGION BELONGS TO GOD, THE NATION TO ALL"

At a meeting of the Arab Club of Damascus held in late February 1919 in honor of General Sir Edmund Allenby, the metropolitan of the Eastern Syrian rite spoke on the meaning of Arabism. "I proclaim a new religion above all others," he announced. "It is the religion of Arab unity which gathers together the children of the nation regardless of their faith."[98] While perhaps an unusual sentiment from a man of the cloth, statements such as this were not uncommon in the eastern zone of Syria during the Faysali period. In November 1919, for example, another orator declaimed to the same audience, "All of us of different religions and homelands profess the religion of patriotism, and we declare openly that all of us are Arabs, the commonalities of language and patriotism uniting us."[99] The next week, a front-page editorial in *al-ʿĀṣima* entitled "Let Us Return to Religion" proclaimed that the three monotheistic religions strove for similar goals—"to reform mankind and to illuminate its hearts with the light of moral excellence." All three religions, the editorial continued, are agreed on several principles: faith in God, belief in the day of judgment, moral virtue, and the "national ties among the sons of one country [and] . . . the patriotic interests that all share."[100] Bashir Yamut's poem, "The Patriotic Brotherhood," also printed in *al-ʿĀṣima,* contained the same sentiment:

> Religion belongs to God. God decreed that
> All religions are from a single source. . . .
> In God's view Jesus and Ahmad are united.
> Why do you think I can differentiate between them?
> They are innocent of hate and ill will.
> Do not create hatred in their names.
> They [i.e., outside observers] charge that we are not united by love of
>   our country.
> So answer these charges.
> We will not accept any haven except brotherhood.[101]

97. This myth is more fully elaborated in L. Carl Brown, "Patterns Forged in Time: Middle East Mind-Sets and the Gulf War," 3–21.
98. *al-ʿĀṣima,* 26 February 1919, 3.
99. *al-ʿĀṣima,* 11 November 1919, 2.
100. *al-ʿĀṣima,* 20 November 1919, 1–2.
101. *al-ʿĀṣima,* 28 August 1919, 4.

While both nationalist discursive communities espoused the cause of intercommunal harmony and circulated the slogan "Religion belongs to God, the nation to all" with more or less enthusiasm, the discursive community to which the Arab government and its allies belonged did so with a particular conviction and zealousness.[102] The Arab government and the Arab Club circulated petitions signed in the name of people of all sects (*ṭawāʾif*), creeds (*madhāhib*), and religions (*adyān*) of a village or quarter; officially sanctioned parades and planned demonstrations, led by spiritual leaders from the Muslim, Christian, and Jewish communities, featured copies of the Old and New Testaments prominently displayed alongside copies of the Qurʾan; and editorialists extolled the common roots and virtues of the three monotheistic religions in newspapers subsidized by, or aligned with, the Arab government.

The fact that Syria included large numbers of both non-Muslims and non-Sunni Muslims naturally encouraged efforts to build a political community that treated religious affiliation with disinterest. But promoting intercommunal harmony had the additional effect of furthering governmental designs both domestically and internationally. At home, the Arab government aspired to quiet the fears of religious minorities who questioned the Hijazi commitment to secularism and were leery of the sharif's caliphal ambitions. Amir Faysal himself worried that their apprehensions about joining a state that contained a Muslim majority might cause them to call upon France for protection, an act that would, of course, have devastating consequences for Syrian unity.[103] Abroad, guaranteeing protection and full political participation to minorities served the tactical purposes of those who hoped to win independence by demonstrating to the entente powers that Syria was "a nation worthy of life and independence."[104] Thus, as *al-ʿĀṣima* outlined in a proclamation to "our most exalted Muslim brothers," "We want Europe and the whole world to know that the ancient reli-

102. al-Ḥuṣrī, *Yawm Maysalūn*, 77. In the leaflet "Independence or Death!" cited earlier, for example, the slogan is attached, but parenthetically and at the end of the text. The popular committees, which, as will be seen below, more often appropriated Islamic symbols or combined the slogan and Islamic symbols in the same text, used the slogan to dispel the fears of minorities who were alarmed by the "volunteer movement" and the organization of armed (Muslim) militias, and who questioned, in the words of the Greek Orthodox patriarch, "whether it was wise to arm those who might misuse their weapons." See *al-ʿĀṣima*, 7 November 1919, 5.

103. Sulṭān, *Tārīkh Sūriyya 1918–1920*, 133–134; Mūsā, *al-Murāsalāt al-tārīkhiyya*, 1:244–245.

104. This expression was twice used by ʿAli Rida al-Rikabi during his stay in Aleppo. See Mardam Bek, *Dimashq wal-Quds fī al-ʿishrīnāt*, 28, 43.

gious struggles have died and are finished, and we are now sons of one nation and one fatherland."[105] In his proclamations to the Syrian people, Faysal consistently linked religious toleration in Syria with favorable decisions at the peace conference. "If we are divided into parties and sects," he told an audience in Aleppo, "[the civilized world] will despise us, because they regard all religions as equal and do not distinguish between peoples."[106]

Nevertheless, the Arab government and its allies did not show support for minority rights merely on utilitarian grounds, nor were the conspicuous displays of revulsion at incidents such as the February 1919 massacre of Armenians in Aleppo just cynical ploys contrived for foreign consumption.[107] Rather, because of their predilection for positivist ideas and modernist apologetics, the *mutanawwirūn* who supported the Arab government and articulated the ideals upon which the program of the government was constructed believed that the freedoms and constraints imposed by the modern age had made "religiosity a weaker influence in building social and political nations over time."[108] "We are in the twentieth century," read a proclamation published in *al-ʿĀṣima,* "and true patriotism is above everything else, and the Muslim is the brother of the Christian whether he wants it or not."[109] The *mutanawwirūn* believed that communally based social structures and identities, the remnants of a more primitive time, would thus naturally disappear with the exposure of Syrian society to the exigencies of modernity and the construction of social institutions compatible with the contemporary era.[110]

It was the function of the *mutanawwirūn* to catalyze this process not only by constructing such institutions, but by inducing Syrians to accept their vision for the modern nation state as well. The dissemination of the slogan, "Religion belongs to God, the nation to all," was thus only part of a broader process through which the *mutanawwirūn* sought to instill in the population a "civic" model of the nation in which the bonds of citizenship and shared legal practice and political ideals would supersede the bonds

105. *al-ʿĀṣima,* 7 November 1919, 6.
106. *al-ʿĀṣima,* 16 June 1919, 3.
107. For one such display, see telegram from Faysal to Zayd reprinted in *al-ʿĀṣima,* 25 March 1919, 3.
108. *al-Kawkab,* 8 October 1918, 4–5.
109. *al-ʿĀṣima,* 7 November 1919, 6.
110. In an article published in *al-ʿĀṣima,* Faʾiz al-Khuri quotes from Herbert Spencer, who compared the socialists of Europe to persons "consumed by religion." Both, according to al-Khuri, are bound more by faith and wishful thinking than by scientifically demonstrable laws, which should be the foundations of society. See *al-ʿĀṣima,* 14 June 1919, 1.

of ethnicity and religion.[111] Theirs was a conception of nation born of historic accident and the exigencies of diplomacy, imposed by a self-conscious political elite upon a population that, in the words of Amir Faysal, "like children . . . does not understand the meaning of nationalism, freedom or independence."[112]

As evinced by a variety of unofficial texts, from graffiti to leaflets to slogans chanted in unauthorized demonstrations, both the program of civic nationalism promoted by *mutanawwirūn* and the goal of joining the ranks of "civilized nations" lacked inherent appeal for many Syrians. On the contrary, texts confirm that much of the discourse used by the Arab government and its supporters in their communications with the Syrian population—a discourse represented by slogans such as "Religion belongs to God, the nation to all"—was a discourse that M. M. Bakhtin characterized as "authoritative." In contrast with "internally persuasive discourse," authoritative discourse cannot be integrated with previously held beliefs through concurrence or piecemeal assimilation; instead, since it is inextricably linked to the authority that promulgates it and gains support solely on the basis of its connection to that authority (and not on the basis of its intrinsic merit), its acceptance or rejection depends on circumstances extrinsic to the cogency of its argument or its associability with previously held beliefs.[113] That such state-sponsored discourse is relatively impervious to widespread concurrence or piecemeal assimilation is to be expected: as Emile Durkheim argues in his *Professional Ethics and Civic Morals,* the complexity of modern societies ensures that only the vaguest or most banal platitudes promulgated by a state can win broad approbation among a heterogeneous population.[114] Thus, with the manifest failure of the strategy of achieving independence by proving that Syria was a civilized nation "worthy of life and independence," the emergence of the popular committees as credible claimants to authority, and the disintegration of internal conditions, the authority of the Arab government and its *mutanawwirūn*

111. See Smith, *National Identity,* 9–11; Anthony D. Smith, "The Myth of the 'Modern Nation' and the Myths of Nations," 8–12. By civic nationalism, Smith means "a political commitment not simply to particular boundaries, however they originated, but to a particular spatial and social location among other territorial nations. The basis of this commitment is a belief in the importance of residence and propinquity, as opposed to descent and genealogy." *National Identity,* 117.

112. See statements of Amir Faysal in Aleppo, 11 November 1918, transcribed in al-Ḥuṣrī, *Yawm Maysalūn,* 213.

113. M. M. Bakhtin, *The Dialogic Imagination,* 342–346.

114. Emile Durkheim, *Professional Ethics and Civic Morals,* 63.

allies collapsed, and slogans such as "Religion belongs to God, the nation to all" remained only vestigially, appearing in (usually official) political oratory but, for the most part, absent from the street.[115]

In contrast with the attempts made by the *mutanawwirūn* to use slogans to inculcate nonconventional and modernist values, the popular committees and their supporters consistently reasserted symbols which were familiar to most Syrians—symbols that "could mobilize certain varieties of feelings of collective belonging which already existed"[116]—all the while investing them with new meanings by placing them within a nationalist discursive field. Significantly, while the use of these symbols by the popular committees and their supporters, like the overabundance of eurogenic symbols in the discourse of the *mutanawwirūn,* was hardly elective, it was nonetheless self-conscious. In an article published, ironically, on the front-page of *al-ʿĀṣima,* Muhibb al-Din al-Khatib took the *mutanawwirūn* to task not just for failing to use symbols and slogans that had resonance with the population but for using symbols that actually worked at cross-purposes with their goals. Public opinion, he wrote, is derived from a synthesis of historical traditions and those transitory events that "the people compel . . . to be compatible with their traditions."

> Syrian public opinion combines that which is constant and that which is novel because it borrows from past tradition and is faithful to eternal goals. It links that which is novel with tradition according to the dictates of the time, attempting thereby to balance new exigencies and ancient tradition; it is satisfied with the new as long as it does not contradict the old, or it will resist it unto death if the two remain in contradiction. This is the secret of the Syrian's optimism toward new things, an optimism that has lasted from the earliest days through today; it is also the reason for his pessimism in regard to all he wishes to safeguard.[117]

As exhortations for intercommunal harmony disappeared from leaflets distributed on the streets of Damascus after the departure of the King-Crane Commission, conspicuously Islamic symbols—calls for jihad and

115. The slogan "Religion belongs to God, the nation to all" appears in 14 percent of the sample leaflets distributed during the period October 1918-June 1919; it appears in none of the sample leaflets distributed after the King-Crane Commission departed Damascus. Among leaflets from the former period, 32 percent call for the preservation of minority rights or for equality of all Syrians regardless of religion; this number is reduced to 7 percent after June 1919.

116. E. J. Hobsbawm, *Nations and Nationalism since 1780: Programme, Myth, Reality,* 46.

117. *al-ʿĀṣima,* 23 October 1919, 1–2.

Islamic unity, salutations addressed to Muslims or "Defenders of Islam," quotes from the Qur'an, the slogan "God is with us"—took their place.[118] The following leaflet, distributed in Damascus during the autumn of 1919, provides typical examples:

> To the Defenders of Religion
>
> Remember the words of God: Struggle and wage jihad. Where is this jihad? Attend to God's injunction: Prepare all force of which you are capable against them. Where is this force that you are to provide to defend your religion and your country? Enough of their falsehoods and deceptions. Enough of your tolerance and inaction. They have lied to you, deceived you, betrayed you. They want to partition you even after they have made pledges to you. They will swallow you up after they have sworn to be faithful. Do not trust those who profess to believe your religion. Draw your swords and sharpen them. Prepare your guns and your ammunition. I swear by God that the enemy will not be able to stand against you, for God is with us and God is the buttress of believers.[119]

By the spring of 1920 even Amir Faysal acquiesced to the use of Islamic symbols within texts promulgated by the Arab government. In April 1920, for example, the amir presided over a ceremony held to dedicate the standard of the first infantry division of the Arab army. The inscription on one side of the standard was

> In the name of God the merciful, the beneficent
> Struggle in the path of God
> God is with us
> Our victory will be manifest

On the obverse was

> There is no God but God, Muhammad is the messenger of God
> First Infantry Brigade
> Year: 1338

118. Among the sample leaflets that were distributed after the departure of the King-Crane Commission from Syria, 53 percent contain one or more of the following symbols or slogans that had not appeared in leaflets distributed before the arrival of the commission: the call for Islamic unity (22 percent); the call for jihad (17 percent); the slogan "God is with us" (31 percent). During the same period, 22 percent of the sample leaflets were addressed to Muslims or "Defenders of Islam"; neither form of address appeared in leaflets collected immediately before and during the visit of the King-Crane Commission to Damascus.

119. AD 2344/643, Cousse to HC, 30 October 1919 (enclosures in Arabic and French). See also FO 371/4186/162128/495, Dispatch from the Acting Spanish Consul in Damascus, 11 December 1919.

Faysal delivered a speech after the army paraded the banner through the streets of Damascus, declaring, "At this time it is incumbent on the division that dedicates this flag to prove that it is worthy of this gift and that it knows how to sanctify it by sacrificing its blood defending the honor of the army and protecting the fatherland."[120]

European and American observers ascribed the Islamization of political rhetoric to both the resurgence of atavistic characteristics among the population of Syria and to the efficacy of Kemalist propaganda that called for Islamic unity against the common Christian enemy. While there is evidence that the Turkish insurgents did distribute money and propaganda to the popular committees and the guerrilla bands with which the committees were affiliated,[121] it is important to note that the use of Islamic symbols was hardly atavistic. Islamic symbols did not dislodge nationalist symbols from popular texts; rather, in most texts the two sets of symbols were fully conjoined. Thus, on the eve of the French invasion of inland Syria, for example, *al-Kināna* published a full-page proclamation summoning Syrians "to enter the barracks," using both sets of symbols in combination.

> Your honor, your independence, your holy religious rites, and your freedom are in imminent danger and if you do not rise up and defend them, the first will be oppressed, the second will disappear, and the third will be trampled by divisions of your enemy—the enemy of God and the fatherland. Muhammad the Arab calls you to sacrifice your spirits and money to save your country. Remember the commandments of God and His prophet and follow the examples of Ibn Walid, Tariq, ʿUqba, Ibn al-ʿAs, and Ibn al-Khattab. . . . Come forward and do not hesitate to enter the barracks, to enlist, and to trust in God—for He is the best of helpers. And if you support God, God will not abandon a believing nation.[122]

The placement of Islamic symbols within the popular nationalist discursive field extricated those symbols from the contexts in which they had previously been situated and transformed their meaning to connote the bonds of "nation" that united Syrians with one another and differentiated them

120. *al-ʿĀṣima,* 29 April 1920, 5; MD 4H58/1, "Rapport hebdomadaire: 27 avril au 3 mai 1920."

121. FO 371/4184/144109/I.4405, GHQ (Egypt) to DMI, 30 October 1919; FO 371/4184/150560/I.618/S, GHQ (Egypt) to DMI, 4 November 1919; FO 371/4185/158008, "Summaries of Telegrams," 29 November 1919; MD 20N171/2, "Rapport hebdomadaire 18–25 janvier 1920"; MD 4H58/1, "Rapport hebdomadaire: 9 au 16 février 1920"; MD 4H58/1, "Rapport hebdomadaire: 17 au 23 février 1920"; AD 2345/no no., "Le cri du droit," 5 March 1920; MD 4H114/2/146, Cousse to Gouraud, 30 March 1920; AD 2358/526, Cousse to HC, 10 June 1920.

122. *al-Kināna,* 15 July 1920, 2.

from the imperialist enemies "of God and the fatherland." Syrians thus did not "retreat" from a national identity to a religious identity; instead, in the frenzied atmosphere of post-San Remo Syria,[123] as the numbers of Syrians participating in politics increased dramatically, the bonds of Islam came to exemplify, not contravene or replace, the bonds of nation, and the defense of Islam, like the familiar call for the defense of female virtue against defilement by the French *ṭāmiʿūn,* came to connote the defense of nation and communal purity:[124]

> If the brave sons of Syria were to shrink from death on behalf of their fatherland
> How would our girls protect their honor?
> How would our people safeguard their souls?
> How would the nation be freed from the filth of the enemy?[125]

Thus, as described in the Introduction, by the spring of 1920, those "brave sons of Syria" who volunteered to fight at Maysalun left for the front proclaiming the defense of their country to be "*al-jihād al-waṭanī*"—the patriotic jihad—compelled by conflation of religious and nationalist duty.

DEMOCRACY AND PROGRESS

In the early spring of 1920, around the time that the recently reconvened Syrian General Congress took up debate on independence and a constitution, the delegates to that body divided themselves into three blocs. Al-

123. In a letter to his friend Saʿid Shuqayr, a physician working in the foreign ministry of the Arab government wrote, "Individual dementia is among the greatest afflictions I know. But worse still is the complete dementia of a nation. . . . I am not a prophet, yet I see the end result very clearly if the afflicted do not return to their senses. DU SA/493/6/51, Amin Maʿluf to Saʿid Shuqayr, 1 June 1920.

124. Take, for example, the following extract from a pamphlet entitled "The Bitterness of Occupation: A Lecture by a Tunisian in the City of Damascus the Night of Friday 8 of jumādā al-thānia 1333," reissued by the committee of national defense of Damascus: "France feels that it is not possible to influence the hearts of the Islamic peoples so long as the light of faith burns in their breasts, and thus they have made the commission of offences against religious feelings and duties an overriding principle so that they might cause true beliefs to waver in the breasts of youths." Original in MD 4H114/2, "Brochures anti-françaises éditées pendant la guerre et remises un moment en circulation par le comité de la défense nationale à Damas," 3 February 1920. See also BL AJB/Add. Mss./49749, 21 April 1919; AD 2344/629, Cousse to HC, 23 October 1919; 4H112/2b, n.d.; MD 4H112/2b, al-Rayah: "Méfaits des soldats" (in French), 18 April 1920; MD 4H114/4, *al-Difāʿ*, 22 June 1920.

125. *al-ʿĀṣima* cited this poem, by Ahmad Shakir al-Karami, as a model for a "new, nationalist poetry." 13 May 1920, 2–3.

though contemporary observers and historians have disputed the exact number of members in each, most affirm that a majority of members belonged to a coalition that called itself the Progress Party (*ḥizb al-taqaddum*), while the remainder participated either in the Democratic Party (*al-ḥizb al-dimuqrāṭī*) or in a third, less coherent grouping (identified, variously, as the Moderate Liberal Party [*ḥizb al-ḥurr al-muʿtadil*] or simply, because they did not belong to one of the other parties, "independents" [*istiqlāliy-yūn*]).[126] Members of the Progress Party were al-Fatat stalwarts who generally supported the policies of the Arab government, while members of the Democratic Party were either affiliated with or supported the goals of the Higher National Committee. The independents tended to vote with the Progress Party.

Since the Arab government and the popular committees provided the institutional framework that supported the two main nationalist discursive communities, it is natural that their rivalry would carry over into the Syrian General Congress. But what is perhaps most interesting about the intra-parliamentary rivalry was the names chosen by the two blocs. The decision made by the representatives to call their respective caucuses "progress" and "democracy" was not haphazard. The rival blocs chose these names because each name functioned within its community as a key symbol, summarizing and representing both the foundations of political legitimacy and the fundamental goals of the national movement for those who participated in that community.

In the Introduction, I traced the resonance of the concept of "progress" in the Middle East primarily to the emergence of new social classes and the reconfiguration of established classes that constructed (or reconstructed) their worldview under the influence of the nineteenth-century expansion of market relations and state capabilities. In the latter years of the Ottoman Empire, individuals from this milieu formulated the symbols and discur-

126. Muhammad ʿIzzat Darwaza claims that *ḥizb al-taqaddum* initially included thirty-five members (Balawi puts the membership at thirty), later expanding to sixty-five, while *al-ḥizb al-dimuqrāṭī* and the centrist bloc each included about twenty members. Farzat claims there were thirty members of *al-ḥizb al-dimuqrāṭī*. Besides faulty memory, the dispute about numbers might be attributed to three factors: the fluidity of party allegiances, the evolving nature of party politics within the congress, and the delayed arrival in the capital of representatives from areas outside of Damascus. See Darwaza, *Mudhakkarāt*, 2:145, 188–189; Darwaza, *Ḥawla al-ḥaraka al-ʿarabiyya al-ḥadītha*, 1:115–116; Balāwī, "al-Aḥzāb al-siyāsiyya fī Sūriyya," 28; Farzat, *al-Ḥayā al-ḥizbiyya fī Sūriyya*, 75. For an enumeration of representatives present in Damascus, see Russell, *First Modern Arab State*, 236 n. 6.

sive field and shaped the institutional setting for one of the two main communities of discourse that dominated nationalist politics during the immediate postwar period. For those within this community, the concept of universal progress not only possessed the same intrinsic resonance that it had for their European counterparts, but as with nationalists from similar backgrounds in other parts of the world, the concept supplied a principal rationale for their activities: the national movement, under the leadership of the *mutanawwirūn* and their political stewards, would deliver to the population of Syria the material benefits associated with civilization and, through the appropriation of relevant cultural supports upon which continued progress depended, align Syria with the community of "civilized" nations and Syrians with the universal project of modernity.

The association of nationalism with national advancement and human progress was thus a familiar theme that permeated the writings and oratory of the *mutanawwirūn*. For example, sermons distributed by the Arab government to mosques throughout Damascus in April 1919 presented the case for progress and "civilization" to Friday worshipers in the idiom of Islamic modernism:

> Independence consists of training minds to interpret the truth. It is the effort made by all for the interests of all, the appeal made to true and useful sciences so that the mind might expand and cast aside the veils of ignorance, so that men might worship God in total humility and obedience and utilize to the fullest extent possible the ideas of progress and civilization. It is by independence that men will be able to expend their efforts in the pursuit of their interests which are also the interests of their nation. Among these are the improvement of communications, the construction of railroads, and the fostering of commerce, agriculture, and all other forms of economic activity. This is the independence of which the prophet approved, the independence advocated by Islam.[127]

Other texts contained visions of the glorious Syrian future that would be secured by investment in or application of industrial and agricultural technology,[128] praised the Arab government and the sharifians ("the princes of today, like the princes of yesterday, revering knowledge and striving to expand it"[129]) for their commitment to the advancement of science and knowledge, or announced the formation of scientific and literary societies, the commencement of lecture series, the founding of schools, and the ini-

127. AD 2343/286, Cousse to HC, 24 April 1919 (Arabic text and French translation enclosed).
128. See *al-Fallāḥ*, May 1919, 16–18; *al-ʿĀṣima*, 7 May 1919, 1.
129. *al-Fallāḥ*, May 1919, 18.

tiation of civic institutions such as a national library and national museum—all of which simultaneously functioned as exemplars and (for the benefit of both the entente powers and skeptics at home) proof of the advance of civilization in Syria.

For the *mutanawwirūn*, harmonizing the nation with the exigencies of universal progress required a fundamental restructuring of social life, including the role accorded women in Syrian society. Newspapers such as *al-ʿĀṣima* and *al-Kawkab* offered a constant barrage of articles discussing the importance of women in building the new Syria, urging them to prepare for independence by studying and emulating their more liberated counterparts in the West. In these articles, the *mutanawwirūn* called on women to apply themselves in culture and the arts, to undertake acts of charity, and to renounce frivolity and frippery in order to devote themselves to the nation: "Damascene women possess gold jewelry whose value exceeds a million lira. . . . If all this money were collected and placed in a savings account, it could be used to establish an academy." [130] But beneath these calls was the effort to create a facsimile of the two spheres that had defined idealized gender roles among the (nonfeminist) bourgeoisie of nineteenth-century Europe—a public sphere dominated by men, supported and nurtured by a sphere of domestic femininity:

> If woman is not held back, she will be a treasure house of knowledge and a depository of the humanities and art. However, she does not want the divine aptitude that would prepare her to be an engineer or lawyer or *khaṭība* or journalist, but she wishes that it make her a mother and mistress of the house and nursemaid to her infants and children. Those who attempt to fill her head with various sciences and arts on the contrary fill the void in her thoughts with matters that separate her from what was created for her sake and drive her away from the execution of her natural functions.[131]

Because Syrian nationalists confronted conditions that differed from those existing in Europe, the activities that the *mutanawwirūn* apportioned to women included both those enjoined on European women and others from which European women were barred. For example, some *mutanawwirūn* (one of the most prominent and, to conservatives, vexing of

130. *al-ʿĀṣima*, 28 August 1919, 5–6. See also *al-ʿĀṣima*, 5 February 1920, 5; *al-Kawkab*, 11 November 1919, 11; *al-Kawkab*, 13 January 1919, 11.

131. *al-Kawkab*, 28 October 1919, 7–8. See also *al-ʿĀṣima*, 11 September 1919, 1–2; and the account of Gertrude Bell's visit to the "School for the Daughters of Martyrs" (*madrasat banāt al-shuhadāʾ*) in Damascus in IO L/PS/10/802, Gertrude Bell, "Syria in October 1919," 15 November 1919, 11.

whom was Satiʿ al-Husri, minister of education) argued that Syrian girls should receive education like European girls; after all, if women were expected to raise children who would build the Syria of the future, they needed training in the sciences and national culture so that they might tutor their offspring. "Arab women need to realize that the awakening of the East needs capital—that is, knowledge," an editorialist in *al-ʿĀṣima* wrote.

> As Imam Ghazali said: Your children grew up fifty years before they were born in terms of the ideas that influenced you [their mothers]. Thus women from their earliest youth must be fed with the milk of knowledge and virtue in order to raise children of virtue.[132]

But members of the Progress Party used the same rationale to argue that Syrian women should be exposed to politics as well. As a result, the party championed the cause of women's suffrage within the Syrian General Congress. According to several accounts, it was the proposal to extend the franchise to women that precipitated the split between rival blocs: the Democrats and their extraparliamentary allies opposed not only women's suffrage but the efforts of Satiʿ al-Husri to expand education for girls. Furthermore, the attendant debate effectively paralyzed the congress up to a week before the French invasion of inland Syria.[133] Ironically, France did not enfranchise its women for another quarter-century.

For the Democratic Party and its allies outside the Syrian General Congress, "progress" did not hold the allure that it did for their rivals, nor did they consider adherence to the principle a criterion for legitimation. On occasion, the party and its allies even held the idea of progress and its proponents up to ridicule. "The French in Syria do not care whether their territory is destroyed or not, whether its economic life comes to a standstill or not, whether the population lives or dies, nor whether villages are wiped out or are populous," one writer declared in *al-Kināna*. "They only care that the authorities there should possess the sources of wealth and turn the free population into slaves in the name of progress, and that only the Syrians feel the effects of all this upon them."[134] In place of the uncertain

132. *al-ʿĀṣima*, 28 August 1919, 5–6.

133. *al-ʿĀṣima*, 12 July 1920, 1; Darwaza, *Ḥawla al-ḥaraka al-ʿarabiyya al-ḥadītha*, 1:115–116; Farzat, *al-Ḥayā al-ḥizbiyya fī Sūriyya*, 75; Ḥasan al-Ḥakīm, *Khubarātī fī al-ḥukm*, 46; al-Ḥaffār, "al-Ḥukūmāt allatī taʿāqabāt 1(15 tishrīn al-thānī 1372): 10; AD 2374/938/CP/dossier: TEO zone ouest, "Situation politique," 29 April 1920. According to *al-ʿĀṣima*, 31 May 1920, 1, the Syrian General Congress accepted a resolution granting women the right to vote by acclamation on 29 May 1920.

134. FO 371/5188/E7808/42, "Arabic Press Abstracts for Week Ending June 14 1920."

blessings of progress, the Democratic Party and the popular committees with which the party was affiliated based their legitimacy on their claim to represent the "will of the nation."

This claim constituted a central theme of texts disseminated by the popular committees. For example, in early March 1920, on the eve of the reconvening of the Syrian General Congress, the Higher National Committee posted a broadsheet throughout Damascus entitled "The Nation Dictates Its Wishes to the Syrian Congress." The declaration first reminded the representatives of their mission by opening with a salutation greeting "the noble Syrian Congress which convenes during this political storm to echo the aspirations of the nation." Following a brief introduction, the declaration listed the nation's demands, which the congress had to enact to "obtain the nation's confidence and become its true representative." Starting each refrain with the assertion "The nation wants," the declaration underscored the democratic principles that had to govern an independent Syria:

> The nation wants from [the congress] a civilian, democratic, representative government. . . .
>
> The nation wants that when [the congress] proclaims its august amir as king of the country that it proclaim him a just, constitutional, and democratic king. . . .
>
> The nation wants [the congress] to base its fundamental law on the principle of a representative, democratic, decentralized monarchy. . . .

The notice was signed by Kamil al-Qassab, "in the name of the Syrian nation."[135]

To enhance their claim to represent the "will of the nation," the popular committees circulated their own idealized founding myth, just as the Arab government had done before them. The myth presented the committees as the inevitable product of popular enthusiasm that had been aroused by the Evacuation Crisis. According to the preamble to the charter of the Higher National Committee:

> Public action for the nation cannot succeed if the individuals of the nation are not prepared for it. The requirement [for public action] is mutual assistance, which is necessary to foster it. Thus were the circumstances when the matter of patriotic formations arose in the capital of Syria. The need for them was felt in homes of every neighborhood and in the heart of every individual. Thus, the people rushed to realize this undertaking on

135. Original text in SL:LW. Reprinted in *al-Ahrām*, 12 March 1920, and in USNA 165/2558–16, Military Attaché (Cairo) to Director Military Intelligence, 16 March 1920.

> every front, and the people of [each] district played their part without collusion, compelled by the feeling of patriotic duty. This glorious creation, which was given the name "Higher National Committee," along with the branch committees, arose from the totality of their labors.[136]

Thus engendered, the popular committees assumed the function of consolidating and rendering effective the inchoate aspirations of Syrians by transforming "the entire nation into a single powerful bloc which feels one feeling and strives for one powerful interest."[137]

For those associated with or sympathetic to the popular committees, the symbol of democracy thus cohered with the overall representation of Syria as an organic community that possessed a common will derived from a common history and identity. Although the *mutanawwirūn* also attended to democracy, they situated it within a very different discursive field—one that assigned pride of place to "progress." Thus, although they accepted democracy as doctrinally consistent with "the spirit of the age," they argued that the nation was as yet ill-prepared for democracy and would thus have to undergo extensive preparation (under their tutelage) before democratic principles could be applied in Syria:

> All the miseries that democracy has inflicted in other countries comes from its establishment without preparation; it is not reasonable that we demand to arrive at the second stage before passing through the first. . . . Therefore I say to my brothers among the *mutanawwirūn:* If we are to be trusted in our claims of serving the nation, every one of us must gird himself to reform education and awaken the spirit in today's sons so they can become tomorrow's men.[138]

The training for democracy advocated by the *mutanawwirūn,* and even their notion of what the democratic society of the future might look like,[139]

136. SL:LW, "Niẓām al-lajna al-waṭaniyya al-ʿulyā fī al-ʿāṣima al-sūriyya," 17 November 1919.

137. SL:LW, "Niẓām al-lijān al-waṭaniyya al-farʿiyya fī bilād Sūriyya," 17 November 1919.

138. *al-ʿĀṣima,* 26 January 1920, 1–2. The editorial from which this quote was taken, "Education for Democracy—and the Principles of Democracy," was written by Muhibb al-Din al-Khatib, illustrating once again al-Khatib's ambiguous position as editor of *al-ʿĀṣima* and secretary of the Higher National Committee.

139. According to an unsigned editorial in *al-ʿĀṣima,* "Complete Arab democracy will come about when subjects see His Highness shaking hands with them, acting like an equal, and entertaining them in accordance with the practice of his first ancestors. . . . Thus, we have seen His Royal Highness, the King of England, descend to the public arena to answer an Egyptian villager with kind words. 'Thank you, my son, for your kind support; God bless you.' (Signed with the royal seal.) The reader will see in this answer the spirit of true democracy, which takes shape in England

enabled them to retain their fundamentally disjunctive view of Syrian society and complemented their advocacy of governance by specialists and technocrats. As will be seen in the next chapter, this view permeated the discourse of the *mutanawwirūn,* limiting its appeal at the very moment when expanded popular participation in politics demanded the utilization of a discourse that a wider audience could embrace.

---

daily and which ignites pride." "Democracy for the Arabs," *al-ʿĀṣima,* 21 April 1919, 1–2.

4 The Integrative and Prescriptive Powers of Rival Nationalist Discursive Fields

The previous chapter discussed the diversity of meanings that the two main nationalist discursive communities derived from a variety of slogans and key symbols, some of which they held in common, some of which were peculiar to one or the other community. The purpose of this chapter is to demonstrate the interrelationship of these symbols and their community-specific meanings, and to place them in the broader context of the integrated sets of values, obligations, and goals enjoined through the discursive field of each community.

In some respects, this task has already been begun. It was, of course, impossible to discuss the central role played by the key symbols "progress" and "democracy," for example, without referring to the framework that transformed these terms into exemplary symbols. The approach that will be taken in this chapter, however, differs from that of the previous chapter in two respects. First, this chapter reverses the direction of the investigation: since the discursive field itself prescribes the set of connotations that participants in the discursive community might ascribe to each enclosed symbol, the analysis of discursive fields must begin with an examination of the fields in their totality rather than with extrapolation from discrete, selected symbols. Second, this chapter will be more restrictive of its subject matter than was its predecessor: even though the discursive fields under examination sanctioned a comprehensive set of beliefs that addressed a multitude of public and private concerns, this chapter will confine its focus to the approach each discursive field took to the particular problem of establishing an ideal political community and reconstituting the proper ordering of society.

What makes this discussion critical for understanding the political and social transformation of post-Ottoman Syria is the fact that discursive fields do more than just portray an idealized world; they also inspire their proponents and provide guidance for their activities. As mentioned at the beginning of Chapter 3, a symbol within the discursive field acts as a bridge between a symbolic referent and a particular range of meanings. Consequently, the discursive field reflects the environment in which it is created.[1] But because the discursive field itself imposes coherence on an array of possible symbolic meanings, it simultaneously separates itself from its social context and acquires the characteristics of paradigmatic truth; that is, the discursive field acts as the source of its own authority.[2] As a result, the integrated symbol system acts as a prescriptive map for behavior: because the enclosed symbols, whose meanings are derived from the aggregate of symbols within the discursive field, distinguish licit from illicit endeavor, the field steers its adherents through a set of sanctioned activities. As Robert Wuthnow has noted, the field often performs this function by directly juxtaposing symbols that connote actions and values that are advocated and those that are considered baneful in the manner that, for example, Christian theology juxtaposes heaven and hell and the entrance requirements for each.[3] As will be discussed in more detail below, in post-Ottoman Syria the juxtaposition of "progress" and "stagnation" in the discursive field of the *mutanawwirūn,* like the juxtaposition of "the nation" and its enemies (such as "those who would sell the nation like a commodity") in the field of their nationalist rivals in the popular committees, served to commend behavior appropriate for those within each discursive community.

One example that illuminates the process by which the discursive field mediates social experience and symbolic meaning comes from the discursive field associated with the Arab government and its extragovernmental allies: the discursive field of this particular community of discourse transformed the objective categories of occupation and social standing denoted by the term *middle strata* into symbolic categories (*mutanawwirūn, mustanīrūn,* etc.) from which its adherents derived a circumscribed number of meanings and possible courses of action. In turn, these meanings and authorized actions, which will be described in detail below, confirmed the congruent meanings connoted by the other symbolic forms that constituted

1. Wuthnow, *Communities of Discourse,* 3, 13–14, 554–558.
2. Bruce Lincoln, *Discourse and the Construction of Society: Comparative Studies of Myth, Ritual, and Classification,* 24–25. See also Wuthnow, *Communities of Discourse,* 555; Castoriadis, *Imaginary Institution of Society,* 368–369.
3. Wuthnow, *Communities of Discourse,* 14–15, 554–558.

the discursive field, thereby strengthening the comprehensiveness of the field itself.

It is this discursive field—the field that was not only framed but inhabited by the *mutanawwirūn* and their allies—that will constitute the subject of the first part of this chapter.

THE VIEW FROM THE TOP

The community of discourse with which the Arab government and allied political and cultural societies were identified included two groups that might be described as "outsiders" to Syrian society as it had been constituted before World War I. The first consisted of the military men, the sharifians and their retainers, and so on, who had come to Damascus from other places—the Hijaz, Iraq, and Palestine—with the Arab army or in the wake of the Ottoman withdrawal from Syria. Basing their right to political authority on their participation in the Arab Revolt, their presence in the Arab government sparked protests from many native-born notables who had customarily controlled local politics. The second group of outsiders was made up of the *mutanawwirūn,* who believed that education or profession qualified them to play a special role in postwar Syria regardless of their wartime activities.

A commonality of interests united these two groups. Both, for example, chafed at the strictures of a political system that promised nothing to accommodate their ambitions. Both therefore sought to reconstruct that system, albeit in different ways: although many of the immigrants would no doubt have been satisfied merely to insert themselves within the preexisting social and political formations, the *mutanawwirūn* believed that shifts in relationships of power had lagged so far behind the economic and social developments that had transformed Syrian society over the previous half-century that rectification was possible only through a more radical alteration in the status quo. In addition to their shared goals, each group possessed attributes that complemented those of the other: while the immigrants provided the *mutanawwirūn* with legitimation (through the myth of the Arab Revolt and the capacity to secure international recognition) and access to power and financial resources, the immigrants needed the *mutanawwirūn* to articulate a nationalist program, link them as far as they could to indigenous social and political structures, and construct and direct unfamiliar institutions that were necessary for the proper functioning of a modern nation state.

For the most part, then, the *mutanawwirūn* set the agenda and formulated the discursive field for the Arab government. Because, as discussed earlier, progress and other modernist axioms constituted an indispensable element of their social imaginary, the discursive field of the *mutanawwirūn* reproduced many of the polarities popular among nineteenth- and early-twentieth-century European intellectuals who had inhabited a similar milieu. The field of the *mutanawwirūn* thus contrasted civilization with barbarism,[4] progress with stagnation,[5] the moderation of secularism with the fanaticism of communalism,[6] and meritocratic advancement with patronage politics[7]—tropes common to nationalist elites throughout the late colonial world. For the *mutanawwirūn,* these polarities acted as guideposts that would mark the contours of the new Syria. Modeled on the "young" nations of Europe and the United States, the Syria of the future would likewise be inhabited by a population committed to the principles of progress, liberal political values, and even individual initiative and free enterprise. One contributor to *al-Kawkab* argued for these last values in the following manner:

> It is necessary for us to leave aside the government and its affairs while it is preoccupied with performing its usual duties, for we must not impose on it that for which it has no aptitude. We must turn our attention to progress by ourselves, without the help of the government . . . which is not able to do what we do. It is time for us to depend on ourselves, and to follow in the footsteps of other living nations that reached the highest levels of progress and perfection by virtue of depending on the individual and [his] diligence in work.[8]

While some pairs of contrasting images embedded within the discursive

4. See, for example, *al-ʿĀṣima,* 7 May 1919, 1–2, 5–6; *al-ʿĀṣima* 24 (n.d.); MAE L:SL/vol. 15/340/92–95, Picot to Pichon, 21 July 1919; MD 7N4182/4/340, Picot to MAE, 21 July 1919; *al-ʿĀṣima,* 28 August 1919, 5–6; *al-Kawkab,* 28 October 1919, 7–8.

5. See analysis of Gilbert Clayton, chief political officer attached to the British army, in FO 371/3054/227658, Clayton to Sir Mark Sykes, 28 November 1917; *al-ʿĀṣima,* 16 June 1919, 3; *al-Kawkab,* 21 October 1919, 7–8.

6. *al-ʿĀṣima,* 26 February 1919, 3; *al-ʿĀṣima,* 7 May 1919, 5–6; MAE L:SL/vol. 6/20–21, Mercier to Picot, 10 December 1918; AD 2372/dossier: propagande anti-française/219/41/bureau b5/d, 19 December 1918.

7. According to Amir Faysal, in a speech delivered in May 1919, "in private affairs we should respect people of noted families, but we should not give them responsible posts unless they are fit for them, and then it is their education and character that entitles them to the post." *al-ʿĀṣima* 24 (n.d.). See also *al-ʿĀṣima,* 16 June 1919, 3; *al-Kawkab,* 30 September 1919, 7–8.

8. *al-Kawkab,* 21 October 1919, 7–8. In the wake of a series of strikes that crippled the tram system, electrical generation, and manufacturing in Damascus, *al-ʿĀṣima* published an editorial that argued that "strikes are the right of workers just

field of the *mutanawwirūn* explicitly conveyed community goals, others merely intimated paradigmatic ideals through metaphor and allusion. For example, writers and orators of the period frequently contrasted the dynamism of modernity with the stagnation of the (Ottoman) past by celebrating the vitality of youth, implicitly disparaging what they considered to be hidebound traditionalism. The Arab Club claimed to represent "all cultured youth,"[9] "young" was an adjective of choice used to describe those patron saints of the nationalist movement, the "martyrs,"[10] and Amir Faysal professed a special bond with the youth of Syria: "If I said to the youth, 'Throw yourselves into the sea,' they would do so and no one would hesitate, because they know that I speak wisdom and because the youth of the country understand everything."[11] The names of political associations sponsored by and for *mutanawwirūn* also reflected the preoccupation with youth—not only al-Fatat (actually *jamʿiyyat al-umma al-ʿarabiyya al-fatāt*, the Young Arab Society), but also the Arab Youth Club; the Association of Young Syrians; the Association of Young Lebanese (which later merged with Young Syria); Young Mesopotamia; the Patriotic Youth; The Sword, the Fire, the Ardor of Youth; and the Youth of the Jazira (*fityān al-Jazīra*), a group that began as a Syrian affiliate of the Egyptian-based Syrian Union but later merged with the Democratic Party of Kamil al-Qassab.[12]

The resonance of the trope that counterposed youth and age in the discursive field of the *mutanawwirūn* came about as a result of several factors. As discussed in Part I, the youth/age dichotomy corresponded to an actual generational conflict: most of those who identified themselves by the signification "*mutanawwirūn*" were members of a cohort that was young in comparison with the patriarchate of notables that had held power in Damascus during the late Ottoman period. But the trope must be read on another level as well: the counterposing of youth and age paralleled the struggle of

---

as the lowering of wages and dismissals are the right of employers." The editorial ended by condemning a strike by artisans because their demands for higher prices and wages "would create destructive monopolies." *al-ʿĀṣima*, 16 June 1919, 1–2.

9. MD 7N4182/4, Laforcade to Pichon, 19 August 1919.

10. AD 2343, "Protestation" (in French and Arabic), 5(?) February 1919; *al-Kawkab*, 27 May 1919, 9; *al-ʿĀṣima*, 11 September 1919, 4–6.

11. *al-Kawkab*, 5 August 1919, 6–7. Interestingly, the title of the article that reprinted Faysal's musings was "Is This Democracy?"

12. For these often short-lived organizations, see AD 2368/10/2, Report to Lt. Wiet on Yusuf Estifan, 2 January 1919; AD 2372/no no.; MD 7N4182/4/340, Picot to MAE, 21 July 1919; FO 371/4183/136154/346–351, Lutfallah to Lloyd George, 16 September 1919.

the *mutanawwirūn* and the sharifians to upset previously existing relations of authority in Syria (both as they existed and as they were imagined), to associate Syria with the universal project of modernity, and to impose new notions of political community and a social order that was itself hierarchically divided.[13]

In the same vein, the discursive field of the *mutanawwirūn* derived similar connotations from a trope that contrasted the vitality of wakefulness—the present condition of the *mutanawwirūn,* which they sought to instill in the population of Syria—with the lethargy of slumber, calling upon Syrians "to awaken from their slumber and clear off the dust of ignorance that had accumulated over the centuries." "If the masses had sucked the milk of true knowledge instead of having as teachers a bunch of ignoramuses who almost ended their lives with silliness and idle talk," complained one editorialist, "they would have awakened from their sleep and kept up with other nations, treading the path of progress."[14] As with *youth* and *young,* the *mutanawwirūn* appropriated *wakefulness* and *reawakening* for organizational titles, such as the Committee for Intellectual Awakening (led by Sami al-Bakri, ʿAbd al-Rahman al-Safarjalani, Nadim al-Sawwaf, and Yahya al-Shamʿa) and the Committee for Palestinian Awakening.[15]

The raison d'être of the *mutanawwirūn,* then, was to provide the "milk of true knowledge" commended by the above-cited editorialist. "The great mass of the nation is not confined to the educated, the notables, and the merchants of the cities who read the daily newspapers, follow international and domestic politics, and who are concerned with scientific discoveries and technological innovation," Muhibb al-Din al-Khatib complained on the pages of *al-ʿĀṣima.*

13. For comparable examples of the "youth" trope and its meaning, see George L. Mosse, *Fallen Soldiers: Reshaping the Memory of the World Wars,* 54–69; Anderson, *Imagined Communities,* 118–119. Elie Kedourie presents a different argument ("nationalist movements are children's crusades") in *Nationalism* 82–83, 96.

14. *al-Kinānа,* 2 June 1920, 1–2. See also *al-Kawkab,* 27 May 1919, 9; *al-ʿĀṣima,* 20 October 1919, 1–2; FO 371/5187/500, Extracts from *al-Urdunn* in "Arabic Press Abstracts for the Week Ending February 9 1920"; al-Ziriklī, *Dīwān al-Ziriklī,* 24–25. While Benedict Anderson also discusses the popularity of this trope among nationalist movements, his argument differs from the one employed here. See *Imagined Communities,* 195–196.

15. FO 371/4183/136154/346–351, Lutfallah to Lloyd George, 16 September 1919.

> Rather, the great mass of the nation is composed of working people, those who dwell in villages and mountains, those who are devoted to breaking the soil and planting it. It is to these that the educated [*mutaʿallimīn*] must devote their zeal, to enlighten their hearts and advance their talents and intellectual abilities.[16]

To bring about their modernist apotheosis, the *mutanawwirūn* directly attacked popular practices and offered Syrians didactic slogans (including "Religion belongs to God, the nation to all") and hectoring advice. For example, *al-ʿĀṣima* reprinted a speech delivered by the recently deceased Andrew Carnegie in 1885 "to give to the youth of this awakening nation a summary of the experiences of which American youth have been able to take advantage and which hold the key for wealth and success." It is difficult to imagine what Syrians could have thought of Carnegie's advice for young people to work hard, save their earnings, and avoid the evils of alcohol, stock speculation, and IOU's.[17] In a front-page editorial entitled "A Danger Threatens Our Domestic Life," another edition of the same newspaper blamed the proliferation of coffeehouses in Syria for a variety of social ills, from unemployment ("If a city had no coffeehouses, then the idle would focus their attention on finding work") to family breakdown ("Those who flee from their homes to coffee shops do not feel the sweetness and beauty of a happy family, but instead offer a bad example to the mistress of the house, who will take every opportunity to flee to the house of a neighbor"). The editorial added the warning that "knowing that the greatest city on earth—and by this I mean London—lacks coffeehouses, it follows that coffeehouses are one thing and civilization another."[18] Ten months later, on the eve of the French invasion of inland Syria, the newspaper even blamed Syria's economic collapse on the profligacy of the lower classes:

> People plunge into drink and pleasures and clothes and waste. This is what makes the peasant raise the price of his land—so that he can preserve his social standing. Thus, he becomes proud and pampered, resulting in increased inflation, the abandonment of work, and harshness in transactions.[19]

16. *al-ʿĀṣima,* 16 October 1919, 1–2.
17. *al-ʿĀṣima,* 25 August 1919, 1–2. See also "At the Grave of Carnegie" in *al-ʿĀṣima,* 28 August 1919, 6–7. Carnegie was well-known as a proponent of the philosophy of Herbert Spencer, whose writings were influential among the *mutanawwirūn.*
18. *al-ʿĀṣima,* 11 September 1919, 1–2.
19. *al-ʿĀṣima,* 17 July 1920, 5–6. See also *al-ʿĀṣima,* 27 March 1919, 4; *al-ʿĀṣima,* 7 May 1919, 1–2.

To combat the unwholesome practices of the popular classes, the *mutanawwirūn* championed diversions that they claimed were morally uplifting, civilized, and patriotic. Not coincidentally, these diversions could be easily observed and supervised by official agencies. In the wake of popular agitation against the Faysal-Clemenceau Agreement, for example, *al-ʿĀṣima* published a series of articles calling on the Arab government to build racetracks in cities throughout the eastern zone of Syria. Before the war, the article stated, the popular classes

> passed much of their time [watching horseracing], but when the war was announced, this activity stopped. Under these circumstances it is to the advantage of those who love horses that they have a place for racing in which to spend their time, for it is better for them to spend their time there than in the corners of coffeehouses. They will gain material and hygienic benefits from this activity, and they will take on a vitality that they did not know before.[20]

In exchange for the counsel they provided the nation, the *mutanawwirūn* claimed special prerogatives for themselves, such as preferment to choice administrative positions, the deference of those who had formerly been their social betters, and access to or entrée into the highest ranks of society. These claims naturally placed the *mutanawwirūn* at odds with much of the traditional notability—depicted as the guardians of privilege and purveyors of patronage (*ittikāliyya*)—against whom the *mutanawwirūn* contrasted themselves.[21] An article entitled "The Fatherland above Everything," published in *al-Kawkab,* detailed the intense animosity that separated the two groups, comparing it to "a dangerous disease [that] has become deeply rooted among us Easterners."

> The notables [*aʿyān*] and the men of enlightenment [called, variously, *ʿulamāʾ*, *mustanīrūn,* and *ʿiṣāmiyyūn*[22] in the article] have engaged in a violent quarrel, and each side has begun working to supplant its oppo-

20. *al-ʿĀṣima,* 5 February 1920, 2.
21. *al-ʿĀṣima,* 26 January 1920, 1–2.
22. For use of the term *ʿiṣāmiyyūn* during a later period, see Joseph Vashitz, "*Dhawat* and *ʿIsamiyyun:* Two Groups of Arab Community Leaders in Haifa During the British Mandate." Although, according to Vashitz, in mandated Palestine the term denoted economic achievement, the author of "The Fatherland above Everything" uses it interchangeably with "*mustanīrūn.*" Furthermore, while Vashitz argues that in his texts the relationship between the *dhawāt* (notables) and the *ʿiṣāmiyyūn* was not antagonistic, the article published in *al-Kawkab* demonstrates that the *aʿyān*/*ʿiṣāmiyyūn* dichotomy in postwar Syria was the bellwether of the previously described status revolution.

> nent and obtain the leadership and influence it covets for itself. [Each side] uses everyone else for [its own] designs. . . . It is not for us to tell them to end their quarrel and adhere to the principle of unity or forswear predominance and seize the bond of concord, because a dispute between two dissimilar classes is something that is impossible to extirpate or abandon. However, we hope that [mutual] assurances and natural boundaries will circumscribe the quarrel, and that it not extend to that which touches the general interests of the fatherland.[23]

The author of this article continued his analysis of the wrangling that divided established and emergent elites with a description of a meeting that had been called to decide "an important matter concerning the life of the nation and the future of the country." The participants elected one of the *ʿiṣāmiyyūn* to lead them rather than one of the notables who was in attendance, thereby angering the latter, "who was not pleased that he was subordinate to this upstart." Although admonishing the *ʿiṣāmī* for not dealing with his rival in a more diplomatic manner, the author delivered a harsh rebuke to the notable, reminding him that

> we do not ignore the fact that the semblance of the presidency or leadership is important, inasmuch as this brings rapture and happiness to the soul. But this cannot be allowed to eclipse our reason and come between us and our dreams; [nor can it be allowed to] lead us to take gambles from which we shall derive only failure and disappointment.

The article concludes by situating the conflict between the notables and men of enlightenment within the broader framework of the evolution of social systems, warning the traditional notability that it must bow to the inevitable:

> In times past, power and influence went to those who were endowed with physical strength; after that came a period in which those who did not have strength had power, and the following eras brought us chiefs who differed in their talents and specialties until this age arrived. [Now] only those intellectuals rule who are given a share of the light which lights the gloom for its master and guides him on his way. If a group of people are sorry that they see at the head of our community people of this sort, they should not take it personally, for they know that this matter reflects accurately the spirit of the age and is necessary. There is no profit or benefit to be gained by resisting this. They must realize that knowledge is the route to advancement and the means to high rank and the greatness they seek. If there is any sublime love in their souls, then this should guide them and dictate their affairs.

23. *al-Kawkab,* 30 September 1919, 7–8.

The prerogatives claimed by the *mutanawwirūn* and their allies among the sharifians placed them at odds not only with the traditional notability but with the majority of the population of Syria as well. For example, in June of 1919, Fa'iz al-Khuri published a two-page disquisition on socialism in *al-ʿĀṣima* that was little more than a thinly veiled defense of rule by the educated elite of society.[24] In his article, al-Khuri—a graduate of the School of Law and Imperial War College in Istanbul, a member of the Literary Society of Istanbul before the war and of the Arab Club of Damascus during the Faysali period, and an advocate of the philosophy of Herbert Spencer[25]—challenged the social leveling advocated by European socialists by raising the question "Can those who are informed and those who aren't be equal?" and by answering it negatively. Men earn their rights by performing duties that advance the fatherland, he asserted; as a result, "it is not equality when the educated man [*ʿālim*] who works for the benefit of his country is equal to the savage ignoramus under law." Al-Khuri cited two examples to bolster his assertion that the *mutanawwirūn* should be treated differently from the rest of society. First, he cited (with implied approbation) electoral systems that grant the educated (*mutaʿallimīn*) a greater voice than the ignorant. He then asked whether it is just for a criminal who attacks a merchant to receive the same punishment as a criminal who attacks a governor or a judge; after all, the latter serves his subjects while the former merely serves himself. For al-Khuri's intended audience—other *mutanawwirūn* and government employees who subscribed to *al-ʿĀṣima*—the answer was obvious.

Like the *mutanawwirūn,* sharifians and their retinue similarly partitioned Syrian society into those who, like themselves, were fit to rule and those who were fit only to be ruled. However, because they lacked the credentials—or, perhaps, the pretensions—of the *mutanawwirūn,* they did not adopt the airs of a cultural elite. Instead, as outsiders and conquerors, these newcomers to Damascene politics maintained that their presence was necessary to integrate and order a society that they claimed had been divided for centuries into autonomous, vertically organized parochial communities. ʿAli Rida al-Rikabi, although himself of Damascene origin, articulated their view when he wrote on the pages of *al-ʿĀṣima,*

> The Arab government has been vigilant in preserving the peace, upholding the law, and organizing the administration with a spirit of unity, con-

24. *al-ʿĀṣima,* 14 June 1919, 1–2.
25. For Khuri's background, see al-Charkas, *al-Dalīl al-muṣawwar,* 1:72–73.

> cord, harmony, and cooperation among peoples of all sects, religions, and nationalities so that there will be no difference in rights. . . .
>
> The relationship of the government to the people is the relationship of a compassionate mother to her son, and the people should act toward the government with faithfulness and devotion.[26]

For al-Rikabi and his associates, the ties between the Arab government and the population of Syria were "indissoluble because they are guaranteed by the hand of Faysal."[27] But Faysal was more than the glue that united the disparate "sects, religions, and nationalities" of Syria. Faysal's presence in Damascus sanctioned the very presence of Hijazis and Iraqis as well as the political and social aspirations of the *mutanawwirūn.* Faysal thus became a national icon, "a stern but benevolent father," a doctor who treated the diseases of the nation, "the spirit of the national movement," the "destroyer of oppression, protector of right, guardian of the Arabs, son of nobility and glory."[28] In one text he was the Dr. Edward Jenner of Syria because of his ability to "cure" the nation. In another he was the modern Khalid b. Walid of the Arabs.[29] Faysal himself participated in the creation of this cult by placing himself at the center of ritual, accepting homage (*mubāyaʿa*) like an Abbasid caliph,[30] reviewing parades held to celebrate national festivals, and touring Syria in well-publicized excursions during which he was welcomed with victory arches constructed specially for the occasion. In short, Faysal, in his own words, was the person "whom [Syrians] entrusted with [their]

26. *al-ʿĀṣima,* 7 May 1919, 5–6.

27. The first civilian cabinet of Syria echoed this sentiment in its statement to the Syrian General Congress of 27 May 1920: "The Arabs were liberated by virtue of the glorious deeds of King Hussein and his brave son, deeds that the people will always remember with gratitude. He is thus the founder of the Arabs' modern history with which the nation started its second golden age.

"Chapters of thankfulness and esteem will also be devoted in our history to his talented son, His Majesty Faisal the First, King of Syria, who has taken up the Syrian case and pledged to continue to work for the liberation of the entire country and to defend it to the last. He is the creator of the Syrian Kingdom and the one most responsible for its deliverance and establishment on the basis of freedom and regeneration." al-Husri, *Day of Maysalun,* 124–126.

28. USNA 165/2266-AA-45/58, Yale to War Department, proclamation of Amir Faysal, 3 October 1918; *al-ʿĀṣima,* 7 May 1919, 5–6; FO 3371/5032/81–83, From *al-Ahrām,* 1 February 1920; AD 2346/c1a, Speech delivered by ʿAbd al-Rahman al-Kayyali in "Remembrance of Syrian Independence Day."

29. *al-ʿĀṣima,* 2 May 1919, 1; *al-Fallāḥ* 1 (May 1919), 16.

30. *al-ʿĀṣima* 24, n.d.; FO 371/4181/89850/24, Clayton to Curzon, 17 June 1919; *al-ʿĀṣima,* 11 March 1920, 3.

interests and to whom [they] handed over political leadership."[31] Only Faysal and members of his cabinets among all the political actors of post-Ottoman Syria referred to the population of Syria as *raʿāyā* (subjects), a word that was, by the second decade of the twentieth century, both outmoded and patronizing.[32]

Thus, Syrian society for the *mutanawwirūn* and their associates in the Arab government was a dichotomous society, one in which the cultured and educated were strictly differentiated from the vulgar. As historian Keith Wrightson has written, such a worldview not only envisions a society of hierarchically ranked degrees, a society "pregnant with conflict" pitting the "better sort" against the "inferior sort," it also produces a "language of dissociation" that stigmatizes and alienates a vast majority of the population.[33] In other words, what began as a differentiation based on skills and military prowess developed into a differentiation based on moral qualities.[34] As a result, the *mutanawwirūn* failed to articulate an inclusive vision of the Syria of the future that would resonate with a majority of the Syrian population. Their inability to formulate an image that would have meaningful cultural referents for Syrian society thus left the field open to those who could, such as the leadership of the popular committees and their allies.

THE DISCURSIVE FIELD OF THE POPULAR COMMITTEES

As discussed in Chapter 2, participants in the popular committees came from a wide range of social backgrounds: wealthy grain merchants and neighborhood-bound *petits-bourgeois,* landowning notables and merchant ulama, bedouin shaykhs and *qabaḍāyāt.* In part, shared *ressentiment* unified this diverse group. To some of those who joined the popular committees, the

31. *al-ʿĀṣima,* 11 September 1919, 4–6. See also *al-ʿĀṣima,* 16 June 1919, 3; MAE L:SL/vol. 14/873, Picot to MAE, 24 June 1919; FO 371/5032/81–83, Excerpts from *al-Ahrām,* 1 February 1920; USNA 59/890d.00/8/468, Jackson to Secretary of State, 4 March 1920.

32. *al-ʿĀṣima,* 3 May 1920, 2–3. For the evolution and use of the word *raʿāyā,* see Ami Ayalon, *Language and Change in the Arab Middle East: The Evolution of Modern Political Discourse,* 48–50.

33. Keith Wrightson, "Estates, Degrees, and Sorts: Changing Perceptions of Society in Tudor and Stuart England," 44–47.

34. Cp. Geoffrey Crossick's analysis of "moral terminology" in Victorian Britain in "From Gentleman to the Residuum: Languages of Social Description in Victorian Britain," 163–164.

European political interference in Syrian affairs that culminated in the Arab Revolt and the impending imposition of mandates not only stripped them of much of the prestige and/or authority that they had previously enjoyed but resulted in the twin calamities of territorial division and foreign (French, Hijazi) rule. Their hostility to the new political order was shared by many others among the secondary leadership and rank and file of the committees who had been overwhelmed by the disruptive power of late-nineteenth-century capitalism, the expansion of state capabilities, or both.

For both these groups, "progress," "civilization," and other eurogenic abstractions intoned by the *mutanawwirūn* and their allies not only held little appeal but acted as a reminder of their tribulations. Furthermore, the attempt to impose structures and categories of thought that many Syrians considered alien, in conjunction with the social and economic disruptions endured by Syrians during the nineteenth and early twentieth centuries, catalyzed an ideological reaction that took the form of a rigid and self-conscious traditionalism. In response to the assemblage of seemingly hollow values and imported social constructs espoused by the *mutanawwirūn,* popular orators and writers not only selectively drew upon and ideologized hitherto nonideologized images of a timeless and egalitarian past but, by surrounding contemporaneous dogmas with an aura of immutability, they provided the principles and moral imperative for community reconstruction and day-to-day social conduct.

At the core of the discursive field that suffused the speeches, leaflets, articles, and manifestos of propagandists associated with the popular committees in post-Ottoman Syria was a set of interconnected images: the organicism and historic continuity of the Syrian nation and the interdependence of members of the national community; the autonomy of civil society and its primacy over the institutions of state; the virtue of traditional values and their vulnerability in the face of alien conspiracies, traitors, and "those who would sell the nation like a commodity."

As outlined in the previous chapter, the national community envisioned by organizers for and activists in the popular committees was larger than the narrow confines of quarter or town but smaller than the pan-Arab state originally advocated by the sharifians. This community was a *Syrian* national community, composed of inhabitants who lived within the "natural boundaries" of Syria and who shared natural affinities derived from a common culture and economy. Since this community had existed for centuries, even when it had been submerged in larger political entities such as the Ottoman Empire, its right to absolute independence was not based on the

Arab Revolt but on a common ancestry and on the soil that "has soaked up the blood of our grandfathers and fathers":[35]

> You have been directed from numerous generations toward the aspiration of right, and right appeared in front of you and fled as a fugitive and you followed it. In your race is the blood of your forefathers and in your hearts is their freedom and noble attributes. You want to live as your forefathers lived, as the lion lives in his lair and the eagle in the sky.[36]

The bond that united Syrians was thus not a political bond but rather the commonality of worldview and interests derived from race and the historic experience of the Syrian nation.

This organic notion of Syria held by popular leaders and their constituents governed their attitude toward the nature of the state and its proper relation to society. While in the eyes of many the Arab government lacked legitimacy for a number of reasons—the prominent role played by "foreigners," particularly "barbaric" Hijazis; the incompetence of its economic policies; its seemingly sycophantic and overly conciliatory foreign policy—the "language of dissociation" used by the *mutanawwirūn* to divide the ruling elite from their charges, a language that reflected the dominance of an imperious state over a compliant society, affirmed a cleavage that appeared particularly unnatural and provocative. In contrast, the popular committees and their allies posited the independent existence of the nation (*umma*) and its precedence over the state.[37] This theme appeared constantly in the propaganda of the popular committees, from Kamil al-Qassab's description of the January 1920 demonstration quoted at the beginning of Chapter 3 to the broadsheet entitled "The Nation Dictates Its Wishes to the Syrian Congress" that also appeared over his signature. "I am not inter-

35. From a speech delivered by Kamil al-Qassab, transcribed in *al-Kināna*, 15 July 1920, 2–3.

36. Included in a speech delivered by Felix Faris transcribed in AD 2346/c1a, "Remembrance of Syrian Independence Day." See also leaflets and transcriptions contained in the following: MAE L:SL/vol. 43/62–171, Original copies of "nombreux tractes, affiches, et manifestes . . . répandus à profusion à travers la ville (Damas) avant et pendant le séjour des délégués (Américains)," n.d.; AD 2345, 5 March 1920; AD 2372/dossier: propagande anti-française, 8–9 March 1920.

37. During the Faysali period, the term *umma* was perhaps the most commonly used term for "nation." While originally referring to the community of Muslim believers, it was one of a group of terms derived from religion used to denote nonreligious referents when other terms were lacking or inadequate or when such usage was already commonplace, as it was by the first decades of the twentieth century. It was employed by both discursive communities.

ested in the government, inasmuch as it is a shadow of the nation and it governs you as you are," an editorialist wrote on the pages of *al-Difāʿ*. "If I want reform, I must first start with the nation."[38]

The *umma* was, for the discursive community that contained the popular committees and their allies, self-regulating and normally harmonious, able to organize itself without the interference of government. Thus, for those within the popular committees, Syria was not merely a collection of autonomous communities requiring the intervention of government or the *mutanawwirūn* to effect its consolidation, nor was it horizontally stratified. Syrians, with historic ancestors and contemporaneous brothers, were (to cite a common metaphor) family. "Do not accept the dismemberment of your country, your family, your fatherland. Syria is one and indivisible," a "Devoted Arab Citizen" wrote in a leaflet distributed on the eve of the arrival of the King-Crane Commission to Damascus.[39] Article three of the charter establishing the branches of the Higher National Committee reiterated this theme, in effect conferring on the popular committees the role of family guardian:

> The committee of each quarter, neighborhood, or community will guide the people of the neighborhood or community to do what they must for their fatherland [in order to realize] the goals stated in the previous article. It attends especially to strengthening the harmony, affection, and mutual understanding among the people of the quarter so that they can be like one family, and to strengthening the patriotic and national ties among all the sons of the fatherland.[40]

Just as a family is composed of discrete but interdependent members united by ties of kinship, Syria, according to those orators and writers who were affiliated with the popular committees, was composed of discrete but interdependent *ṭabaqāt* (singular, *ṭabaqa*)—a term that, although usually rendered into English as "classes," more closely resembles "estates" when situated in the discursive field of the committees. The use of the words *ṭabaqa*/*ṭabaqāt* was, like the use of many words found in nationalist texts, not restricted to one particular community of discourse. Amir Faysal, for example, occasionally used the term as a synonym for "beliefs" or "creeds" (*madhāhib*), and the progovernment journalist Khalil Mardam Bek divided the people of Hama into two *ṭabaqāt*—the "gentlemen" or "upper classes"

38. *al-Difāʿ*, 13 January 1920, 1.
39. MD 7N4182/4/340, Picot to MAE, 21 July 1919; MAE L:SL/vol. 43/86, 88.
40. SL:LW, "Niẓām al-lijān al-waṭaniyya al-farʿiyya fī bilād Sūriyya," 17 November 1919.

(*sāda, khāṣṣa*) and the "masses" (*ʿāmma*)—based on what he called their "social upbringing."[41] As should be expected, however, the term's connotations shifted significantly when integrated into the discursive field identified with the popular committees. For example, an article published in the progovernment newspaper *al-Kawkab* used *ṭabaqāt* in a sense that approximates that of Mardam Bek—that is, to bifurcate Syrian society. "In Syria today there is a large organized party striving urgently for independence and happiness without halting in the face of difficulties," an editorialist wrote.

> I would not be exaggerating if I said that the *ṭabaqa* of common people, laborers, and peasants all help this party without exception in its demands. It recognizes but one word, "Independence, Independence"—no foreigner in the country—without needing commentary on this word and without outlining a philosophy. The enlightened *ṭabaqa* [*al-ṭabaqa al-mutanawwira*] works day and night explaining this word in terms of language and politics. . . . If those who hold different opinions were to renounce some of their interpretations and strive for the ties of mutual understanding, we would see all Syrians treading a single road, without obstacles and difficulties.[42]

For the members of the popular committees and their allies, on the other hand, the division of society into *ṭabaqāt* differed from this division of society in two ways: first, although texts presented different categories of *ṭabaqāt* (including, for example, merchants, wealthy merchants, workers [*ʿummāl*], peasants, ulama, government functionaries, etc.), they always presented Syrian society as composed of more than two parts. Syrian society was thus not bifurcated into hierarchic and opposing factions. As opposed to the "language of dissociation" used by the *mutanawwirūn*, the division of society into a number of distinct but fundamentally analogous *ṭabaqāt* connoted a social order that was both inclusive and democratic. Second, since each *ṭabaqa* had a different function in society, all *ṭabaqāt* had to act in harmony for society to operate smoothly. Petitions circulated by the popular committees expressing the so-called "will of the nation," as well as speeches by such popular spokesmen as Kamil al-Qassab, underscored the essential interrelationship among *ṭabaqāt* by commonly using

41. *al-ʿĀṣima,* 6 May 1920, 4; Mardam Bek, *Dimashq wal-Quds fī al-ʿishrīnāt,* 148.

42. *al-Kawkab,* 13 January 1920, 12. See also *al-ʿĀṣima,* 11 September 1919, 6; *al-ʿĀṣima,* 16 October 1919, 1–2; *al-ʿĀṣima,* 8 December 1919, 1–2.

the phrase *kull ṭabaqāt* (all *ṭabaqāt*) to mean the totality of the Syrian nation. In contrast, the propaganda of the popular committees treated those who opposed committee activities as a *ṭabaqa* beyond the pale of the community: "There is among the sons of man a *ṭabaqa* that cannot see life as pleasurable except by retaining influence, even if this leads to the crushing of reality and the destruction of the sons of man."[43]

For the discursive community of the popular committees, the *ṭabaqāt* that constituted society were linked by ties of mutual obligation. The wealthy citizens of Syria, for example, had an obligation to help the poor by paying the traditional alms (*zakāt*). Shaykh Muhammad Hamdi al-Safarjalani, one of the founding members of the Higher National Committee, pleaded for the payment of such charity in a guest editorial that appeared on the front page of *al-ʿĀṣima:*

> Is it not the duty of the rich to construct hospitals for the poor of the nation, as well as eating places and schools for the education of their children, since they are all vital members of the nation, not dissevered limbs begging on the roads? . . . Thus, I encourage people of good will of every quarter to form associations whose purpose is the collection of *zakāt* from the rich to transfer to the poor, and for all endeavors aimed at creating harmony among the individuals of the *umma*.[44]

Poverty in Damascus, epitomized by the "residue of the alleys"—abandoned or neglected children—would be alleviated only when the wealthy, who were "aloof from an important duty, like the duty of the aorta whose function it is to guide the blood to other veins,"[45] fulfilled their obligations.

For members of the popular committees and their supporters, the interdependence of the *ṭabaqāt*, as well as the primacy of the historically determined and self-regulating Syrian *umma* and a rigorously applied traditionalism, influenced the configuration of all categories within the discursive field that guided mores and public behavior, including those that conjoined gender and social function. Between the mid-nineteenth century and the

43. *al-Kināna*, 26 June 1920, 2. See also *al-Kawkab*, 27 January 1920, 5; SL:LW, al-Qassab, "Important Notice," (in Arabic), early March 1920; USNA 165/2558–16, Military Attaché (Cairo) to DMI (reprint of speech by al-Qassab from *al-Ahrām*), 16 March 1920; FO 371/5188/E4515/35, "Arabic Press Abstracts for Week Ending April 26, 1920"; USNA DC RG84/vol. 24/674, Shahbandar to US Consul (Damascus). Arabic transcription of protest delivered by the Higher National Committee, 18 May 1920.

44. *al-ʿĀṣima*, 17 November 1919, 1–2.

45. *al-ʿĀṣima*, 12 January 1920, 1.

first decades of the twentieth, a variety of factors contributed to the disarrangement of the social and economic position that had been previously held by women in Syrian society. Among these factors were the restructuring of urban space; the decline of rural autarchy and the simultaneous expansion of links coupling town and countryside; the reorganization of artisanal production and shifting patterns of employment engendered by new technologies (such as the introduction of sewing machines to Damascus); demographic irregularities brought about by war and migration; and the mobilizing activities of the Arab government and its allies.[46] The discourse employed by the popular committees facilitated social reconstruction and the re-equilibration of gender roles by exhorting activities and values that were congruent with the new realities, while simultaneously protecting those activities and values from the imputation of innovation by wrapping them in the garb of "tradition."

Through these acts of authentication, the local popular committees authorized women to engage in a variety of activities in the public sphere, including many that had previously been denied them. Like the Arab government and its allies, for example, the popular committees of Damascus and Aleppo encouraged women to participate in planned demonstrations. Unlike their rivals, however, the popular committees reportedly permitted and even encouraged women to assess and collect money to support local branch committees. Furthermore, if anecdotal evidence and the accounts of foreign observers are accurate, women joined—and perhaps in some cases were conscripted into—militias organized by the popular committees, not just as auxiliaries but as combatants.[47] "The wife of the prophet waged ji-

46. See, for example, FO 371/2770/189602, I.C.E.C. (Switzerland), 19 September 1916; FO 371/3058/137867, "Internal Conditions," 11 May 1917; FO 371/3400/100453, "Enemy Treatment of Armenians," Clayton to Sec. of State for Foreign Affairs, 19 May 1918; FO 371/4227/77186, Report by Major Davenport (APO Amman), 22 April 1919; MD 4H112/2a, "Report on Independence Day Celebrations at Aleppo," Lt. Kouadi, 10 March 1920; James Anthony Reilly, "Women in the Economic Life of Late-Ottoman Damascus"; Reilly, "Origins of Peripheral Capitalism," 155–156, 158.

47. MAE L:SL/vol. 21/44, Roux to MAE, 22 January 1920; Interviews with Kamil Daghmush (2 November 1989) and Abu Ribah al-Jaza'iri (15 November 1989), both veterans of the Battle of Maysalun. An article in *al-ʿĀṣima*, 22 December 1919, 3, describes two women from Iraq who also joined the military. Unfortunately, the article fails to note whether the unit(s) they joined consisted of regulars or irregulars.

had," one female volunteer reportedly told her brother before departing to fight at Khan Maysalun. "How can you go and not me?"[48]

The discursive field of the popular committees thus invested women with a different set of responsibilities from those found in the discursive field of the *mutanawwirūn*. As described in the previous chapter, under the rubric of progress the *mutanawwirūn* confirmed a distinctive space for women's activities alongside and supplementary to that for men's. Consequently, from the perspective of the *mutanawwirūn*, women were to contribute to the nation by undertaking acts of charity through philanthropic societies (such as the Women's Charitable Thrift Society [*jamʿīyat al-iqtiṣād al-nisāʾī al-khayrī*] of Aleppo and the Awakening of Arab Women [*yaqẓat al-fatāt al-ʿarabiyya*] and Charitable Affairs for Muslim Women [*al-umūr al-khayriyya lil-fatayāt al-muslimāt*] of Beirut),[49] by organizing women's affiliates to established nationalist associations, by educating their children, and by participating in those public activities (demonstrations, petition campaigns, voting) that would prepare them for their role as "mothers of the nation." According to an article in *al-ʿĀṣima*, for example, at the founding meeting of a women's association in Aleppo in December 1919, the obviously upper-class participants resolved the following: to spend less on clothes and other commodities, and to postpone purchases; to promote and use "national" cloth rather than cloth imported from Europe; to abandon high fashion and return to simpler styles; to give up extravagant customs, such as refusing to wear the same dress to two different weddings; to create a place to teach tailoring and styling, and to appoint a council and president to supervise its operation; and to "spread a nationalist spirit among women . . . [so that they might] train the men of the future."[50]

Similarly, while "cultured" women also enlisted in the Arab army, their activities—wrapping bandages and tending to the wounded—replicated

48. Jān Alexān, "Zaynab fī Maysalūn." Interviewed forty years after the Syrian rout, she also told the reporter, "I cannot describe my feelings exactly. We all knew that the invading army was stronger than ours, but our faith was strong. We hoped that we would be martyred on the field of battle and [thus] revive the fatherland." According to her recollections, three women from her village volunteered to fight at the Battle of Maysalun.

49. *al-ʿĀṣima*, 5 February 1920, 5; Lybyer Papers, R.S. 15/13/22, "Statement of the Moslem Women Presented to the Commission at Beirut, July 8, 1919." The latter document lists two other organizations that comprised the "Societies of Moslem Women in Beirut": *dār al-ṣināʿāt al-bayrūtiyya*, and *madrasat nādī al-fatayāt*.

50. *al-ʿĀṣima*, 18 December 1919, 3–4; *al-Kawkab*, 11 November 1919, 11; IO L/PS/10/802/12, Gertrude Bell, "Syria in October 1919," 15 November 1919 (particularly pages 12ff.).

the role established for them by the *mutanawwirūn* in society in general. One such woman, Nazik al-ʿAbid, the future wife of the Beiruti litterateur and Syrian General Congress representative Muhammad Jamil Bayhum, even received the title "honorary president" of the Arab army "in recognition of her efforts on behalf of the daughters of the martyrs, for her community service, and for her participation in women's [*nisāʾiyya*] activities."[51]

The discursive field of the popular committees, on the other hand, did not sanction either progress as a paradigmatic principle or the "civilized" nations of Europe as archetypes. Thus, because their discursive field did not recognize women as an autonomous category within the *umma,* the committees regarded the unprecedented and conspicuously eurogenic attempts made by the *mutanawwirūn* to extend the franchise to women and state-sponsored educational opportunities to girls as both treacherous and divisive, a threat to the indivisibility and purity of the historic Syrian community. Hence the vehemence with which the Democratic Party and its supporters waged their campaign against women's suffrage, for example: like the widely circulated stories of assaults against Syrian women committed by French soldiers stationed in the western zone, the activities of the *mutanawwirūn* metaphorically signified imperialism's violation of the integrity of the *umma.* Conversely, neither the depth of these feelings nor its causes was lost on the *mutanawwirūn:* months before lower-class Damascene youths began to assault women who dressed in Western fashions, *al-ʿĀṣima* warned women to avoid activities and ostentatious displays that might be interpreted as a "challenge [to] others" and to comport themselves in a manner that "is strictly in accordance with [others'] social life and customs" when venturing out in public.[52]

The battle over women's suffrage and education was thus but one front in a war that the popular committees and their supporters waged in the name of the nation against "false traitors"[53]—fifth-columnists and other dupes of Western imperialism. The resignification of the terms *mushāghib* (agitator) and *mankūb* (oppressed, unfortunate)[54] by the popular committees illustrates how these groups appropriated labels that originally held pejorative meaning and transformed them into symbols that affirmed the autonomy and cohesion of the *umma.*

51. Bayhum, *Sūriyya wa Lubnān 1918–1922,* 167.
52. *al-ʿĀṣima,* 12 January 1920, 1–2.
53. *al-Kināna,* 15 July 1920, 3.
54. For copies of leaflets signed "*mankūb*" see MAE L:SL/vol. 43/62, 64, n.d.; MD 7N4182/4/340, Picot to MAE, 21 July 1920.

The Arab government first employed the term *mushāghib,* for example, to describe those who challenged or demonstrated against its policies. ʿAli Rida al-Rikabi used the term in a speech delivered on the occasion of Faysal's return from his first trip to Europe in May 1919, contending "the esteemed sons of the nation are naturally prepared to assimilate modern civilization, no matter how much *mushāghibūn* agitate and no matter what liars purport."[55] The term was adopted by al-Rikabi's successor as military governor (Mustafa Niʿmat[56]) who, at the height of the Evacuation Crisis, condemned those *mushāghibūn* who "in their fervor forget their duty and foment arguments at a time when complete calm is called for."[57] In reply, the newspaper *al-Difāʿ* printed a scathing front-page editorial in which the author, who identified himself only by the title *mushāghib,* compared himself to his adversaries:

> I do not want a chair in one of the offices of the palace.
> I do not want the presidency of one of the large associations.
> I do not want to offend one who believes he should precede me, although he is not better than I.
> I do not want money from the treasury, although by lacking this money I am impoverished.
> I do not want distinction in the city where the title *sayyid* or *zaʿīm* would delight me.
> I do not want to bring a *zaʿīm* to his chair, my being with him being like butter and honey.
> I do not want to pay the price of silence.
> I do not want to return to a custom which benefits me alone and which injures the nation as a whole.
> I do not want a stance like the stance taken by Samson when he shook the pillars of the temple and collapsed it, saying, "Upon myself and your enemies, O Lord."[58]

The discursive field of the popular committees and their supporters

55. *al-ʿĀṣima,* 7 May 1919, 5–6.
56. ʿAbd al-Hamid al-Qaltaqji held the post for a few days between al-Rikabi and Niʿmat.
57. *al-ʿĀṣima,* 15 December 1919, 5.
58. *al-Difāʿ,* 13 January 1920, 1.
59. See AD 2372/dossier: propagande anti-française, 19 December 1918; MD 7N4182/dossier 4/340, Picot to MAE, 14 April 1919; AD 2430/dossier confidentiel—départ, Cousse to HC, 17 May 1919 (Arabic enclosure); AD 2329/dossier a-1, Unsigned, untitled leaflet, 25 June 1919; MAE L:AH/vol. 4/48 (undated Arabic leaflets and broadsheets); MAE L:SL/vol. 43, Original leaflets, 21 July 1919; FO 371/4185/156060 B.II/6946 (M.I.2), DMI to Under Sec. of State, 26 November 1919. Amir Faysal also adapted the phrase in a June 1919 speech delivered in

counterposed the community of *mushāghibūn* to its antithesis in the form of a conspiracy of those "who would sell their nation like a commodity."[59] While this particular trope is not unique to Faysali Syria (cp. the conspiracy of the *vendepatria* in Peronist Argentina), it was particularly germane to this period because it accommodated anti-imperialism, the antimarket economic paternalism advocated by the popular committees and supported by their constituents, and Qur'anic allusion.[60] "Down with those who have sold their fatherland," read one leaflet distributed by Black Hand. "Awaken, Syrians, and take care: your fatherland has been sold, and you have yet to take vengeance on those who have done it." Another leaflet warned Syrians to "Rescue the nation before it is lost. . . . Overthrow the sellers [of the nation] before they commit the crime of treason."[61]

Like the "aristocratic plot" conjured up by the radical democrats of the French Revolution and analyzed by, among others, François Furet and Lynn Hunt,[62] the conspiracy of "those who would sell their nation like a commodity" served two purposes for the popular committees and their allies. First, it served to legitimate the activities of the committees by elevating what many might otherwise have considered a mere contest for power to a struggle of Promethean proportions:

> O nation! O sons of Syria—My brothers! . . . He who charges you with fickleness is a cunning hypocrite, a traitor, or an ignoramus who pretends to know. He is to be considered a fool at least. It is possible that an individual sell his principle and enslave his honor. As for the totality of the people, there is not enough money in the whole world to buy them, and there is no power in the whole world able to crush them, because they demand in every step the right which God granted them in life. And he who defends the right of God is too noble to be sold and too powerful to be annihilated.[63]

Second, the plot provided the revolutionaries with a mirror image—an

---

Damascus: "I spoke [at the peace conference] and I asked that the independence of Iraq and Syria should not be sold for the little help she needs from the outside, but Syria should be allowed to buy that help for what it is worth." FO 371/4181/89850/24, Clayton to Curzon, 27 June 1919.

60. An editorialist for *al-Difāʿ* hinted at this last association when, alluding to the story of Jacob and Esau, he wrote, "I do not want to sell my right of the first-born for a bite of lentil." *al-Difāʿ*, 13 January 1920, 1.

61. AD 2329/a-1, 25 June 1919; MAE L:SL/vol. 43/63, 21 July 1919.

62. Furet, *Interpreting the French Revolution*, 53–56; Lynn Hunt, *Politics, Culture, and Class in the French Revolution*, 38–48.

63. Included in a speech delivered by Felix Faris transcribed in AD 2346/c1a, "Remembrance of Syrian Independence Day."

"anti-principle" of conspiracies designed to defend privilege and parochial interests—against which the new order might contrast itself.

On the other hand, while the denunciations of traitors, slanderers, and renegades "who speak to foreigners in the name of [the nation] while following ambitions and personal interests that are incompatible with [it]"[64] are a common recourse for groups forced to confront the realities of mass politics for the first time, they inevitably coarsen political debate. The propaganda of the partisans of the popular committees in Syria, like the propaganda of the French radicals before them, was filled with violent images and calls for vigilance against the enemies of the nation. An Independence Day speech delivered by Sami al-Sarraj before the Arab Club of Aleppo is representative of this new militant idiom:

> Before I spoke, princes of words did well, and they formed ideas and played on the heartstrings in mild tunes. However, I wish to shake the strings of energy in the hearts of the people. Perhaps children sleep because of lively rocking and the chanting of the mother. I hand the people over to God that they sleep after this.
>
> How far is sleep from the camps of men in the desolate desert when savage beasts, crouching, penetrate the rocks and find hiding places, and hungry vultures circle in the sky, and snakes and vipers slither in the gravel?
>
> How far is sleep from those who set out on a night when the moon is absent and shadows are murky and the gloom increases?
>
> How far is sleep from a nation such as the Arab nation, which having put on the sword belt and taking the bow of courage from its shoulder, brandishes the sword of the *futūwa* so that the cosmos becomes terrified and the age becomes disturbed?
>
> The eye of the lion does not sleep while the jackal rips out its cub.[65]

This coarsening of political rhetoric was, of course, not confined to the discursive community of the popular committees; the violence of these denunciations (which, in the immediate aftermath of the Faysal-Clemenceau Agreement, counted the amir himself among the traitors) placed a premium on militancy by all nationalist factions. In this atmosphere, even Faysal was forced to adopt a militant posture when he was out of earshot of

64. AD 2372/dossier: propagande anti-française, "To the Noble Arabs," 19 December 1918; *al-Difāʿ*, 13 January 1920, 1. See also al-ʿIyāshī, *al-Īḍāḥāt al-siyāsiyya*, 105–106. The leaflet contained in the first citation, reportedly distributed by the Arab Independence Party, uses the phrase to warn against those who would divide the nation by appealing to sectarianism. This demonstrates how familiar phrases were later invested with new meaning when recontextualized.

65. AD 2346/c1a, "Remembrance of Syrian Independence Day," 17–20.

the diplomats assembled in Paris. The amir thus interlaced his speeches—even those that counseled patience—with the face-saving slogan, "Independence is taken, not conferred," which he had first enunciated upon his return from Paris after initialing his agreement with Clemenceau.[66]

Overall, the tone and content of the discursive field employed by the popular committees and their allies, its traditionalism and distinctive assemblage and counterposition of images—the dissociation of the "nation" (as represented by the committees and their sympathizers) from its enemies (as represented by those who "would sell their nation like a commodity"), the organic bonds that united the diverse members of the former and the dangers posed by the conspiracies hatched by the latter, and so on—link the popular movement that arose in Faysali Syria with populist movements that have emerged in other places during other periods. Like the Syrian popular movement, populist movements have historically arisen as a political response to a societal disjuncture, such as that prompted by the rapid and uneven spread of market-oriented relations. Not only does the variable scope and timing of social transformation cleave society into dissimilar and competing segments, it facilitates the formation of a new political bloc from among the disaffected and excluded.[67] The discursive options open to this political bloc reflect both the circumstances of its origins and its vulnerability to disruption by the power of capital and state that impelled its creation in the first place. Hence, the repetitiveness of populist tropes through time. While the discursive field of the popular committees

66. See, for example, USNA 59/890d.00/8/468, Jackson to Sec. of State, 4 March 1920; MD/4H114/dossier 4/459, Cousse to Gouraud, 27 May 1920; FO 371/5188/E7808/42, "Arabic Press Abstracts for Week Ending June 14 1920." According to the 29 May 1920 edition of the Beirut newspaper *al-Ḥaqīqa,* for example, Faysal repeated the slogan in a speech that contained the following paragraph: "The Syrian nation has declared its independence in accordance with its own interests. The powers, although they have acknowledged this independence, have laid down certain conditions safeguarding their interests. While we have declared our independence, we have promised to respect the interests of all nations so that we may be united in friendship with the peoples that we fought beside as allies. The powers have laid down their conditions and have said: 'Come, let there be no friction between our interests and yours.' It appears from this that we have suffered no wrong hitherto. The gates of negotiation are still open to both sides, and we must know that we are regarded as an independent nation."

67. J. B. Allcock, "'Populism': A Brief Biography," 382, 386; Kenneth Minogue, "Populism as a Political Movement," 200; William F. Holmes, "Populism: In Search of Context," 37–41; Margaret Canovan, "Two Strategies for the Study of Populism," 544–552; Angus Stewart, "The Social Roots"; Donald MacRae, "Populism as an Ideology"; Carlos M. Vilas, "Latin American Populism: A Structural Approach," 391.

was thus hardly unique, it does display the common set of concerns experienced by a population or segment of a population that, perceiving itself the victim of economic, social, and/or political peripheralization, sets about reconstituting itself as "the nation" in opposition to a politically dominant "antination."

SYMBOLS, FIELDS, AND NATIONALIST HISTORIES

In a recent essay, Philip Khoury pointed out that "[w]here studies of the rise of Arab nationalism fall short is their neglect to explain how and why the idea of Arabism is translated into a full-blown political movement."[68] Although attempts to resolve this problem have generated a contentious debate among historians of modern Middle Eastern history, the question is unanswerable as posed because it is premised on two assumptions that do not stand up to scrutiny: that there was a singular evolutionary path for nationalism in the Arab Middle East, and that this nationalism was the exclusive product of a particular group of thinkers who then propagated it ("with revolutionary abruptness," according to Elie Kedourie[69]) among the rest of the population.

While salon habitués, ambitious military officers, and belletrists did provide an outline for a post-Ottoman Arab polity, their influence was circumscribed by their inability (and reluctance) to address popular concerns in a compelling idiom. As a result, the nationalism of nationalist mythopoeia—the nationalism of Arabist intellectuals and al-Fatat and Faysal and "God belongs to the individual, the nation to all"—did not go uncontested in Syria after World War I. It was challenged on multiple levels from within the nationalist tendency by Syrian Unionists and their collaborators who distrusted the sharifians and the Arab Revolt, by Syrian nativists who resented the interference by "foreigners" in Syrian affairs, by traditionalist ulama and their merchant allies who took exception to the imposition of alien conceits and feared marginalization at the hands of rising elites, and by a heterogeneous political bloc that not only drew from the previous three categories but included large numbers of Syrians whom the sharifians and their allies had mobilized but failed to win over to their program. Because the popular committees were able to articulate the concerns of this last group in a language that was germane to their needs, these Syrians did not remain indifferent to nationalist controversies, nor did their participation

68. Philip S. Khoury, "Syrian Political Culture: A Historical Perspective," 19.
69. Elie Kedourie, "Pan-Arabism and British Policy," 213.

in politics subside as the coercive power of the Arab government diminished. Spokesmen for the popular committees drew from an assortment of symbols that were evocative, while reshaping those symbols by recontextualizing them within an integrated discursive field. By means of this process, those symbols accrued new meanings pertinent to a population unsettled by decades of crisis and faced with the task of community reconstruction.

There is no denying that adding a popular dimension to the nationalist legend provides for a more troublesome nationalism, a nationalism in which a Syrian "territorial" identity challenges an Arab one, Islamic imagery embellishes the legend of the "martyrs," and rumors of French sexual assaults against Muslim women weigh as heavily on the minds of those who volunteered to fight at Khan Maysalun as the example of the Arab Revolt. Nevertheless, if historians of nationalism in the Arab Middle East have overlooked these sentiments, they might at least take consolation from the peculiar blindness of ʿAbd al-Qadir al-Muzaffar, the first president of the Damascus branch of the Arab Club, who also failed to comprehend the popular dimension of nationalist politics in Syria. A little more than a month before a Damascus crowd stormed the Syrian General Congress, looted weapons from the Damascus Citadel, fought loyalist soldiers on the streets of Damascus, then massed at Baramki Station for transportation west to wage *"al-jihād al-waṭanī"* against the French, al-Muzaffar told French officials, "If you would want to provoke a demonstration, we would have difficulty bringing together fifty men."[70]

70. AD 2374/dossier: TEO zone ouest: adm., cabinet politique/1193/CP, "Zone est: situation générale," 15 June 1920.

Part Three

THE CEREMONIES OF NATIONALISMS

5 Mobilization from Above and the Invention of Traditions

Part II identified the sometimes shared, sometimes idiosyncratic symbolic components of the two main nationalist communities of discourse in post-World War I Syria—the community of the Arab government and its *mutanawwirūn* allies, on the one hand, and the community of the popular committees and their supporters, on the other—and outlined both the individual and composite connotations that community participants derived from them. The competition between the rival communities to effectuate what they considered to be suitable boundaries and attributes for their national community—a competition that involved both the creation and arrogation of symbols and slogans as well as attempts to delineate an appropriate array of meanings for them—often took place in public and semipublic spaces. Orators delivered speeches in restricted clubs and at public demonstrations; actors performed didactic plays in theaters and municipal squares; patrons of coffeehouses listened to and argued over newspaper editorials that other customers read aloud; and parades, organized according to some ritual specialist's idea of the proper representation of society, marched through winding neighborhood streets and on main thoroughfares.[1] In this chapter and the next, I shall examine one means by which rival groups of nationalists contested and substantiated their ideas: collective ceremonies. The analysis of collective ceremonies is necessary not only to understand the diverse messages with which competing political associations sought to attract and instruct the population of Syria, but also to understand the process by which a political public was created and mobilized.

1. I have borrowed the term *ritual specialist* to designate the individuals responsible for planning public ceremonies from Christel Lane's extremely useful *The Rites of Rulers: Ritual in Industrial Society—The Soviet Case.*

As defined by anthropologists Sally F. Moore and Barbara Myerhoff, a collective ceremony is "a dramatic occasion, a complex type of social behavior that usually has a purpose, but one that alludes to more than it says, and has many meanings at once."[2] An effective collective ceremony in the secular sphere acts in the same manner as an effective religious rite: it connects the participant, both as an individual and as a member of a community, to an exemplary order so that "the world as lived and the world as imagined, fused under the agency of a single set of symbolic forms, turn out to be the same world."[3] Those who participate in an effective ceremony thus temporarily leave the profane world and enter a world in which only symbolic activity takes place, a world in which men walking down the street are transformed into a parade.[4]

Ceremonies use symbols in two ways: they not only contain symbols, but the ceremony itself, in its entirety, acts as a symbol. Symbols contained within a ceremony—the flags carried by a ceremony's participants or the uniforms worn by them, the slogans shouted in a line of march, enunciated in speeches, or inscribed on placards or banners, and so on—might be read by applying the same techniques as are employed in the analysis of symbols contained within other texts. The analysis of the symbolism contained in the morphology of a ceremony, however, requires the adoption of an additional methodology, a methodology suggested by Clifford Geertz.

Ceremonies, according to Geertz, consist of two forms of modeling: they provide a "model of [social] reality," which entails "the manipulation of symbolic structures so as to bring them, more or less closely, into parallel with the pre-established non-symbolic system," and a "model for [social] reality," which entails "the manipulation of the non-symbolic system in terms of the relationships expressed in the symbolic."[5] Geertz's formulation allows those who are investigating ceremony to escape both the one-dimensional bounds of Durkheimian functionalism (implicit in Geertz's conception of ceremony as a "model of [social] reality"), according to which ceremony acts exclusively as symbolic representation of social solidarity, and the vulgar Marxist view (corresponding to Geertz's conception of ceremony as a "model for [social] reality"), according to which ceremony

2. Sally F. Moore and Barbara Myerhoff, "Secular Ritual: Forms and Meanings," 5.

3. Clifford Geertz, "Religion as a Cultural System," 28.

4. Mosse, *Nationalization of the Masses*, 50–51, 208.

5. Geertz, "Religion as a Cultural System," 28; Lane, *Rites of Rulers*, 12. Don Handelman succinctly characterizes the dual role of ceremony in the title of his book, *Models and Mirrors: Towards an Anthropology of Public Events.*

functions as the means by which society's dominant groups impose their values on subordinate groups.[6] As Geertz appreciates, the very potency and veridicality of ceremony is rooted in the fact that it is not unidimensional; on the contrary, a ceremony's potency and veridicality come from the fact that it functions as a "multivocal" symbol, simultaneously celebrating the individual in society both as he is and as he ought to be.

Although most ceremonies simultaneously provide a "model of" and a "model for" reality, they rarely balance the two functions of modeling equally. Didactic ceremonies, commonly celebrated among new and/or revolutionary regimes, naturally seek to downplay the "model of" aspect of ceremony, which would only reinforce the social divisions and goals of the *ancien régime.* Thus, ceremonies of such regimes, designed by ritual specialists to inculcate a specific mapping of the new regime's ideology, attempt to emphasize the "model for" aspect of ceremony to the point of excluding all traces of the "model of" aspect. Such an emphasis is not unproblematic: there is, of course, an inherent contradiction between the desire of ritual specialists to create ceremonies to inculcate a pat, formulaic "model for" reality and the ceremonial process itself. The effectiveness of symbols depends on their multivocality, but it is this very multivocality that the ritual specialist employed by the new and/or revolutionary regime must eliminate in order to instruct the population in a set of prescribed values. In the process of constructing ceremony, the ritual specialist thus reduces symbols to mere signs; in other words, for every symbol/signifier, there will be one and only one meaning/signified. Thus, the closer a ceremony approaches the didacticism of a pure "model for" society, the less likely it is to have resonance with a population.[7]

The various ceremonies organized by the Arab government, such as demonstrations, parades, and theatrical productions, with their didacticism and overdeveloped "model for" component, lacked efficacy and power in part for this reason. As will be seen below, however, the form that these ceremonies took was not chosen arbitrarily; rather, their form was necessarily derived from both the tactical approach adopted by the Arab government to achieve independence and the express model of social relations embedded within the government's ideology. In contrast, because the "model for" society prescribed by the ritual specialists in the popular committees more closely substantiated the social relations of the participants as those participants believed or preferred them to be, the ceremonies spon-

6. Emile Durkheim, *Elementary Forms of the Religious Life,* 245.
7. Lane, *Rites of Rulers,* 13, 192–193, 281.

sored by the popular committees could and did forgo many of the more obviously prescriptive elements contained within the demonstrations organized by their rivals. As a result, they acquired a cogency for participants that, if eyewitness accounts are to be believed, was unmatched by other ceremonies mounted in Faysali Syria.

MOBILIZATION FROM ABOVE: CREATING THE CROWD

In its attempt to implant the principles of sharifian legitimacy and to inculcate the nationalist values associated with the *mutanawwirūn* among the Syrian population, the Arab government faced a dilemma. The urgency to establish and maintain authority within the eastern zone, to disseminate the ideals of the *mutanawwirūn*, and to demonstrate to the entente powers not only that Syria was prepared to assume its place among civilized nations but that Syrians were united in their desire for independence and sharifian representation at the Paris conference compelled the Arab government to undertake a controlled mobilization of the Syrian population. But because many of those who had previously held the reins of local authority considered the Arab government to be composed of upstarts, intruders, or both, the government, its representatives and supporters in cities and towns throughout Syria, and its allies among the *mutanawwirūn* could not rely upon preexisting networks to mobilize the Syrian population for them. Furthermore, unlike the traditional notability and the local leadership of the popular committees, members and agents of the Arab government frequently had little knowledge of the neighborhoods and villages they sought to control. As a result, they adopted a multiplicity of strategies to bypass or co-opt their rivals. These strategies ranged from the previously mentioned distribution of bribes to troublemakers and potential competitors to the subvention of newspapers and the restructuring of institutions to link the government directly with the population. By undertaking these measures, the Arab government and its supporters not only accelerated the ongoing enfeeblement of traditional structures of authority but unintentionally expedited the emergence of the popular committees.

To enhance its capacity to scrutinize and penetrate villages and urban quarters, for example, the Arab government enlisted the assistance of *makhātīr*, functionaries who had traditionally acted as intermediaries between the state and the population. During the Ottoman period, *makhātīr* had collected taxes, distributed government largesse, and transmitted information from the government to the population and vice versa. Under the Arab government, *makhātīr* did all this and more: working alongside members of the local Arab Clubs, they enforced the controversial conscription policies of the Arab government, assembled the inhabitants of their quarters for government-sponsored demonstrations and celebrations, ensured the prominent display of government-sanctioned posters throughout the quarters and villages they administered, reported on unsanctioned political activities in their districts, and supervised the closing of shops on official holidays and days of protest.[8] The *makhātīr* of Faysali Syria thus promoted the political mobilization of the population, disseminated and enforced the Arab government's ideological views, and brought villages and urban quarters that had remained relatively free of government intrusion during the Ottoman period directly and consistently under the purview of the state for the first time.[9]

The campaign mounted by the Arab government and its allies to protest remarks made by French foreign minister Stephen Pichon illustrates the close working relationship that connected the Arab government, local functionaries, leaders of extragovernmental organizations, and *makhātīr.* On 29 December 1918, on the eve of the commencement of the Paris peace conference, Pichon delivered a speech before the French chamber of deputies reaffirming France's historic interests in Syria. The speech became a cause célèbre among all Syrian nationalists, particularly those associated with the Arab government and its sympathizers in al-Fatat and the Arab Club, who saw in the speech an opportunity to launch a campaign to expand the popular base of the government.

The mobilization against the speech began with a meeting of *makhātīr* of Damascus convoked by Nasib al-Bakri, the head of Faysal's chancellery and a member of the executive committee of the Arab Club of Damascus. During the war, al-Bakri had traveled through the Hawran dispensing

8. *al-ʿĀṣima,* 27 January 1920, 5; *al-ʿĀṣima,* 5 February 1920, 4; al-ʿAllāf, *Dimashq fī maṭlaʿ al-qarn al-ʿishrīn,* 42; Balāwī, "al-Aḥzāb al-siyāsiyya fī Sūriyya," 26; Gabriel Baer, *Fellah and Townsman in the Middle East: Studies in Social History,* 119, 134–135. According to Howard M. Sachar, the Arab government also attempted to enlist *makhātīr* who lived in the coastal zone in nationalist activities. *Emergence of the Middle East,* 263.

9. Although their job required that they act as the eyes and ears of the government, some *makhātīr* joined or worked with the popular committees. See: SL:LD, Letter to al-Qassab, 18 December 1919; SL:LW, Qa'id fawj [?] to presidency of LW, 20 December 1919; AD 2430/dossier confidentiel—départ/634, Cousse to HC, 24 October 1919; FO 371/5076/E8007, "Note by Miss G. L. Bell—May 22, 1920." According to the above documents, *makhātīr* from Dayr al-ʿAtiya, Kara, Dayr al-Zur, and from the Damascus quarters of ʿAmara, Maydan, and Salihiyya participated in the activities of the Higher National Committee, its branches, or the local committee of national defense.

money to Druze chieftains on behalf of the Arab Revolt. After the Arab army entered Damascus, al-Bakri once again took on an intermediary role, this time between the Arab government and extragovernmental political organizations. In this capacity, he allocated money drawn from the government's "secret service account" for a variety of clandestine purposes.[10] In the wake of the meeting with al-Bakri, the *makhātīr* of Damascus circulated two petitions in their neighborhoods, one protesting the statements made by Pichon, the other affirming the choice of Faysal as the nation's representative to the peace conference.[11] According to a French report, the executive committee of the Arab Club drafted both petitions. British sources also challenged the credibility of the petitions, complaining not only that the *makhātīr* who gathered signatures did so in the company of gendarmes, but that they forged signatures and stamped the petitions with seals that local residents had left with them for safekeeping. The French liaison officer received a total of 200 such petitions to forward to his government, while his British colleague collected 350.[12] The petitions were so similar that the British representative sent only a sample copy of the petition protesting Pichon's remarks to his superiors in London:

> We Syrian and non-Syrian inhabitants of liberated territory, sinking all differences of caste and religion, write in protesting that the SECULAR rights claimed by France have absolutely no foundation and that we do not admit to any nation any right whatever—ancient or not—within the limits of our Motherland. Business relations based on the freedom of commerce cannot constitute any right whatever over the inhabitants, their liberty, or their national independence.
>
> In consideration of the fact that it has been announced by every great politician and particularly by the Honourable President of the United States that this war has been fought for no other end than the liberation of peoples and the cancellation of Treaties which compromise the liber-

10. al-Charkas, *al-Dalīl al-muṣawwar lil-bilād al-ʿarabiyya*, 1:62–63; SL:LW, Fawzi and Nasib al-Bakri to Higher National Committee, n.d.; AD 2367/10/1/117, Cousse to HC, 5 February 1919; DU SA 493/13/25–35, Shuqayr to Waters-Taylor, 3 September 1919; AD 2380/5/67/386, ʿAli Rida al-Rikabi to Military Governor of Aleppo, 17 February 1920; MAE L:SL/vol. 12/32–38, Cousse to HC, n.d.

11. Faysal had earlier sent a telegram to his brother Zayd in Damascus requesting that such petitions authorizing him to act as the Arab representative be forwarded to him in Paris. The anti-Pichon protests came in the wake of this request. For Faysal's authorization of the above campaign, see Mūsā, *al-Murāsalāt al-tārīkhiyya*, 2:61.

12. MAE L:SL/vol. 10/19–23, Cousse to HC, 12 February 1919; MAE L:SL/vol. 9/240, Picot to MAE, 13 February 1919; AD 2367/10/1/181, Cousse to HC, 5 March 1919; AD 2430/no no., Cousse to HC, 18 March 1919.

> ties of small nations[,] Treaties concluded without our consent we will not recognise (? gp. omitted). When our nation joined the Allies she joined them for nothing but to fight for her independence. With every fibre of our being we protest against the declaration of the Honourable Minister of Foreign Affairs of the French Republic and we trust that the Allies will help us to defend our rights and obtain our independence.[13]

The similar wording and demands contained in the petitions lend credence to French charges that they all emanated from a single source.

The Arab government supplemented the efforts of the *makhātīr* by invoking the assistance of artisanal guilds to circulate petitions and swell crowds at demonstrations. By the beginning of the twentieth century, the power and responsibilities of the guilds had diminished substantially as a result of the twin processes of Ottoman administrative revitalization and the accelerating integration of the empire into the world capitalist system. But even if, as one contemporary observer complained, the guilds of Damascus could no longer even ensure a minimal level of professional competence among their members, they still performed a variety of support and welfare functions and provided a network for intraquarter and interquarter communication.[14] The masters (*arbāb*) of each craft in Damascus, for example, acted as important conduits for the dissemination of news and information. Traveling in a circuit (*dawr,* plural *adwār*) that spanned their neighborhoods or quarters, they held court every week in the home of a different guild member, discussing both private and public affairs. After visiting the last home in their circuit, the masters returned to the first to restart the process.[15]

The Arab government and its allies in organizations such as the Arab Club sought to take advantage of these ready-made networks by using the guilds as building blocks for demonstrations and rallies.[16] For example, guilds played a major role in the demonstration organized by the Damascus municipality to greet Amir Faysal upon his return from France at the be-

13. FO 371/4179/47227/74, Clayton to Balfour, 18 March 1919.

14. al-ʿAllāf, *Dimashq fī maṭlaʿ al-qarn al-ʿishrīn,* 137.

15. In his memoirs, Hasan al-Amin reports that three *adwār* traversed his neighborhood, *ḥayy al-kharāb.* See al-Amīn, *Dhikrayāt,* 38–43.

16. See, for example, *al-ʿĀṣima,* 11 September 1919, 4–6; AD 2430/dossier confidentiel—départ/240, Cousse to HC, 11 August 1919. The popular committees also encouraged the participation of guilds in their parades and demonstrations (see, for example, Kamil al-Qassab's description of a demonstration organized on 17 January 1920 in *al-Kawkab,* 27 January 1920, 5). However, as will be discussed below, the structure of these ceremonies lent very different connotations to their participation.

ginning of May 1919. The municipal government ordered the guilds to gather along the Barada River in a prescribed order, beginning with jewelers, cereal merchants, and leather merchants, continuing through carders, innkeepers, millers, dyers, cobblers, café owners, drivers, saddlers, manufacturers of starch, blacksmiths, barbers, carpenters, bathkeepers, greengrocers, manufacturers of containers, bakers, fitters, shoemakers, licorice merchants, tinsmiths, ironworkers, butchers, potters, weavers, printers, pastry chefs, and grain merchants, and ending with merchants of the Suq al-Arwam, Suq al-Buzuriyya, and Suq al-ʿAttarin. The government directed that each guild participating in the demonstration carry a banner proclaiming "Long Live Arab Independence!" with the name of the guild or profession written, sewn, or attached below. When the amir passed in front of their position, the guildsmen were instructed to greet him with shouts of "Long Live the Amir!" and "Long Live Complete Arab Independence!" and with cheers. To ensure compliance, the municipality warned that it would assign police to monitor the activities of demonstrators at strategic intervals.[17]

To facilitate its oversight of the guilds, the Arab government supervised the reorganization of existing guilds and mandated the creation of new ones.[18] Although there exists little information about the attitude of most guild members to the restructuring and politicization of their associations, evidence indicates that some members, in particular those from religious minorities, were less than enthusiastic about the activities of the government and its allies. While more than fifty guild representatives appeared before the King-Crane Commission when the commission visited Damascus (in most cases to testify in favor of the Damascus Program promulgated by the Syrian General Congress), the commission also received a petition from Christians of Aleppo, who disputed the credentials of such associations. "[The Arab Club] has organized, with official help, guilds that must present themselves before you and speak in the name of artisans," they complained.

17. MAE L:AH/vol. 4/237–238, Picot to Pichon, 22 May 1919, (in Arabic and French).

18. See Mardam Bek, *Dimashq wal-Quds fī al-ʿishrīnāt,* 6. This is also hinted at in the broadsheet posted throughout Damascus by the municipal government on the eve of the demonstration just described: "The merchants or artisans who have not yet formed their guilds should send delegates who will assemble at the rear of the aforementioned guilds and act in accordance with the stipulations of the present program."

> At the slightest examination, you could verify that these guilds are but small groups mandated by the Arab Club for the purpose of endorsing its views. This club and the guilds are composed exclusively of Muslims, although many of the crafts are practiced almost entirely by Christians or Jews.[19]

As it did with guild members, the Arab government mobilized teachers and schoolchildren for its demonstrations and ceremonies, and as early as the spring of 1919, schoolchildren—sometimes mobilized separately, sometimes mixed in among other groups—became a regular component of the urban crowd assembled to celebrate the amir or the policies of the Arab government.[20] But because the Arab government and the *mutanawwirūn* aspired not only to enlist the young in their activities but to instill their variety of nationalism among them, the interest expressed by the government and its allies in schoolchildren extended beyond ceremonial occasions. For example, the Arab government sponsored conferences at (ironically) the Madrasa al-Kamiliyya and the normal school to acquaint administrators and teachers with a curriculum that had been drafted under government supervision so that they, in turn, might disseminate it among other primary-school teachers.[21] In the wake of this meeting, schoolchildren throughout the zone were instructed to memorize and recite panegyrics to Syria and to the values of the *mutanawwirūn*. For example,

1. The clatter of tablets[?], the squeaking of pens
   Sever the chains, throw off oppression.
   Without them we won't succeed.
   These are the life of nations.

2. We are the youth of al-Jazira,
   We are youths of the country.
   We inherited an ancient glory
   From a time that has returned.

19. MAE L:SL/vol. 43/24–32, "Rapport des Syriens Catholiques et Orthodoxes d'Alep," 18 July 1919. See also Harry N. Howard, *The King-Crane Commission: An American Inquiry in the Middle East,* 120. The Arab Club was not the only political organization that understood the value of guilds in politics. The program of the Syrian Patriotic Party called for the party to "encourage charitable, trade, and guild organizations" (*jamʿiyyāt al-ʿumāl*). Farzat, *al-Ḥayā al-ḥizbiyya fī Sūriyya,* 77.

20. AD 2430, Cousse to Dame, 18 March 1920. See also FO 371/4181/89850/24, Clayton to Curzon, 17 June 1920.

21. *al-ʿĀṣima,* 27 June 1919, 4. The overall efficacy of the efforts of the government is not known.

3. You, Syria, are my country,
You are the epitome of splendor.
All who will come to you, some day,
Covetous, will meet their death.

4. We are the ones who venture to the throes of death and, seeking dangers,
We give ourselves no choice except glory or death.[22]

Private schools and extragovernmental political associations also encouraged "patriotic instruction." In October 1919, Gertrude Bell visited the School for the Daughters of the Martyrs (*madrasat banāt al-shuhadā'*), a private school established in Damascus and financed by charitable donations. The school included among its students the orphaned daughters of members of the Arab army who had died during the Arab Revolt, as well as girls between the ages of sixteen and eighteen who came from "good Damascene families." In her report, Bell described a ceremony held in her presence:

> Girls and children were brought out into the large garden which surrounds the house to sing patriotic songs. In one of them a chorus of the elder girls addressed the orphans, reminding each one that her father died in the cause of liberty and bidding her never to forget that she was "bint al-ʿArabi" (daughter of the Arabs) while the children replied that they would never forget their birth, or King Hussein who fought for their race, nor finally (this stanza was specially prepared for the American Commission) President Wilson who laid down—save the mark—the principles of freedom.[23]

Since the public mission of the Arab Club was to raise Syria to the level of "civilized" nations and to inculcate nationalist values among the population, local chapters of the club also sponsored instruction in patriotism throughout the eastern zone and beyond. A British agent in Jerusalem complained that both the local Arab Club and the Literary Society "teach pan-Arab ideals to children, especially those in the Rashidiyya and Rawdat al-Maʿrifa Schools," while every Thursday, just after school had adjourned for the week, the Arab Club of Damascus "encouraged" schoolchildren to circulate through the city singing the praises of the sharifians:

22. Ṣāfī, *ʿAlā janāḥ al-dhikrā,* 1:231.
23. IO L/PS/10/802, Gertrude Bell, "Syria in October 1919," 15 November 1919.

O great lord, the pride of all Arabs
Your dominion is a glorious dominion,
The dominion of your ancestor, the prophet.[24]

One school in particular was a hotbed of nationalist organizing. Maktab ʿAnbar (renamed *tajhīz,* i.e., preparatory school, in the winter of 1918), had existed as the only government secondary school in Damascus during the late Ottoman period. Immediately before World War I, the school annually educated (and frequently housed) as many as six hundred students. Although these students came from outlying towns and villages as well as from local areas, there was an especially close relationship between the school and wealthier merchants of the Suq al-Hamidiyya, who frequently enrolled their children. Demonstrations organized by instructors at the school and composed predominantly of students started at the site of the *tajhīz* and wound their way through the suq, often terminating at the amir's saray. Along the path of their parade, according to one participant, "the people of the city" joined the marchers, chanting slogans that had been written and practiced at the school.[25]

As tensions escalated along the border that divided the eastern and coastal zones during and after the Evacuation Crisis, teachers and students at the *tajhīz,* like many other Damascenes, responded to the increasingly militarized atmosphere of the city by undertaking preparations for war. Shaykh ʿAbd al-Qadir al-Mubarak, for example, an Arabic instructor who taught both at the *tajhīz* and the military academy (*al-madrasa al-ḥarbiyya*), facilitated the transfer of students from the former school to the latter. By the spring of 1920, one observer recalled, teachers and students had converted the *tajhīz* "into a military barracks," and weapons were distributed to the students, who used them in their daily drills. One student who attended the school during this period, Jamil Saliba, later recalled that "[w]e [students] slept with our rifles at the sides of our beds." A contingent of students mustered from the school subsequently fought as volunteers at the Battle of Maysalun.[26]

24. Sulṭān, *Tārīkh Sūriyya,*108.

25. Khoury, *Syria and the French Mandate,* 410–412; Fakhrī al-Bārūdī, *Mudhakkarāt al-Bārūdī,* 1:30–31; al-Qāsimī, *Maktab ʿAnbar;* Interview with Kamil Daghmush, 2 November 1989; Interview with Dr. ʿAbd al-Karim al-Yafi (alumnus of the *tajhīz*), 21 November 1989; Interview with Ihsan Haqqi, 10 November 1989.

26. Munīr al-Rayyis, *al-Kitāb al-dhahabī lil-thawrāt al-waṭaniyya fī al-mashriq al-ʿarabī: al-Thawra al-sūriyya al-kubrā,* 103; al-Qāsimī, *Maktab ʿAnbar,* 102–103.

The *mutanawwirūn* were not the only ones in Faysali Syria who recognized the potential of linking educational activity and nationalist organizing. Many ulama, particularly those who were affiliated with the popular committees, also linked the two. As a result, even those nationalist organizations hostile to the policies of the government and the ideals of the *mutanawwirūn* followed their lead and competed with the government and the Arab Club to enlist students in political activities. The popular committees not only collected donations from schoolchildren, they also recruited volunteers from among older students to train in local militias. In Damascus, instructors at Qur'an schools, most notably those located in the Jamiʿ Tankiz and the Umayyad Mosque, brought their students to demonstrations sponsored by the Higher National Committee and its affiliates. Like the students at the *tajhīz*, many of these students had also come to the capital from surrounding villages.[27]

Although the efficacy of the attempt made by the short-lived and financially strapped Arab government and various nationalist associations to use schools to inculcate patriotic values among the young must remain a matter of conjecture, one memoirist has left a record of his experience as a schoolchild mobilized to participate in a demonstration organized by the government. Rida Safi was attending the Madrasa al-Husayniyya al-Sultaniyya in Homs when Amir Faysal, who had just been crowned king of Syria, visited the city to receive the homage of its inhabitants. Under the supervision of their teachers, students from all the schools of the city assumed posts along the path of the procession. As might be expected, what left the greatest impression on the young Safi was not the political significance of the event but the pomp of the amir's cortege, the disappointingly prosaic appearance of the king, and the penalties that would be meted out if any student mishandled the miniature Arab flag issued to each child:

> It was up to each schoolchild to hold his flag vertically and wave it, for if he was lax in this, his flag would be taken from him as punishment, since such discourtesy was unbecoming the Arab flag. I will never forget the tears that flowed as a result of this punishment, and the righting of the flag or a faithful promise that 'he would be worthy of this trust, and would preserve his dear flag to wave forever' was of no avail.[28]

27. Interview with Dr. ʿAbd al-Karim al-Yafi, 21 November 1989; FO 371/4182/125609/M56, "Arab Movement and Zionism," Major J. N. Camp (Jerusalem) to CPO, Cairo, 26 August 1919; *al-Kawkab*, 16 December 1919, 11; *al-Kawkab*, 6 January 1920, 10; Darwaza, *Mudhakkarāt*, 2:26; Akram Ḥasan al-ʿUlabī, *Khiṭaṭ Dimashq: Dirāsa tārīkhiyya shāmila*, 62–63.

28. Ṣāfī, *ʿAlā janāḥ al-dhikrā*, 1:233–234.

Perhaps the easiest and most inexpensive means for the government to disseminate information and mobilize the population was through the press. Newspapers sympathetic to or controlled by the government published announcements of public ceremonies, instructions for participants, and parade routes to be followed, as well as the texts of speeches that had been delivered, petitions supporting the demands of demonstrators, and patriotic verses lauding the cause or holiday being celebrated. For particularly important occasions, such as Faysal's return to Damascus from the Paris conference in spring 1919, the arrival of the King-Crane Commission in Damascus, the reconvening of the Syrian General Congress, and the declaration of Syrian independence and the coronation of Faysal as king of Syria, the print campaigns lasted days or even weeks.

Although the rate of literacy in Syria was low, especially in the countryside,[29] and although the number of printed copies of each newspaper in circulation tended to be small, newspapers played a significant role in mobilization. By publishing exegeses on nationalism and other topics that were compatible with the policies it pursued, and by printing its own version of events in the official chronicle, *al-ʿĀṣima,* the Arab government and the *mutanawwirūn* who wrote for the newspaper clearly hoped to influence and direct the activities of those literate Syrians upon whom, it was perceived, popular mobilization and the dissemination of nationalist ideology depended. Since all government employees who earned more than 1,000 *qurūsh* had to subscribe to *al-ʿĀṣima,* the government acquired what was, in effect, a captive audience. Furthermore, since government censors prohibited other newspapers from reporting local news until it had first been published in *al-ʿĀṣima,* the Arab government was able to put its own "spin" on events before its rivals could do so.[30]

The influence of newspapers was not limited to the literate, however: not only were newspapers passed around and read aloud in informal settings like coffeehouses, but much to the annoyance of French diplomats posted to Damascus, street-corner vendors shouted out the headlines of the latest editions—especially those headlines that were particularly provocative or scandalous, such as those that reported atrocities committed by

29. According to French data accumulated ten years after their occupation of inland Syria began, only 28 percent of the population of the State of Syria was literate. In the Jabal Druze, the figure was 6 percent. Khoury, *Syria and the French Mandate,* 411. A French report issued two years after the occupation of inland Syria puts the literacy rate much higher. See Haut-commissariat de la République Française en Syrie et au Liban, *La Syrie et le Liban en 1922.*

30. *al-Kawkab,* 11 March 1919, 12.

French soldiers. The French government found this practice so vexing that it lodged a formal complaint with the Arab government, demanding that the government take steps to stop it. After receiving the complaint, the Arab government threatened to arrest vendors who so much as shouted the names of the newspapers they were selling.[31] On occasion newspapers even functioned as signs, printing slogans (sometimes in English or French) in banner headlines on a single page or one side of a folio for posting as a broadsheet or for holding aloft as a placard in demonstrations.

While not all newspaper publishers and editors participated in promotional efforts on behalf of the Arab government, those who did were not always motivated by personal conviction or loyalty to the sharifians. The government enlisted the support of journalists by applying both the carrot and the stick. The Arab government offered monetary inducements to publishers and editors to print favorable articles and editorials. The records of the financial adviser to the Arab government, Sa'id Shuqayr, contain lists of allocations made for this purpose, including a grant of 480 P.E. to proprietors of newspapers from the amir's secret service account; the "irregular or extraordinary expenditure" of 450, 400, and 415 P.E. made for the same purpose in, respectively, January, May, and June of 1919; and payments of 200 P.E. to Muhammad Kurd 'Ali, editor of *al-Muqtabas*, and 85 P.E. to the director of another newspaper from a special "donations" fund. Other sources reveal the disbursement of 200 P.E. to Habib Kahala, proprietor of *Sūriyya al-jadīda*, and 150 P.E. to Rushdi al-Salih and Ma'ruf al-Arna'ut, the proprietors of *Istiqlāl al-'Arab*. Payments made to al-Salih and al-Arna'ut on the eve of Faysal's departure from Europe underwrote the distribution of five hundred free copies of their newspaper in the

31. MAE L:SL/vol. 56/147, Cousse to M. l'administrateur en chef, 22 July 1919; MD 4H1/5, Commandants Sciard, Gérard, "Rapport avec annotations sur un voyage en Syrie (29 juin-25 juillet 1919) et compte rendu sur la situation au Levant"; MAE L:SL/vol. 56/220/152, Cousse to Picot, 1 August 1919. One typical headline was "Defilement by Soldiers" and ran in the Aleppan newspaper *al-Rāya*. The following story ran underneath: "The quarter of Rumayla is one of the most beautiful quarters of Beirut. Situated on the edge of the sea, it is inhabited by the best Christian families. Encamped in the neighborhood of this quarter is a troop of French soldiers who immediately began ransacking homes by night and hounding women in plain daylight, haranguing them rudely. The inhabitants of this quarter, roused to action by this barbaric behavior, complained to the head of the quarter who relayed their complaint to the administrative council, which is supervised by General Gouraud. Do you know what happened? The complaint was shelved because no one dared speak of the matter to the Great Conqueror. One resident of the quarter is now recommending to others that they emigrate to Egypt or America with their families!" MD 4H112/dossier 2b, 18 April 1920.

Damascus quarters of Qanawat, the Maydan, Salihiyya, ʿAmara, and Bab Tuma, and the sale of the newspaper below cost in other quarters.[32]

In part, the economics of newspaper publishing in post-Ottoman Syria strengthened the government's hand in dealing with the press. The average run of a newspaper in Damascus was fifteen hundred copies; of these, approximately three to four hundred were sold and the remainder were distributed without charge.[33] Without outside subsidies, printing alone would have made the cost of newspaper publishing prohibitive. The Arab government, which controlled the allocation of newsprint and rates for mail and telegraphy could thus buy influence for as little as 25 P.E. and a load of newsprint, the price reportedly offered by the ministry of the interior to newspaper publishers in June 1920. Little wonder, then, that after the owners of *Sūriyya al-jadīda*, *al-Kināna*, and *Lisān al-ʿArab* refused the offer of government subsidies, the French representative to the Arab government predicted that the threat of censorship and shortage of paper would soon weaken their resolve.[34]

The bargain basement rates for which journalists and newspapers could be bought made their subornation irresistible, and foreign representatives and various political associations (such as the Arab Club of Aleppo, which supervised the publication of two newspapers) joined the Arab government in purchasing influence. The French, who wanted not only to counter nationalist and Kemalist propaganda but to plant false economic data that contrasted the prosperity of the coast with the plight of the eastern zone, were particularly active and offered grants to at least nine newspapers. Enterprising journalists such as Muhammad Kurd ʿAli and Habib Kahala were thus able to supplement their support from the Arab government with remuneration from France, while, after a brief flirtation with financial independence, an equally enterprising Ibrahim Hilmi of *Lisān al-ʿArab* offered the pages of his newspaper to both French and British representatives for the modest sum of 100 P.E.[35]

32. DU SA 493/13/2, 4, 5, Letter from Shuqayr to Waters-Taylor: Appendices B, D, E, 3 September 1919; MAE L:SL/vol. 5/58–61, Mercier to HC, 20 November 1918; AD 2368/10/2/66, Cousse to HC, 21 January 1919; MAE L:SL/vol. 12/32–39, Cousse to HC, 6 April 1919; Fakhrī Nūrī al-Kaylanī, "Qirāʾa fī milaff al-ṣiḥāfa bayna ʿāmī 1727 wa 1928 fī bilād al-shām" (n.p., n.d.) (Handwritten manuscript).

33. AD 2368/10/2/56, Cousse to HC, 18 January 1919.

34. *al-Kawkab*, 11 November 1919, 11; MD 4H114/4/482, Cousse to Gouraud, 2 June 1920; MAE L:SL/vol. 12/32–38, Cousse to HC, 6 April 1919.

35. AD 2430, Picot to Cousse, 2 January 1919; AD 2368/10/2/56, Cousse to HC, 18 January 1919; AD 2368/10/2/66, Cousse to HC, 21 January 1919; MAE L:SL/vol. 12/32–38, Cousse to HC, 6 April 1919; AD 2342, "Rapport sur les

In addition to offering the carrot of money, however, the Arab government, following in the footsteps of the entente powers, also brandished the stick of censorship. Entente censorship of newspapers published in the eastern zone lasted until October 1919. Included among the press regulations was a list of permitted and proscribed topics: newspapers were permitted, for example, to publish articles calling for the intervention of the League of Nations in Syrian affairs, either directly or through a mandatory power. They could also advocate the establishment of an Arab confederation on the Swiss model, so long as they included the recommendation that this take place within some sort of trusteeship arrangement. On the other hand, newspapers were not allowed to make derogatory statements about any of the entente powers, nor were they allowed to print articles calling for "complete independence" or containing "pan-Arab" or "pan-Islamic sentiments" without first submitting those articles for prepublication review.[36]

The Arab government continued the policy of direct censorship initiated by the entente powers. Before they could begin publication, the proprietors of newspapers had to deposit 100 P.E. with the government, to be held against any fines that they might incur for future violations of censorship rules. The government also warned the proprietors that it would hold them personally responsible for any infractions. Derogatory statements about

troubles survenus le 28 février 1919 à Alep—1er échelon GHQ," 14 April 1919; AD 2209/158, Pilley to Picot, 18 April 1919; AD 2343/87, Pilley to Picot, 22 May 1919; MD 7N4184/1, "Renseignements politiques," 20 April 1920; MD 7N4184/1, "Renseignements politiques," 20 May 1920; MD 4H114/4/594, Cousse to Gouraud, 24 June 1920. Gertrude Bell wrote the following of Ibrahim Hilmi: "I had several visits from Ibrahim Hilmi, a Baghdadi of 25 or rather younger, editor in Damascus of a paper called 'Lisan al Arab'. His knowledge of Arabic is so scholarly that Pere Anastase, one of the best judges, tried to induce him to return to Baghdad to assist him when he was editing our vernacular paper. He is pro-British, and has published in the Lisan a number of articles favourable to our administration. He discussed the possibility of his paper's obtaining a circulation with us and urged that such advocacy as his, coming from Syria and not from the Government press in Baghdad, would make an impression. He is probably not without hope that we would ultimately subsidize the Lisan. He hinted that he would be willing to undertake editorial work in Baghdad if we would offer him high enough terms, but his requirements would not be modest. He is however a capable young man." IO L/PS /10/802, Gertrude Bell, "Syria in October 1919," 15 November 1919.

36. MAE L:SL/vol. 9/214, Hornblower (Chief Censor), 13 February 1919; DU SA 493/15/74–84, Report of the "Conférence des administrateurs en chef" (Haifa), 12–14 May 1919; MAE L:SL/vol. 56/147, Cousse to M. l'administrateur en chef, 22 July 1919; *al-Kawkab*, 14 October 1919, 10. Even after the entente powers ceased their direct censorship of newspapers, however, they continued to exert indirect pressure by lodging diplomatic protests with the Arab government following the publication of articles of which they did not approve.

Sharif Husayn and his sons, the Arab government, the entente powers and their representatives, and the Zionist movement, among other topics, were forbidden, as was the republication of stories first carried by the French press agency Havas or the newspaper *Le Temps*.[37]

While the Arab government applied these regulations inconsistently, they did have a chilling effect on the press. In February 1919, for example, the government suspended the publication of *Sūriyya al-jadīda* and called its owners before a military court for publishing an article entitled "Things Seen," which purportedly "slandered patriotic feelings." The government acted in a similar manner at various times against *al-Difāʿ*, *Lisān al-ʿArab*, and *al-Urdunn*.[38] It is therefore probable that opposition newspapers adopted their idiosyncratic style—the use of irony to mask criticism (as in the *al-Difāʿ* article, "Did the Emir Agree with France on Its Mandate for Syria? Is It Possible?" cited in Chapter 3) and the publication of "transcripts" of speeches in the place of editorials—as a defense against similar charges of slander.

PUBLIC HOLIDAYS

It was primarily through the mobilization of the above-cited networks—institutions of governance and their functionaries, guilds, schools, and the press—as well as members of the military, that the Arab government, working in conjunction with allied political associations such as the Arab Club, constructed its public ceremonies. By celebrating an assortment of expressly designated heroes (the martyrs, Amir Faysal, the soldiers of the Arab army), anniversaries (such as those marking the dates on which the Arab Revolt was launched, Damascus was "liberated," and the martyrs hanged), and events (the return of Faysal from Europe in May 1919 and January 1920), the government sought to formulate a suitable national narrative, affirm a specific ordering of society and political community, validate its legitimacy, and inculcate the values it associated with nationalism. In short, the Arab government designed its ceremonies to mark the beginning of a new political and social dispensation.

37. *al-Kawkab*, 18 February 1919, 1; *al-Kawkab*, 27 January 1920, 11; *al-Kawkab*, 11 November 1919, 11; MAE L:SL/vol. 56/220/152, Cousse to Picot, 1 August 1919; WO 95/4374, Copy of telegram from Cousse to Picot, 14 October 1919; MD 4H114/1/373–374, Cousse to Gouraud, 5 December 1919; MD 4H114/4/617, Cousse to Gouraud, 30 June 1920.

38. *al-Kawkab*, 27 January 1919, 11; *al-Kawkab*, 18 February 1919, 1. The government again suspended publication of *Sūriyya al-jadīda* in November 1919, in the aftermath of the Evacuation Crisis. *al-Kawkab*, 11 November 1919, 11.

There is no doubt that sharifians and their allies understood the importance of symbolic action for advancing their prestige and affirming their legitimacy. Within the first four days of their appearance in the city, the sharifians disputed with the Jaza'iri brothers over which flag—the flag of the Arab Revolt or the flag once presented by Sharif Husayn to ʿAbd al-Qadir al-Jaza'iri—would fly over the city, released several thousand prisoners interned by the Turks (in the process creating what a British observer delicately called a "security problem"), dispatched a representative to Beirut to oversee the raising of the Arab flag in that city by a sister of one of the martyrs, removed a bronze wreath that Kaiser Wilhelm II had installed at the tomb of Saladin in 1898, and staged two ceremonial entrances. The first entrance, made on 1 October 1918 and led by Sharif Nasr, Nuri al-Saʿid, and "other famous men," rode from the Maydan to the saray amidst a "dense throng" that, according to reports, showered "flowers, gifts of scent and all manner of tokens of affection" on the sharifians. Two days later, Amir Faysal himself led a second entrance into the capital. As reported by a British observer, the amir rejected the automobile offered him and, "with a strong sense of historical fitness," made his way instead on horseback, leading an entourage of twelve to fifteen hundred supporters. This, the observer added, "undoubtedly impressed the inhabitants of the city with the reality of his arrival far more vividly than an orderly procession of innumerable battalions following upon the unimpressive passage of high-powered cars."[39]

In addition to the nationwide commemorations of the martyrs held (tentatively) in October 1918 and (more confidently) in May 1920, the Arab government designated three dates for the celebration of national holidays: 27 April, to commemorate the anniversary of the launching of the Arab Revolt (*ʿīd al-thawra*); 30 September, to commemorate the anniversary of the entrance of the Arab army into Damascus and the "liberation" of Syria (*ʿīd al-fatḥ*); and 8 March, to celebrate the declaration of Syrian independence and the coronation of Faysal as king of Syria (*ʿīd al-istiqlāl*). Because they commemorated events that had taken place before the establishment of the Arab government, the first two holidays differed from the last: unlike the third celebration, whose date was imposed by events that

39. AD 2429/9/no no., Telegram marked HC Beyrouth, 21 October 1918; USNA 59/867.00/955, "Report of Elias Khouri, 1st Dragoman of Beirut Consulate," 8 September 1919; al-Ḥaffār, "al-Ḥukūmāt allatī taʿāqabat" 1(3 shawwāl 1372): 18–19. Quotes taken from FO 371/3383/169562/559ff., Clayton to FO, 8 October 1918.

begged commemoration, *ʿīd al-thawra* and *ʿīd al-fatḥ* celebrated anniversaries that had been consciously selected by a government intent on inventing traditions. As might be expected, the anniversaries of events that did not contribute to the Sharifian mythos—the withdrawal of Ottoman forces from Damascus, the liberation of Jerusalem (by British forces), the first raising of the Arab flag over the city (by the Jaza'iri brothers)—were neither singled out for commemoration nor even mentioned in the press.[40]

Interestingly, whether planned or not, the calendrical sequencing of *ʿīd al-thawra* and *ʿīd al-fatḥ*, separated by the day set aside for the commemoration of the martyrs, loosely traced a plot structure that reaffirmed both the authoritative national narrative and the symbolic importance of the holidays. The commemorative season began with the observance of the beginning of the Arab Revolt in April (the initial conflict), continued by recalling the passion of the martyrs in May (temporary reversal), and ended with the liberation of Damascus in September (ultimate triumph). Ceremony thus recreated and compressed a drama that had lasted two and a half years into a five-month season.[41] Thus, only the abrupt removal of the Arab government in July 1920 prevented the further reinforcement of the sharifian saga through the yearly repetition of the holiday cycle.

The celebration of ʿīd al-fatḥ in Damascus consisted of two segments. First, a parade composed of a military band, mounted and unmounted units of the Arab army, fire engines, police and gendarmes, and students from military, vocational, and primary schools marched before a reviewing stand on which Amir Zayd, representing his brother who was once again on his way to Europe, stood at attention.[42] Reviewing the parade alongside Zayd were the military governor, the president of the war council, and "impor-

40. The first *ʿīd al-thawra* was tentatively celebrated in May 1919 in Aleppo. Documentation is poor. According to the French liaison officer in Aleppo, Naji Bey al-Suwaydi, at that time assistant to the local governor and member of the Arab Club, was the chief organizer of the event. Because the Arab Club organized the Aleppo commemoration less than three months after the Armenian massacre, it was reportedly used as an occasion to foster reconciliation among the elites of the Arab and Armenian communities. Representatives of the two communities met at the club's headquarters and listened to speeches expressing regret for the "events" and declaring that "henceforth, Armenians and Muslims will be brothers." AD 2343/87/8–10, Pilley to Picot, 22 May 1919. See also AD 2209/153, Pilley to Picot, 14 April 1919.

41. For a discussion of calendrical sequencing, see Eviatar Zerubavel, *Hidden Rhythms: Schedules and Calendars in Social Life*, 46; Hunt, *Politics, Culture, and Class in the French Revolution*, 34–35.

42. *al-ʿĀṣima*, 2 October 1919, 3; *al-Kawkab*, 14 October 1919, 10. According to *al-Kawkab*, the review was "the most important event of this celebration."

tant members of the government and royalty, soldiers, representatives of the allies, notables, and great men of the nation."[43] A statue representing "the spirits of the martyrs" stood at the side of the reviewing stand, a silent reminder of the bond connecting the Arab Revolt, the Arab government, and the sacrifice of the "sons of Syria." As reported in *al-ʿĀṣima,*

> The passing of infantry, cavalry, and artillery units of the Arab army continued to music that stirred the hearts until thousands of people cheered with a deafening noise. While schoolchildren trembled, the Arab flag waved above them, and the breeze scattered the echoes of their voices, which sang patriotic songs.

The parade began at ten o'clock in the morning; forty-five minutes later, the parade finished and the crowd dispersed. A twenty-one-gun salute signaled the completion of the brief public phase of the celebration.[44]

The second segment of the celebration took place that evening, when the amir hosted a private reception held at his residence in Salihiyya. Those invited included government functionaries, delegates to the Syrian General Congress, leaders of the Arab Revolt, and "men of distinction" (*ʿilyat al-qawm*). "A beautiful table was laid before them, decorated with flowers, and cups of tea and trays of sweets and fruit were served to the guests, who talked pleasantly among themselves." To remind those who were neither political leaders nor "men of distinction" that this was, indeed, a special occasion, the Arab government ordered the closure of government offices, the garlanding of government buildings with strings of electric lights, and the display of the Arab flag throughout the city.[45]

Although taking place after the symbolically discordant celebration of Syrian independence, the celebration held in Damascus seven months later to mark *ʿīd al-thawra* followed much the same format as had its predeces-

43. *al-ʿĀṣima,* 2 October 1919, 3.

44. A report in *al-Kawkab* put the time of the parade at nine o'clock. *al-Kawkab,* 14 October 1919, 10.

45. Historians have given all or part of the credit for the design of the Arab flag to several sources, including the Literary Society of Istanbul (which purportedly suggested the flag's striped pattern as early as 1909–1911), Sir Mark Sykes of the British War Office, the Ottoman Administrative Decentralization Party, al-Fatat, Sharif Husayn, field commanders of the Arab Revolt, and finally, the Syrian General Congress. Whatever its origins, the Arab flag, like all national flags, took on the role of what Sherry Ortner calls a "summarizing symbol" (see Chapter 3), and as such stood above day-to-day politics. Images of the flag and use of its colors were ubiquitous. Posters announcing municipal events and opposition platforms

sor. As had taken place during *ʿīd al-fatḥ,* the Arab government ordered the suspension of official business, the nighttime illumination of government offices, and the display of the Arab flag and four-color bunting reminiscent of the flag throughout the capital. Like the previous celebration, this one also consisted of two segments: a public ceremony that began with a military review, and a private reception for prominent Syrians and foreign guests held at the amir's residence.[46] Only one modification distinguished the celebration of *ʿīd al-thawra* from the celebration of *ʿīd al-fatḥ:* during the former, the public sequence recommenced in the evening. For this twilight sequence, the Arab government once again gathered a crowd composed primarily, according to *al-ʿĀṣima,* of soldiers and schoolchildren be-

---

were decorated with pictures of the flag, often printed in color, and even policemen's billy clubs were painted to resemble the flag. The flag also played a central role in demonstrations and national holidays, as is illustrated by the following excerpts from an article that appeared in *al-Kawkab* in the aftermath of the *ʿīd al-fatḥ* festivities, which, according to the newspaper, commemorated "the deliverance of Syria from the hands of the Turks and the raising of the Arab flag [by the sharifians] in place of the Turkish flag":

> Hardly had the sun risen and spread its light when the Arab flag was raised from every place in Damascus—on homes, shops, clubs, hotels, government ministries, and coffeehouses. It was as if Damascus wore a cloak of four colors that veiled the sun. People who stirred could not fix their eyes on sights other than these streaming Arab flags. But everyone knew the meaning of the flags, that they were an open declaration of the demands of the nation in the presence of the men of the great powers. Even the trams and railroads bore the flags on their roofs. . . . Infantry, artillery, cavalry, machine-gunners, police, gendarmerie, and firemen [passed in review], but what brought people most joy and raised the most applause and cheers was when they saw the Arab flag that the Arab army brought last year and raised for the first time, watching it being borne with courage, fortitude, and pride.

See FO 371/2136/42812, 25 May 1919; USNA 59/867.00/955, "Report of Elias Khouri, First Dragoman of Beirut Consulate," 8 September 1919; IO MSS EUR 152 (Frank Lugard Brayne Mss.)/18b, "Palestine and Syria Autumn 1918," 7 October 1918; *al-Kawkab,* 28 October 1919, 10; USNA 165/2558–16, Military Attaché to D.M.I., 16 March 1920; A. L. Tibawi, *A Modern History of Syria, Including Lebanon and Palestine,* 272; Sulaymān Mūsā, *al-Ḥaraka al-ʿarabiyya: al-Marḥala al-ūlā lil-nahḍa al-ʿarabiyya al-hadītha, 1908–1924,* 135–140; Kasmieh, *al-Ḥukūma al-ʿarabiyya fī Dimashq,* 48; Fromkin, *A Peace to End All Peace,* 315.

46. MD. 4H58/1, "Rapport hebdomadaire, 27 avril au 3 mai"; MD 4H114/2/327, Cousse to Gouraud, 28 April 1920. During the latter event, ʿAli Rida al-Rikabi, Hashim al-Atasi, Shaykh al-Islam Taj al-Din al-Hasani, and the Greek Orthodox Patriarch delivered speeches in which they thanked Sharif Husayn and his son for their service to the nation and expressed hope for entente recognition of Syrian independence. In his reply, Faysal recalled that the Arabs had joined the war at a time when the entente cause appeared doubtful and that he aspired to maintain the same relationship of friendship with the great powers in the future that he had enjoyed during the conflict.

low the balcony of Faysal's residence. First, Fakhri al-Barudi, who was at this time serving as Faysal's chamberlain, congratulated the king on the completion of the fourth year of the Arab Revolt, recalled the memory of the martyrs, and wished the nation happiness "in the shade of His Beloved Highness." Following three other brief speeches that reiterated similar themes, Faysal himself "offered precious pearls [of wisdom to the crowd] and wished the nation happiness and his congratulations now and in the future." The crowd dispersed after Faysal's benediction.[47]

Two aspects of these celebrations merit special attention. First, the public ceremonial sequences used a variety of techniques to assert the precedence and legitimacy of the sharifians: the act of reviewing parades that passed beneath the amir's residence; the preeminent placement of Faysal or his surrogate among a selection of noteworthy citizens of Syria who were invited onto the amir's "private balcony" (as *al-ʿĀṣima* took pains to inform its readers) and into his home as his guests; the association of Faysal and the Arab Revolt with the passion of the martyrs; the staged adulation of the crowd and the tributes proposed by citizens of the first rank; and the benediction offered to the nation. Second, the division of the celebrations into public and private ceremonial sequences and, as newspaper accounts make clear, the privileging of the latter, as well as the brief participation and passive role of the crowd, depicted in concrete form the division of the nation into two unequal parts that was favored in the discourse of the *mutanawwirūn.*

The staging of the celebrations marking Syrian independence was a radical departure from the staging of other public celebrations for two reasons. First, the reaction of Faysal to the declaration of Syrian independence was, at best, ambivalent; whatever his public demeanor, the declaration forced the amir to choose between outraging either the entente powers or the popular committees and their constituents.[48] Second, the popular committees and the Syrian General Congress, not the Arab government, initiated and dominated the campaign that led to the declaration. Thus, although the celebrations marking Syrian independence included many of the symbolic elements of the previously described celebrations, it transformed their meaning in a manner that rendered the sharifians respondents to a more generalized popular will.

47. *al-ʿĀṣima,* 29 April 1920, 4.
48. See Russell, *First Modern Arab State,* 136–140.

In early March 1920, Amir Faysal, "consider[ing] that the [Syrian General] Congress would serve as a vent for the great excitement existing in the country," reconvened the representative body.[49] Addressing the congress on 6 March, the amir asked it to determine the form of a future Syrian state and to draft a constitution. While asserting that Syria was independent as a result of the Arab Revolt and by virtue of Wilsonian principles, the amir did not at that time charge the congress with declaring independence, and indeed seemed to hold open the possibility of compromise with the entente powers.[50] The subsequent actions of the congress were, however, consistent with proposals made by Kamil al-Qassab in his speech to the assembly—a speech that the popular committees reprinted, distributed, and posted on the streets of Damascus under the title "The Nation Dictates Its Wishes to the Syrian Congress" (see Chapter 3). "Let [the congress] hold fast to every word of the desire of the nation," al-Qassab's speech concluded, "and let it learn that conferring power in the name of the nation without any safeguard to ensure it will be wielded as the nation desires will be considered the most unpardonable of errors." On 7 March 1920, the Syrian General Congress voted for the independence of Syria within its natural boundaries, with Faysal as constitutional monarch.

Damascenes celebrated Independence Day in a manner that was in accord with al-Qassab's demand that the nation (as represented by the Syrian

49. IO L/PS/10/802/P1896/EA3004, Allenby to FO, 7 March 1920. Allenby goes on to say, "In the event of his either refusing to convoke Congress, or refusing to accept the Crown, he [Faysal] considers that he will be disowned by the people and that immediate hostilities will commence both against the British and the French." Nuri al-Saʿid, Faysal's military adviser and confidant, concurred with Allenby's analysis. In a conversation with a British representative, al-Saʿid stated, "Faysal saw that there was great danger of the whole of Syria becoming disaffected. It was with the intention of leading public opinion round in the right direction that he agreed to summon the Congress at Damascus, but before doing so he had tried hard to induce them not to assemble. It was only when he realised that he would lose his own position as the ruler of the Syrian Arabs that he had to agree to the action of the Congress." FO 371/5034/E2522, "Record of Conversation between Major Young and Nuri as-Sa'id," 1 April 1920. See also: AD 2346/c1a/204, Cousse to HC, 9 March 1920; FO 371/5216/E2896, Major H. Garland, "A Talk with Sheikh Abdul Malik of the Arab Agency, Cairo," 18 March 1920.

50. *al-ʿĀṣima,* 7 March 1920, 1–2. As recorded in *al-ʿĀṣima,* Faysal's remarks included the following: "I do not believe that any nation wishes to enslave us. Based on my official trips to Europe and conversations and correspondence with the [entente] leaders, I have no doubt of their good intentions." For the complete text of Faysal's speech, see Ḥasan al-Ḥakīm, *al-Wathāʾiq al-tārīkhiyya,* 137–139.

General Congress and civil institutions) take precedence over the ruling institution.[51] On 8 March, at ten o'clock in the morning, the Syrian General Congress convened to select a congressional delegation to present its decision to the amir; three hours later, the delegation, led by Hashim al-Atasi, president of the congress, filed to the amir's residence, where it invited the amir to accompany it to Martyrs' Square.[52] By this time, crowds, mobilized by the municipal government, the popular committees, the Arab Club, and "representatives of the nation," had already begun to gather at the square to greet the amir. Posters displayed throughout the capital the day before the ceremony attest to the fact that the municipal government relied upon guilds and schools to swell the crowd.[53]

The arrangement of the cortege that accompanied the amir from his residence to the square appears to have been carefully planned. The amir's carriage followed behind a line of deputies from the Syrian General Congress, cabinet ministers, and the president of the congress. Faysal and Zayd were dressed in military uniforms and surrounded by unmounted generals of the Arab army. Members of the Royal Guard rode behind the amir's carriage. Ihsan al-Jabiri, the president of the Aleppo municipality, led a final contingent composed of military officers, notables, lancers, and attendants.

51. *al-ʿĀṣima,* 8 March 1920, 2; MAE L:SL/vol. 25/285–290, "Extrait du journal Difah," 9 March 1920; MD 4H112, Toulat to Gouraud, 10 March 1920; *al-ʿĀṣima,* 11 March 1920, 3; USNA 165/2558–16, Military Attaché (Cairo) to DMI, 16 March 1920; IO MSS/Eur/F152 (Frank Lugard Brayne Mss.)/20, Pierre Bardakjy (?) to Capt. Bichon, 18 March 1920; *al-ʿĀṣima,* 25 March 1920, 4; AD 2346/144, Cousse to Millerand, 8 April 1920; al-Charkas, *al-Dalīl al-muṣawwar lil-bilād al-ʿarabiyya,* 1:109–112.

52. The delegation was, interestingly, composed of individuals who held widely divergent political views: Hashim al-Atasi, Ahmad Qadri, ʿAbd al-Qadir al-Kaylani, ʿAbd al-Qadir al-Khatib, Ahmad al-ʿIyashi, Riyad al-Sulh, Tawfiq al-Bissar, ʿAbd al-Rahman al-Yusuf, Tayduri Antaki, Rashid Rida, Subhi al-Tawil, Fath al-Marʿashli, Mahmud al-Faʿur, Amin Bayhum, and Saʿd al-Din al-Jabiri. al-ʿIyāshī, *al-Īḍāḥāt al-siyāsiyya,* 50.

53. The posters, which were in color and prominently displayed the Arab flag, began as follows:

1. All inhabitants of the capital will meet on the 8th of March at 11:00 A.M. at Nasr St. and Salihiyya.
2. The groups will proceed quietly, led by the heads of parties, to the places assigned to them.
3. All tradespeople, students, male and female, will take part in the procession.
4. The groups will meet at 2:00 P.M. at Martyrs' Square.
5. At 3:00 independence will be proclaimed from the balcony of the municipal building by reading the decision of the Syrian congress.

USNA 165/2558–16, U.S. Military Attaché (Cairo) to DMI, 16 March 1920.

From the saray to the Salihiyya Bridge, the cortege traveled between two lines of soldiers; at the bridge, lines of schoolchildren, stretching as far as the municipal building, stood as a phalanx on the fringes of the parade route.[54]

At three o'clock, Muhammad ʿIzzat Darwaza, who was at that time the secretary of the Syrian General Congress, climbed out onto the balcony of the municipal building where religious leaders, tribal leaders, and the consuls of France, Italy, the United States, Spain, and Persia were already waiting. He read out the proclamation ending military rule in the eastern zone, the declaration of independence, and the resolution of the congress that authorized Faysal to assume the post of king of Syria. Following a 101-gun salute and a speech by Faysal "assuring his devotion to the interests of the nation," the secretary of the congress of Iraq read the decision of that body to proclaim Faysal's brother, ʿAbdallah, king of Iraq. This document was ceremonially handed to Faysal, as if a further confirmation of the separation of Syria within its natural boundaries from its eastern neighbor.

A military parade, reviewed by Faysal, capped this segment of the celebration. Following the review, Faysal and selected religious leaders adjourned to a room inside the municipal building where they participated in a well-publicized ceremony of allegiance.[55] Unlike the pledge of loyalty offered by notables, tribal leaders, and others to Faysal when he returned from his first trip to Europe, however, the compact (*ṣakk*) linking Faysal and religious leaders who acted in the name of the nation was reciprocal.[56] "When the Syrian nation had chosen to crown His Highness Amir Faysal, son of His Majesty King Husayn I, king of Syria in its natural boundaries," the document began,

> we spent the day in the municipal building of Damascus, the capital, to perform the duty of *mubāyaʿa* personally and by proxy. This action is undertaken in accordance with the seven binding conditions stipulated in our first interview with His Highness held on Monday, 6 October 1918. These conditions are: obedience to God; respect for [all] religions; con-

54. *al-Difāʿ*, 9 March 1920, 1.

55. Detailed accounts of the ceremony were carried in local newspapers. See, for example, *al-ʿĀṣima*, 11 March 1920, 3.

56. According to *al-Difāʿ*, the following religious leaders took part in the ceremony: the patriarch of the Greek Orthodox Church, the patriarch of the Greek Catholic Church, the Syrian Catholic bishop, a representative of the Maronite patriarch, a representative of the Syrian Jacobite bishop, a representative of the Armenian Jacobite bishop, a representative of the Armenian Catholic patriarch, the head of the Protestant community, and the chief rabbi of Damascus. *al-Difāʿ*, 9 March 1920, 1.

> sultative rule in conformity with the laws and statutes enacted for such rule; equality under law; establishment of order; propagation of knowledge; and the allocation of jobs and positions to the [most] qualified.
>
> With the acceptance by His Highness of these conditions, one by one, we acknowledge him king of this country, pledging obedience and devotion to His Majesty and support for his government in any capacity possible. We give him this legal document which is over our signatures and seals, humbly requesting that His Majesty act, for the length of his life, in accordance with what it contains for the good of the country and the advancement of its people.[57]

Following this ceremony, Faysal reemerged onto the balcony of the municipal building, where he once again reviewed a military parade and, in an inversion of an analogous ceremonial sequence held during the celebration of *ʿīd al-thawra,* accepted the good wishes (*tabrīkāt*) of various ministers, members of congress, and religious leaders.[58] Faysal then returned to his residence in a procession that reversed the order of the earlier line of march. Abandoning his carriage, the newly crowned king now rode on horseback at the head of the procession, followed by the chairman of the council of state and the president of the congress, who rode in a carriage surrounded by a troop of the Royal Guard.

Celebrations continued for three days, during which time the Arab government proclaimed full amnesty for any deserter from the Arab army who turned himself in within fifteen days and a partial amnesty for most prisoners (except those imprisoned for "disgraceful or abominable crimes"). The municipality ordered flags to fly throughout the city, suqs to remain open until midnight, and public and private buildings and shops to remain lit until the same hour. In the evenings, detachments of troops toured the city with torches.[59] The day after Faysal's coronation, the Syrian General

57. Ibid., 3.

58. Among the well-wishers were the president and members of the council of ministers, a deputation from the Syrian congress, a qadi, the mufti and the *naqīb al-ashrāf* (the head of the estate representing the descendants of the prophet), the Greek Orthodox patriarch, the Catholic patriarch, bishops of the Latin, Syriac, and Old Armenian churches, the leaders of the Protestant community, and rabbis. *al-ʿĀṣima,* 8 March 1920, 2.

59. USNA 165/2558–16, Military Attaché (Cairo) to DMI, 16 May 1920; *al-ʿĀṣima,* 25 March 1920, 4. According to a French report, "In Damascus, Faysal has tried to release from prison members of the party that opposes him. These have refused to leave and have declared that they will remain in prison until a Syrian ruler governs Syria." MD 4H112/2a, Lt. Kouadi, "Report on Independence Day Celebrations at Aleppo," 10 March 1920.

Congress proclaimed that 8 March would henceforth be celebrated as Independence Day.[60]

Independence Day was celebrated not only in Damascus but in cities throughout the eastern zone. Since ritual specialists in Damascus enjoined these celebrations by telegram and dictated their format, they all contained common elements: each lasted for three days; local garrisons, guilds, and schools supplied the manpower for the processions; outlying cities sent delegations to Damascus with gifts for the king; the municipalities imposed holiday regulations similar to those imposed in Damascus; and the local governor read out the declarations of the Syrian congress and hosted receptions for local notables. In Aleppo, where about one thousand members of the volunteer militias marched alongside regular units, government authorities distributed handbills announcing the slogans to be shouted, including "In spite of himself, the Muslim is the brother of the Christian and the Jew," "The Arabs were Arabs before Moses, Christ, and Muhammad," "Independence and Faysal are the two treasures of Syria," and, of course, a variation of "Religion belongs to God, the nation to all" (rendered, in this case, "Religion is God's, and the fatherland belongs to his children").[61]

Ostensibly, the celebration held in Damascus to mark Independence Day resembled the celebrations marking *ʿīd al-thawra* and *ʿīd al-fatḥ*. All three celebrations featured reviews of military parades, ceremonial sequences held behind closed doors, and a distinct role reserved for important personages that offset the nonparticipatory or restricted role reserved for the crowds. Nevertheless, the celebration of Independence Day held in the capital imbued these shared attributes with new meaning. Through their structure and use of symbols, the ceremonies of independence contrasted an active "nation" with a passive amir/king. This theme appeared prominently in three separate dramatic sequences. First, a procession escorted Faysal from his residence and transported him before the populace to a public building where he agreed to abide by the decision of the congress and a

60. AD 2346/144, Cousse to Millerand, 8 April 1920. ʿAwni ʿAbd al-Hadi puts the date of the session a day earlier, at which time the Syrian congress also approved the design for the national flag. AD 2346/III-e, ʿAwni ʿAbd al-Hadi to Cousse, 31 March 1920. Three weeks later, the Syrian foreign ministry confirmed both decisions. IO L/PS/10/802/P2905/59, Meinertzhagen to FO, 29 March 1920.

61. See MD 4H112/2a, Lt. Kouadi, "Report on Independence Day Celebrations at Aleppo," 10 March 1920; USNA 59/890d.00/9/473, Jackson to Sec. of State, 13 March 1920; IO MSS Eur F152 (Frank Lugard Brayne Mss.)/20, Letter from Pierre Bardakjy(?) to Capt. Bichon, 18 March 1920; AD 2347(?)/série c/carton 5/dossier a/67/l, Trenga to HC, 20 April 1920; Ṣāfī, *ʿAlā janāḥ al-dhikrā*, 1:233–234.

compact presented by the nation's spiritual leaders. Second, the amir rode to his coronation in a carriage behind the nation's representatives; after the ceremonies at the municipal building, the king led the procession back to his residence on horseback. Finally, while on other occasions the king bestowed his blessing on the nation, on this occasion he instead received the blessing of the nation. As will be seen in the next chapter, much of the symbolism contained in these Independence Day ceremonies bore a striking resemblance to that contained in demonstrations organized by the popular committees. Thus, rather than underscoring sharifian power, the ceremonies organized in Damascus to mark Independence Day reflected the changing balance of power between politics as represented by the Arab government and its allies, on the one hand, and the emergent politics of the street, as represented by the popular committees in particular, on the other.

THEATER

The magnitude of the ceremonies discussed so far, like that of many of the demonstrations to be discussed in the next chapter, was enormous, mobilizing tens and, reportedly, even hundreds of thousands of Syrians and converting whole areas of the cities in which they took place into ceremonial space. But the Arab government and its allies in the Arab Club and Literary Society also designed ceremonies on a scale of such intimacy that their performance could be bounded by the walls of a coffeehouse, theater, or movie house. Like their grander counterparts, theater pieces such as plays, poetry recitals, dramatic readings, revised renderings of *karakūz* shadow plays, and even cinema,[62] produced singly or in conjunction with other ceremonies, fulfilled an important function for the government and the *mutanawwirūn:* the inculcation of nationalist values. For this reason, the Arab government and local governments both inside and outside the eastern zone, in association with their extragovernmental allies, encouraged and supported the staging of theatrical performances. They did this in

62. An article in *al-ʿĀṣima* gave an account of a "movie party" sponsored by the municipal government of Damascus at Cinema al-Manakh to which Faysal, Zayd, representatives of the entente powers, notables, *mutanawwirūn,* and merchants were invited. Three films were shown. The first was about the scouting movement "and how it instills, through physical and mental activity, a love of good and shunning of bad, and the preparation of bodies [so that young people] can take on their national duties." The second film showed Faysal's negotiating activities in Paris, his triumphal first return from Europe to Beirut and Damascus, and "the great reception for him." The final film was a comedy. *al-ʿĀṣima,* 11 September 1919, 6.

a variety of ways, from organizing acting troupes and constructing theaters (such as a municipal theater built by the local government in Ram Allah) to establishing at least one acting school, the appropriately named Theater School (*al-masraḥ al-madrasī*), in Aleppo. The Arab government was so enthusiastic about the value of theatrical performances that even the War College in Damascus boasted a curriculum that offered instruction in drama. In the spring of 1919, the cadets even produced a play, *ʿAbd al-Rahman or the Second Umayyad Dynasty in al-Andalus*, to which the public was invited.[63]

While the Arab government was an enthusiastic supporter of theater, most productions were sponsored by the Arab Club and Literary Society. The latter group in particular was a firm advocate of the political uses of theater during the postwar period. According to its charter, the Literary Society was established "for the good of the Arab nation and the revival of its glory, the spread of its history and noble traditions, the teaching to its sons true knowledge [for] the training of their minds and their unification, and the establishment of charitable works and projects benefiting literature, knowledge, art, society, agriculture, culture, trade, economics, health, and morals, which will bring the Arab nation ample benefit and gain." To this end, members of the society both integrated nationalist themes into the texts of old plays and commissioned the writing of new plays.[64]

An article in *al-Kawkab*, a newspaper that frequently reported on plays produced by branches of the Arab Club and Literary Society, outlined in detail the benefits that the nation would derive from such dramatic presentations. According to the newspaper, although plays that depicted events from Islamic history already existed, they were inadequate and "need[ed] a new formulation that fits the spirit of nationality spreading among nations and peoples." Playwrights, the article continued, should write plays that had a "Syrian shape." These plays would depict Syrian history and Syrian heroes, critique contemporary affairs, and "call attention to the shortcomings in our customs and conduct so that people can purify their morals and improve their circumstances." Only after such plays have been written and performed, the article concluded, would the "descendants [of these heroes] be able to pursue the ideals of their fathers."[65]

63. *al-Kawkab*, 3 June 1919, 8; *al-Kawkab*, 29 July 1919, 10; ʿAdnān Ibn Dhurayl, *al-Masraḥ al-sūrī mundhu al-Qabbānī ilā al-yawm*, 94.
64. See *al-Kawkab*, 8 April 1919, 11; Birrū, "al-Muntadā al-adabī."
65. *al-Kawkab*, 12 August 1919, 7.

Stage productions—even those that served as political propaganda—were not new to Syria in the immediate post-Ottoman period. Theater had played an important part in the literary *nahḍa* that had taken place in greater Syria during the mid-to-late nineteenth century. Prominent playwrights and actors like Farah Antun (who rendered the *Oedipus* cycle into Arabic) and Khalil Matran translated and produced the works of Sophocles, Molière, and Shakespeare as part of the Arabist project to create a new Arab identity that would be rooted in high culture and literary Arabic. Some actors, such as the popular ʿUthman Jalal who specialized in the performance of the works of Molière, cultivated a devoted following among educated audiences. The political/cultural associations and acting troupes that proliferated during the Faysali period took up the mantle of the Arabists by continuing to produce "neoclassical" works, often with the support of the Arab government and local governments, which sought to extend the reach of genteel culture at home and gain prestige abroad from such productions. The Independence Day celebrations that were held in Damascus, for example, included two performances of a new production of *Romeo and Juliet*, produced by the distinguished actor Salama Hijazi. They were reportedly received with enthusiasm.[66]

Nevertheless, neoclassicism and "plain drama" appealed to only a thin layer of the population of Syria.[67] As a result, during the late Ottoman period, playwrights and producers such as Abu Khalil al-Qabbani began to experiment with new themes and forms of popular theater, and staged plays that integrated music, drama, and dance or depicted historical themes. In the interval between the turn of the century and World War I, acting troupes inspired by al-Qabbani and led by his epigones toured the Levant.[68] One particularly popular theater company, led by Salama Hijazi and actor/director George Abyad, offered a selection of historical dramas such as *Salah al-Din and the Kingdom of Jerusalem*, and *al-Ḥākim bi-ʿAmr Allah*.[69] The performances of the Syrian-born, Paris-trained Abyad were

66. Rushdī Ṣāliḥ, *al-Masraḥ al-ʿarabī*, 69–70; al-Charkas, *al-Dalīl al-muṣawwar lil-bilād al-ʿarabiyya*, 1:112.

67. When critics rebuked actor George Abyad for replacing classical pieces with mere "melodrama," the actor and producer defended himself by arguing that people "would support only lighter fare." Ṣāliḥ, *al-Masraḥ al-ʿarabī*, 70–71.

68. Ibn Dhurayl, *al-Adab al-masraḥī fī Sūriyya: Dirāsa fī al-masraḥiyya al-ʿarabiyya al-sūriyya mundhu Abī Khalīl al-Qabbānī ilā al-yawm*, 14, 18; Nadīm Muʿalla Muḥammad, *al-Adab al-masraḥī fī Sūriyya: nashʾa—taṭawwur*, 9–10; M. M. Badawi, *Early Arabic Drama*, 56–64.

69. Ṣāliḥ, *al-Masraḥ al-ʿarabī*, 69. See also Jacob M. Landau, *Studies in the Arab Theater and Cinema*, 75–80.

so well received that he obtained the patronage of the Arab Club and became, in effect, the court actor of the Arab government.[70]

Playwright and political agitator Maʿruf al-Arnaʾut, whose activities during the Faysali period were recounted earlier, also penned a succession of plays with political and historical messages, including *ʿAmr b. al-ʿĀṣ, The War in Tripoli* (*al-Ḥarb fī Ṭarāblus*), *ʿUmar b. al-Khaṭṭāb* (written during World War I), and *Edirne Ablaze* (*Adirna fī al-nār*). Although the text of the last play, also called *Return to Edirne,* has disappeared, its subtitle bears witness to its message: "A Tragedy with an Introduction and Four Acts, Representing the Fall of Edirne on 26 March, and the Ensuing Calamities through the Third Balkan War, and the Recovery of Edirne under the Leadership of the Hero Anwar Bek." Al-Arnaʾut has also been credited with the invention of a dramatic technique that was new to the Syrian stage: immediately before or after the performance of his play, an actor, assuming the role of a fortune-teller or other seer, would turn to his audience and address it directly, offering political commentary in the form of predictions about the future.[71]

Plays produced during the postwar period by the Arab Club and Literary Society embraced a variety of dramatic themes. Some were shameless contributions to sharifian mythopoeia. The Arab Club of Homs, for example, sponsored an amateur performance of a play entitled *The Arab Revolt* (*Thawrat al-ʿArab*), while the Patriotic Club (*al-nādī al-waṭanī*) of Tulkarm produced *The Battle of Tafila,* a play that depicted the sharifian victory over Ottoman forces in January 1918, as a fundraiser for widows and orphans of the district. In Hama and Aleppo, Amin al-Kaylani, the scion of a prominent family heavily involved in Arab Club activities, produced plays such as *Wādī Mūsā, The Battle of al-Hasa* and *The Battle of Maʿan,* which likewise celebrated important battles of the Arab Revolt.[72] Other plays celebrated nationalist virtues, depicted the suffering endured by Syrians during World War I, or commemorated important events or individuals from history, such as the ever-popular sagas of Salah al-Din and the conquest of

70. In his review of a play performed by al-Abyad's company in Damascus and attended by Amir Zayd and ʿAli Rida al-Rikabi, the critic for *al-ʿĀṣima* gushed that Abyad had not only "held up the banner of refined Arab theater for the past six years . . . as befits this awakening nation," but had pioneered the art of the future. *al-ʿĀṣima,* 22 September 1919, 4.

71. Ibn Dhurayl, *al-Adab al-masraḥī fī Sūriyya,* 33–36.

72. Ibn Dhurayl, *al-Masraḥ al-sūrī,* 107; Ibn Dhurayl, *al-Adab al-masraḥī fī Sūriyya,* 68; *al-Kawkab,* 7 October 1919, 12.

Spain.[73] One double bill, coproduced by the Committee for the Advancement of Arab Drama in Palestine and the Association of Brotherhood and Virtue, included plays from each of the first two categories. The evening began with a presentation of *The Fall of a Young Girl,* a play that portrayed the heroine's "surrender to desire and appetite, her torment of shame and degradation, and her [eventual] repentance." The second play on the program, *Famine in Syria,* depicted the wartime plight of a mother and her starving children and the noble actions of an Arab soldier in the Ottoman army whose situation was not much better. The patriotic message of the play, according to a review in *al-Kawkab,* was convincingly imparted "in a manner that caused hearts to bleed."[74]

Possibly the most widely produced plays during the postwar period were those that portrayed the activities of the "villainous" Ottoman governor of Syria, Jamal Pasha, and the suffering of the martyrs. Productions of *Jamal Pasha the Butcher* and *Jamal Pasha and the Martyrs of the Arab Community* —probably two plays derived from a single *Urtext* that has been attributed to Maʿruf al-Arnaʾut[75]—were a staple of Arab Club and Literary Society repertoires and appeared in theaters in Jerusalem, Jaffa, Beirut, Tulkarm, Homs, and Damascus. Reportedly, al-Arnaʾut himself was so adept at its staging that "he terrified the masses of Damascus."[76]

Although presenting what was, fundamentally, the same story for much the same reason—"so that the people could see in this piece the outrages with which this shedder of blood was enamored and which he used against the men of the Arab nation"[77]—the actual performances of plays about Jamal Pasha differed from city to city. In Tulkarm, the production was sponsored by the local Patriotic Club, an association that, according to an article in *al-Kawkab,* had been founded not only *by* notables and intellectuals but *for* them. Before the play, the actors appeared on stage in costume to sing an "Arab anthem." A member of the club then delivered a speech "[urging] his fellow countrymen on to unity and harmony, and, by pointing out the

73. See *al-Kawkab,* 3 June 1919, 8; *al-Kawkab,* 29 July 1919, 9–10; MD 4H112/2b/68, Officier liaison d'Alep, "Renseignements," 10 June 1920.

74. *al-Kawkab,* 8 October 1918, 8.

75. While no copies of the play or plays exist, ʿAdnan Ibn Dhurayl writes that "most historians" agree that the play (or perhaps the text upon which the play or plays were based) was the work of al-Arnaʾut. *al-Adab al-masraḥī fī Sūriyya,* 36. See also Muḥammad, *al-Adab al-masraḥī fī Sūriyya,* 20–21.

76. Ibn Dhurayl, *al-Adab al-masraḥī fī Sūriyya,* 36; Ibn Dhurayl, *al-Masraḥ al-sūrī,* 107; *al-Kawkab,* 11 February 1919, 9; MAE L:SL/vol. 12/32–38, 39, Cousse to HC, 6 April 1919; *al-Kawkab,* 15 July 1919, 10–11.

77. *al-Kawkab,* 15 July 1919, 10–11.

greatness, civilization, and might that the Arabs had possessed in bygone ages, he inspired them to exert [every] effort for the future." Between scenes, schoolchildren took to the stage to sing patriotic songs.[78] In Jerusalem, on the other hand, the local Arab Club began the evening's performance with a skit in which actors, dressed as spirits of great Arab men, hovered about a scaffold to remind the children in the audience of their "patriotic duty." The club closed the evening with a rendition of a tribute to Faysal reportedly composed by the local belletrist Khalil al-Sakakini while on his way to join the Arab army with three hundred young men:

> O great king, the pride of all Arabs!
> Your reign is the grand reign, the reign of your ancestor the prophet.
> March toward this reign before it is too late.
> Display zeal toward the enemy to purify the fatherland.
> Renew the ancient era, the era of glory.
> Follow the true way, comply with correct opinion.
> We are no longer a subservient nation.
> Relaxation and happy nights are not for us.
> In the time of war we come forth in droves.
> We attack the enemy—none of us flees.
> If we live, we live honorably; if we die, we die honorably.
> It would grieve us to die ignobly, for our purpose is to end that which is ignoble.[79]

The differences between the presentations in Tulkarm and Jerusalem, although more structural than significative, suggest a more profound problem encountered by the Arab government and the *mutanawwirūn* in their efforts to use theater to inculcate a predetermined nationalist agenda. Prescribed ceremonial sequences, constant surveillance, and the authority inherent in ceremonial planning enhanced the ability of the government and its allies to control the form and symbolic content of large-scale ceremonies and thus to delimit the array of meanings they conveyed to participants and observers alike. Local and frequently autonomous chapters of political associations, on the other hand, often sponsored or produced plays and other staged events in numerous small venues. The informal and unsupervised nature of the performances increased the possibility that the message the government and the *mutanawwirūn* were attempting to instill would be compromised or even totally garbled. Theatrical events also provided a forum in which antigovernment messages might be expressed, par-

78. Ibid., 10–11.
79. *al-Kawkab*, 11 February 1919, 9.

ticularly after the onset of the Evacuation Crisis. Sometimes, orators and recruiters from the popular committees took the stage to deliver speeches; at other times, they disrupted the gatherings with impromptu harangues and calls to action.[80] As recounted in Chapter 2, theaters in Aleppo were popular sites for the recruitment of young men into the armed gangs that dominated the countryside.

Coffeehouses, located both on main thoroughfares in the heart of cities and in suqs adjacent to semiprivate lanes, provided another venue for the staging of patriotic theatrical events. At the close of World War I, it was common for the more popular and centrally located coffeehouses to cater to several hundred clients a day who passed their time sipping coffee, playing backgammon (*ṭāwula*), smoking narghiles, trading gossip, reading newspapers, and watching shadow plays and other entertainments.[81] The attitude of the Arab government to this forum was ambivalent. As recounted in Chapter 4, *al-ʿĀṣima* charged coffeehouses with corrupting morals, destroying family life, and fostering a culture of idleness. Furthermore, members of the government, fearing that coffeehouses provided space in which unrestricted discussion and political conspiracy could take place, took steps to regulate them during the martial law regime that preceded the French invasion. Such conspiracies were not entirely imaginary: those who allegedly plotted the assassination of Amir Faysal in June 1919 formulated their plans in daily gatherings held in the Syrian Café in Damascus.[82]

On the other hand, some *mutanawwirūn* sought to take advantage of these ready-made platforms. In Hama, for example, where from fifty to sixty coffeehouses plied their trade during this period, two in particular were famous for the theatrical productions they housed. One was owned by Tawfiq al-Shishakli, a physician, graduate of Maktab ʿAnbar, and one of

80. MD 4H112/2b, "Excerpts from *al-Rayeh* 236," 3 May 1920; MD 4H112/2b, Notebook entitled "Habib Bey Estephane," 13 May 1920; USNA 59/890d.00/17/507, Jackson to Adm. Bristol, 19 May 1920.

81. Interview with Fakhri Nuri al-Kaylani, 8 November 1989; Interview with Abu Ribah al-Jazaʾiri, 15 November 1989; Interview with ʿUmar Khadim al-Saruji, 31 December 1989.

82. *al-ʿĀṣima,* 15 July 1920, 2–3; AD 2324/A-1, 25 June 1919. In one anti-Zionist drama, *The Ruin of Palestine,* produced by the Arab Club of Nablus in January 1920, the patronage of a coffee shop by the two protagonists leads directly to their downfall: while visiting a coffee shop, a young Zionist woman gets them drunk, steals their money, and, inspired by a "Zionist leader" to "do your best for your country and nation," tricks the men into registering their property in her name. Having lost all, the two rush into the market shouting, "The country is ruined, the Jews have robbed us of our land and honor." They then commit suicide. Muslih, *Origins of Palestinian Nationalism,* 169.

the principal leaders of that city's Arab Club. The other, al-Salon, was owned by the municipal government, which rented out its theatrical space to acting troupes. The productions these and other coffeehouses housed were often performed by amateurs—for example, young members of prominent families who had a passion for acting—who charged their audiences a small fee that they shared with their Arab Club patrons and coffeehouse proprietors.[83]

In contrast with the Arab government and the Arab Club, the popular committees do not seem to have sponsored theatrical presentations in coffeehouses or in any other location. The reason for this is probably twofold. First, not all the constituencies represented by the committees considered theater and acting to be seemly. For example, when Dr. Asʿad al-Hakim—who taught acting at the Madrasa al-Kamiliyya while Kamil al-Qassab was still director—produced two plays, he not only caused a stir in Damascus, but his plays were censured by the magazine *al-Ḥaqāʾiq*, and conservative ulama collected formal legal opinions condemning such activities.[84] But perhaps a more important factor militating against popular committee sponsorship of theatrical performances was the fact that dramatic presentations physically replicated the unequal division of society championed by the sharifians and the *mutanawwirūn:* by instructing their passive audiences in "appropriate" nationalist myths and virtues, actors in theatrical productions, who often came from the self-described layer of "enlightened" or "cultured" youth, labored to create a mass audience for nationalist doctrines while they simultaneously discouraged mass participation in nationalist politics.[85] As will be seen in the next chapter, the ceremonies constructed by the popular committees not only reflected a very different notion of the proper ordering of society but, through both their form and their content, conformed to that ordering as well.

83. Interview with Fakhri Nuri al-Kaylani, 8 November 1989; Interview with Abu Ribah al-Jaza'iri, 15 November 1989. Al-Kaylani himself participated in amateur theatricals that were performed in coffeehouses during the French mandate (he once played the role of Jean Valjean in a dramatic production of *al-Buʾasāʾ* [*Les Misérables*]) in a theatrical company organized by Muhammad al-Barudi.

84. al-Qāsimī, *Maktab ʿAnbar*, 23.

85. George L. Mosse explores this same contradiction in his analysis of *Thing* plays in Nazi Germany. *Nationalization of the Masses*, 114–118.

6 Demonstrating Communities

The celebration of public holidays and the staging of theatrical productions were not the only ceremonical activities sponsored by the Arab government and its allies. Ritual specialists associated with the government also planned and staged demonstrations the form and content of which, like the form and content of the ceremonies described in the previous chapter, reveal not only the political goals professed by their planners but their underlying assumptions about the proper ordering of society. However, unlike the ceremonies analyzed in the previous chapter—ceremonies which were predominantly the work of the government and its supporters—the popular committees and their allies also organized demonstrations. The fact that both nationalist blocs represented themselves through a common medium adds another dimension to the study of ceremonies: a side-by-side comparison of the demonstrations staged by the two blocs enables the historian to contrast directly their respective guiding principles. Analysis of demonstrations is useful for another reason as well: as will be argued below, because affirmational (i.e., "proactive") demonstrations of the type mounted by the popular committees only take place in societies in which broad horizontal and associational affiliations exist either alongside or in place of vertical and communal affiliations, their staging in Syria provides evidence to confirm an underlying transformation of social and political relations during the late Ottoman and early post-Ottoman periods. As argued in the Introduction, such a transformation is a prerequisite for the emergence of mass-based nationalist movements.

GOVERNMENT-SANCTIONED DEMONSTRATIONS

Demonstrations were not a novelty introduced into the Arab Middle East after World War I, nor was the Arab government in Syria the first government in the region to sanction and organize them. Throughout the Ottoman period, Syrians had staged parades and demonstrations to celebrate a number of events, including the coronations of Ottoman sultans and royal births. During these observances, they not only displayed decorations in shop windows and festooned local government buildings, but notables of each quarter planned and organized parades that typically included a march to the local seat of the imperial government.

The order of march and activities performed during these demonstrations were similar to—and likely borrowed from—the order of march and activities performed in parades held to celebrate religious festivals and marriages: marchers sang the same or similar songs and brandished customary ceremonial weapons, such as swords and canes. As took place in religious or matrimonial parades, processional leaders stood on the shoulders of one of the lead participants to supervise the action and direct the participants in celebratory cheers. The march itself served as the central event of the ceremony, and marchers stayed only a brief time at their destination to "display their feelings of fealty and joy," in the words of one contemporary observer.[1]

The local government in Damascus also organized demonstrations to dramatize popular sentiment during international crises, such as the conflicts with European powers over Crete (1896–1897) and Bosnia and Herzegovina (1908), and the Tripolitanian War (1911), assigning each *thuman* of the city a day on which to demonstrate, either alone or with other *athmān*. In this way, the government ensured a weeklong series of demonstrations. As they had done during the previously cited demonstrations, the crowd first marched to government offices, brandishing weapons and shouting slogans such as "We fast and we pray—the Island of Crete belongs to the Osmanlis," or "Who told you to go to war, Italian sons of dogs?" Demonstrators then marched to the gates of foreign consulates, where they continued to chant slogans while their leaders presented petitions of protest to the foreign legates. The route of the march (from the residential quarters to the foreign consulates, by way of the government offices) and the ceremony of petitioning enabled the crowd to display to foreign observers both its loyalty to the Ottoman government and its opposition to European actions. Concomitantly, the sacralization of the Ottoman cause through its representation in ceremony, as well as popular participation in that ceremony, enabled the Ottoman government to induce the popular sacrifices (such as acquiescence to conscription and supplementary taxes) that were

1. al-ʿAllāf, *Dimashq fī maṭlaʿ al-qarn al-ʿishrīn,* 120–123; J. Lecerf and R. Tresse, "Les *ʿarada* de Damas."

necessary to reverse the effects of foreign aggression. The demonstrations thus fulfilled both an inwardly directed and an outwardly directed purpose.

In July 1908, local branches of the Committee of Union and Progress also organized quarter-based demonstrations in support of the restoration of constitutional rule. Similarly, their opponents in the Muhammadan Union all too hastily organized demonstrations to celebrate the triumph of the attempted countercoup mounted against the committee in 1909. According to a dispatch written by Nasif Mashaka, acting agent of the United States consul, the demonstrations held on the former occasion were a daily—and for him a frightening—occurrence. "Imagine some five hundred illiterate young men, some with swords in their hands, others with revolvers and many with prohibited rifles stolen from the government, this whole crowd followed by a great multitude pass through the streets and the bazaars shooting and shouting," he reported.

> On the 8th instant, the orations in general were exceptionally liberal. A 'Young Turk' having the grade of 'Usbashy' stood on the platform, took out his sword and asked the people to stand up and repeat after him an oath to the meaning that if tyranny shall reign again, they would overthrow it no matter how dear it might cost them. They solemnly declared that they were ready to sacrifice for liberty their wives, their children and their blood! After this solemn oath three times three cheers were given for liberty, the Army and the sultan.[2]

Less than a year later, local representatives of the Muhammadan Union mobilized residents of the Maydan, which had been decorated and illuminated in honor of the occasion, to parade through the quarter for a day and a night chanting, "God has granted victory to the sultan."[3]

Because the Arab government was committed to a tactic of achieving independence by showing the entente powers that Syrians were prepared for and united in their desire for independence, it also sponsored demonstrations to present its case to the outside world. These demonstrations were of two types: petition demonstrations, in which the central drama consisted of the presentation of a list of demands directly or indirectly to representatives of the entente powers, and celebratory demonstrations, during which the Arab government and/or associated political organizations such as the Arab Club assembled the population so that they might display their devotion to the government, Amir Faysal, or both.

2. Quoted in Elie Kedourie, *Arabic Political Memoirs and Other Studies*, 137. See also Lecerf and Tresse, "Les ʿ*arada* de Damas," 261; Khoury, *Urban Notables*, 56.

3. Lecerf and Tresse, "Les ʿ*arada* de Damas," 261.

A generic blueprint for both types of demonstrations appeared in an unusual article that was published on the front page of *al-ʿĀṣima* on the eve of the arrival of the King-Crane Commission in Damascus.[4] The article, entitled "A True Vision," was written in the form of a prophetic parable that outlined the brilliant future of independence and progress awaiting Syrians if only they could convince the commission—and through the commission, the entente powers—that they could behave in a "civilized" manner.

The article began with a description of the author at his desk, contemplating the news of demonstrations held in Egypt to show popular support for Egyptian independence: "We hardly see such good order in the demonstrations of the most advanced Western nations," the author proclaims in a statement that would soon be echoed by ʿAli Rida al-Rikabi himself in personal correspondence.[5]

> I said to myself, "By God! They unjustly accuse the East and its people of savagery, immaturity, and an inability to imitate the civilization of the West. What is more indicative of their readiness [for independence] than this admirably ordered and perfect demonstration?"

Lulled into sleep, the author dreams of meeting a soothsayer who takes him on a tour of the future—a tour that includes a glimpse of the upcoming visit of the commission to Damascus. In the dream, "the sons of the nation," guided by their intellectuals (*al-mufakkirūn*), "held an orderly demonstration showing their national sentiments and desires in a way that would demonstrate to the delegation that the nation was worthy of independence." All Syrians, regardless of religious or sectarian affiliation (as the author is careful to point out), participated in the demonstration, placing on their forearms or breasts bindings printed with the slogan "We demand complete independence." Small boys wore the slogan on their fezzes while girls embroidered it on their frontlets. The owners of shops, hotels, and homes publicly displayed the same slogan in English and Arabic. So ubiquitous was the slogan that "one could not walk down the street without seeing the signs on every building and wall."

> I laughed when I saw a bald man with the slogan written on his head. I saw the owners of carriages and horses who placed this slogan on the faces of their horses. The sweets seller put the slogan on the containers

4. *al-ʿĀṣima,* 7 May 1919, 1–2.
5. In November 1919, al-Rikabi wrote to Saʿid Shuqayr, "I do not think that the demonstrations taking place in the most advanced nations are better organized and more peaceful." DU SA/493/6, 25 November 1919.

> of sweets and milk. I was truly amazed when I saw the work of the residents of Salihiyya—they had written this slogan on Mt. Qasyun by night in letters two parsangs long. The people kept up this sort of activity until the delegation left Damascus.

Nevertheless, while all Damascenes displayed the slogan and attended the demonstration—the author assures his readers that those who refused to take part were abused and compelled to join in—their participation, like their participation in the public ceremonies described in the previous chapter, was passive. "The demonstration that the people put on was perfect—quiet, without tumult, no speeches—yet through its silence the demonstration announced the advancement of the people." The commission, impressed by the "wisdom, advancement, and worthiness for complete independence" they found in Syria, returned to Paris to recommend that Syrians be allowed their independence. "The matter was decided accordingly." The article concludes with a summation, quoted in the Introduction of this book, of the brilliant future of economic advancement brought about by technological progress that was awaiting Syrians as a reward for their efforts.

As will be seen shortly, while most demonstrations organized by the government fit the pattern outlined in "A True Vision," the author could not help but omit mention of one indispensable aspect of these demonstrations: the Arab government did not stage demonstrations solely to impress the entente powers. Like the demonstrations organized by the Ottoman government to protest foreign aggression, and like the public holidays inaugurated by the Arab government and discussed in the previous chapter, government-sponsored demonstrations were designed to sway the beliefs of the participants and onlookers as well. Thus, while providing the entente representatives with a (largely deceptive) "model of" Syrian society, the Arab government simultaneously used demonstrations to provide the population of Syria with an officially sanctioned "model for" society.

Often, the Arab government began imposing its "model for" society even before the first demonstrators gathered. For example, in those demonstrations in which the central drama was the presentation of petitions to representatives of foreign powers, the circulation of the petitions and the gathering of signatures contributed to this end. As has been previously noted, because the petition campaigns were centrally coordinated by the Arab government, often in conjunction with the Arab Club, all petitions circulated in a given campaign contained demands that were virtually identical. But in addition to disseminating government-approved demands, the petitions followed a standardized formula that reinforced notions of social stratification endorsed by the government and their *mutanawwirūn* allies. The first sentence of each petition stated the district or town in which the petition had been circulated ("We, the undersigned residents of . . . "), then, before listing the demands, enumerated the categories into which the Arab government divided residents of the area (for example, "members of all creeds" (*madhāhib*), "members of all sects" (*ṭawāʾif*), "members of all religions" (*adyān*). To underscore these divisions, the signatures following the body of the petition were often likewise divided according to the government's view of the natural cleavages within Syrian society, which could be bridged only through the person of Amir Faysal.[6] The Arab government frequently reproduced these divisions physically when arranging the line of march of the demonstrators who assisted in the ceremony of petition presentation.

Because their dissemination was supported by the Arab government and Arab Club affiliates, these petitions, and the notions of stratification they promoted, circulated widely. While the role of quarter-based *makhātīr* in petition campaigns has already been described, the circulation of petitions extended far beyond urban boundaries. During the petition campaign that preceded the demonstration of 20 February 1919, for example, agents of the Arab government and the Arab Club roamed not only throughout the eastern zone but throughout neighboring zones as well. For example, Sami al-ʿAzm, a member of the executive committee of the Arab Club of Damascus, drew up and oversaw the distribution of petitions in the districts of Qatana (to the southwest of Damascus) and Duma (to the northeast). Al-ʿAzm used the occasion of the distribution of petitions in Qatana to establish branches of the Arab Club both there and in the surrounding region. According to French reports, the *qāʾimmaqām* of the district, ʿAbdallah Ustuwani—an Istanbul-trained lawyer and son of ʿAbd al-Muhsin Ustuwani, a member of the council of state of the Arab government—dispatched thirty cavalrymen to accompany al-ʿAzm on his rounds. Arab Club representatives gathered signatures in a similar manner in districts as far away as Amman, al-Salt, al-Karak, and Beirut.[7]

6. Originals and translations of petitions have been preserved in various archives in Britain, France, and the United States. In addition, many petitions were printed in Syrian newspapers such as *al-ʿĀṣima* and *al-Kawkab*.

7. AD 2368/10/2/162, Cousse to HC, 21 February 1919. According to French reports, in Druze and Christian villages in Qatana, where the Arab Club did not anticipate support for the petition, representatives of the club allegedly obtained signatures by presenting the petition as a protest against changes in the tax collection system—changes that would have increased the tax burden placed on cultivators.

The purpose of the demonstration held in Damascus on 20 February 1919 was to present the petitions gathered by al-ʿAzm and his colleagues to the representatives of the entente powers. Although, as will be seen below, the demonstration did not actually take place as planned, the Arab government and the Arab Club did distribute a program for the event that attests to the plans and motivations of those who organized it. According to the program, the planners intended for the participation of the crowd to be brief (less than one hour) and its role marginal. In effect, the crowd would present itself as a tableau vivant staged for the benefit of the petition recipients: under the direction of their local *makhātīr,* demonstrators, arranged according to a predetermined line of march, were to parade from their quarters to the city hall. There, while they patiently listened to speeches delivered not only in Arabic but also in French and English—languages incomprehensible to most demonstrators—delegations of *mutanawwirūn,* handpicked by the Arab Club, would present the petitions to foreign legates. As stipulated by the program, the presentation of the petitions—the central drama of the demonstration—was to take place offstage and behind closed doors.[8]

Over the course of the next year—that is, until the Arab government lost control of the streets to the popular committees—the government and its supporters organized a series of demonstrations that shared significant characteristics with this petition demonstration.[9] As in the ceremonies organized by the Arab government to celebrate national holidays, the fundamental building blocks of these demonstrations were primary and secondary schools supported by the government; the Arab army and functionaries of the Arab government; and any one of a number of government-allied political or charitable associations, newly reconstituted guilds, and

---

The reports also assert that in Muslim villages, the petition was presented in the context of a choice between a French/Christian government and an Arab/Muslim government. Those who had been identified as potential recalcitrants were put into detention for twenty-four hours during the time of the petition's circulation. In addition, the French liaison officer complained that the residents of Duma were asked to sign a blank piece of paper on which was written afterwards, "We, the undersigned, delegate Amir Faysal to act in our name and to represent us before the peace conference to demand the complete independence of Syria. . . . " AD 2430/154, Cousse to HC, 19 February 1919; AD 2430, Cousse to HC, 18 March 1919.

8. AD 2430/no no., Cousse to HC, 21 February 1919; AD 2430/dossier confidentiel—départ/65, Cousse to HC, 21 February 1919.

9. For descriptions of these demonstrations, see AD 2429/42, Mercier to Pichon, 11 November 1918; AD 2430, Cousse to Dame, 20 March 1919; MAE L:AH/vol. 4/237–238, Picot to Pichon, 22 May 1919; AD 2430/240, 11 August 1919.

"cultural" organizations such as the Arab Club. The enlistment of these groups in demonstrations served two purposes for the Arab government. First, it enabled the government to effect a controlled mobilization of the Syrian population while simultaneously bypassing—and therefore potentially enervating—its rivals, such as oppositional members of the indigenous Damascene notability and, later, the popular committees. Furthermore, the process of assembling each demonstration—the selection and physical organization of the participants, their arrangement in the line of march, their participation or nonparticipation in various sequences of the ceremony—permitted the government to define, reinforce, and expand the institutional networks under its control while once again providing the population of Syria with an officially sanctioned "model for" society.

In addition, because in their planning all government-supported demonstrations shared a common outwardly directed purpose—to show the entente powers that the Syrian population was prepared for independence and stood united behind the Arab government and Amir Faysal—they scripted similar roles for the schoolchildren, guild members, political activists, soldiers, and functionaries they incorporated. Unlike many of the demonstrations organized by the popular committees in the aftermath of the Evacuation Crisis—demonstrations that would, in effect, celebrate the crowd itself—the participants in government-sponsored demonstrations were rarely the focus of the ceremony or even the principal actors in the drama. Often the government and its allies assembled demonstrators to act as a backdrop to the true focus of attention, such as the presentation of petitions. At other times, they cast demonstrators as bit players in a drama that primarily concerned Amir Faysal, the *mutanawwirūn,* and the entente powers. Because government-sponsored demonstrations could thus convey their meaning and fulfill their function without the active participation of the crowd in the central drama, and because the government feared that the unruliness of the crowd would discredit it in the eyes of foreign powers and cast doubt on the preparedness of Syrians for independence,[10] the crowd's presence at government-sponsored demonstrations was uniformly fleeting and its participation restricted.

The demonstration held in Damascus in the spring of 1919 to greet Amir Faysal upon his first return from Europe was typical of the celebra-

10. See, for example, AD 2430/no no., Cousse to HC, 21 February 1919; MD L:AH/vol. 4/237–238, Picot to Pichon, 22 May 1919; MD L:SL/vol. 43/39–41, "Renseignements d'agent," 12 July 1919; AD 2344/c1/310, Cousse to Picot, 3 November 1919.

tory demonstrations organized by the Arab government and its allies. Faysal, who had been away from Syria for over five months, returned to Damascus to direct the preparations for the upcoming visit of the King-Crane Commission. As soon as word of the amir's departure from Europe reached Damascus, the Arab government began preparing ceremonies of greeting. "It is unnecessary to tell you that all activity here is directed to assure him a grand reception," the French liaison officer resident in Damascus reported.

> . . . the police have personally invited all the inhabitants to fly the Arab colors; the schools have been mobilized; victory arches have begun to be raised practically all over, and there promise to be innumerable speeches. The arrival of the amir will certainly be a capital event in Syrian affairs.[11]

For days before his arrival in the capital, local newspapers carried news of the amir's journey from Rome to Beirut, reported on celebrations held in his honor in Beirut, then followed his progress to Damascus.[12] To ensure a fitting reception in the Syrian capital, *al-ʿĀṣima* printed a front-page editorial on 2 May entitled "His Exalted Highness Amir Faysal," which praised Faysal's efforts in Europe and recounted his qualities as an Arab hero "who was and still is working tirelessly to guarantee the future of the nation" and who "rescued the nation from slavery and the misfortunes of slavery."[13]

The demonstration organized in Damascus to greet the amir, like the above-cited demonstration that provided the background for the delivery of petitions to entente representatives, was coordinated by the municipal government of Damascus. It was staged as a triumphal celebration of the amir, whose entrance into the city was described by a Syrian observer as follows:

> When His Highness Amir Faysal arrived at Damascus, he rode in a carriage drawn by eight horses. On the carriage were trimmings of gold and silver. Victory arches had been set up for him and were decorated with jewels donated by the women of Damascus. Spread before him in his path were 25,000 carpets.[14]

According to *al-ʿĀṣima*, crowds of Syrians had turned out to greet Faysal; nevertheless, the public ceremony was mere window dressing planned for the benefit of the entente powers. After briefly acknowledging the crowd, Faysal adjourned to a nearby park to speak with a small group that had been

11. AD 2430, Cousse to Dame, 20 April 1919.
12. See, for example, *al-ʿĀṣima*, 2 May 1919, 2.
13. Ibid., 1.
14. al-ʿIyāshī, *al-Īḍāḥāt al-siyāsiyya*, 32.

invited to attend this invitation-only event.[15] In the park, orators delivered speeches of greeting and recited specially composed poems. In response, the amir thanked the entente representatives in attendance for the support of their governments, which had "saved the nation from the enemy" and "offered [the Arabs] independence." In addition, the amir thanked the population of Syria "for remaining calm during the past five months, enabling him to push on for complete independence." Following the ceremony in the park, the military governor hosted a banquet in Faysal's honor, to which "members of the [Arab] government, groups of ulama, [progovernment] notables, spiritual leaders from the minority communities, and delegations from the surrounding areas" were also invited.

The public and private aspects of the ceremony greeting Faysal, like the public and private aspects of the celebration of national holidays, thus replicated the binary division of Syrian society into sorts: while selected notables, heads of separate communities, *mutanawwirūn*, and so on, decided affairs of state, ritual specialists removed the populace from center stage and cast them in a passive role. Ironically, then, this demonstration, like others organized by the Arab government, affirmed the fact that real political decisions were to be made neither democratically nor in the streets.

The meaning of government-sponsored demonstrations was not just propounded through their form, however. As described in the previous chapter, the Arab government carefully vetted the slogans shouted by demonstrators and the messages inscribed on their banners. Moreover, the Arab government took advantage of the theatricality of demonstrations and the casting of the populace in a passive or secondary role to inculcate the proper "model for" Syrian society and nationalist politics. This was perhaps most evident in the parade that preceded the demonstration held in Damascus on 16 November 1919. According to official accounts, the purpose of the parade was to display the unity of the Syrian population and reaffirm its desire for complete independence and its rejection "of any patriotism or nationalism but Arab nationalism in any part [of Syria]." Embedded within the ranks of the marchers were floats constructed to symbolize this message. Some demonstrators, for example, carried a table decorated in the black, white, and green colors of the Arab flag. On the table, parade organizers had placed copies of the Old Testament, the New Testament, and the Qur'an, an obvious reference to the unity of the separate Jewish, Christian, and Muslim communities within the framework of

15. *al-ʿĀṣima*, 7 May 1919, 5–6.

the "new religion" of Arab nationalism.[16] Also included in the parade was a cart on which a man stood, wearing a costume representing a map of Syria divided into sections labeled "eastern zone," "southern zone," and "coastal zone," corresponding to the entente's division of the Arab provinces of the Ottoman Empire. As reported in the official government journal, "This man, representing the nation, asked the people if they would be satisfied with his division or colonization, and they answered in unison, expressing principles upon which the nation had decided unanimously."[17] To ensure that the theme of the demonstration was not lost on the population, another float, containing newspapermen working a printing press, printed nationalist slogans and distributed them to the crowd.

In the end, the demonstrations organized by the short-lived Arab government accomplished neither their outwardly nor their inwardly directed goals. As can be ascertained from the dispatches sent home by the foreign legates based in Syria, the entente representatives regarded the demonstrations sometimes with bemusement, sometimes with contempt. "I have the honor to send you . . . a copy of the order of the Damascus municipality addressed to the corporations, regulating the tiniest details of the ceremony organized to greet Amir Faysal," François Georges-Picot wrote to his superiors at the Quai d'Orsay. "This document has no interest except to show [you] . . . how one can organize a spontaneous popular demonstration that displays unanimous support for whatever opinion you desire."[18]

Likewise, while the Arab government was ultimately unable to instill its brand of nationalism among the Syrian population for a variety of reasons unconnected to the manner in which it arranged demonstrations, the demonstrations it sanctioned did little to bolster its support among the populace. The demonstrations were ineffective for several reasons. First, government-sponsored demonstrations relied on didactic signs that were relatively weak in comparison with the resonant and multivocal symbols of which the popular committees took advantage. The message of the demonstrations was further diluted because there was no inherent connection between the central drama of the demonstrations—the presentation of petitions, for example—and the physical organization of the participants. This was hardly accidental: while a primary function of the demonstrations organized by the Arab government was to display the "civilized" nature of the Syrian population and its readiness for self-government, the govern-

16. AD 2344/c1/149–151, 17 November 1919.
17. *al-ʿĀṣima*, 17 November 1919, 3–4.
18. MAE L:AH/vol. 4/237–238, Picot to Pichon, 22 May 1919.

ment had to hold the demonstrators virtually incommunicado lest they display their indifference to European standards of civilization and their frustration with the tactical approach taken by the government to achieve independence. In addition, because the Arab government could not maintain control of the streets (as indicated, for example, by the placement of machine-gun nests on the main thoroughfares of Damascus on at least three separate occasions), it expended as much effort repressing demonstrations as it did promoting them.[19] Finally—and perhaps most important—the nationalism that the Arab government attempted to promote through the demonstrations just did not resonate with the population.

The circumscribed capacity of government-sponsored demonstrations to instill among the population a worldview and ideology that appeared alien to many Syrians becomes apparent when the plans for the demonstrations are compared with accounts describing their actual realization. At times, political activists who disagreed with government policies deliberately subverted the meaning of government-sponsored demonstrations. For example, during the demonstrations held in Damascus to celebrate Faysal's return to Syria after the amir had initialed the Faysal-Clemenceau Agreement—demonstrations that reportedly generated significantly less enthusiasm than those held to mark his first return from Europe—unknown individuals, obviously rankled by the amir's attempts to reach a compromise with the entente powers and Zionists in Paris and by the kidnapping of Yasin al-Hashimi by the British, climbed onto the roof of the Arab Club building and tossed to the crowd papers on which antigovernment, anti-Faysal slogans had been printed. Among the slogans were "Death to those who betray Palestine," "Faysal, protect the patrimony of prophets and of our ancestors," "Where is your generalissimo, Faysal?" and "The Arab nation is indivisible."[20]

On other occasions, the crowd itself refused to play the role that the government and its allies had scripted for it. The demonstration held in

19. AD 2344/c1/310, Cousse to Picot, 3 November 1919; AD 2344/325, Cousse to Picot, 10 November 1919; MD 4H114/1/434, Cousse to Gouraud, 28 December 1919. For the placement of machine-gun nests in Damascus during the visit of the King-Crane Commission, after its departure, and during the final days of the Arab government, see MAE L:SL/vol. 14/897, Picot to MAE, 27 June 1919; FO 371/4182/125032, "CPO: Report on a Conversation in Cairo with Michel Bey Lotfullah on His Return from Syria August 5th 1919"; MD 4H114/dossier 5/no no., Cousse to Gouraud, 20 July 1920; MD 4H60/dossier 1, "Bulletin quotidien 1270," 23 July 1920; IO L/PS/10/802/P5841, GHQ (Egypt) to WO, 24 July 1920.

20. AD 2372/dossier: propagande anti-française, 17 January 1920.

February 1919 to accompany the presentation of petitions to the entente representatives was, in reality, neither as popular nor as disciplined as planners had anticipated. As estimated by an obviously pleased French observer, only three or four hundred participants—including a number of curious onlookers—attended the ceremony, a far cry from the thousands expected by the Arab government. Moreover, the performance of music and the display of decorative flags and bunting, which lent the demonstration a festive quality, belied the seriousness of the occasion.[21] It was perhaps for this reason that, instead of a protracted series of speeches, only two were delivered to the crowd. In addition, through their activities the demonstrators seemed to flaunt both their detachment from and inattention to the principal themes of the ceremony. According to Asʿad Daghir, who claims to have been present at the event, although the Arab government arranged the demonstration to serve as a backdrop for the presentation of petitions drawn up to demonstrate to foreign legates that Syrians supported the efforts of Amir Faysal to negotiate with the entente powers on their behalf and that Syria was ready to join the "civilized" nations of the world, the impatient crowd chanted a slogan that was fundamentally at odds with this purpose: "The religion of Muhammad is the religion of the sword."[22]

Nevertheless, the crowd did not remain entirely detached from the central drama of the demonstration. To the contrary, the focus of the demonstration shifted from the delegated and almost secretive presentation of petitions to foreign representatives to a collective presentation of copies of the petitions to the military governor, ʿAli Rida al-Rikabi, who assumed responsibility for passing them on.[23] Thus, whether as a result of last-minute adaptation on the part of its organizers acting in response to the indifference or antipathy of the population, the active or passive resistance of the demonstrators itself, or a combination of both, those who had been mobilized to bear witness to the central drama of the demonstration instead both recast the ceremony and assumed the role of active participants in it. As will be seen in the next section, the alteration in the central dramatic sequence of the demonstration, which in effect transformed an event that had

21. AD 2430/no no., Cousse to HC, 21 February 1919; AD 2430/dossier confidentiel—départ/65, Cousse to HC, 21 February 1919.

22. AD 2367/10/1/146, Cousse to HC, 14 February 1919; AD 2430/no no., Cousse to HC, 21 February 1919; AD 2430/65, Cousse to HC, 21 February 1919; Dāghir, *Mudhakkarātī*, 105.

23. AD 2430/no no., Cousse to HC, 21 February 1919; AD 2430/65, Cousse to HC, 21 February 1919.

been designed to confirm a specific structuring of society and political program into one that challenged that structuring and program, attests to the underlying tension, present in all didactic ceremonies, between the designs of the mobilizers and the aspirations of the mobilized.

THE DEMONSTRATIONS OF THE POPULAR COMMITTEES

In early September 1919, the Arab Club of Damascus, responding to the same impetus that precipitated the formation of the voluntary militias, mobilized a demonstration that was unlike any previously planned by the Arab government or allied political association. Even though the September 15 Accord, the kidnapping and exile of Yasin al-Hashimi, and the organization of the popular committees were still in the future, the Arab government was particularly vulnerable at this time: the King-Crane Commission had come and gone, and although its recommendations still remained secret, provocations such as the British acceptance of the mandate for Palestine in the late summer fueled the skepticism felt by many Syrians about the efficacy of the Arab government's diplomatic efforts and its commitment to complete independence and Syrian unity. According to *Sūriyya al-jadīda,* for example,

> Syria has gained nothing from the American Commission but schism and distress of mind. No one doubts that Europe will throw the demands of the nation to the wall, and is striving to solve this question in her own political interests.[24]

Placed on the defensive, the Arab government and its allies could not but respond to the public agitation that the government itself, through its efforts at mobilization during the spring and summer of 1919, had unintentionally nurtured. As a result, on 9 September, Amir Faysal and his retinue participated in a demonstration held, according to a report in *al-ʿĀṣima,* "to glorify the Arab army . . . by insisting on the right to unity and independence."[25]

24. Cited in Russell, *First Modern Arab State,* 91–92.
25. *al-ʿĀṣima,* 11 September 1919, 4–6. This demonstration was actually the second demonstration held in as many weeks to champion an expansion of military recruitment and, implicitly, a more forceful foreign policy. According to a sketchy French report, in the first demonstration, led by Amir Zayd and Yusuf Istifan (one of the principal speakers at the 9 September demonstration), a detachment of troops from the regular Arab army along with three to four hundred volunteer fighters marched to Faysal's residence. I have not been able to obtain any further information about this demonstration. AD 2430/dossier confidentiel—départ/257, Telegram to HC, 4 September 1919.

Several pieces of evidence indicate that government officials, including the amir and the military governor, viewed participation in the demonstration as a means to co-opt and assuage adverse public opinion. For example, rather than ignoring or striving to suppress the agitation for armed defense (the British would soon attempt suppression by removing al-Hashimi to Palestine after he called for the enlistment of twelve thousand volunteers), government representatives, including many whose subsequent actions indicate that they still maintained confidence in the entente powers and the Paris negotiations, adopted the call for defense as their own. In an interview published in *al-Kawkab,* for example, ʿAli Rida al-Rikabi thus differentiated between defense as advocated by "the intellectuals, men of leadership, and the righteous"—defense "by all effective, rational means compatible with the preservation of order and tranquility"—and defense as advocated by "demagogues." "He is prepared to exert every effort, both materially and spiritually, for the purpose of true national defense, to join his trustworthy, patriotic brothers in serving the nation, and to establish a reasonable organized defense," the article reported. It then warned of the consequences of adopting the alternative approach to defense: "The beloved fatherland will be held back if the fangs of discord and selfish and personal interest toy with it."[26] Moreover, although the presence of high government officials, including Amir Faysal and his immediate cohort, lent official sanction to the demonstration, a close examination of the symbolism embedded in the demonstration, its morphology, the activities of the demonstrators, and the content of the speeches delivered by the designated orators reveals a government prepared to concede symbolic ground to its opponents.

The program of the demonstration was complex, consisting of several successive sequences. As described in *al-ʿĀṣima,*[27] the demonstration began when representatives of political parties, guilds, and "youths of nationalist organizations . . . of every quarter," organized by the Arab Club, converged on the club's headquarters to call for military service ("*tajnīd fī sabīl al-waṭan*"). At the clubhouse, they were joined by another procession that, as the ensuing speeches pointed out, was the true focal point of the demonstration. Led by a cavalry unit drawn from the regular Arab army, this group of marchers included "young men and the sons of notables" from

26. *al-Kawkab,* 6 January 1920, 5.

27. The following description of the demonstration, along with transcriptions of speeches delivered during its staging, can be found in *al-ʿĀṣima,* 11 September 1919, 4–6.

Shaghur, the Maydan, Qaymariyya, ʿAmara, and other quarters who had registered in a battalion sponsored by the Arab Club and who now marched behind the club's banner. Immediately behind them, a phalanx of newly enlisted youths from the Qanawat quarter of the city followed a litter-bearing camel "which served as a symbol for the glory of the nation, which the sons of the nation would have to protect to their last soul."

From the Arab Club, the entire assemblage marched a short distance to a location where Amir Faysal, his brother, and their retainers awaited them and where an exchange of speeches between the marchers and the sharifians took place. Three speakers, all chosen by the Arab Club, spoke for the marchers: Shaykh ʿAbd al-Qadir al-Muzaffar, president of the club; Muhammad Shurayqi, who, as the Arab Club poet, often recited his own verses on ceremonial occasions;[28] and a former Maronite priest, Yusuf Istifan, who, in the months following this demonstration, would put his fervent anti-French rhetoric at the service of the popular committees.[29] After Faysal replied to the three, the crowd adjourned to Martyrs' Square for another ceremony, this time without the amir. Istifan once again addressed the crowd, but now from the Municipal Building balcony overlooking the square that government officials customarily used for their ceremonial addresses. Istifan invoked the image of the martyrs, who, he proclaimed, "look to the youth from their particles of dust to complete the task they had begun." After Istifan's speech, the crowd returned to the Arab Club building and disbanded.

At first glance, this demonstration appears similar to other ceremonies and demonstrations planned by the Arab government or its allies before

28. For information on Shurayqi, see AD 2430/dossier confidentiel—départ/634, Cousse to HC, 24 October 1919; *al-ʿĀṣima*, 12 July 1920, 1; FO 317/5040/E13211/ 1171, Report by GL Easton, 18 October 1920; Darwaza, *Ḥawla al-ḥaraka al-ʿarabiyya al-ḥadītha*, 1:27; Darwaza, *Mudhakkarāt*, 2:99, 112, 143–144; Mardam Bek, *Dimashq wal-Quds fī al-ʿishrīnāt*, 29, 47–48; Joarder, *Syria Under the French Mandate*, 209–211.

29. For Yusuf Istifan, see AD 2368/10/2, "Rapport à lieut. Wiet," 2 January 1919; AD 2437/dossier: propagande arabe/43, "Rapport sur les journaux du 26 et 27 mai," 28 May 1919; AD 2430/dossier confidentiel—départ/216, 21 July 1919; AD 2430/dossier confidentiel—départ/257, Telegram to HC, 4 September 1919; AD 2430/dossier confidentiel—départ/260, Telegram to HC, 18 September 1919; MD 4H112/2B/44, "Renseignements du 8 au 15 mai, 1920 (Ça et là dans Alep)"; MD 4H112/2B, Untitled notebook by French agent; FO 371/5036/E6983/24–27/748, Shahbandar to Easton, 1 June 1920; *al-Kināna*, 15 July 1920, 3; MD 4H114/5/no no., Cousse to Gouraud, 20 July 1920; Angelil, "L'occupation d'Homs," 180–191; FO 371/5040/E13211/212–218/1171, G. L. Easton to Curzon, 18 October 1920.

and subsequently: a parade before the amir, the exchange of speeches, the invocation of the martyrs, didactic exhibits, and a list of speakers ("an *ʿālim*," "a priest," and "an educated youth," in the words of *al-ʿĀṣima*) carefully chosen as representatives of exemplary categories befitting a government-sanctioned "model for" society. Even Faysal's speech to the demonstrators differed little from others he had delivered and would continue to deliver: having introduced himself as "the person to whom you have entrusted your interests and handed over your political leadership," he defended the integrity of the entente powers, assured his audience that those powers would not renege on their wartime promises, and declared that, contrary to newspaper accounts, he had not done nor would he do anything to jeopardize Syrian unity and independence.

In spite of these similarities, however, this demonstration differed from previously described ceremonies in significant ways. During other ceremonial occasions, for example, it had become common practice for a crowd to pay symbolic obeisance to Faysal by gathering below the balcony of his residence or government building; on this occasion, not only did the amir ride out from his residence to wait for the crowd at a location midway between his residence and the Arab Club building, but the crowd then withdrew from the amir to hold its own ceremony to which the amir was not invited. This ceremony took place below the very balcony associated with official pronouncements. Furthermore, as can be determined through the speeches delivered by the crowd's representatives, the encounter with the amir was not petitionary; rather than representing the focal point of power—the dispenser of beneficence and intercessor with the outside world—the amir assumed the role of an icon of national unity who bore witness to the activities of the nation. In the words of Yusuf Istifan, "We have come to this place in order to renew in front of you and under this Arab banner a covenant made between us [the volunteers] and the nation." If the newspaper transcription is accurate, Istifan repeated the formula "a covenant made between us and the nation" twice in his speech.

This demonstration might also be distinguished from those described earlier by the role assigned to its participants. Unlike other demonstrations and ceremonies with which the Arab government and its allies were associated—demonstrations in which the crowd, barred from direct participation in the focal ceremonial sequence, assumed the passive role of backdrop or, at best, audience—this one had participants assume a central, performative role. But not only were the participants the principal celebrants, they were also the object of the celebration. "We have become at this hour soldiers . . . ," proclaimed ʿAbd al-Qadir al-Muzaffar. "The youth of this nation meet now because they feel that our freedom and independence will necessarily continue because we are soldiers."

Two aspects of this demonstration foreshadowed the demonstrations sponsored by the popular committees. First, as the initial speech of Istifan, the encounter between the demonstrators and Faysal, and the subsequent ceremony held in Martyrs' Square all make clear, the demonstration symbolically separated the "nation" from the ruling institution and privileged the former over the latter. Because the popular committees claimed to embody the nation and represent its will, and because the demonstrations they sponsored thus symbolized the nation assembled, this separation and privileging was a consistent theme in their demonstrations as well.

Second, the demonstration held on 9 September not only presented the crowd as instrumental but confirmed both its instrumentality and autonomy by engaging it in activity that was entirely self-referential. The use of the participants as the motive force to advance the central drama of the demonstration would come to characterize all demonstrations sponsored by the popular committees. Furthermore, as the authority of the Arab government weakened further during the spring and early summer of 1920, and as the government increasingly ceded control of the streets of urban Syria to the popular committees, the committees attenuated or even eliminated from the demonstrations they sponsored ceremonial sequences that dramatized dissent from the policies of the Arab government and/or the entente powers. By deleting all referents extraneous to the demonstrators themselves, the popular committees were in effect sponsoring demonstrations that had no purpose other than to represent in microcosm a nation that was self-directed and self-contained. In these demonstrations, the celebration of the nation and its autonomy did not merely accompany other symbolic messages, it superseded them.

The first and most common large-scale demonstrations organized by the popular committees were petition demonstrations. In most cases, these demonstrations might be differentiated from those organized by the Arab government on the basis of their central dramatic sequence, during which the crowd submitted petitions to representatives of the Arab government. These petitions were either to be acted on by the government itself or to be passed on to the entente powers. This shift in the identity of the petition recipient had important symbolic connotations: by means of the presentation of a list of demands to the Arab government in the name of the nation, demonstrators, under the leadership of the popular committees, not only reenacted the confrontation between the nation and the government but symbolically reestablished the proper equilibrium between the two adversaries. As a result, even those demonstrations that included the submission of petitions beginning with professions of devotion to an iconocized amir—like the demonstration of 17 January 1920, described below—were confrontational rather than supplicatory.

In the aftermath of the kidnapping of al-Hashimi, for example, the newly formed Higher National Committee staged a petition demonstration in Damascus to protest the abduction. During the demonstration, Kamil al-Qassab and Asʿad Daghir, representing the committee, submitted a petition to Amir Zayd to be forwarded to the entente powers in the name of the nation. The warning contained in the petition was clearly not addressed to the entente powers alone: "The nation considers General al-Hashimi to be one of the foremost representatives of the national movement, which was one of the most important factors in the victory of the allies in the east," the petition declared about the man who, although an early member of al-Fatat, had chosen to remain in the Ottoman army rather than join the sharifians. "The nation will not be responsible for the consequences that might result from [the arrest of] the general, nor from any other act contrary to its aspirations and sacred rights."[30] Thus, like the petition cited in Chapter 3 entitled "The Nation Dictates Its Wishes to the Syrian Congress"—a petition that derived its emotive power from the reiteration of the confrontational motif "the nation wants" before each of many demands directed at the congress—the tone of this petition was neither deferential nor suppliant.

Perhaps the largest demonstration held in Damascus during the Faysali period, estimated by British authorities to have exceeded one hundred thousand participants, was the petition demonstration staged by the commit-

30. AD 2332/dossier a/sous-dossier Loutfallah/1, Kamil al-Qassab and Asʿad Daghir to Amir Zayd, n.d. (in Arabic and French). In cities outside Damascus, demonstrators addressed their petitions to local representatives of the Arab government, whom they charged with sending their list of demands to the capital. See, for example, MD 4H112/2bB/215, "Manifestation de protestation contre les actes du gouvernement du littoral," 14 April 1920. In his memoirs, Muhammad ʿAli al-ʿAjluni, the head of the royal guard and rival of al-Hashimi, offers a more derisive perspective with respect to the demonstrations organized to protest the arrest of al-Hashimi. During one demonstration, which he attributes to the Arab Club, students from the professional schools, and so on, he writes that he was on the balcony of the amir's residence when the raucous crowd gathered below. When someone leaned down from the balcony and shouted at the crowd, "Why do you want al-Hashimi?" the crowd responded, "We want to punish him and cut him up." al-ʿAjlūnī, *Dhikrayāt ʿan al-thawra al-ʿarabiyya al-kubrā*, 85.

tees of national defense on 17 January 1920.[31] The day before the demonstration, Amir Faysal, having initialed a tentative agreement with French premier and acting foreign minister Georges Clemenceau, arrived home in Damascus for the second time in eight months. While neither the French nor the Arab governments had, by the time the amir arrived in Damascus, published the text of the Faysal-Clemenceau Agreement, rumors of its contents circulated widely in Damascus.[32] The demonstration (the subject of the two newspaper articles cited at the beginning of Chapter 3) began with a march from the Hamidiyya Barracks to the seat of the Arab government. When Faysal emerged from the building to meet with the demonstrators on the street, they presented him with "their national demands" framed in the form of a declaration calling for the complete independence of Syria within its natural boundaries and for the recruitment "of a national army that will defend its independence and will maintain the security of the interior and exterior of the country."[33]

By the spring of 1920, the popular committees, often acting in coalitions that reflected local conditions, mounted a series of petition demonstrations throughout the eastern zone that underscored the autonomy and primacy of the nation even more bluntly. Instead of petitioning the government to intercede with the entente powers on behalf of the nation, these protests ignored the Arab government entirely and petitioned the entente powers directly. The Higher National Committee in Damascus, along with local affiliates in Aleppo, Homs, and Hama, organized several demonstrations of this type throughout the spring and early summer of 1920 to protest issues that were of particular concern to their constituents, including Zionist immigration to Palestine, French actions in Lebanon (the issuance of the new

31. FO 371/5144/E360, "Letter of Proceedings #59," Egypt and Red Sea Command, 30 January 1920. For a similar estimate, see *al-Kawkab*, 27 January 1920, 5. The French liaison officer also described the demonstrators as "extremely numerous." MD 4H114/2/37, Cousse to Gouraud, 17 January 1920. The same report attributes the demonstration to a coalition of "extremist" groups, including the Higher National Committee, the Committee of National Defense, and the Arab Club. A leaflet that was used to advertise the demonstration (contained in AD 2372/dossier: propagande anti-française) was signed "Congress [*muʾtamar*] of the Committees of Defense."

32. For rumors circulating in Damascus, see *al-Difāʿ*, 17 January 1920, 1; FO 371/5144/E360, "Letter of Proceedings #59," Egypt and Red Sea Command, 30 January 1920.

33. AD 2372/dossier: propagande anti-française, 17 January 1920; AD 2375/chemise: division de Syrie/392/2, Arlabosse to GCDS, 17 January 1920; *al-Kawkab*, 27 January 1920, 5.

Syrian currency, restrictions on Friday *khuṭab*), and the San Remo Agreement dividing Syria into separate mandated territories.[34]

While the popular committees continued to organize demonstrations that alluded to the autonomy and primacy of the nation while protesting entente actions or Arab government irresolution, they also organized demonstrations solely to celebrate that autonomy and primacy. These demonstrations were a radical departure from petition demonstrations because, by eliminating ceremonial sequences that adverted to external events or authorities, they were comprehensive in themselves. Furthermore, unlike the demonstrations discussed above, many of these demonstrations were frequently festive, small-scale, ostensibly leaderless, and/or haphazardly organized. On some occasions, armed demonstrators chanting slogans or singing songs marched through residential quarters. On others, the demonstrations culminated with speeches lauding the Syrian nation or with the administration of an actual or symbolic oath of allegiance that pledged the participants to defend the fatherland or reformulated the social contract that united Syrians with each other or the nation with the state.[35] Kamil al-Qassab conducted one such swearing-in ceremony on the eve of the French invasion. According to a report in *al-Kināna,* the ceremonies began at the Arab Club headquarters with a meeting that included more than three hundred participants. From there, the entire convocation, singing "patriotic songs," paraded to a meeting of the Democratic Party that was being held in the quarter of Ma'dhanat al-Shahm. After delivering a speech in which he recalled all that the Higher National Committee had been able to accomplish "in spite of the depravity of the corrupt and the wiles of the haughty," al-Qassab called on his audience to "renew their covenant." He

34. See, for example, IO L/PS/10/802/P4953, "Renseignements: semaine du 18 au 24 mai 1920"; AD 2346, "Extraits des renseignements du 19 mai 1920."

35. See, for example, AD 2344/327, Cousse to Picot, 10 November 1919; MAE L:SL/vol. 121/1–2, "Rapport de renseignements hebdomadaires," 10–17 November 1919; FO 371/4185/152060/I.707S, GHQ (Egypt) to DMI, 11 November 1919; FO 371/4238/160100/8–11, "Situation in Egypt, Syria, and Arabia," 14 November 1919; AD 2344/c1/149–150–151, 17 November 1919; FO 371/4185/158008/408–409, "Summaries of Telegrams," 29 November 1919; USNA 59/867.00/1035/1682, US Consul (Aleppo) to Sec. of State, 1 December 1919; *al-Kawkab,* 2 December 1919, 6–7; FO 371/4186/165787/I.1224, GHQ (Egypt) to DMI, 23 December 1919; FO 371/4186/174490/FO 10 (CPO331/6), Meinertzhagen to GHQ, 13 January 1920; MD 4H114/5/700, Cousse to Gouraud, 16 July 1920; MD 4H60/1, "Bulletin quotidien 1264," 20 July 1920; MD 4H60/1, "Bulletin quotidien 1266," 21 July 1920.

then administered an oath to an estimated fifteen hundred recruits to the party.[36]

The thematic content of both the celebratory and the petition demonstrations organized by the popular committees was further reinforced through their internal structure. Unlike the demonstrations staged by their adversaries—demonstrations that presented an idealized and unfamiliar "model for" society to the targeted population that constituted its domestic audience—the demonstrations organized by the popular committees were designed in a manner that confirmed a "model of" society as experienced by a participative population cast in the role of performers. The fundamental building block of these demonstrations was the local popular committee, and most individuals who participated in them did so under the auspices of the local committees with which they were affiliated. Because, as described in Chapter 2, these local committees had assumed responsibility for a variety of day-to-day functions usually associated with governance—the policing and provisioning of urban quarters, the organization of locally based militias, and so on—and because these committees were linked in a pyramidal structure that included quarter-based committees, regional defense committees, and a national committee, the demonstrations did, in effect, recreate a "model of" society while articulating programs of action that were functional in intent and national in scope.[37]

In more elaborately structured demonstrations, the popular committees allowed groups other than the committees to maintain their individual or corporate identities in the line of march. However, because these groups were placed behind a vanguard representing the popular committees, and because their positions in the demonstration were seemingly haphazard and nonhierarchical, individuals and groups not affiliated with the committees were symbolically subsumed in the committees, and therefore in the Syrian nation. For example, committees of national defense arranged the line of march for the demonstration held on 17 January in the following manner: Leading the march, as if to consecrate the undertaking, were widows and daughters of the martyrs and ulama and other religious leaders, representing the spiritual unity of the nation. Marching immediately behind them were members of the popular committees and representatives of the Higher National Committee. Finally, there followed, in no apparent

36. *al-Kināna,* 15 July 1920, 3.

37. For a similar analysis, see Mary Ryan, "The American Parade: Representation of the Nineteenth-Century Social Order," 137–138.

order, notables and members of the municipal council, government functionaries, military pensioners, doctors, pharmacists, members of the press, representatives of political parties, students of the professional and preparatory schools, merchants, artisans, and finally the heads of the guilds and quarters.[38]

Demonstrations of the type sponsored by the popular committees generated enthusiasm during those periods when participation in government-sponsored demonstrations waned. On 9 November 1919, for example, a demonstration that ended with participants marching to Faysal's residence while shouting, "To war, to war," attracted a crowd estimated at between fifteen and twenty thousand. The next day, only a fraction of that number participated in a demonstration that culminated in the presentation of a petition by the president of the municipality of Damascus to foreign consuls.[39] French observers noted a similar phenomenon when demonstrations organized by the Arab government and the popular committees competed on 16 and 17 January 1920 in the wake of Amir Faysal's return to Damascus from Europe.[40] Such occurrences cannot be attributed simply to the ability of the popular committees to mobilize resources more effectively than the Arab government, or to their ability to exert social pressure on residents of those quarters in which they were active; these capabilities were, after all, derived from the prestige already enjoyed by the popular committees. Furthermore, while the Arab government's capacity for coercion and suasion did decline as a result of ongoing financial difficulties, it never entirely disappeared. Indeed, the government-sponsored demonstration held on 16 January reportedly consisted entirely of police, gendarmerie, the Arab army, schoolchildren, and the heads of the guilds. Overall, then, demonstrations organized by the popular committees were successful because they reenacted in ceremony and symbolized in form a construction of society that reflected more accurately than did demonstrations mounted by the Arab government the social ordering envisaged by the participants.

This conclusion is borne out by As'ad Daghir, who, in his memoirs, compared the activities and deportment of participants in demonstrations

38. The order of march for the demonstration on 17 January 1920 can be found in a leaflet contained in AD 2372/dossier: propagande anti-française, 17 January 1920. See also al-Qassab's report in *al-Kawkab*, 27 January 1920, 5.

39. AD 2344/296, Cousse to HC, 28 October 1919; AD 2430/dossier confidentiel—départ/325–326, Cousse to HC, 10 November 1919; FO 371/4185/152060/I.707S, GHQ (Egypt) to DMI, 11 November 1919; FO 371/4238/160100, Admiralty Report, "Situation in Egypt, Syria, and Arabia," 14 November 1919.

40. MD 4H114/2/37, Cousse to Gouraud, 17 January 1920.

sponsored by the Arab government and those in demonstrations sponsored by the popular committees. According to Daghir, during the demonstration mounted by the Arab government in the wake of the first nationwide petition campaign, demonstrators who had been herded into the capital from villages surrounding Damascus acted as if they were on an outing—shouting, firing guns in the air, and so on. During later demonstrations organized by the popular committees and observed by Daghir, participants appeared more disciplined and focused on national issues. In addition, Daghir noted that during the latter demonstrations, the competition normally found among youths from various quarters was replaced by a spirit of "cooperation against the foreigners," and that parade organizers did not need to rely on vertical networks of patronage for mobilization.[41]

Overall, Daghir found in the demonstrations sponsored by the popular committees evidence that the horizontal, associational, and national ties linking the participants with one another superseded ties that were vertical, "primordial" (i.e., kinship- or communally-based), and purely localist. While it is difficult to take all of Daghir's recollections at face value—the manner in which he compresses the time separating the two demonstrations in his account, for example, calls into question his ability to recall the details of events that occurred over three decades before the publication of his memoirs—the plausibility of his conclusion that these demonstrations evince an underlying shift in political and social relationships among Syrians is further supported by the work of Charles Tilly.

Tilly's argument might be summarized in the following manner: In all societies there exist a limited number of options available for the expression of dissent. Two factors determine the variety and scope of activities that constitute these "repertoires of contentious collective action": the extent to which capitalist relations have permeated society (and have thereby affected the organization not only of economic relations, but of social relations as well) and the strength and diffusion of modern institutions of governance (which generate similar effects).[42] Because these same factors simultaneously determine the organization of relations of power, and be-

41. Dāghir, *Mudhakkarātī,* 105, 107.

42. Charles Tilly, *The Contentious French,* 10; Tilly, Tilly, and Tilly, *Rebellious Century,* 253–254. It is important to note that, according to the Tillys, different repertoires of contentious collective action may coexist in a society as a result of the asynchronous and unequal spread of capitalism and state influence. See *Rebellious Century,* 54.

cause the "forms, frequencies, and personnel of collective action depend intimately on the existing structure of government and politics,"[43] not only do contentious collective actions embody and display underlying but otherwise hidden political and social relationships, but shifts in the nature of collective actions parallel and reveal shifts in those relationships.

The repertoire of contentious collective action in societies where capitalism is not the only or the predominant mode of production, where centralized market relations are balanced by or subsumed in other relations, and where state structures are either weak or distant includes, according to Tilly, local, often communally based and/or vertically organized competitive collective actions such as feuds and intervillage rivalries. As capitalist relations and state intrusiveness expand, popular resistance increasingly erupts in the form of short-lived reactive collective actions, such as land occupations and tax revolts. While often larger in scale than competitive collective actions, these outbursts are fundamentally defensive and socially conservative. Finally, the organizational revolution associated with the victory of "the merchants and statemakers"—a revolution that, ironically, fosters the expansion of associational life and, in some cases, the emergence of mass parties-cum-movements—renders possible contentious collective actions that are national in scope and autonomous and complex in structure. These actions are proactive; their purpose is not merely to display popular displeasure or defy legal authority but to enable participants seeking to control institutions of state to articulate demands for "rights, privileges, or resources not previously enjoyed."[44]

In post-Ottoman Syria, each local popular committee, each committee-organized neighborhood simultaneously mirrored and offered a microcosmic model for the organization of a horizontally bound national community. As a result, dissentient demonstrations that provided an alternative "model of" political community became an option in the "repertoire of contentious collective action" of the Syrian populace. It is ironic, then, that while the Arab government matched a modernizing discourse with advocacy and representation of a "traditional" political sociability that was communally bound and vertically linked, the popular committees utilized a "traditionalizing discourse" to defend a political sociability that was relatively new to Syria.

43. Charles Tilly, *From Mobilization to Revolution,* 170.
44. Tilly, Tilly, and Tilly, *Rebellious Century,* 49–54, 253–254.

CEREMONIES AND THE TRANSFORMATION OF SYRIAN POLITICS

In his *The Nationalization of the Masses,* George L. Mosse defines the "new politics" that emerged in eighteenth-century Europe as a political style that naturally attended the development of the notion of popular sovereignty and the equation of "the nation" with the "general will." "The general will became a secular religion, the people worshipping themselves, and the new politics sought to guide and formalize this worship," Mosse contends. "The new politics attempted to draw the people into active participation in the national mystique through rites and festivals, myths and symbols which gave a concrete expression to the general will."[45] In addition to long-term shifts in economic and administrative practices that contributed to the transformation of Syrian politics by altering the face of cities, expanding general mobility, breaking down neighborhood cohesion and previously existing modes of social organization, enlarging the rôle and capabilities of the state, and so on, activities undertaken by the Arab government, its allies, and its rivals during the Faysali period expedited the appearance of the new politics in Syria.

The Arab government and its allies were the first to use the techniques of mass organizing during the post-Ottoman period in their attempts to demonstrate to the entente powers that their program had the support of the majority of the inhabitants of the eastern zone. They decreed national holidays designed to commemorate those events that would affirm a suitable national narrative. They deployed *makhātīr* and gendarmes throughout urban quarters and villages proximate to large cities to gather the crowds for these and other ceremonies, to solicit signatures on petitions, and to compel shopkeepers and homeowners to display banners and/or political slogans in their windows. Chary of relying on established structures for either governance or mobilization, they constructed or reconstructed schools, guilds, and a state apparatus and then herded schoolchildren, guild members, and government functionaries to demonstrations. Overall, in conjunction with other government activities—the dissemination of national symbols, conscription, the reorganization of municipal structures, educational reform, and so on—the mobilization for ceremonies enabled the Arab government to expand into areas that had previously been relatively

45. Mosse, *Nationalization of the Masses,* 1–2.

free of state supervision and control, further shattering the parochialism of quarter-based politics and paving the way for the popular committees.

But even though the Arab government and its allies initiated the use of ceremonies during the Faysali period, their worldview and their tactical approach to achieving independence precluded their undertaking more than a partial and highly circumscribed mobilization of the population. No such constraints restricted the mobilizing activities of the popular committees. In the autumn of 1919, with the apparent failure of the Arab government to prevent the division of Syria and the imposition of British and French mandates in the Levant, the popular committees, taking advantage of the previous mobilizing activities of the Arab government, sparked an organizational revolution by institutionalizing the horizontal, associational, and national relationships of power germane to the lives of many urban Syrians. These are the relationships that the committees displayed and celebrated in their demonstrations. Thus, like the German festivals described by Mosse—festivals that, as Mosse describes them, represented the "objectification of the general will"—the demonstrations staged by the popular committees both symptomatized and galvanized the appearance of the "new politics" in Syria.

Conclusions

This book began with a description of the physical attacks on the institutions and symbols of the Arab government that occurred in Damascus, Aleppo, Homs, and Hama on the eve of the July 1920 French invasion of inland Syria. As argued in the Introduction, the specificity of the targets, the slogans shouted, and the prior and subsequent activities of the crowd preclude either disregarding these incidents altogether or dismissing them as the anarchic activities of an undifferentiated "mob." The attempt to integrate these incidents into a comprehensive narrative of nationalism in the Arab Middle East raised questions about historiographic conventions; after all, if the so-called "Arab nationalist movement" was as homogeneous as has been presented in most canonical writings on its origins and early evolution, why would such attacks have taken place? The answer, as should by now be obvious, is that the presumption that there existed a singular and undifferentiated "Arab nationalism" and "Arab nationalist movement" is not borne out by the evidence. In contrast with those historians who would essentialize Arab nationalism or hold the other nationalisms that arose among the inhabitants of the region to be somehow incomplete or an "unnatural truncation of a 'true' Arab" nationalism, I have attempted to identify both the reasons why alternative constructions of nation and nationalism originated in Syria during the late nineteenth and early twentieth centuries and the characteristics of those constructions as they took shape in the immediate aftermath of World War I.

Part I of this book compared the prewar and wartime nationalist formations with the popular committees that emerged during the second year of the Faysali period. Neither al-Fatat nor the Arab Club of Damascus was structurally or ideologically prepared to lead or channel the emergent popular politics that represented the interests of an increasingly disquieted and politicized Syrian population. Not only was al-Fatat crippled by internal cleavages and organizational deficiencies, but as the capacity of the Arab government to dominate the politics of Syria deteriorated in the wake of decisions made in Paris, the behind-the-scenes manipulation of government policy and personnel choices that preoccupied the organization, even if they could be effected, became increasingly irrelevant to the Syrian future. Similar problems undercut the efficacy of the Arab Club of Damascus, although that organization's mobilizing activities on behalf of the Arab government—an essential part of the Arab Club's raison d'être—certainly facilitated and informed activities later undertaken by the popular committees.

In contrast to al-Fatat and the Arab Club, the popular committees were not only organizationally and functionally independent of the Arab government, but their structure reflected and reified both the changing nature of urban political authority in Syria and an alternative but previously inchoate consciousness of "national" community. In Damascus and other cities, representatives to the Higher National Committee and the leadership of its branch committees were chosen through elections that enfranchised all adult males. The committees thus sanctioned the empowerment of a new type of nationalist leadership and integrated into nationalist politics large numbers of Syrians who had heretofore been excluded from all but the most perfunctory participation in organized political activity. In the process, the popular committees substantiated the representative principle and eliminated the differentiation between ruler and ruled that marked the structure and, as described in Part III, the representational activities of the Arab Club and the Arab government. Even in those neighborhoods and villages in which the organization of local branches of the popular committees seemingly replicated previously existing social arrangements, the committees transformed those relationships by integrating networks of kinship or clientage within a national political machine that assumed the functions of governance and privileged the electoral process. The emergence of the popular committees thus heralded a transformation in relationships of power upon which mass politics—George L. Mosse's "new politics"—depended.

The popular committees did not attract support just through their structure, however; rather, as discussed in Part II, the committees, like the Arab government and the Arab Club, acted as the institutional core of a distinct community of discourse. They assured the autonomy and perpetuation of this community by providing a forum and support for propagandists, by assembling like-minded activists into a tangible and mutually reinforcing community, and by transforming the ideas of this cohort into concrete actions and institutions. Conversely, the discursive field synthesized and disseminated by propagandists and activists linked to the popular committees legitimated the committees and their activities by validating the vision of national community and social organization that the committees offered.

The discursive field with which the popular committees were associated contrasted sharply with the field of the self-styled *mutanawwirūn.* While the *mutanawwirūn* sought to propagate among the population of Syria their own vision of society and the Syrian future that was both hortatory and comprehensive, it was a vision sustained by images of universal progress, liberal values, the benefits of "civilization," and so on. It was, in other words, a vision that conceded little to the world inhabited by a majority of Syrians. On the other hand, those affiliated with or sympathetic to the popular committees employed a traditionalizing discourse to convey an image of an organic and interdependent Syrian community imperiled by foreign imperialists and conspiracies of "those who would sell their nation like a commodity." The prestige accorded those who were affiliated with the committees, the widespread participation in committee-sponsored activities such as meetings, elections, demonstrations, and militia activities during periods of political crisis (the onset of the Evacuation Crisis, the initialing of the Faysal-Clemenceau Agreement, the declaration of Syrian independence, the final days before the French invasion), and the preeminent position of tropes introduced or popularized by the committees in popular nationalist discourse all testify to the ability of the committees to articulate a nationalism that simultaneously corresponded to and reconfigured the beliefs held by many Syrians.

Part III, an examination of ceremonies, brought together themes introduced in the previous two parts. The Arab government and its allies staged celebrations of public holidays, theatrical productions, and demonstrations for both inwardly and outwardly directed purposes. On the one hand, the government and its *mutanawwirūn* supporters used public and semipublic spaces to inculcate "patriotic values" among the population, to display symbolically what they deemed to be the proper ordering of society, and to disseminate a specific rendition of the national narrative that would vindicate their right to rule. On the other hand, they mounted ceremonies for the benefit of outside observers to exhibit a nation that was "civilized" (i.e., prepared for independence according to the standards set by the League of Nations and Wilsonian principles) and programmatically united. To ensure that these ceremonies remained orderly and their meaning transparent, the Arab government and its allies effectively barred most Syrians from active participation and cast them as spectators or backdrop to a drama with which they were only tangentially connected. As a result, these ceremonies reenacted in dramatic form the divide that separated the nationalist elites from the remainder of the population—a divide that, regardless of the activities of the entente powers, foreordained the failure of the nationalist project envisioned by the sharifians and the *mutanawwirūn.*

While many of the demonstrations mounted by the popular committees ostensibly resembled those staged by the Arab government and its allies, others eliminated dramatic sequences associated with petitioning or protest. These demonstrations not only portrayed a structuring of society and national narrative that contrasted sharply with those presented in government-sponsored demonstrations, they were in large measure self-referential. By eliminating outwardly directed ritual sequences and by breaking down the distinction between audience and participant, these demonstrations symbolically recreated the nation in microcosm and confirmed an underlying transformation of social relations in urban Syria that rendered sustained and proactive contentious collective action possible.

Despite the swells of enthusiasm that the popular committees had generated during the second year of the Faysali period, however, neither the Higher National Committee nor the urban infrastructure for the committees of national defense lasted much beyond the French invasion of inland Syria. The repression of the popular committees in the cities, begun even before French troops crossed the border separating the western and eastern zones, was rapid and thorough. On 12 July 1920, the interior ministry of the Arab government announced that it was closing the offices of the Higher National Committee because the organization had been founded "without complying with the law." The government ordered the organization's papers impounded and threatened additional legal sanctions against it.[1] With the possibility of further and even harsher government repression looming, particularly after the imposition of the martial law regime the next day, many of the committee leaders in Damascus fled the capital. Among them was Kamil al-Qassab, who reportedly escaped to Qunaytra where he took refuge with Mahmud Faʿur.[2] With the advance of General Gouraud's army, others fled to Palestine, Egypt, Iraq, or the eastern parts of Syria.

1. *al-ʿĀṣima,* 12 July 1920, 2. According to the same source, the Arab government took similar actions against the Arab Club because, although it had been founded "for scientific and literary purposes . . . it delved into political matters contrary to its founding principles."

2. Général C. J. E. Andréa, *Thawrat al-Durūz wa tamarrud Dimashq,* 32. Al-Qassab soon thereafter left Qunaytra for Haifa.

French military forces entered Aleppo on 23 July 1920, and Damascus two days later. The occupation authorities expanded the repression of the committees that had begun under the Arab government. In early August, a court-martial sentenced a cross section of the nationalist leadership to death in absentia. Among those condemned were leading activists from the Higher National Committee and the committees of national defense: Kamil al-Qassab, ʿAli Khalqi (who had been in the Hijaz with al-Qassab during the war and who led a band of five hundred Mutawalli and bedouin *ʿiṣābāt* in the Marjʿayun area during the Faysali period[3]), Ahmad Muraywid, Mahmud Faʿur, Shukri al-Tabbaʿ, Rashid al-Taliʿa, ʿUmar Bahlawan (a merchant and member of the Higher National Committee of Damascus[4]), ʿAbd al-Qadir al-Sukkar, Tawfiq Yaziji (editor of the newspaper *al-Difāʿ*, which supported the activities of the popular committees), ʿUthman Qasim (who allegedly led the attack on the citadel of Damascus discussed in the Introduction[5]), Yasin Diab, ʿId al-Halabi, Nabih al-ʿAzma, Sami al-Sarraj, Subhi Barakat, and Munib al-Natur. Twenty-three of the combatants who had taken part in the events of Jabal ʿAmil and Tall Kalkh also received death sentences. These included ʿAbdallah al-Kanj al-Dandashi, Khalid Rustum, and Hasan Ibrahim al-Dandashi, all members of the local committee of national defense.[6]

Along with the death sentences they handed down, the French arrested and imprisoned a number of secondary leaders of the popular committees and committee supporters on a variety of charges, including brigandage, conspiracy, and the illegal possession of weapons. Among those seized were

3. For more on Khalqi, see MD 4H114/1/83, "Rapport journalier de Damas," 25 November 1919; MD 4H114/2/141, Cousse to Gouraud, 26 March 1920; IO L/PS/10/802/P5598/48, Wratislaw to Secretary of State, 22 June 1920; FO 371/5049/E6473/216 ff., Report of French Liaison Officer, 18–24 May 1920; MAE L:SL/vol. 33/119, Gouraud to Millerand, "Note au sujet des rapports entre le haut-commissionaire de la République Française en Syrie-Cilicie et l'emir Fayçal," 22 September 1920; MD 4H114/8, Arlabousse to Catroux, 13 October 1920.

4. Khayr al-Dīn al-Ziriklī, *Ma raʾaytu wa ma samiʿtu*, 14–16.

5. For more on Qasim, see Qadrī, *Mudhakkarātī*, 248; Hindī, *Maʿrakat Maysalūn*, 61–62; AD 2324/a1, 25 June 1919; FO 371/4183/136154, Lutfallah to Lloyd George, 16 September 1919; AD 2375/chemise: division de la Syrie, 1919–1920/361a, Col. Sousselier to GC, 7 February 1920.

6. On 9 August 1920, the French recommended that thirty-six members of nationalist organizations and the Arab government be executed; overall, Khayr al-Din al-Zirikli lists fifty-eight names of those sentenced to die. MD 4H109/1, Général Gouraud, 12 August 1920; al-Ziriklī, *Ma raʾaytu wa ma samiʿtu*, 14–16; Hindī, *Kifāḥ al-shaʿb al-ʿarabī al-sūrī*, 89.

Tawfiq al-Bissar and al-Hajj Nur al-Jisri, members of the Syrian General Congress from, respectively, ʿAkkar and Aleppo, who had acted as intermediaries between the Arab Club of Aleppo and the armed bands operating outside the city.[7] The French pursued former members of the popular committees in Damascus with particular fervor: fearing that the success of bedouin and irregulars in the immediate area and in the Hawran would trigger open revolt in the capital, French authorities arrested so-called "agitators" en masse within a month of their occupation of the Syrian capital.[8] The sentences that the courts-martial handed down were harsh: one of the condemned, whom the French charged with plotting a raid on a village, received twenty years in prison; another was deported from Syria for the same crime.[9] Occupation authorities imposed these and similarly severe sentences not only to punish those whom they considered to be a menace but to intimidate the remainder of the population and, in the words of one French report, to "decapitate" the most influential families of Syria that harbored anti-French sentiments. Overall, the occupation authorities adopted a strategy explicitly designed to ensure that Syrians "understood that politics is risky and that it is sometimes wiser to remain on the sidelines."[10]

In addition to courts-martial, French authorities undertook a variety of other actions to pacify the population, boost support for its position as mandatory power, and efface the effects of committee organizing and propaganda. In Damascus, for example, the occupation authorities "discreetly" encouraged Rida al-ʿAbid to establish a club modeled on the dismantled Arab Club of Damascus for the purpose of disseminating pro-French propaganda. They underwrote the journalistic endeavors of Muhammad Kurd ʿAli in Damascus, distributed monthly subventions ranging from 20 to 40 P.E. to six newspapers in Aleppo (*al-Taqaddum, al-Sāʾiqa, al-Umma, al-Barīd al-sūrī, al-Nahḍa* and *Le Franco-Syrien*), and quite probably suborned the Damascus newspapers *Fatāt al-ʿArab* and *Sūriyya al-jadīda*. They replaced recalcitrant quarter and village leaders, enlisted the support of friendly tribes (such as the ʿAnaza) to act as irregulars in the battle against guerrilla units organized by the popular committees, circulated petitions in

7. FO 861/68, "Report on the Situation in Aleppo," 9 September 1920.

8. MAE L:SL/vol. 116/1726–1733, Gouraud to Guerre section orientale, 28 August 1920.

9. MD 4H109/dossier 1, Gouraud to Générals commandants 2ème et 4ème divisions, 12 August 1920.

10. MAE L:SL/vol. 33, La Marine dans le Levant, "Rapport hebdomadaire sur la situation politique," 20 August 1920.

Aleppo to demonstrate that "popular will" favored autonomy for the northern province, and organized mass demonstrations to signal an end to "the fanaticism and exactions" of Arab rule and to display the military power of France.[11] Ironically, then, many of the strategies that the Arab government, its allies, and the popular committees had pioneered in their efforts to mobilize, superintend, and win the support of the Syrian population were applied by the French occupiers in order to establish their authority.

The anarchic conditions that the French found in inland Syria abetted their designs. During the final days before the French army entered their cities, most urban Syrians faced a series of hardships that encumbered daily life and frustrated organized resistance to the occupation. The martial law regimen imposed by the Arab government not only disrupted the usual patterns of urban activity, it also limited the capacity of the population to resist the French: before the Arab government took flight, it had imposed curfews, closed markets, embargoed news, banned political assemblies, broken up demonstrations, arrested dissidents, and, within the limits of its capacity, commandeered transportation and confiscated stockpiled weapons. Even had Syrians chosen to resist these measures, the influx of large numbers of bedouin into the cities of the eastern zone—an estimated ten thousand in Damascus and its immediate environs, three thousand in Aleppo, and fifteen hundred in Homs and Hama—dissuaded many from venturing outside their homes.[12] With the withdrawal of Amir Faysal and his entourage to the village of Kiswa south of Damascus, and with the collapse of local institutions of governance, the anarchy spread. In Damascus, shopkeepers attempted to dissuade looters by flying Italian flags over their shops; in Homs, families that lived on the outskirts of town were evacuated from their homes and put to work barricading buildings in the center of the city while armed volunteers stood guard; in Aleppo, it was left to the American consul to persuade the local military commander and chief of police to

11. MD 4H109/1, "Projet d'instructions pour le général Goybet," 30 July 1920; MD 4H60/1, "Bulletin quotidien 1324," 11 August 1920; FO 861/67, "General Report on the Situation at Aleppo," 21 August 1920; FO 861/68, "Report on the Situation at Aleppo," 9 September 1920; MAE L:SL/vol. 33, Capitaine de Lestapis, "Notes de la presse 10," 15 September 1920.

12. *al-ʿĀṣima,* 15 July 1920, 1–2; IO L/PS/10/802/P6248, Consul General, Beirut to FO, 16 July 1920; FO 371/5037/E8509, Mackereth to FO, 16 July 1920; MD 4H114/dossier 5, Cousse to Gouraud, 17 July 1920; MD 4H60/dossier 1, "Bulletin quotidien 1260," 19 July 1920; MD 4H60/1, "Bulletin quotidien 1266," 21 July 1920; FO 371/5037/E8880/80, Mackereth to FO, 23 July 1920; Kersante, "Syrie: L'occupation d'Alep."

remain at their posts and to organize armed patrols to maintain order.[13] Under these circumstances, it should not be surprising that foreign observers commonly used terms such as "sullen" and "weary" when describing the emotions expressed by many Syrians at the time of the invasion.[14]

There were, of course, exceptions: residents of two quarters of Damascus—the Maydan and Shaghur—did engage French forces in gun battles during the initial occupation of the Syrian capital; the ongoing struggles in the countryside waged by Ibrahim Hananu, Salih al-ʿAli, Mahmud Faʿur, and others continued; and French sources attest to clandestine attempts—perhaps real, perhaps the product of colonial fantasy—made by an assortment of political activists to regroup elements of the nationalist movement that had gone underground.[15] French apprehensions were not entirely delusory: on 30 August 1920, a *chete* reconnaissance column penetrated the center of Aleppo, sparking not only a gun battle with French forces but also a rumor that the column was the precursor of an all-out assault on the city by the Turks, who were intent on liberating it from French control. At around the same time, unknown assailants ambushed and killed ʿAla al-Din al-Durubi and ʿAbd al-Rahman al-Yusuf, the prime minister and president of the consultative council, whom Faysal had appointed to the last Arab government and who had remained in office to collaborate with the occupation forces.[16]

Notwithstanding these incidents, most of the resistance encountered by the French was not only defensive and unorganized but nonviolent as well. French and British sources indicate widespread evasion of their order directing Syrians to surrender their weapons, and in spite of threats, large numbers of Muslim residents of Aleppo avoided signing the French-circulated petition calling for Aleppan autonomy. Instead, they circulated a petition

13. MD 4H60/dossier 1, "Bulletin quotidien 1266," 21 July 1920; FO 371/5039/E10316, J. B. Jackson, 30 July 1920; Angelil, "L'occupation d'Homs"; Kersante, "Syrie: L'occupation d'Alep."

14. MD 4H58/dossier 2, "Rapport hebdomadaire: 29 juillet à 4 août"; MD 4H60/dossier 1, "Bulletin quotidien 1324," 11 August 1920; 23.12 MD 4H60/dossier 1, "Bulletin quotidien 1327," 12 August 1920; MAE L:SL/vol. 33, "Rapport hebdomadaire sur la situation politique," 20 August 1920; FO 861/67, "General Report on the Situation at Aleppo," 21 August 1920; Angelil, "L'occupation d'Homs"; Kersante, "Syrie: L'occupation d'Alep."

15. See MD 4H58/2, "Rapport hebdomadaire: 29 juilletà 4 août"; MD 4H114/5/714, Toulat to HC, n.d.; MD/4H60/1, "Bulletin quotidien 1324," 11 August 1920; MD 4H60/1, "Bulletin quotidien 1327," 12 August 1920; MAE L:SL/vol. 116/1726–1733, Gouraud to MD, 28 August 1920.

16. FO 861/68, Report on the Situation at Aleppo, 9 September 1920; Khoury, *Syria and the French Mandate*, 98–99.

addressed to the local American consul, complaining of the French tactics and asking for the intervention of the other entente powers on behalf of the Syrian population.[17] Syrians also engaged in petty acts of sabotage against their occupiers. According to one story, for example, when General Gouraud first arrived in Damascus, Abu Shukri al-Tabbaʿ, the father of a Higher National Committee organizer who had fought at the Battle of Maysalun, and a companion loosed the horses of the general's carriage.[18] The feeling of defiance tempered by powerlessness experienced by many Syrians during the first months of the French occupation ultimately found expression in widespread rumors that foretold of impending liberation and even miraculous delivery. Among the most prevalent rumors spread in the eastern zone during the late summer of 1920 were reports that the British had issued an ultimatum to the French demanding that the occupiers withdraw from the eastern zone, that British troops had occupied the southern town of Darʿa in preparation for a march north, that gangs of Turkish-supported guerrillas were preparing to invade Aleppo, and that the end of time was approaching.[19]

But while anecdotes of scattered acts of resistance and rumors of liberation demonstrate that, after brief skirmishing at Khan Maysalun, the inhabitants of the eastern zone did not respond to the French invasion and occupation with a uniform passivity or fatalism, they hardly constitute evidence that the mobilization of the Syrian population that had occurred over the previous months was of singular significance. In recounting these events, and in describing the opposing constructions of nation and nationalism that vied for dominance during the twenty-two months of the Faysali period, it has not been my intention to provide such evidence. Nor has it been my intention to substitute one nationalist myth for another. Instead, underlying this study has been the contention that the Faysali period is noteworthy for two reasons. First, the interval separating the withdrawal of Ottoman forces from Syria and the beginning of the quarter-century French occupation marked a clearly bounded episode in the history of nationalism in the Arab Middle East during which the struggle over nationalist issues was especially manifest and contentious. This period thus provides a particularly revealing glimpse into the broader sweep of that history.

17. FO 861/68, "Report on the Situation at Aleppo," 9 September 1920.

18. al-Amīn, *Dhikrayāt*, 28.

19. MD 4H58/2, "Rapport hebdomadaire: 29 juilletà 4 août"; MD 4H60/1, "Bulletin quotidien," 12 August 1920; FO 861/68, "Report on the Situation at Aleppo," 9 September 1920.

Second, the mobilization of the Syrian population that took place during this period accelerated and reinforced two processes that had been under way since the mid-nineteenth century: the diffusion of a nation state framework for the reconstruction of communities disrupted by social and political upheaval, and the transformation of relationships of power in such a way as to facilitate the diffusion of nationalist ideologies.

By the early twentieth century, the preconditions necessary for a nationalist breakthrough were already in place throughout much of the Arab Middle East. Over the previous half-century, a number of factors—the expansion of markets integrated on a regional and global scale, the enhancement of state capabilities, the growth of urban concentrations, the introduction of new transportation and communications technologies, the intensification of labor commodification, and so on—had expedited the breakdown of economic parochialism, reduced the overall efficacy of local, informally constituted bonds of clientalism, and disarranged the lives of an ever-increasing portion of the population. While the appearance of these preconditions was not in itself sufficient to ensure the diffusion of nationalist ideologies, it did enhance the likelihood that, given the proper circumstances, nationalist organizers would find a constituency receptive to their ideas. Over time, as the numbers of those affected by the processes of change mounted, that constituency expanded.

While the broadening and deepening of what Benedict Anderson calls the "cultural system" of nationalism among the inhabitants of the Arab Middle East was a long-term process, it was neither a continual nor an undifferentiated one. Rather, it was an episodic process, driven by crises and effected by organizers who learned from and enlarged upon the efforts of their predecessors. This book has focused upon both the long-term and the immediate crises that fueled one such episode and on the activities of political activists who defined and shaped a national community temporarily embraced much of the Syrian population. The mobilizing activities undertaken by these activists during the Faysali period proved to be both precursor to and progenitor of numerous similar episodes. The Syrian Great Revolt of 1925–1927 and the Palestine Great Revolt of 1936–1939 are just two examples of subsequent nationalist uprisings the roots of which might be traced to the events discussed in this book.[20]

20. A number of those who participated in the events recounted in this book later took part in subsequent nationalist uprisings in Syria and Palestine. Among the members and supporters of the popular committees during 1919–1920 who played prominent roles in the Syrian Great Revolt of 1925–1927 were ʿAbd al-

While the interplay of the local, regional, and international determinants that ignited and shaped each episode was unique, and while the ideological predicates that inspired—and in turn were disseminated by—nationalists active during these episodes frequently differed, all had two attributes in common. First, the unevenness and differential effects of the transformative processes described above defined not only the shape of the insurgent alliance but the program it articulated and the strategies it employed to realize that program. As a result, each alliance made use of discursive tropes and organized itself and its activities in a manner characteristic of populist insurgencies the world over.[21] Second, each insurgency promoted a further social transformation that, in the absence of a comprehensive political resolution, virtually guaranteed that similar insurgencies would occur in the future. Far from being an isolated historical curiosity, then, the events of the Faysali period heralded the advent of a popular nationalist politics in the Arab Middle East that, in one form or another, has persisted to the present day.

Qadir al-Sukkar, Ramadan Shallash, Muhammad al-ʿAshmar, ʿId al-Halabi, Hasan al-Kharrat, and Ahmad Muraywid.

Shaykh ʿIzz al-Din al-Qassam, the popular *ʿālim* whose organizing activities and subsequent death at the hands of the British in 1935 during an ill-fated raid was a major factor in sparking the Palestine Great Revolt, was also intimately acquainted with the activities of the popular committees in Syria. Not only had al-Qassam participated in the guerrilla activities of Salih al-ʿAli's irregulars in the Latakia region during the Faysali period, but after the French invasion of inland Syria, he fled to Haifa with the assistance of Kamil al-Qassab. The two continued their collaboration in exile, first teaching together at Madrasa al-Burj al-Islamiyya (until they quarreled in 1925), then touring the countryside preaching resistance to the British and Zionists. See al-Jundī, *Tārīkh al-thawrāt al-sūriyya fī ʿahd al-intidāb al-faransī;* al-Ḥāfiẓ and Abāẓa, *Tārīkh ʿulamāʾ Dimashq;* Khoury, *Syria and the French Mandate,* 174–182; Ḥamūda, *al-Waʿī wal-thawra,* 42–43, 45, 50.

21. A selection of common tropes used during the Palestine Great Revolt can be found in Nels Johnson, *Islam and the Politics of Meaning;* Ted Swedenburg, *Memories of Revolt: The 1936–1939 Rebellion and the Palestinian National Past.*

Bibliography

ARCHIVAL SOURCES

Archives diplomatiques, Nantes, France
Boston University Archives (William Yale Papers)
British Library, London (Arthur James Balfour Papers)
Foreign Office, London
India Office, London
Markaz al-wathā'iq al-tārīkhiyya, Damascus
Ministère de la défense, Vincennes, France
Ministère des affaires étrangères, Paris
National Archives of the United States, Washington, D.C.
Salafiyya Library, Cairo (Lajna Waṭaniyya, Lajnat al-Difāʿ, al-Fatāt, Kāmil al-Qassāb files)
Sudan Archives, University of Durham, England (Shuqayr Papers, F. R. Wingate Papers)
University of Illinois, Urbana-Champaign (Albert H. Lybyer Archives)
War Office, London

NEWSPAPERS AND MAGAZINES

al-Ahrām
Arab Bulletin
L'Asie français
al-ʿĀṣima
al-Bashīr
al-Difāʿ
al-Fallāḥ
al-Ḥaqiqa
al-Jundī
al-Kawkab

al-Kināna
al-Manār
al-Muqtabas
The Near East
Petite relations d'orient
al-Qibla
Sūriyya al-jadīda

BOOKS, ARTICLES, AND UNPUBLISHED MANUSCRIPTS

Abrahamian, Ervand. *Iran Between Two Revolutions*. Princeton, 1983.

Adamson, Walter L. *Hegemony and Revolution: A Study of Antonio Gramsci's Political and Cultural Theory*. Berkeley, 1980.

al-ʿAjlūnī, Muḥammad ʿAlī. *Dhikrayāt ʿan al-thawra al-ʿarabiyya al-kubrā*. Amman, 1956.

Alexān, Jān. "Zaynab fī Maysalūn." *al-Jundī*, 19 April 1960: 32–33.

al-ʿAllāf, Aḥmad Ḥilmī. *Dimashq fī maṭlaʿ al-qarn al-ʿishrīn*. Edited by ʿAlī Jamīl Nuʿīysa. Damascus, 1976.

Allcock, J. B. "'Populism': A Brief Biography." *Sociology* 5 (September 1971): 371–387.

Althusser, Louis. *For Marx*. London, 1969.

al-Amīn, Ḥasan. *Dhikrayāt, al-Juzʾ al-awwal: Min al-ṭufūla ilā al-ṣibā*. Beirut, 1973.

Anderson, Benedict. *Imagined Communities: Reflections on the Origin and Spread of Nationalism*. London, 1983.

Andréa, Général C. J. E. *Thawrat al-Durūz wa tamarrud Dimashq*. Translated into Arabic by Ḥāfiẓ Abū Musliḥ. Beirut, 1985.

Angelil, P. G. "L'occupation d'Homs: Angoisses et délivrance." *Petite relations d'orient* 6 (November 1920): 180–191.

Antonius, George. *The Arab Awakening: The Story of the Arab National Movement*. London, 1938.

Arjomand, Said Amir. "Traditionalism in Twentieth-Century Iran." In *From Nationalism to Revolutionary Islam*, edited by Said Amir Arjomand, 195–232. London, 1984.

ʿAskar, Iḥsān. *Nashʾat al-ṣiḥāfa al-sūriyya: ʿArḍ lil-qawmiyya fī ṭawr al-nashʾa min al-ʿahd al-ʿuthmānī ḥattā qiyām al-dawla al-ʿarabiyya*. Cairo, 1972.

Ayalon, Ami. *Language and Change in the Arab Middle East: The Evolution of Modern Political Discourse*. New York, 1987.

al-ʿAẓm, Khālid. *Mudhakkarāt Khālid al-ʿAẓm*. Vol. 1. Beirut, 1973.

al-ʿAẓma, ʿAbd al-ʿAzīz. *Mirʾāt al-Shām: Tārīkh Dimashq wa ahlihā*. London, 1987.

Bābīl, Naṣūḥ. *Ṣiḥāfa wa siyāsa: Sūriyya fī al-qarn al-ʿishrīn*. London, 1987.

Badawi, M. M. *Early Arabic Drama*. Cambridge, England, 1988.

Baer, Gabriel. *Fellah and Townsman in the Middle East: Studies in Social History*. London, 1982.

———. "Village and Countryside in Egypt and Syria: 1500–1900." In *The Islamic Middle East 700–1900*, edited by A. L. Udovitch, 595–652. Princeton, 1981.

Baker, Ray Stannard, and William E. Dodd, eds. *Public Papers of Woodrow Wilson.* Vols. 5–6: *War and Peace: Presidential Messages, Addresses, and Public Papers (1917–1925).* New York, 1927.

Bakhtin, M. M. *The Dialogic Imagination.* Edited by Michael Holquist. Translated by Caryl Emerson and Michael Holquist. Austin, 1981.

Balāwī, Muṣṭafā. "al-Aḥzāb al-siyāsiyya fī Sūriyya (1920–1939)." M.A. thesis, University of Damascus, 1985.

Balibar, Etienne. "The Nation Form: History and Ideology." In *Becoming National: A Reader,* edited by Geoff Eley and Ronald Grigor Suny, 151–178. Oxford, 1996.

al-Bārūdī, Fakhrī. *Mudhakkarāt al-Bārūdī.* 2 vols. Beirut, 1951.

Baṣrī, Mīr. *Aʿlām al-siyāsiyya fī al-Irāq al-ḥadīth.* London, 1987.

Bayhum, Muḥammad Jamīl. *Sūriyya wa Lubnān 1918–1922.* Beirut, 1968.

Bernstein, Michael André. *Bitter Carnival: Ressentiment and the Abject Hero.* Princeton, 1992.

Berque, Jacques. *Egypt, Imperialism and Revolution.* Translated by Jean Stewart. New York, 1972.

Birrū, Tawfīq. "al-Muntadā al-adabī wa dawruhu fī al-niḍāl al-ʿarabī." *al-Maʿrifa* 38 (April, 1965): 35–44.

Bourdieu, Pierre. "The Disenchantment of the World." In *Algeria 1960,* 1–94. Translated by Richard Nice. Cambridge, England, 1979.

———. *The Logic of Practice.* Translated by Richard Nice. Stanford, 1990.

———. *Language and Symbolic Power.* Edited by John B. Thompson. Translated by Gino Raymond and Matthew Adamson. Cambridge, Mass., 1991.

———. *Outline of a Theory of Practice.* Translated by Richard Nice. Cambridge, England, 1972.

Breuilly, John. *Nationalism and the State.* Chicago, 1982.

Brown, L. Carl. "Patterns Forged in Time: Middle East Mind-Sets and the Gulf War." In *The Political Psychology of the Gulf War,* edited by Stanley A. Renshon, 3–21. Pittsburgh, 1993.

Calhoun, Craig Jackson. "The Radicalism of Tradition: Community Strength or Venerable Disguise and Borrowed Language?" *American Journal of Sociology* 88 (March 1983): 886–914.

Cannadine, David. "The Context, Performance and Meaning of Ritual: The British Monarchy and the 'Invention of Tradition,' *c.* 1820–1977." In *The Invention of Tradition,* edited by Eric Hobsbawm and Terence Ranger, 101–164. Cambridge, England, 1983.

Canovan, Margaret. "Two Strategies for the Study of Populism." *Political Studies* 30 (December 1982): 544–552.

"The Case of Emir Feisal." *Current History* 13(2) (February 1921): 254.

Castoriadis, Cornelius. *The Imaginary Institution of Society.* Translated by Kathleen Blamey. Cambridge, Mass., 1987.

al-Charkas, Maḥmūd. *al-Dalīl al-muṣawwar lil-bilād al-ʿarabiyya.* Vol. 1. Damascus, 1930.

Chatterjee, Partha. "Colonialism, Nationalism, and Colonized Women: The Contest in India." *American Ethnologist* 16 (1989): 622–633.

———. *The Nation and Its Fragments: Colonial and Postcolonial Histories.* Princeton, 1993.

———. *Nationalist Thought and the Colonial World: A Derivative Discourse?* Minneapolis, 1986.

Chevallier, Dominique. "Consciences syriennes et représentations cartographiques à la fin du XIXe siècle et au début du XXe siècle." In *The Syrian Land in the Eighteenth and Nineteenth Century: The Common and the Specific in the Historical Experience,* edited by Thomas Philipp, 1–10. Stuttgart, 1992.

Clark, John et al. "Sub Cultures, Cultures, Class." In *Culture, Ideology, and Social Process: A Reader,* edited by Tony Bennett et al., 53–79. London, 1981.

Cleveland, William L. *The Making of an Arab Nationalist: Ottomanism and Arabism in the Life and Thought of Satiʿ al-Husri.* Princeton, 1971.

Cohen, Anthony P. *The Symbolic Construction of Community.* London, 1985.

Coke, Richard. *The Arab's Place in the Sun.* London, 1929.

Comaroff, John L. "Of Totemism and Ethnicity." *Ethnos* 52 (1987): 301–323.

Commins, David Dean. *Islamic Reform: Politics and Social Change in Late Ottoman Syria.* New York, 1990.

———. "Religious Reformers and Arabists in Damascus, 1885–1915." *International Journal of Middle East Studies* 18 (1986): 405–425.

Cotler, Julio. "State and Regime: Comparative Notes on the Southern Cone and the "Enclave" Societies." In *The New Authoritarianism in Latin America,* edited by David Collier, 255–282. Princeton, 1979.

Crossick, Geoffrey. "From Gentleman to the Residuum: Languages of Social Description in Victorian Britain." In *Language, History, and Class,* edited by Penelope J. Corfield, 150–178. Oxford, 1991.

Dāghir, Asʿad. *Mudhakkarātī ʿalā hāmish al-qaḍiyya al-ʿarabiyya.* Cairo, 1956.

Darwaza, Muḥammad ʿIzzat. *Ḥawla al-ḥaraka al-ʿarabiyya al-ḥadītha.* Vol. 1. Sidon, 1950.

———. *Mudhakkarāt wa tasjīlāt.* Vol. 2. Damascus, 1984.

Davis, Eric. "The Concept of Revival and the Study of Islam and Politics." In *The Islamic Impulse,* edited by Barbara Freyer Stowasser, 37–58. Washington, D.C., 1987.

Davis, Natalie Zemon. "The Rites of Violence: Religious Riot in Sixteenth-Century France." *Past and Present* 59 (1973): 51—91.

Dawn, C. Ernest. *From Ottomanism to Arabism: Essays on the Origins of Arab Nationalism.* Urbana, 1973.

———. "The Origins of Arab Nationalism." In *The Origins of Arab Nationalism,* edited by Rashid Khalidi et al., 3–30. New York, 1991.

de la Torre, Carlos. "The Ambiguous Meanings of Latin American Populisms." *Social Research* 59 (Summer 1992): 385–414.

Deringil, Selim. "Legitimacy Structures in the Ottoman State: The Reign of Abdulhamid II (1876–1909)." *International Journal of Middle Eastern Studies* 23 (1991):345–359.

di Tella, T. S. "Populism and Reform in Latin America." In *Obstacles to Change in Latin America,* edited by C. Veliz, 47–74. Oxford, 1962.

Doumani, Beshara. *Rediscovering Palestine: Merchants and Peasants in Jabal Nablus, 1700–1900.* Berkeley, 1995.

Drake, Paul W. "Requiem for Populism?" In *Latin American Populism in Comparative Perspective,* edited by Michael L. Conniff, 217–245. Albuquerque, 1982.

Duara, Prasenjit. *Rescuing History from the Nation: Questioning Narratives of Modern China.* Chicago, 1995.

Dubois, Jean. *Le Vocabulaire politique et social en France de 1869 à 1872: à travers les oeuvres des écrivains, les revues et les journaux.* Paris, 1962.

Duggan, Stephen P. "Syria and Its Tangled Problems." *Current History* 13(2) (February 1920): 238–248.

Durkheim, Emile. *The Elementary Forms of the Religious Life.* Translated by J. S. Swain. New York, 1961.

———. *Professional Ethics and Civic Morals.* Translated by Cornelia Brookfield. Glencoe, Ill., 1958.

Eagleton, Terry. *Ideology.* London, 1991.

Esherick, Joseph W., and Jeffrey N. Wasserstrom. "Acting Out Democracy: Political Theater in Modern China." *Journal of Asian Studies* 49 (November 1990): 835–865.

al-Fāḍil, Ilyās, and Rāmiz Ḥīthāwī. *al-Kitāb al-dhahabī lil-mujāhidīn al-sūriyyīn.* Damascus, 1972.

al-Farḥānī, Muḥammad. *Fāris al-Khūrī wal-ayyām la tunsā.* Beirut, 1965.

Farzat, Muḥammad Ḥarb. *al-Ḥayā al-ḥizbiyya fī Sūriyya: Dirāsa tārīkhiyya li-nash'at al-aḥzāb al-siyāsiyya wa tatawwurihā bayna 1908–1955.* Damascus, 1955.

Fawaz, Leila Tarazi. *Merchants and Migrants in Nineteenth Century Beirut.* Cambridge, Mass., 1983.

Femia, Joseph V. *Gramsci's Political Thought: Hegemony, Consciousness, and the Revolutionary Process.* Oxford, 1987.

Fromkin, David. *A Peace to End All Peace: The Fall of the Ottoman Empire and the Creation of the Modern Middle East.* New York, 1989.

Furet, François. *Interpreting the French Revolution.* Translated by Elborg Forster. Cambridge, England, 1981.

Geertz, Clifford. "After the Revolution: The Fate of Nationalism in New States." In *The Interpretation of Cultures,* 234–254. New York, 1973.

———. "Religion as a Cultural System." In *Anthropological Approaches to the Study of Religion,* edited by Michael Banton, 1–46. London, 1966.

Gellner, Ernest. "The Sacred and the National." In *Encounters with Nationalism,* 59–73. Oxford, 1994.
———. *Nations and Nationalism.* Ithaca, 1983.
Gelvin, James L. "Demonstrating Communities in Post-Ottoman Syria." *The Journal of Interdisciplinary History* 25(1) (summer 1994): 23–44.
———. "Demonstrating Communities in Post-Ottoman Syria, *Journal of Interdisciplinary History,* 25 (summer 1994): 23–44.
———. "The Ironic Legacy of the King-Crane Commission." In *The Middle East and the United States: A Historical and Political Reassessment,* edited by David W. Lesch, 11–27. Boulder, 1995.
———. "The Other Arab Nationalism: Syrian/Arab Populism in Its Historical and International Contexts." In *Rethinking Nationalisms in the Arab World,* edited by James Jankowski and Israel Gershoni, 231–248 . New York, 1997.
———. "The Social Origins of Popular Nationalism in Syria: Evidence for a New Framework." *International Journal of Middle East Studies* 26 (November 1994): 645–662.
Ghazzī, Kāmil. *Nahr al-dhahab fī tārīkh Ḥalab.* 3 vols. Aleppo, 1923–1926.
al-Ghuṣayn, Fā'iz. *Mudhakkarātī ʿan al-thawra.* Damascus, 1956.
Gilbar, Gad G. "Changing Patterns of Economic Ties: The Syrian and Iraqi Provinces in the 18th and 19th Centuries." In *The Syrian Land in the Eighteenth and Nineteenth Centuries: The Common and the Specific in the Historical Experience,* edited by Thomas Philipp, 55–68. Stuttgart, 1992.
Gilsenan, Michael. "Against Patron-Client Relations." In *Patrons and Clients in Mediterranean Societies,* edited by Ernest Gellner and John Waterbury, 167–183. London, 1977.
Gontaut-Biron, Roger de. *Comment la France s'est installée en Syrie (1918–1919).* Paris, 1923.
Graham-Brown, Sarah. "Agriculture and Labour Transformation in Palestine." In *The Rural Middle East: Peasant Lives and Modes of Production,* edited by Kathy and Pandeli Glavanis, 53–69. London, 1989.
Gramsci, Antonio. *Selections from the Prison Notebooks.* Edited and translated by Quintin Hoare and Geoffrey Nowell Smith. New York, 1987.
Guha, Ranajit. *Elementary Aspects of Peasant Insurgency in Colonial India.* Delhi, 1983.
———. "On Some Aspects of the Historiography of Colonial India." In *Selected Subaltern Studies,* edited by Ranajit Guha and Gayatri Chakravorty Spivak, 37–44. Oxford, 1988.
Habermas, Jurgen. *The Structural Transformation of the Public Sphere: An Inquiry into a Category of Bourgeois Society.* Translated by Thomas Burger and Frederick Lawrence. Cambridge, Mass., 1993.
al-Ḥaffār, Wajīh. "al-Ḥukūmāt allatī taʿāqabat ʿalā al-ḥukm fī Sūriyya." *al-Shurṭa wal-amn al-ʿāmm* 1(2 ramaḍān 1372–ḥazīrān 1373).
al-Ḥāfiẓ, Muḥammad Muṭīʿ, and Nizār Abāẓa. *Tārīkh ʿulamāʾ Dimashq fī al-qarn al-rābiʿ ʿashar al-hijrī.* Damascus, 1986.
Haim, Sylvia. *Arab Nationalism: An Anthology.* Berkeley, 1962.

al-Ḥakīm, Ḥasan. *Khubarātī fī al-ḥukm*. Amman, 1978.
———. *al-Wathā'iq al-tārīkhiyya al-muta'alliqa bil-qaḍiyya al-sūriyya fī al-'ahdayn al-'arabī al-fayṣalī wal-intidābī al-faransī, 1915–1946*. Beirut, 1974.
al-Ḥakīm, Yūsuf. *Dhikrayāt*. Vol. 3: *Sūriyya wal-'ahd al-fayṣalī*. Beirut, 1966.
Hall, Stuart. "Ethnicity: Identity and Difference." In *Becoming National: A Reader*, edited by Geoff Eley and Ronald Grigor Suny, 339–351. Oxford, 1996.
Ḥamūda, Samīḥ. *al-Wa'ī wal-thawra: dirāsa fī ḥayāt wa jihād al-Shaykh 'Izz al-Dīn al-Qassām, 1868–1935*. Amman, 1987.
Handelman, Don. *Models and Mirrors: Towards an Anthropology of Public Events*. Cambridge, England, 1990.
Hassan, Najate Kassab (Ḥasan, Najāt Qassāb). *Ḥadīth dimashqī 1884–1983*. Damascus, 1988.
Haut-commissariat de la République Française en Syrie et au Liban. *La Syrie et le Liban en 1922*. Paris, 1922.
Hindī, Iḥsān. *Kifāḥ al-sha'b al-'arabī al-sūrī, 1908–1948*. Damascus, 1962.
———. *Ma'rakat Maysalūn*. Damascus, 1967.
Hobsbawm, E. J. *The Age of Empire, 1875–1914*. New York, 1987.
———. "Introduction: Inventing Traditions." In *The Invention of Tradition*, edited by Eric Hobsbawm and Terence Ranger, 1–14. Cambridge, England, 1983.
———. "Mass-Producing Traditions: Europe, 1870–1914." In *The Invention of Tradition*, edited by Eric Hobsbawm and Terence Ranger, 263–308. Cambridge, England, 1983.
———. *Nations and Nationalism since 1780: Programme, Myth, Reality*. Cambridge, England, 1990.
———. *Primitive Rebels: Studies in Archaic Forms of Social Movements in the Nineteenth and Twentieth Centuries*. New York, 1959.
Hofstadter, Richard. *Age of Reform*. New York, 1955.
Holmes, William F. "Populism: In Search of Context." *Agricultural History* 64 (fall 1990): 26–58.
Hourani, Albert. "*The Arab Awakening* Forty Years After." In *Emergence of the Modern Middle East*, edited by Albert Hourani, 193–215. Berkeley, 1981.
———. *A History of the Arab Peoples*. Cambridge, Mass., 1991.
———. "Ottoman Reform and the Politics of Notables." In *Beginnings of Modernization in the Middle East*, edited by W. R. Polk and R. L. Chambers, 41–68. Chicago, 1968.
Howard, Harry N. *The King-Crane Commission: An American Inquiry in the Middle East*. Beirut, 1963.
Hroch, Miroslav. *Social Preconditions of National Revival in Europe: A Comparative Analysis of the Social Composition of Patriotic Groups Among the Smaller European Nations*. Translated by Ben Fowkes. Cambridge, England, 1985.

Hunt, Lynn. *Politics, Culture, and Class in the French Revolution.* Berkeley, 1984.
Hurewitz, J. C. *The Middle East and North Africa in World Politics: A Documentary Record.* Vol. 2: *British-French Supremacy, 1914–1945.* New Haven, 1979.
al-Ḥuṣnī, Muḥammad Adīb Āl Taqī al-Dīn. *Kitāb muntakhabāt al-tawārīkh li-Dimashq.* 3 vols. Beirut, 1969.
al-Ḥuṣrī, (Abū Khaldūn) Sāṭiʿ (al-Husri, Abu Khaldun Satiʿ). *The Day of Maysalun: A Page from the Modern History of the Arabs.* Translated by Sidney Glazer. Washington D.C., 1966.
———. *Yawm Maysalūn.* Beirut, 1947.
al-Ḥuṣrī Khaldūn Sāṭiʿ. *Mudhakkarāt Ṭaha al-Hāshimī, 1919–1944.* Beirut, 1967.
Ibn Dhurayl, ʿAdnān. *al-Adab al-masraḥī fī Sūriyya: Dirāsa fī al-masraḥiyya al-ʿarabiyya al-sūriyya mundhu Abī Khalīl al-Qabbānī ilā al-yawm.* Damascus, n.d.
———. *al-Masraḥ al-sūrī mundhu al-Qabbānī ilā al-yawm.* Damascus, 1971.
Ibrāhīm Pāshā, Jamīl. *Niḍāl al-aḥrār fī sabīl al-istiqlāl.* Aleppo, 1959.
al-ʿIyāshī, Ghālib. *al-Īḍāḥāt al-siyāsiyya wa asrār al-intidāb al-faransī ʿalā Sūriyya.* Beirut, 1955.
———. *Tārīkh Sūriyya al-siyāsī min al-intidāb ilā al-inqilāb: 1918–1954.* Beirut, 1955.
Izutsu, Toshihiko. *Ethico-Religious Concepts in the Qurʾan.* Montreal, 1966.
Jamāl Bāshā. *Mudhakkarāt Jamāl Bāshā.* Translated into Arabic by ʿAlī Aḥmad Shukrī. Cairo, 1923.
James, Daniel. *Resistance and Integration: Peronism and the Argentine Working Class, 1946–1976.* Cambridge, England, 1988.
Jankowski, James. "Egypt and Early Arab Nationalism, 1908–1922." In *The Origins of Arab Nationalism,* edited by Rashid Khalidi et al., 243–270. New York, 1991.
Joarder, Safiuddin. *Syria Under the French Mandate: The Early Phase, 1920–1927.* Dacca, 1977.
Johnson, Michael. "Political Bosses and Their Gangs: Zuʿama and Qabadayat in the Sunni Muslim Quarters of Beirut." In *Patrons and Clients in Mediterranean Societies,* edited by Ernest Gellner and John Waterbury, 207–224. London, 1977.
Johnson, Nels. *Islam and the Politics of Meaning in Palestinian Nationalism.* London, 1982.
al-Jundī, Adham. *Shuhadāʾ al-ḥarb al-ʿālamiyya al-kubrā.* Damascus, 1960.
———. *Tārīkh al-thawrāt al-sūriyya fī ʿahd al-intidāb al-faransī.* Damascus, 1960.
Kandiyoti, Deniz. "Identity and Its Discontents: Women and the Nation." In *Colonial Discourse and Post-Colonial Theory: A Reader,* edited and introduced by Patrick Williams and Laura Chrisman, 376–391. New York, 1994.

Karpat, Kemal H. "The Transformation of the Ottoman State, 1789–1908." *International Journal of Middle East Studies* 3 (1971): 243–281.
Kasaba, Resat. "Populism in Turkey, 1946–1961." In *Rules and Rights in the Middle East: Democracy, Law, Society,* edited by Ellis Goldberg, Resat Kasaba, and Joel S. Migdal, 43–68. Seattle, 1993.
Kasmieh, Khairia (Khayriyya Qāsimiyya). "An Evaluation of the Arab Government in Damascus, 1918–1920." In *State and Society in Syria and Lebanon,* edited by Youssef M. Choueiri, 27–31. New York, 1993.
———. *al-Ḥukūma al-ʿarabiyya fī Dimashq bayna 1918–1920.* Beirut, 1982.
al-Kawākibī, Nazīh. "al-Maẓhar al-ʿumrānī li-Dimashq fī al-muntaṣaf al-thānī lil-qarn al-tāsiʿ ʿashr." In *Dimashq: dirāsāt tārīkhiyya wa athariyya,* 187–201. Damascus, 1980.
al-Kaylanī, Fakhrī Nūrī. "Qirāʾa fī milaff al-ṣiḥāfa bayna ʿāmī 1727 wa 1928 fī bilād al-Shām." n.p., n.d. (Handwritten manuscript.)
Kedourie, Elie. *Arabic Political Memoirs and Other Studies.* London, 1974.
———. "The Capture of Damascus, 1 October 1918." In *The Chatham House Version and Other Middle Eastern Studies,* 33–51. Hanover, N.H., 1970.
———. *Nationalism.* Oxford, 1993.
———. *Nationalism in Asia and Africa.* London, 1971.
———. "Pan-Arabism and British Policy." In *The Chatham House Version and Other Middle Eastern Studies,* 213–235. Hanover, N.H., 1970.
Kersante, Jules. "Syrie: L'occupation d'Alep." *Petite relations d'orient* 6 (November 1920): 170–177.
Khalidi, Rashid. "ʿAbd al-Ghani al-ʿUraisi and *Al-Mufid:* The Press and Arab Nationalism before 1914." In *Intellectual Life in the Arab East, 1890–1939,* edited by Marwan Buheiry, 84–91. Beirut, 1981.
———. "Arab Nationalism in Syria: The Formative Years, 1908–1914." In *Nationalism in a Non-National State: The Dissolution of the Ottoman Empire,* edited by William W. Haddad and William Ochsenwald, 207–238. Columbus, 1977.
———. "The Origins of Arab Nationalism: Introduction." In *The Origins of Arab Nationalism,* edited by Rashid Khalidi et al., vii–xix. New York, 1991.
———. "Ottomanism and Arabism in Syria Before 1914: A Reassessment." In *The Origins of Arab Nationalism,* edited by Rashid Khalidi et al., 50–69. New York, 1991.
———. "Society and Ideology in Late Ottoman Syria." In *Problems of the Middle East in Historical Perspective: Essays in Honour of Albert Hourani,* edited by John Spagnolo, 119–131. Reading, England, 1992.
al-Khaṭīb, Muḥibb al-Dīn. "Mudhakkarāt Muḥibb al-Dīn al-Khaṭīb." *al-Thaqāfa* (Algiers) 1–3 (January 1972–August / September 1973).
———. *al-Muʾtamar al-ʿarabī al-awwal.* Cairo, 1913.
Khoury, Philip S. *Syria and the French Mandate: The Politics of Arab Nationalism, 1920–1945.* Princeton, 1987.
———. "Syrian Political Culture: A Historical Perspective." In *Syria: Society,*

Culture, and Polity, edited by Donald Quataert and Richard T. Antoun, 13–27. Albany, 1991.
———. *Urban Notables and Arab Nationalism: The Politics of Damascus 1860–1920.* Cambridge, England, 1983.
Kohn, Hans. *A History of Nationalism in the East.* London, 1929.
Kubik, Jan. *The Power of Symbols against the Symbols of Power: The Rise of Solidarity and the Fall of State Socialism in Poland.* University Park, 1994.
Kurd ʿAlī, Muḥammad. *Khiṭaṭ al-Shām.* 6 vols. Damascus, 1983.
Laclau, Ernesto. *Politics and Ideology in Marxist Theory: Capitalism—Fascism—Communism.* London, 1977.
Landau, Jacob M. *Studies in the Arab Theater and Cinema.* Philadelphia, 1958.
Landes, Joan B. *Women and the Public Sphere in the Age of the French Revolution.* Ithaca, 1988.
Lane, Christel. *The Rites of Rulers: Ritual in Industrial Society—The Soviet Case.* Cambridge, England , 1981.
Lasswell, Harold D. "The Language of Power." In *Language of Politics: Studies in Quantitative Semantics,* edited by Harold D. Lasswell et al., 3–19. New York, 1949.
Lawrence, T. E. "Emir Feisal II: The Sykes-Picot Treaty, Impatient Arabs." *Times* (London), 11 August 1920, 9.
———. *Evolution of a Revolt.* Edited by Stanley and Rodelle Weintraub. London, 1968.
Lecerf, J., and R. Tresse. "Les ʿ*arada* de Damas." *Bulletin d'études orientales* 7–8 (1937–1938): 237–264.
Lesch, Anne Mosely. *Arab Politics in Palestine, 1917–1939: The Frustration of a Nationalist Movement.* Ithaca, 1979.
Lincoln, Bruce. *Discourse and the Construction of Society: Comparative Studies of Myth, Ritual, and Classification.* New York, 1989.
Link, Arthur S., ed. *The Papers of Woodrow Wilson.* Vols. 56, 58. Princeton, 1987.
Loder, John de Vere. *The Truth About Mesopotamia, Palestine, and Syria.* London, 1923.
Longrigg, Stephen Hemsley. *Syria and Lebanon under French Mandate.* London, 1958.
Lukitz, Liora. "The Antonius Papers and *The Arab Awakening,* Over Fifty Years On." *Middle Eastern Studies* 30 (October 1994): 883–895.
Luxemburg, Rosa. "The Mass Strike, the Political Party, and the Trade Unions." In *Rosa Luxemburg Speaks,* edited by Mary-Alice Waters, 153–218. New York, 1970.
MacCallum, Elizabeth P. "The Arab National Movement." *Muslim World* 25 (October 1935): 359–374.
Mach, Zdzislaw. *Symbols, Conflict, and Identity: Essays in Political Anthropology.* Albany, 1993.
MacRae, Donald. "Populism as an Ideology." In *Populism: Its Meaning and*

National Characteristics, edited by Ghita Ionescu and Ernest Gellner, 153–165. London, 1969.

Mallon, Florencia E. *Peasant and Nation: The Making of Postcolonial Mexico and Peru.* Berkeley, 1995.

Maʿoz, Moshe. "The Impact of Modernization on Syrian Politics and Society during the Early Tanzimat Period." In *Beginnings of Modernization in the Middle East: The Nineteenth Century,* edited by William R. Polk and Richard L. Chambers, 333–350. Chicago, 1968.

Mardam Bek, Khalīl. *Dimashq wal-Quds fī al-ʿishrīnāt.* Edited by ʿAdnān Mardam Bek. Beirut, 1978.

Masters, Bruce. "Ottoman Policies toward Syria in the 17th and 18th Centuries." In *The Syrian Land in the 18th and 19th Century: The Common and the Specific in the Historical Experience,* edited by Thomas Philipp, 11–26. Stuttgart, 1992.

Meinertzhagen, Richard. *Middle East Diary, 1917–1956.* New York, 1960.

Minogue, Kenneth. "Populism as a Political Movement." In *Populism: Its Meaning and National Characteristics,* edited by Ghita Ionescu and Ernest Gellner, 197–211. London, 1969.

Moghadam, Val. "Islamic Populism, Class, and Gender in Postrevolutionary Iran." In *A Century of Revolution: Social Movements in Iran,* edited by John Foran, 189–222. Minneapolis, 1994.

Monroe, Paul et al. *Reconstruction in the Near East.* New York, 1924.

Moore, Sally F., and Barbara Myerhoff, , eds. *Secular Ritual.* Amsterdam, 1977.

Mosse, George L. *Fallen Soldiers: Reshaping the Memory of the World Wars.* New York, 1990.

———. *Nationalism and Sexuality.* Madison, 1985.

———. *The Nationalization of the Masses: Political Symbolism and Mass Movements in Germany from the Napoleonic Wars through the Third Reich.* New York, 1975.

Mouzelis, Nicos. "On the Concept of Populism: Populist and Clientalist Modes of Incorporation in Semiperipheral Polities." *Politics and Society* 14 (1985): 329–348.

Muḥammad, Nadīm Muʿalla. *al-Adab al-masraḥī fī Sūriyya: nash'a—taṭawwur.* Damascus, 1982.

Mūsā, Sulaymān. *al-Ḥaraka al-ʿarabiyya: al-Marḥala al-ūlā lil-nahḍa al-ʿarabiyya al-ḥadītha, 1908–1924.* Beirut, 1986.

———. *al-Murāsalāt al-tārīkhiyya.* Vol. 1: 1914–1918. Amman, 1973.

———. *al-Murāsalāt al-tārīkhiyya.* Vol. 2: 1919. Amman, 1975.

———. *al-Murāsalāt al-tārīkhiyya.* Vol. 3: 1920–1923. Amman, 1978.

Muslih, Muhammad Y. *The Origins of Palestinian Nationalism.* New York, 1988.

———. "The Rise of Local Nationalism in the Arab East." In *The Origins of Arab Nationalism,* edited by Rashid Khalidi et al., 167–185. New York, 1991.

Nairn, Tom. "The Modern Janus." *New Left Review* 94 (1975): 3–29.

Nietzsche, Friedrich. *On the Genealogy of Morals.* Edited by Walter Kaufmann. Translated by Walter Kaufmann and R. J. Hollingdale. New York, 1969.

———. *The Will to Power.* Edited by Walter Kaufmann. Translated by Walter Kaufmann and R. J. Hollingdale. New York, 1967.

Ochsenwald, William. "Ironic Origins: Arab Nationalism in the Hijaz, 1882–1914." In *The Origins of Arab Nationalism,* edited by Rashid Khalidi et al., 189–203. New York, 1991.

Ortner, Sherry B. "On Key Symbols." *American Anthropologist* 75 (1973): 1338–1346.

Owen, Roger. *The Middle East in the World Economy, 1800–1914.* London, 1981.

Ozouf, Mona. *Festivals and the French Revolution.* Translated by Alan Sheridan. Cambridge, Mass., 1988.

Ozveren, Y. Eyup. "Beirut." *Review* 16 (fall 1993): 467–497.

Pascual, Jean-Paul. "La Syrie à l'époque ottomane (le XIXe siècle)." In *La Syrie d'aujourd'hui,* edited by André Raymond, 31–53. Paris, 1980.

Peukert, Detlev J. K. *The Weimar Republic: The Crisis of Classical Modernity.* Translated by Richard Deveson. New York, 1989.

Philipp, Thomas. *The Syrians in Egypt, 1725–1975.* Stuttgart, 1985.

Porath, Yehoshua. *The Emergence of the Palestinian-Arab National Movement, 1918–1929.* London, 1974.

Qadrī, Aḥmad. *Mudhakkarātī ʿan al-thawra al-ʿarabiyya al-kubrā.* Damascus, 1956.

al-Qāsimī, Ẓāfir. *Maktab ʿAnbar: ṣuwar wa dhikrayāt min hayātina al-thaqāfiyya wal-siyāsiyya wal-ijtimāʿiyya.* Beirut, 1964.

Rafeq, Abdul-Karim. "Arabism, Society, and Economy in Syria, 1918–1920." In *State and Society in Syria and Lebanon,* edited by Youssef M. Choueiri, 1- 26. New York, 1993.

al-Rayyis, Munīr. *al-Kitāb al-dhahabī lil-thawrāt al-waṭaniyya fī al-mashriq al-ʿarabī: al-Thawra al-sūriyya al-kubrā.* Beirut, 1969.

Reilly, James Anthony. "Origins of Peripheral Capitalism in the Damascus Region, 1830–1914." Ph.D. dissertation, Georgetown University, 1987.

———. "Women in the Economic Life of Late-Ottoman Damascus." *Arabica* 42 (1995): 79–106.

Rengger, N. J. *Political Theory, Modernity and Postmodernity.* Oxford, 1995.

Riḍā, Rashīd. *Mukhtārāt siyāsiyya min majallat "al-Manār".* Edited and introduced by Wajīh Kawtharānī. Beirut, 1980.

al-Rifāʿī, Anwar. *Jihād nuṣf qarn: Sumūw al-amīr Saʿīd al-Jazāʾirī.* Damascus, n.d.

al-Rīḥānī, Amīn. *Mulūk al-ʿarab, aw riḥla fī al-bilād al-ʿarabiyya.* Beirut, 1951.

al-Rīmāwī, Suhayla. *Jamʿiyyat al-ʿarabiyya al-Fatāt al-sirriyya : Dirāsa wathāʾiqiyya, 1909–1918.* Amman, 1988.

———. *al-Tajriba al-fayṣaliyya fī bilād al-Shām.* Amman, 1988.

Robin, Regine. *Histoire et Linguistique.* Paris, 1973.

Roded, Ruth. "Ottoman Service as a Vehicle for the Rise of New Upstarts among the Urban Elite Families of Syria in the Last Decades of Ottoman Rule." *Asian and African Studies* 17 (1983): 63–94.

Rothenberg, Winifred Barr. *From Market-Places to a Market Economy: The Transformation of Rural Massachusetts, 1750–1850.* Chicago, 1992.

Rowe, William, and Vivian Schelling. *Memory and Modernity: Popular Culture in Latin America.* London, 1991.

Rudé, George. *The Crowd in History: A Study of Popular Disturbances in France and England, 1730–1848.* London, 1964.

Ruedy, John. *Modern Algeria: The Origins and Development of a Nation.* Bloomington, 1992.

Russell, Malcolm. *The First Modern Arab State: Syria under Faysal 1918–1920.* Minneapolis, 1985.

Ryan, Mary. "The American Parade: Representation of the Nineteenth-Century Social Order." In *The New Cultural History,* edited by Lynn Hunt, 131–153. Berkeley, 1989.

Sachar, Howard N. *The Emergence of the Middle East: 1914–1924.* New York, 1969.

al-Safarjalānī, Muḥī al-Dīn. *Fājiʿat Maysalūn wal-baṭal al-ʿaẓīm Yūsuf al-ʿAẓma.* Damascus, 1937.

Ṣāfī, Riḍā. *ʿAlā janāḥ al-dhikrā.* Part 1. Damascus, 1982.

Sahlins, Marshall. *Historical Metaphors and Mythical Realities: Structure in the Early History of the Sandwich Islands Kingdom.* Ann Arbor, 1981.

Saʿīd, Amīn. *al-Thawra al-ʿarabiyya al-kubrā: Tārīkh mufaṣṣal jāmiʿ lil-qaḍiyya al-ʿarabiyya fī rubʿ qarn.* Vol. 2: *Niḍāl bayna al-ʿArab wal-Faransāwiyyīn wal-Inklīz.* Cairo, 1934.

———. *Thawrāt al-ʿArab fī al-qarn al-ʿishrīn.* Cairo, n.d.

Said, Edward W. *Culture and Imperialism.* New York, 1994.

———. "Third World Intellectuals and Metropolitan Culture." *Raritan* 9 (winter 1990): 27–50.

Ṣāliḥ, Rushdī. *al-Masraḥ al-ʿarabī.* Cairo, 1972.

Scheler, Max. *Ressentiment.* Edited and introduced by Lewis A. Coser. Translated by William W. Holdheim. New York, 1961.

Schilcher, Linda Schatkowski. *Families in Politics: Damascene Factions and Estates of the 18th and 19th Century.* Stuttgart, 1985.

———. "The Famine of 1915–1918 in Greater Syria." In *Problems of the Modern Middle East in Historical Perspective: Essays in Honour of Albert Hourani,* edited by John Spagnolo, 229–258. Reading, England, 1992.

———. "The Impact of the Railways on the Grain Trade of Southern Syria, 1890–1925." In *Infrastructures and Communication: Processes of Integration and Separation in Bilad al-Sham from the Eighteenth Century to the Mandatory Period,* edited by Thomas Philipp and Birgit Schäbler. Gotha, forthcoming.

———. "Violence in Rural Syria in the 1880s and 1890s: State Centralization,

Rural Integration, and the World Market." In *Peasants and Politics in the Modern Middle East,* edited by Farhad Kazemi and John Waterbury, 50–84. Miami, 1991.
Scott, James. *Weapons of the Weak: Everyday Forms of Peasant Resistance.* New Haven, 1985.
Shamir, Shimon. "The Modernization of Syria: Problems and Solutions in the Early Period of Abdulhamid." In *Beginnings of Modernization in the Middle East: The Nineteenth Century,* edited by William R. Polk and Richard L. Chambers, 351–382. Chicago, 1968.
Sharabi, Hisham. *Arab Intellectuals and the West: The Formative Years 1875–1914.* Baltimore, 1972.
Shibutani, Tamotsu. *Improvised News: A Sociological Study of Rumor.* Indianapolis, 1966.
al-Shihābī, al-Amīr Muṣṭafā. *Muḥāḍarāt fī al-istiʿmār.* Vol. 2. n.p., 1956.
al-Shihābī, Qatība. *Dimashq: Tārīkh wa ṣuwar.* Damascus, 1986.
Simon, Reeva S. "The Education of an Iraqi Ottoman Army Officer." In *The Origins of Arab Nationalism,* edited by Rashid Khalidi et al., 151–166. New York, 1991.
Sluglett, Peter, and Marion Farouk-Sluglett. "The Application of the 1858 Land Code in Greater Syria: Some Preliminary Observations." In *Land Tenure and Social Transformation in the Middle East,* edited by Tarif Khalidi, 409–424. Beirut, 1984.
Smith, Anthony D. "Gastronomy or Geology? The Role of Nationalism in the Reconstruction of Nations." *Nations and Nationalism* 1 (March 1995): 3–23.
———. "The Myth of the 'Modern Nation' and the Myths of Nations." *Ethnic and Racial Studies* 11 (January 1988): 1–26.
———. *National Identity.* Reno, 1991.
Stewart, Angus. "The Social Roots." In *Populism: Its Meaning and National Characteristics,* edited by Ghita Ionescu and Ernest Gellner, 180–196. London, 1969.
Sulṭān, ʿAlī. *Tārīkh Sūriyya 1918–1920: Ḥukm Fayṣal b. Ḥusayn.* Damascus, 1987.
al-Suwaydī, Tawfīq. *Mudhakkarātī: Nuṣf qarn min tārīkh al-ʿIrāq wal-qaḍiyya al-ʿarabiyya.* Beirut, 1969.
Swedenburg, Ted. *Memories of Revolt: The 1936–1939 Rebellion and the Palestinian National Past.* Minneapolis, 1995.
———. "The Role of the Palestinian Peasantry in the Great Revolt (1936–1939)." In *Islam, Politics, and Social Movements,* edited by Edmund Burke III and Ira M. Lapidus, 169–203. Berkeley, 1988.
Tabak, Faruk. "Agrarian Fluctuations and Modes of Labor Control in the Western Arc of the Fertile Crescent, *c.*1700–1850." In *Landholding and Commercial Agriculture in the Middle East,* edited by Çaglar Keyder and Faruk Tabak, 135–154. Albany, 1991.
Tauber, Eliezer. *The Arab Movements in World War I.* London, 1993.
———. *The Emergence of the Arab Movements.* London, 1993.

———. *The Formation of Modern Syria and Iraq.* London, 1995.

———. "The Struggle for Dayr al-Zur: The Determination of Borders between Syria and Iraq." *International Journal of Middle East Studies* 23 (1991), 361–385.

Terdiman, Richard. *Discourse/Counter-Discourse: The Theory and Practice of Symbolic Resistance in Nineteenth Century France.* Ithaca, 1985.

Tergeman, Siham. *Daughter of Damascus.* Introduced and translated by Andrea Rugh. Austin, 1994.

Thompson, E. P. *Customs in Common: Studies in Traditional Popular Culture.* New York, 1991.

———. "Eighteenth-Century English Society: Class Struggle Without Class." *Social History* 3 (May 1978), 133–165.

Tibawi, A. L. *A Modern History of Syria, Including Lebanon and Palestine.* New York, 1969.

Tibi, Bassam. *Arab Nationalism: A Critical Enquiry.* New York, 1971.

Tilly, Charles. *The Contentious French.* Cambridge, Mass., 1986.

———. *From Mobilization to Revolution.* Reading, Mass., 1978.

———, Louise Tilly, and Richard Tilly. *The Rebellious Century, 1830–1930.* Cambridge, Mass., 1975.

Turabein, Ahmed. "ʿAbd al-Hamid al-Zahrawi: The Career and Thought of an Arab Nationalist." In *The Origins of Arab Nationalism,* edited by Rashid Khalidi et al., 97–119. New York, 1991.

Turner, Bryan S. "Politics and Society in the Middle East." In *Capitalism and Class in the Middle East: Theories of Social Change and Economic Development, 93–110.* London, 1984.

Turner, James. "Understanding the Populists." *Journal of American History* 67 (September 1980): 354–373.

Turner, Victor. "Hidalgo: History as Social Drama." In *Dramas, Fields, and Metaphors: Symbolic Action in Human Society,* 98–155. Ithaca, 1974.

ʿUbaydāt, Maḥmūd. *Aḥmad Muraywid: 1886–1926.* London, 1997.

al-ʿUlabī, Akram Ḥasan. *Khiṭaṭ Dimashq: Dirāsa tārīkhiyya shāmila.* Damascus, 1989.

al-ʿUmarī, Ṣubḥī. *Maysalūn: Nihāyat ʿahd.* London, 1991.

Vashitz, Joseph. "*Dhawat* and *ʿIsamiyyun:* Two Groups of Arab Community Leaders in Haifa During the British Mandate." *Asian and African Studies* 17 (1983): 95–120.

Vatter, Sherry. "Militant Journeymen in Nineteenth-Century Damascus: Implications for the Middle Eastern Labor History Agenda." In *Workers and Working Classes in the Middle East: Struggles, Histories, Historiographies,* edited by Zachary Lockman, 1–19. Albany, 1994.

Vilas, Carlos M. "Latin American Populism: A Structural Approach." *Science and Society* 56 (winter 1992–1993): 389–420.

Weber, Max. *From Max Weber: Essays in Sociology.* Edited, translated, and introduced by H. H. Gerth and C. Wright Mills . New York, 1958.

———. *The Theory of Social and Economic Organization.* Edited by Talcott

Parsons. Translated by A. M. Henderson and Talcott Parsons. New York, 1947.
White, Hayden. *Metahistory: The Historical Imagination in Nineteenth Century Europe.* Baltimore, 1973.
———. *Tropics of Discourse: Essays in Cultural Criticism.* Baltimore, 1978.
Wiles, Peter. "A Syndrome, Not a Doctrine: Some Elementary Theses on Populism." In *Populism: Its Meaning and National Characteristics,* edited by Ghita Ionescu and Ernest Gellner, 166–179. London, 1969.
Wilson, Mary. "The Hashemites, the Arab Revolt, and Arab Nationalism." In *The Origins of Arab Nationalism,* edited by Rashid Khalidi et al., 204–221. New York, 1991.
Wolf, Eric R. *Peasant Wars of the Twentieth Century.* New York, 1969.
Worsley, Peter. "The Concept of Populism." In *Populism: Its Meaning and National Characteristics,* edited by Ghita Ionescu and Ernest Gellner, 212–250. London, 1969.
Wrightson, Keith. "Estates, Degrees, and Sorts: Changing Perceptions of Society in Tudor and Stuart England." In *Language, History, and Class,* edited by Penelope J. Corfield, 30–52. Oxford, 1991.
Wuthnow, Robert. *Communities of Discourse: Ideology and Social Structure in the Reformation, the Enlightenment, and European Socialism.* Cambridge, Mass., 1989.
Yakobson, Sergius, and Harold D. Lasswell. "Trend: May Day Slogans in Soviet Russia, 1918–1943." In *Language of Politics: Studies in Quantitative Semantics,* edited by Harold D. Lasswell et al., 233–297. New York, 1949.
Zakariyyā, Aḥmad Waṣfī. *ʿAshāʾir al-Shām.* Damascus, 1983.
Zamir, Meir. *The Formation of Modern Lebanon.* Ithaca, 1985.
Zeine, Zeine N. *The Emergence of Arab Nationalism with a Background Study of Arab-Turkish Relations in the Near East.* Delmar, 1958.
———. *The Struggle for Arab Independence: Western Diplomacy and the Rise and Fall of Faisal's Kingdom in Syria.* Delmar, 1960.
Zerubavel, Eviatar. *Hidden Rhythms: Schedules and Calendars in Social Life.* Chicago, 1981.
al-Ziriklī, Khayr al-Dīn. *al-Aʿlām: qāmūsa tarājim li-ashhar al-rijāl wal-nisāʾ min al-ʿArab wal-mustaʿribīn wal-mustashriqīn.* n.p., 1984.
———. *Dīwān al-Ziriklī: al-Aʿmāl al-shiʿriyya al-kāmila.* Amman(?), n.d.
———. *Ma raʾaytu wa ma samiʿtu.* Cairo, 1923.
Zubaida, Sami. *Islam, the People, and the State: Political Ideas and Movements in the Middle East.* London, 1993.

INTERVIEWS

Daghmush, Kamil. Damascus, 2 November 1989.
Daqqar, ʿAbd al-Ghani. Damascus, 2 January 1990.
al-Halabi, Shaykh ʿAbd al-Rizaq. Damascus, 3 January 1990
Haqqi, Ihsan. Damascus, 10 November 1989.

al-Jaza'iri, Abu Ribah. Damascus, 15 November 1989.
al-Kaylani, Fakhri. Damascus, 8 November 1989.
al-Khatib, ʿAdnan. Damascus, 8 November 1989.
al-Khatib, Muhammad Rida. Damascus, 6 January 1990.
al-Qasimi, Shaykh Ahmad. Damascus, 6 November 1989.
al-Saruji, ʿUmar Khadim. Damascus, 31 December 1989.
al-Tabbaʿ, Muhammad Murad. Damascus, 2 January 1990.
ʿUrufa, Shaykh Yasin. Damascus, 2 January 1990, 4 January 1990.
al-Yafi, Dr. ʿAbd al-Karim. Damascus, 21 November 1989.

Index

ʿAbdallah, Amir, 150, 152
ʿAbd al-Hadi, ʿAwni, 251n
ʿAbd al-Hamid II, Sultan, 57
ʿAbd al-Nur, Thabit, 66, 70, 169
ʿAbd al-Rahman or the Second Umayyad Dynasty in al-Andalus, 253
ʿAbduh, Muhammad, 7n, 91, 96
al-ʿAbid family, 57
al-ʿAbid, Nazik, 215
al-ʿAbid, Rida, 292
Abi Tayah, ʿAwda, 29
Abu Shammat, Mahmud, 115
Abu Suʿud, Shaykh Hasan, 80
Abyad, George, 254–55
al-ʿAdli, Fu'ad, 129n, 131
age: as trope, 200–201. *See also* youth
agriculture, 15, 17, 18, 167, 22, 265n, 190. *See also* grain
al-ʿAhd, 54; and Damascus Protocol, 150; Higher National Committee representatives from, 99; Iraqi branch, 57n, 61; members, 56; Syrian branch, 57n, 93n
al-Ahsana tribe, 128
ʿAjlun, 105, 119–20
ʿAjluni, Muhammad ʿAli, 278n
ʿAkkar, 292
al-Akrad, Damascus, 100n
Alawites, 124
Aleppo, 3, 14, 15, 28–29, 30, 32, 59, 75, 81–86, 129–32, 133, 134–35, 146n, 157, 158, 214, 232, 238n, 248, 251, 279, 292, 293–94; Arab Club in, 78–86, 130–31, 134, 173, 218, 255, 292; and Arab Revolt, 30, 172–73; autonomy demanded by, 30; collapse of security in, 42, 43, 90; committee of national defense in, 3, 85, 129–35, 173, 251; economy of, 38, 82–83, 132–33; French occupation of, 134–36, 291–95; July (1920) insurrection in, 3, 45, 131, 287; massacre of Armenians in, 45, 82, 183; pro-Turkish sentiment in, 82–83, 85, 129–30, 132, 146n, 172; refugees in, 43, 45, 122; theater in, 253, 258; World War I and, 27, 43, 82
Alexandretta, 83
al-ʿAli, Salih, 124, 129, 134n, 294, 297n
al-ʿAllaf, Ahmad, 92–93
Allenby, General Sir Edmund H., 27, 30, 31, 170, 181, 247n
Alliance israélite, 29, 74
ʿAmara, Damascus, 229n, 239, 275
Amman, 27, 43, 81, 265; Higher National Committee and, 100, 105, 123
ʿAmmun, Iskandar, 158, 159
Anatolia, 24, 28, 43, 82
ʿAnaza tribe, 43, 292
Anderson, Benedict, 12, 51, 201n, 296
al-Andiya magazine, 79–80

Arabia, 6, 73, 155. *See also* Gulf Arabs; Hijaz
Arabic, 32, 92, 163, 254
"Arab" identity, 5–6, 143, 154, 254. *See also* Arabism
Arab Independence Party, 54n, 56n, 58n, 59–60, 63–66, 70, 93n, 174–75, 218n; and Higher National Committee, 97, 98, 99
Arabism, 7–8, 16, 56, 66, 67, 68, 71, 110, 111, 171, 181, 220, 254. *See also* "Arab" identity; "Arab nationalism"
"Arab nationalism," 4–9, 16, 58n, 63n, 68, 69n, 71, 72, 75, 78, 99, 110, 142–43, 176, 220, 287. *See also* Arabism; nationalism; nationalist elites
Arab Revolt, 4, 25, 26, 68, 83, 89, 93, 94–95, 94n, 110, 141, 147, 150, 153, 154, 161, 163, 168–73, 198, 234, 242, 247; Aleppo and, 30, 172–73; Arab army, 2, 25, 168–69; British and, 25, 26, 68, 69n, 169; ceremonies celebrating, 241, 242–46; Druze and, 230; al-Fatat and, 56; and "martyrs," 178; as symbol, 169–74; and *thawra*, 173–74; theater and, 255
Arab Youth Club, 200
ʿArari, Yusuf, 100n
Armanaz, 134
Armenians: Aleppo massacre, 43, 45, 82, 183, 249n; refugees, 43
al-Arnaʾut, Maʿruf, 74–75, 238, 255, 256
Arslan, ʿAdil, 29, 59, 66, 73
al-Arwam, Suq, 232
al-Asʿad, Kamil, 122–23, 124
al-ʿAsali, Shukri, 66
al-ʿAshmar, Muhammad, 116, 297n
al-ʿĀṣima, 237; on Arab government, 38, 205–6, 247n; on blueprint for demonstration, 263–64; on charity, 212; on coffeehouses, 202, 258; on democracy, 194n; on gender roles, 214, 215; on al-Hashimi's Committee of National Defense, 89; on independence, 164; on intercommunal harmony, 181, 182–83; on public opinion, 185; on racetracks, 203; report on celebration of Arab army, 274–75; report on celebration of *ʿīd al-fatḥ*, 244; report on celebration of *ʿīd al-thawra*, 244–45, 246; report on Faysal's return from Europe, 267–68; report on "movie party," 252n; report on volunteer militias, 90; on role of *mutanawwirūn*, 201–2; on role of women, 192; on socialism, 205; on strikes, 199–200n; on theater, 255
al-ʿAskari, Jaʿfar, 66
Association of Brotherhood and Virtue, 256
Association of Young Lebanese, 200
Association of Young Syrians, 200
al-Atasi family, 128
al-Atasi, Hashim, 64n, 245n, 248
al-Atasi, ʿUmar, 128
al-Atasi, Wasfi, 59
al-Atrash, Nasib, 29
al-Atrash, Sultan, 129
al-ʿAttar, Shaykh Rida, 26
Awakening of Arab Women, 214
ʿAyn Ibl, 123, 124
al-Ayyubi, ʿAta, 26
al-Ayyubi, Shukri, 26
ʿAziz, ʿAli, 66
al-ʿAzm family, 57, 64, 70
al-ʿAzm, Khalid, 64n, 90, 96n
al-ʿAzm, Muhammad Fawzi, 60, 64, 90, 162, 167
al-ʿAzm, Rafiq, 57n, 69n, 93, 157
al-ʿAzm, Sami, 71, 73, 77n, 265–66
al-ʿAzma, ʿIzzat, 66
al-ʿAzma, Nabih, 84, 134, 291
al-ʿAzma, Yusuf, 3, 29, 59, 84

Baʿalbek, 66, 70, 26–28, 126–27
Bab al-Jabiya, Damascus, 105

newspapers (*continued*)
al-Mufīd, 78, 101n; *al-Muqtabas*, 101, 238; *al-Qibla*, 24, 94n; *al-Rāya*, 131, 134–35, 238n; *Sūriyya al-jadīda*, 78, 102–3, 238, 239, 273, 292; as signs, 238; slogans in, 150, 238; street vendors of, 238; subsidies to, 239, 240n, 292; *Le Temps*, 241. See also *al-ʿĀṣima al-Kawkab*
Nietzsche, F., 15
Niʿmat, Mustafa, 216
Nimr, Dr., 95
notables, 30, 199n, 203–4, 244, 261, 267, 274–75, 292; of Aleppo, 15, 30, 82, 84, 85, 130–33; and Arab Club, 64–65, 70, 82, 84, 85; and Arabism, 7–8; of Damascus, 24, 26–27, 57, 64–65, 70, 200; "politics of notables," 80, 104; and popular committees, 21, 104, 207; and volunteer militias, 90–91. *See also* landowners; patronage; vertical ties

Occupied Enemy Territory Administration—East (OETA-E), 1n, 27, 35; Faysal-Clemenceau Agreement and, 36; political authority in, 30; al-Rikabi as military governor, 28–29, 30, 61, 70
Occupied Enemy Territory Administration—North, 27n
Occupied Enemy Territory Administration—West (OETA-West), 27, 35, 36, 39–40, 123
Organization of Religious Scholars, 116
Ortner, Sherry B., 147, 149, 244n
Ottoman Administrative Decentralization Party, 54, 93, 110, 159, 244n; and Syrian Union, 57n, 69n, 154, 158
Ottoman army, 15, 18, 22–24, 26n, 28, 43, 70, 82, 89, 94, 109, 116, 121–22, 243. *See also* Jamal Pasha (the Elder)
Ottoman Empire, 13, 14, 15, 32, 51, 52; partition of, 24–25, 27, 136; transformation of society under, 15–17, 18, 22, 51–52, 136–37, 189–90, 260; World War I and, 22–26, 33, 136, 171. *See also* Committee of Union and Progress; Ottoman army
Ottomanism, 7n, 8, 14, 16
Ottoman Land Code (1858), 13
Ottoman Public Debt Administration, 32

Palestine, 1n, 27n, 31, 40, 69n, 73, 89, 103, 157, 158, 274, 290; Arab Clubs in, 78, 79, 80–82, 99; and Arab Revolt, 169, 170; Britain and, 68, 69, 160, 170, 234, 243, 273, 297n; Great Revolt (1936–1939), 296, 297n; Higher National Committee and, 102, 103, 105, 123; Literary Society in, 66, 68, 81, 234; Zionist immigration, 103, 279–80. *See also* Jerusalem; Nablus; Tulkarm
Palestine Congress, 103
Palestine Great Revolt (1936–39), 296, 297n
Palestinians, 66, 68–69, 78–82, 99, 110, 141, 146n, 198, 234, 296; in Arab government, 20, 83, 110, 198; in Damascus, 123; and al-Fatat, 58
pan-Islamic unity, 119n, 185–86
Parliament, Ottoman, 67, 80, 109, 110
"patriotic agitation," 51, 53–55, 57
Patriotic Club, Tulkarm, 255, 256–57
Patriotic Youth, 200
patronage, 58, 60, 199; popular committees and, 104, 115, 127–28, 137, 283; transformed role of, 14, 19, 52, 104, 137, 288. *See also* notables; vertical ties
peace conference, Paris, 33–35, 72, 85, 95, 163, 168
peasants, 18, 87, 121–22, 127, 128
pensions, 15, 23, 28
petitions, 83, 265, 292–93, 294–95, Arab Club and, 65, 72, 84–85, 100, 182, 264–65; Arab government and, 34, 102, 145, 182, 230–31, 262,

Shafiq Bey, 131
Shaghur, Damascus, 2, 75, 105, 107n, 275, 294
Shaghuri, Ibrahim, 134
Shaghuri, Nicolas, 73
Shahada, Father Mikhail, 98
Shahbandar, ʿAbd al-Rahman, 57n, 58, 59, 66, 68–69, 93n, 96n, 107n, 157
Shakir, ʿUmar, 70, 107–8
al-Shaʿlan, Nuri, 29
Shallash, Ramadan, 66, 174n, 175, 297n
al-Shamʿa, Rushdi, 67
al-Shamʿa, Yahya, 201
al-Shamiyya, Tawfiq, 60, 98, 99, 100n
Shammar tribe, 43
Sharabi, Hisham, 6–7
Shariʿ Nasr, Damascus, 14n
al-Sharkas (al-Masri), Tawfiq (Chewfik), 119n
al-Shawi, ʿIzzat, 64n, 73
Shaykh al-Ard family, 114
al-Shihabi, ʿArif, 67, 93n
al-Shihabi, Fu'ad, 73
al-Shihabi, Ismʿail, 73
al-Shishakli, Tawfiq, 258–59
Shtura, 122
Shuqayr, Najib, 66–67
Shuqayr, Saʿid, 29, 32, 62n, 71, 188n, 238
Shurayqi, Muhammad, 275
al-Sibaʿi family, 114
al-Sibaʿi, Qasim, 129n
slogans, 9, 34, 144, 149–50, 202, 235, 238, 251, 261, 263–64, 269; defined, 149n
Smith, Anthony D., 5, 184n
smuggling, 24, 39, 111, 119, 132
socialists, European, 183n, 205
Spencer, Herbert, 183n, 202n, 205
Storrs, Ronald, 150
strikes, 18, 19, 44–45, 199–200n
al-Sukkar family, 110, 116
al-Sukkar, ʿAbd al-Qadir, 108, 110, 111–12, 113n, 291, 296–97n
Sulayman, Farid, 126
Sulayman, Mustafa, 126
Sulayman, Tawfiq Bek, 126
Sulayman, Yusuf Mukhaybar, 66, 68, 127
al-Sulh, Mukhtar, 157
al-Sulh, Riyad, 248n
Suq al-ʿAttarin, Damascus, 232
Suq al-Buzuriyya, Damascus, 115, 232
Suq al-Hamidiyya, Damascus, 75, 112, 279
Suq Midhat Pasha, Damascus, 115
al-Suwaydi, Naji Bey, 73
Suwayqa, Damascus, 75
"The Sword, The Fire, and The Ardor of Youth," 77–78, 200
Sykes, Sir Mark, 153, 244
Sykes-Picot Agreement (1916), 24–25, 62, 163, 164n
symbols, 9, 22, 145, 197, 220–21; ceremonies and, 10, 226–27, 242; key symbols, 9, 145, 147–50, 189, 296; summarizing, 149, 244n; transforming the meanings of, 96, 144, 153–56, 175, 178–88, 196–98, 215–17, 221, 246, 274. *See also* slogans
Syria, 159; boundaries of, 1n, 73, 155–60, 167, 249; division of, 36, 83, 159, 170, 180, 270, 280; French invasion of inland, 1, 3, 20, 128, 134–36, 192, 290–94; as integral unit, 159–60, 208; as national community, 100, 137, 152, 208–15, 288; as region of Arab nation, 73, 155–60, 164
Syrian Café, Damascus, 258
Syrian General Congress, 47, 102, 111, 122, 132, 133, 206n, 221, 237, 244; blocs within, 188–89; and al-Fatat, 59, 63–64, 122; and Higher National Committee, 102; and Independence Day celebrations, 246, 247–48, 249, 250–52; July insurrections and, 2; "Nation Dictates Its Wishes to the Syrian Congress" (al-Qassab), 193, 209–10, 247–48, 278; reconvening of (March 1920), 47, 247; and women's suffrage, 192

Ustuwani, ʿAbdallah, 265
Ustuwani, ʿAbd al-Muhsin, 265

vertical ties, 19, 52, 91, 260, 284; and mobilization, 9, 19–20, 52, 127–28, 283; popular committees and, 21–22, 283, 288. *See also* patronage

Wahhabism, 6, 110
Walrond, Osmond, 69n
Wasfi, Mustafa, 99
"Watchful Eye," 37
White, Hayden, 4
Wild ʿAli tribe, 128
Wilhelm II, Kaiser, 242
Wilson, Woodrow, 33, 163, 165, 234, 247
wīrkū, 32, 120
women: clothing styles, 148–49; and gender roles, 191–92, 213–15; reports of assaults on, 188, 215, 238n; suffrage, 192, 215
Women's Charitable Thrift Society, 214
World War I, 22–26; Arab army in, 25, 82, 88–89, 144; Arab government after, 26–47; cities during, 14, 23–27, 42–43, 52, 67, 82; Damascus, 23–26, 43, 67; representation of in drama, 255–56; suffering of Syrians during, 4, 22–24, 33, 122, 173. *See also* entente powers
Wrightson, Keith, 207
Wuthnow, Robert, 146n, 197

Yale, William, 63
Yamut, Bashir, 181
al-Yaʿqubi, al-Sharif, 116
Yaziji, Tawfiq, 291
Yemeni troops, in Arab army, 2
Young Men's Party, 119n
Young Mesopotamia, 200
youth: *mutanawwirūn* advice for, 202; as trope, 200–201. *See also* schools, mobilization in
Youth of the Jazira, 200
al-Yusuf family, 57, 58n
al-Yusuf, ʿAbd al-Rahman, 57–58, 60, 64n, 248n, 294

al-Zaghat, Mustafa, 75
al-Zahrawi, ʿAbd al-Hamid, 66
Zayd, Amir, 33–34, 62, 74, 89, 90–91, 102, 148, 169, 175, 178, 230n, 243–44, 248, 255n, 273n, 275, 278
Zeine, Zeine N., 5
Zionism, 4, 146n, 271, 297n; Arab Club of Jerusalem and, 81; Damascus Program and, 167; demonstrations against, 279; in drama, 258n; Higher National Committee and, 98, 99, 103, 279–80; slogans against, 149. *See also* Israel; Palestine; Palestinians
Zirabli, Khalil, 75
al-Zirikli, Khayr al-Din, 70, 71, 78, 93n, 165–66, 176, 291n

Compositor:	G&S Typesetters, Inc.
Text:	10/13 Aldus
Display:	Aldus
Printer:	Haddon Craftsmen
Binder:	Haddon Craftsmen